The Great War

GESCHICHTE - ERINNERUNG - POLITIK

POSENER STUDIEN ZUR GESCHICHTS-, KULTUR- UND POLITIKWISSENSCHAFT

Herausgegeben von Anna Wolff-Powęska und Piotr Forecki

BAND 13

Elżbieta Katarzyna Dzikowska /
Agata Handley / Piotr Zawilski (eds.)

The Great War

Insights and Perspectives

Bibliographic Information published by the Deutsche Nationalbibliothek
The Deutsche Nationalbibliothek lists this publication in the Deutsche
Nationalbibliografie; detailed bibliographic data is available in the internet at
http://dnb.d-nb.de.

Library of Congress Cataloging-in-Publication Data
Names: Dzikowska, Elżbieta Katarzyna, editor. | Handley, Agata, 1979- editor. |
Zawilski, Piotr, editor.
Title: The Great War : insights and perspectives / Elżbieta Katarzyna Dzikowska,
Agata Handley, Piotr Zawilski (eds.).
Description: New York : Peter Lang, 2016. | Series: Geschichte-Erinnerung-
Politik, ISSN 2191-3528 ; Band 13
Identifiers: LCCN 2016010971| ISBN 9783631661116 | ISBN 9783653055870
(ebook)
Subjects: LCSH: World War, 1914-1918–Social aspects. | World War, 1914-1918–
Influence. | War and society–History–20th century.
Classification: LCC D524.6 .G74 2016 | DDC 940.3–dc23 LC record available at
http://lccn.loc.gov/2016010971

This publication was financially supported by the University of Łódź
and the State Archive in Łódź.

Reviewers: prof. Hans-Jürgen Boemelburg, prof. Krystyna Radziszewska

Technical Editor: Karolina Goławska

Translators: Zofia Piwowarska, Marta Moraczewska, Wojciech Pędzich,
Aleksandra Szeliska, Agnieszka Wierzbińska

Cover illustration courtesy of Paweł Kwiatkowski

ISSN 2191-3528
ISBN 978-3-631-66111-6 (Print)
E-ISBN 978-3-653-05587-0 (E-Book)
DOI 10.3726/978-3-653-05587-0

© Peter Lang GmbH
Internationaler Verlag der Wissenschaften
Frankfurt am Main 2016
All rights reserved.
Peter Lang Edition is an Imprint of Peter Lang GmbH.

Peter Lang – Frankfurt am Main · Bern · Bruxelles · New York ·
Oxford · Warszawa · Wien

This publication has been peer reviewed.

www.peterlang.com

Contents

Introduction

The Great War in local perspectives in the Central Europe

The study of publications related to the centenary of the outbreak of the Great War may give the impression that in the European cultural memory the experience related to the events in the west of the continent is more vivid than the experience related to East-Central Europe. Moreover, it may seem that this western viewpoint is dominant not only in media but quite often also in scholarly debates.

The objective of our large-scale, inter-disciplinary project was to approximate local perspectives and to study the Great War through the prism of archive resources stored in locations that today belong to Poland – a country which was not on the map of Europe when the war broke out and which revived in 1918. The citizens of this future state were often forced to fight against their compatriots who were conscripted to foreign armies like other inhabitants of Eastern and Central Europe such as Jews, Ukrainians, Czechs. The war in the east had a more direct impact on daily life of civilian communities which went through the terror of occupation, changes of the frontline, passage of armies. Additionally, the conduct of allied armies also affected the local communities' ordeal.

The authors of the articles used in their research the extensive archival materials from a few regions of Poland in order to investigate the issue of the Great War in these areas. Our focus was also on the question of multiculturalism and multi-ethinicity in face of war, in particular as regards Łódź. The issues regarding the musealisation of memories of the war between Austria and Italy as well as the image of Russia in the propaganda of the central powers add to our perception aspects of memory of culture.

The project concept and the work on the project was coordinated by the Interdisciplinary Centre for Research on Multicultural and Multinational City and Region of Łódź (Ośrodek Badań nad Wielokulturową i Wielonarodową Łodzią i Regionem) of the University of Łódź in collaboration with two other academic institutions: The Department of Literature and Culture of Germany, Austria and Switzerland (Katedra Literatury i Kultury Niemiec, Austrii i Szwajcarii) and the Institute of History (Instytut Historyczny). Our special gratitude is due to the historian, prof. dr hab. Przemysław Waingertner. We are planning two further publications, in German and Polish, in which other project participants: philologists, historians, archivists, political scientists and culture experts, shall present results of their studies of the Great War.

This undertaking could only be successful thanks to extensive support of the Foundation for Polish-German Cooperation (Fundacja Współpracy Polsko-Niemieckiej), our sponsor: Austrian Cultural Forum in Warsaw (Österreichisches Kulturforum Warschau), our partner: Historisches Institut, Osteuropäische Geschichte (JLU Gießen) and Prof. Dr. Hans-Jürgen Bömelburg, State Archives, The City of Łódź Office (Archiwum Państwowe, Oddział w Łodzi), Łódź City Council (Urząd Miasta Łodzi) and Goethe Institute Examination Centre (Prüfungszentrum Goethe-Institut) in Łódź. Our sincere thanks to all the above mentioned institutions.

We would like to thank Ed Lowczowski for his linguistic support and Dr. habil. Frank Schuster from the University of Gießen.

State Archive in Łódź

The Łódź War Losses Assessment Committees (Łódzkie komisje szacunkowe strat wojennych) – an undervalued source for research of the Great War in the Łódź region

The State Archive in Łódź preserves two archival fonds that potentially are an excellent material for extensive research of the history of Łódź and the Łódź region during the Great War.

This refers to the archival material of the War Losses Assessment Committee of the Łódź *powiat*[1] (Komisja Szacunkowa Strat Wojennych Powiatu Łódzkiego) (8244 archival files accounting for almost 12 linear meters) and the Local Assessment Committee in Łódź (Komisja Szacunkowa Miejscowa w Łodzi) (5923 archival files covering over 15 linear meters)[2].

Most likely, this impressive size of the fonds together with the absence of collective or statistical materials (the fonds preserve only appraisal studies of incurred losses) mean that these holdings remain pristine materials, untouched by the hand and unseen by the eye of researchers who prefer to use press materials and general reports[3].

The appraisals comprise: declaration of the injured party concerning the type and value of incurred losses (usually drafted on a printed form which also included

---

1   *Powiat* is the second-level unit of local government and administration in Poland. The term *"powiat"* is most often translated into English as "county" (trans.).

2   The fonds are complex and comprise documents from numerous appraisal committees constituted already in 1914. This paper is not concerned with a complicated history of how the archival files were inherited and taken over. The interested parties should refer to the introduction to inventory of Local Assessment Committee in Łódź by Anna Rynkowska. See: Rynkowska, Anna: *Komisja Szacunkowa Miejscowa w Łodzi* (wstęp do inwentarza). Archiwum Państwowe w Łodzi: Łódź.

3   Vide: Pietras Tomasz *Zniszczenia wojenne z okresu I wojny światowej w okolicach Łodzi* – a paper presented on 18 October 2013 during a conference *Łódź w drodze do niepodległości* organised in the Institute of History of the University of Łódź.

instruction[4]), the injured party interview report, sometimes a separate statement
of the State Main Assessment Committee in Warsaw (Państwowa Komisja Szacunkowa Główna w Warszawie) which functioned in this case as the second instance
entity. The Committee statement was of a decisive nature and determined the final
value of losses (very often it reduced the claims' amount). On many occasions, in
absence of comments from the State Main Assessment Committee, the declaration
was stamped with the Committee's stamp of approval.

The first losses were reported by the injured parties already at the beginning
of 1915 mainly to the Assessment Section (Sekcja Szacunkowa) established at the
Main Civil Committee in Łódź (Główny Komitet Obywatelski) or to the Imperial-
German Police Headquarters (Cesarsko-Niemieckie Prezydium Policji). Appraisal
reports submitted during warfare, i.e. from 1916 to 1917 in front of the Municipal
Assessment Committee (Komisja Szacunkowa Miejska)[5] include such pledge:
"I solemnly swear that, as a party injured in warfare, I will give a truthful evidence
concerning assessment of my losses, knowing that I might be called to account
for my testimony"[6]. Such solution was used probably due to a large number of
submitted declarations. Members of the Municipal Assessment Committee could
estimate the damages first hand and evaluate them in a short time. Based on the
preserved documents it can be stated that in practice the Municipal Assessment
Committee members assessed personally only the damages declared by injured
institutions such as charity associations, religious associations, the railway.

Sometimes we can find in the materials the photographs documenting the
scope of damages as well as technical drawings of destroyed or burnt down houses.
The losses were estimated in the rouble paid in gold according to pre-war rates. If
the injured persons estimated their losses in the German mark (which happened
very rarely), this amount was converted to the Russian currency. The losses were
subdivided into five categories:

---

4   What is interesting is the fact that a separate instruction concerning requisition of
    organ pipes and organs was prepared for parish priests. See: Archiwum Państwowe
    w Łodzi (henceforth: APŁ), Komisja Szacunkowa Strat Wojennych Powiatu Łódzkiego
    (henceforth: KSSWPŁ), sygn. 2490.
5   The Committee was linked to the Department of War Damages Registration of the Cen-
    tral Welfare Council in Warsaw (Wydział Rejestracji Szkód Wojennych Rady Głównej
    Opiekuńczej). It should not be confused with the Local Assessment Committee in Łódź
    which was an agency of the Central Local Assessment Committee (Główna Komisja
    Szacunkowa Miejscowa) in Warsaw.
6   All quotations in the text have been translated by the translator unless stated otherwise.

I.   Losses resulting from army requisitions including lodging infrastructure,
II. General losses (regulations of occupying and civil authorities, confiscations, contributions and penalties, forced sale, administration or operation),
III. Losses due to damages resulting directly from warfare,
IV. Losses due to a direct material losses (theft, robbery, fly from the approaching war front or fly from the areas occupied by enemy, relocation or deportation by authorities),
V.   Losses due to claims (financial).

According to materials included in the fonds the most obvious subject of research seems to be the evaluation and presentation of material losses incurred during the Great War by the Łódź citizens and industry.

Apart from military action, the basic causes of misfortune included: forced sale, confiscation or requisition. They concerned mainly industry machines and facilities, raw materials, fabrics and metals, livestock and fixed assets, food and firewood. Interestingly the injured parties addressed their claims to all three occupant countries[7] but the largest number of them was addressed to the German party[8]. According to the preserved documents, the first requisitions were performed by the Polish civil committees on their own initiative or pursuant to decrees of German authorities and concerned weapons owned by citizens[9].

The order on forced sale of goods and raw materials (only for drastically reduced prices) was applicable not only to production plants and warehouses but also to regular citizens. Together with the introduction of the above mentioned duty, people were banned from selling objects covered by forced sale to any entities apart from the ones indicated by occupation authorities[10]. They were also

---

7   The claims against Austro-Hungarian authorities were related mainly to the legions' residence in Łódź from 11 to 28 October 1914.

8   The last instalment of war reparations for France and Great Britain was paid by the Federal Republic of Germany, a successor of the Reich, on 3 October 2010 i.e. 98 years after the end of World War II. The issue of reparations for Poland has never been finally settled. Our country received a small portion of the allowed 6,5 per cent of German reparations, i.e. 8,5 billion German mark in gold. The reparations were paid in the form of army surplus equipment and railway engines.

9   Among others, Józef Pągowski, a priest from Zgierz handed over as many as two revolvers in October 1914. See: APŁ, KSSWPŁ, sygn. 2520. What is interesting is the fact that in Łódź the Central Committee of Citizens Militia (Centralny Komitet Milicji Obywatelskiej) transferred the confiscated weapons to Legionnaires on a confiscation receipt.

10 Most often it was the War Resources Department, Second Division in Łódź (Kriegsrohstoffstelle Warschau Zweigstelle Lodz) seated by ul. Cegielniana 18 (currently ul. Jaracza).

prohibited to process raw materials. On the sale the Germans usually paid a small advance[11], deposited due amounts in German banks or "paid" them in the form of war loans receipts. Discovery of any earlier undisclosed goods resulted in their confiscation, which was performed on the slightest excuse. Additionally, the persons suspected of non-disclosure of goods were punishable with up to 5 years of prison or with penalty of up to 10 000 German mark[12].

Apart from the list of obvious "goods and products necessary for army" which were subject to requisition and confiscation we will also come across such unique items as: a school globe and 3 blackboards taken from a school in Rzgów[13], a disassembled wooden surface of a bridge on the Ner river in the vicinity of the Zdziechów village[14]. The groundskeeping of a church in Łagiewniki reported, apart from losses resulting from shelling, a theft of "a halter for burying the dead" and 72 candles[15]. Likewise, the injured party – Łódź Nursing Association (Łódzkie Towarzystwo Pielęgnowania Chorych) *Bykur Cholim* reported a requisition of 4 pillows for a Russian field hospital[16]. Administration of Julianów-Marysin property reported a requisition by the Germans of 330 carts with field stones intended for road construction[17]. Mendel Burak, forced to provide lodgings for Prussian officers, reported a theft of bed sheets and a hamper[18].

The requisition receipts or copies thereof that were often attached to appraisal reports indicate the entity that performed the requisition, the exact date of the

---

11 For example, company N. and F. Hanftwurcel in Konstantynów received a cash equivalent of 765,40 rouble for a forced sale of material and equipment worth 8 392,34 rouble. The equivalent equaled only 9% of the due amount. See: APŁ, KSSWPŁ, sygn. 2071.

12 The Łódź textile industry, as already described on numerous occasions, did not pick itself up from war damages and devastation (also the loss of a large outlet in Russia played a part here). During the interwar period the large factories of I.K. Poznański, Scheibler and Grohmann basically fought for survival instead of expanding further. The issue of requisitions and confiscations that devastated industry in Łódź has been discussed broadly by Krystyna Radziszewska, see: Radziszewska, Krystyna: "Korespondencja Związku Przemysłowców Królestwa Polskiego z szefem zarządu Generalnego Gubernatorstwa Warszawskiego 1915–1916. Prezentacja źródła archiwalnego". In: Radziszewska, Krystyna/ Zawilski, Piotr (eds.): *Między wielką historią a codziennością*. Archiwum Państwowe w Łodzi/Wydawnictwo Uniwersytetu Łódzkiego: Łódź 2011, p. 37–48.

13 APŁ, KSSWPŁ, sygn. 1161.

14 Ibid., sygn. 135.

15 Ibid., sygn. 1229.

16 Ibid., sygn. 1697.

17 Ibid., sygn. 1656.

18 APŁ, KSSWPŁ, sygn. 502.

requisition and even about the destination place of the requisitioned materials and raw materials[19].

From the beginning of 1915 requisitions covered also machines and equipment[20]. They were carefully checked before being dispatched from the city. Their files include the manufacturer's name, production date, weight and dimensions as well as their value. Consequently, the researchers are able to assess the condition of machinery in Łódź factories at the outbreak of war. The machine metrics was signed by the Łódź owner, the German "buyer" and a representative of the company where the machine was sent[21].

Another type of losses, a purely financial one, arose in consequence of the lost bank deposits and interest rates[22], a ban on practising law by lawyers and notaries and the loss of income from lease of flats occupied by reservists women (wives of reservists conscripted into the Russian army)[23]. During submission of appraisal reports testimonies were collected from women[24]. The testimonies inform us about the address, the number of occupied rooms and the due rent. Besides, based on the number of crosses used instead of signatures, we can state that about 50% of

---

19 Company M. Kleczewski i ska – a finishing and dyer shop in Zgierz presented confirmations of receipt (certified copies thereof) of velour, satin, cashmere, etc. that were "expropriated" in 1917 and 1918 and sent to Saarbrucken, Królewiec and Munster. See: Ibid., sygn. 2434.

20 Machine Sequester Commission (Maschinen-Beschlagnachme-Kommission) located by ul. Przejazd 30 (now: ul. Tuwima) was responsible for these activities.

21 Machines were transported among others to Altona (now a district of Hamburg), Essen, Ludwigshafen, Kassel.

22 In the situation of general poverty and destruction even the smallest losses were reported. Mariavite Credit-Saving Association (Mariawickie Towarzystwo Pożyczkowo-Oszczędnościowe) in Zgierz reported that 5 rouble, with a due interest rate, was lost in consequence of evacuation by the Russian authorities of the Zgierz Postal Office Savings Bank (Pocztowa Kasa Oszczędnościowa) in which the Association deposited its money. See: APŁ, KSSWPŁ, sygn. 2525.

23 The losses related to this constitute the largest part of the archival material in the Municipal Assessment Committee in Łódź and comprise ca. 1100 files. According to the decree of the Russian government of 10 August 1914, servicemen and their families could not be forced to vacate the flats they occupied. Still, the reservist women, deprived of livelihood, could not pay their rent.

24 Lack of a testimony led to automatic rejection of a claim for payment for a flat occupied by a reservist woman. Only 46 out of the 52 reservist women reported by the Joint Stock Society of Cotton Products of I. K. Poznański (Towarzystwo Akcyjne Wyrobów Bawełnianych I.K. Poznańskiego) submitted their testimonies and the loss was estimated only on the basis thereof. See: APŁ, KSMŁ, sygn. 3818.

women was illiterate. Using the same documents we can also estimate the scale of
conscription into the Russian army. The Joint-Stock Company of Widzew Cotton
Manufacture (Towarzystwo Akcyjne Widzewskiej Manufaktury Bawełnianej) reported a loss resulting from rent that had not been paid by as many as 104 reservist
women. And not all the workers of this factory lived in multi-family houses for
factory workers[25]. Losses due to unpaid rent were also estimated in case of a forced
evacuation of residents by the Russian authorities[26]. Similar losses resulted from
a forced provision of lodgings for servicemen[27]. This was particularly painful for
the Łódź hotels and in particular for the Grand Hotel which had been fully taken
over by the Prussian army and which till October 1916 was banned from renting
rooms to civilians[28]. The appraisal reports contain questionnaires with the family
name and the rank of the lodgings owner, the number of months and sometimes
the name of a military unit.

Declarations presented in front of committees can also provide material for
historians studying the development of industry in the Lodz region. The documents contain for example lists of confiscated machines with indication of the
machine type, manufacturers and even the year of production. Thanks to the lists
of confiscated finished goods it is possible to determine exactly the production

---

25 Ibid., sygn. 1649.
26 This refers to Russian administration clerks evacuated to the East as well as to the
    interned subjects of Germany or Austria-Hungary. The Share Society of K. Scheibler
    Cotton Factories (Towarzystwo Akcyjne Wyrobów Bawełnianych Karola Scheiblera)
    reported a war loss consisting of a rent due for the first 9 months of 1914 for rental of
    the Society's buildings by ul. Konstantynowska 60/62 (now: ul. Legionów), which were
    used as army barracks. See: Ibid., sygn. 4333.
27 Pursuant to the laws concerning provision of lodgings all unoccupied flats were sub-
    ject to registration and had to be made available for servicemen and German clerks.
    A general was entitled to a three-room flat, a staff officer – to two rooms and a captain –
    to one room. Cost of the lodgings was calculated according to the rank: lodgings of a
    general cost 3,50 German mark, lodgings of a captain or a lieutenant – half of this cost,
    i.e. 1, 75 German mark, lodgings of privates and orderlies – 0,50 German mark for 3
    persons. The army of course did not pay for anything. Some facilities were occupied
    throughout the whole war. The Posselt Villa belonging to the Zgierz Cotton Factory
    (Towarzystwo Akcyjne Zgierskiej Manufaktury) was occupied by the Germans from
    17 November 1914 to 13 November 1918. See: APŁ, KSSWPŁ, sygn. 2480.
28 For example General Gerecke paid 3 German mark per day for a room, which before
    the war cost 20 rouble, so he only covered 10% of due amount. See: APŁ, KSMŁ, sygn.
    1806.

profile, its assortment breakdown and the market value of individual products and raw materials[29].

Very detailed lists and declarations presented by the near-Łódź farmers enable determination of farmsteads' condition in terms of livestock, the type and volume of their agricultural produce as well as the farming equipment, furniture and facilities of the farms[30]. This group of the injured persons described their losses in a particularly meticulous way and did not focus on exact determination of the time when their losses occurred.

Foundations and associations that appeared before both Committees often described, apart from their lost assets, also a detailed profile of their business and the composition of authorities. While studying the lists of these organisations we can easily note that they were mostly of a philanthropic and charity nature.

The losses were only partially caused by direct military actions of 1914 (only ca. 10% of claims in the Municipal Assessment Committee and ca. 30% of claims in the War Losses Assessment Committee of the Łódź *powiat*). However, generally, it is thanks to these materials that we can specify exactly a map of sites affected by the German bombing or the route of the front line in November and December 1914.

It is generally believed that contributions were imposed only by occupying authorities but there are materials that indicate the Russian side. For instance, the majority of Starowa Góra inhabitants reported that in November 1914 the Russian army imposed on the village a contribution of 500 rouble for breaking of the field telephone cable lines by unknown perpetrators[31].

---

29 Particularly unfortunate entrepreneurs incurred all possible losses caused by both warring parties. Company Grossbart & Heyman in Konstantynów initially suffered in consequence of collection by the Russians of finished woolen goods worth over 30 thousand rouble. Then, as a result of the German shelling, the factory buildings worth more than 27 thousand rouble were destroyed or damaged. Next, heirloom jewelry worth 2700 rouble was stolen from a broken safe. Finally, during the German occupation, the remaining machinery and raw materials were confiscated. All plagues culminated in a verdict of the German court which imposed a penalty of 300 rouble for selling resources without permission of the occupant authorities. See: APŁ, KSSWPŁ, sygn. 2038.

30 Based on the review of declarations submitted by farmers it can be claimed that the condition of the near-Łódź farmsteads was very good. Nearly every farmer reported a loss of a silver watch. It seems that especially these declarations should be taken with some caution.

31 Ibid., sygn. 597.

It was also common to apply financial penalties for opening business premises or a bakery too early or for closing them too late; for weighing too much or too little goods; for offering for sale too fresh (less than 24 hours) bread.

Confiscation of the church bells is one of the best known facts often quoted to illustrate the policy of the German occupant. This fact is also reflected in the materials of both Committees, in which we can find data concerning not only the weight and the value of bells but also the names of their founders, their proper names, the year of casting, the exact date of confiscation and even information that the bells were destroyed immediately after they had been taken down. The fond of the War Losses Assessment Committee of the Łódź *powiat* contains a surprising information concerning a Catholic parish in Aleksandrów which for 2 big requisitioned bells received 1 smaller bell that had most likely been taken from some cemetery chapel[32]. We do not know what the Aleksandrów parish priest did to deserve such "special" treatment.

The material also depict numerous intermediate losses that are difficult to classify. Yet, the removal of these losses was surely very important for the injured parties. For instance, we can mention "a church organ detuned by soldiers" reported by a church in Łagiewniki[33]. Apparently, the church organ was in the condition that prevented musical setting of the masses and the re-tuning of this very complex instrument required hiring of an expensive tuner. Another unusual loss covered remuneration of forest workers due for the clearance of the forest in Kały which had been hit by shelling[34]. This loss entailed another one – the forest owner not only lost lumber but also had to bear additional costs for the removal of forest down timber. The burning of all accounting documents of the Credit-Savings Bank (Kasa Pożyczkowo-Oszczędnościowa) in Konstantynów, including a register of savings deposits and loans, meant that it "is almost brought to ruin" and unable to enforce liabilities and properly estimate claims of its members who wanted to withdraw their savings[35].

I cannot stop myself from sharing with you the information about a document included in one of the appraisal reports. The archival files include a copy of a confirmation issued in German by the Imperial-German Powiat Bank (Cesarsko-Niemiecka Kasa Powiatowa) in Rawa dated 12 November 1918. This small piece of paper reminds us that the regaining of independence was not an outcome of

---

32   Ibid., sygn. 10.
33   Ibid., sygn. 1229.
34   Ibid., sygn. 1697.
35   Ibid., sygn. 2096.

a one-day upsurge but a continuous, long and complex process[36]. Withdrawal of the German army and administration from the areas of the former Russian annexation was gradual and continued in 1918. Withdrawal from the Prussian annexation (in particular from Pomerania) lasted until 1920.

Due to the limitations of this report, the author has randomly selected only individual sample material chosen from over 1400 files. I hope that the selected examples are interesting enough to attract researches who will study this extensive material in a more disciplined way.

---

36 APŁ, KSSWPŁ, sygn. 4626.

Tomasz Walkiewicz

State Archive in Łódź

Archiwum Państwowe w Łodzi

Polish military formations of the First World War in documents preserved at the State Archive in Łódź

The efforts of Poland to rebuild the state during the First World War were active on two stages: diplomacy and armed combat. In the military sphere, the struggle for independence depended on creating and maintaining Polish military formations. Depending on their organisers' political affiliation, these formations were allied to the Central Powers or the Entente countries. The enlisting volunteers wished to participate in armed combat for an independent Poland. Ready to shed their blood and willing to make the highest sacrifices, they ascertained the Polish nation's inalienable right to their own homeland.

The goal of this paper is to present source material found in the State Archive in Łódź (*Archiwum Państwowe w Łodzi*) concerning a number of Polish military formations of the First World War. Firstly, the information presented below refers to archival material related to military formations emerging by the side of Central Powers – the Polish Legions (*Legiony Polskie*), The Polish Auxiliary Corps (*Polski Korpus Posiłkowy*, PKP) and Polish Armed Force (*Polska Siła Zbrojna*, PSZ), also called *Polnische Wehrmacht*. Further descriptions refer to archival material on the secret Polish Military Organisation (*Polska Organizacja Wojskowa*, POW). The subsequent sections describe source material associated with military formations created by the Russian forces – the Puławy Legion (*Legion Puławski*) and the I Polish Corps (*I Korpus Polski*). Finally I describe archival material referring to the Polish military in France, the Blue Army, serving alongside the allied forces and seen as an allied force.

The source material for each particular military formation is presented within its home fonds. Due to its limited scope, this paper does not include the characteristics of each military formation. Information about their organisational history and combat specifics can be found in related literature[1].

---

1 The history of the creation, organisation and activities of the military formations described in this article may be found in the following publications: Bagiński, Henryk:

On the side of the Central Powers
Polish Legions, Polish Auxiliary Corps, Polish Armed Force

The main fonds for Polish military formations on the side of the Central Powers is the Chief Enrolment Office for the Polish Army in Piotrków. Regrettably, its archive has barely survived and is composed of only 48 units. The individual files

---

Wojsko polskie na Wschodzie 1914–1920. Wojskowy Instytut Naukowo-Wydawniczy: Warszawa 1921; Gąsiorowski, Wacław: *Historia Armii Polskiej we Francji 1915–1916.* Stowarzyszenie Weteranów Armii Polskiej w Ameryce Placówka w Bydgoszczy: Łódź 1939; Klimecki, Michał, Krzysztof Filipow: *Legiony Polskie. Dzieje bojowe i organizacyjne.* Bellona Spółka Akcyjna: Warszawa 2014; Kozłowski, Eligiusz, Mieczysław Wrzosek: *Historia oręża polskiego 1795–1939.* Państwowe Wydawnictwo Wiedza Powszechna: Warszawa 1984; Sienkiewicz, Witold (ed.): *Legenda Legionów. Opowieść o legionach oraz ludziach Józefa Piłsudskiego.* Wydawnictwo Demart S. A.: Warszawa 2010; Lipiński, Wacław: *Bajończycy i Armia Polska we Francji.* Bellona 1929, Vol. 33, Issue 1.: Warszawa 1929; *id., Walka zbrojna o niepodległość Polski w latach 1905–1918.* Oficyna Wydawnicza Volumen: Warszawa 1990 (1ˢᵗ ed., 1931); Nałęcz, Tomasz: *Polska Organizacja Wojskowa 1914–1918.* Ossolineum: Wrocław 1984; Wawrzyński, Tadeusz: "Polski Korpus Posiłkowy (1917–1918)". In: *Studia i Materiały do Historii Wojskowości 1986,* vol. 29; Wojciechowski, Zbigniew: "Polski czyn zbrojny w pierwszej wojnie światowej". In: *Colloquium Wydziału Nauk Humanistycznych i Społecznych Akademii Marynarki Wojennej 2009,* vol. 1; Wrzosek, Mieczysław: *Polski czyn zbrojny podczas pierwszej wojny światowej 1914–1918.* Instytut Wydawniczy PAX: Warszawa 1990; *id., Polskie formacje wojskowe podczas pierwszej wojny światowej.* Sekcja Wydawnicza Filii Uniwersytetu Warszawskiego: Białystok 1977; *id., Polskie korpusy wojskowe w Rosji w latach 1917–1918.* Książka i Wiedza: Warszawa 1969; *id.,* "Polskie ochotnicze formacje wojskowe podczas pierwszej wojny światowej i w okresie następnych dwóch lat (1914–1920)". In: *Białostockie Teki Historyczne 2012,* Vol. 10; Wysocki, Wiesław, Wiktor Cygan and Jan Kasprzyk: *Legiony Polskie 1914–1918.* Volumen: Warszawa 2014; Stawecki, Piotr (ed.): *Zarys dziejów wojskowości polskiej w latach 1864–1939.* Wydawnictwo Ministerstwa Obrony Narodowej: Warszawa 1990. Most of the archive material represented in this paper is related to Łódź, for information on military units active in the city during the Great War cf. Czernielewski, Konrad A.: "Polskie formacje zbrojne w Łodzi. Od przybycia Legionów w październiku 1914 r. do powstania garnizonu Wojska Polskiego w listopadzie 1918 r." *Piotrkowskie Zeszyty Historyczne* 2011, Vol. 12, part 2. Polish Legions' stay in Łódź is also described by: Ajnenkiel, Eugeniusz: *Pierwsze oddziały Legionów Polskich w Łodzi 12–29 października 1914 r.* Księgarnia S. Seipelt: Łódź 1934; Bogalecki, Tadeusz Z.: *Tradycje legionowe w regionie łódzkim 1914–2014.* Drukarnia WIST. Antoni Wierzbowski: Łódź, Zgierz 2014; Jarno, Witold: "Legiony Polskie w Łodzi w okresie I wojny światowej". W: Daszyńska, Jolanta (ed.): *Łódź w drodze do niepodległości.* Księży Młyn Dom Wydawniczy: Łódź 2013; Klimek, Jan: "Park amunicyjny Legionów Polskich w Łodzi (Retkinia – Brus – Srebrna)". *Niepodległość* 1934, Vol. 9.

contain circulars and commands of the Military Department of the Supreme National Commitee (*Departament Wojskowy Naczelnego Komitetu Narodowego*, DW NKN) from 1915–1917[2]; briefings and instructions by the Command of Polish Legions from 1915–1917[3]; orders by the Command of the Polish Legions' Group from 1915–1917[4]; officer orders issued by Polish Auxiliary Corps Command in 1917–1918[5]; memorials and projects concerning the formation of Polish Armed Force[6]; officer orders, communiques and instructions by the Polish Armed Force Enrolment Inspectorate from 1917–1918[7]; orders by the Enrolment Inspectorate in Radomsko from 1917[8]; correspondence related to enlisting volunteers to Polish Legions and Polish Armed Force[9]; reports (daily, weekly and annual) of enlistment procedures conducted in 1915–1918 in the following counties (*powiat*[10] districts): Noworadomsk, Piotrków, Koneck and Opoczno[11]; registers of Legion soldiers employed at the enlistment offices[12]; identity cards of Noworadomsk county enlistment emissaries[13]; files concerning the living conditions of Legion officers[14] and correspondence concerning organising Christmas celebrations for Polish Legion soldiers[15].

These reports contain a considerable amount of interesting information, which sheds light not only on the outcomes of enlistment actions, but sometimes also on the attitudes of local town and village dwellers to the occupants and the new Polish armed forces formed under their auspices. The documents seem to suggest that

---

2 National Archives in Łódź (Archiwum Państwowe w Łodzi, APŁ): Główny Urząd Zaciągu do Wojska Polskiego w Piotrkowie 1914–1920 (Chief Enrollment Office for the Polish Army in Piotrków 1914–1920, GUZWP), ref. 1–2. Duplicates of varying orders of the Military Department of the Supreme National Commitee from 1915–1917 may be found in the fonds of ephementa 1882–2007 (further referred to as ZDiPU), ref. 290.

3 APŁ: GUZWP, sygn. 4–7, 11.

4 Ibid., ref. 12–15.

5 Ibid., ref. 8–9.

6 Ibid., ref. 27.

7 Ibid., ref. 9, 19, 25.

8 Ibid., ref. 10.

9 Ibid., ref. 37, 40.

10 *Powiat* is the second-level unit of local government and administration in Poland. The term "*powiat*" is most often translated into English as "county" (trans.).

11 Ibid., ref. 32, 34, 35, 36, 38, 39.

12 Ibid., ref. 29, 30.

13 Ibid., ref. 43.

14 Ibid., ref. 44.

15 Ibid., ref. 45.

the activities of enlistment emissaries were frequently met with indifference or outright hostility. This prevailing attitude was probably the result of ruthless requisitions of food and wheat, poor treatment of people and common pro-Russian sympathies. A report written by an enlistment emissary at the Enlistment Post in Gorzkowice on 9 February 1917, states:

> Whilst visiting the above towns and villages we have noticed low spirits caused by diverse requisitions. The peasantry is full of bitterness. Requisitions were conducted in an appalling manner – acts such as hitting women with rifle butts were common. The requisitioning officers have no concern for public opinion. As a result, the peasantry declare that they do not intend to break their vows of loyalty to the Emperor. They are undermining whatever good work we do here. […] No one volunteered [to enlist – T.W.][16, 17]

In their reports the emissaries also described the local elites' (represented by the town mayor, local clerk, vicar, organist, and landowners) attitude to the idea of forming a Polish army, and the likelihood of their cooperation.

The second fond containing extensive material associated with Polish military formations allied with Austria-Hungary and Germany is the Ephemeral Print Collection[18]. Numerous affiches and flyers calling Poles to join the ranks of Polish Legions have been preserved. One of the earliest examples is Ignacy Daszyński's proclamation from August 22nd, 1914, in which Daszyński appeals to workers from the Kingdom of Poland: "Whoever considers himself a Pole, hurries to join the ranks of Polish soldiers!"[19]. Another address, published in 1915 by the Chief Enrolment Office for the Polish Army in Piotrków, appeals ardently: "Do not wait! If you can carry arms, go, enlist in the Polish Legions! […] There is no time to hesitate, when Motherland calls. Hurry – fight for the Polish cause, and take the others with you!"[20]. Not all appeals have been written in this stately tone, however; examples of humorous publications include a dialogue titled "A Conversation between the Brave Maciek and the Cowardly Walek" (*Rozmowa dzielnego Maćka z tchórzliwym Walkiem*) printed in a circular published by the Association for the Enlistment to the Polish Armed Forces (*Koło Propagandy na rzecz Wojska*

---

16 Ibid., ref. 36, sheet. 80.
17 Unless stated otherwise, all translations in the text have been provied by the translator.
18 The fonds are currently being completed. In the future, the files will be marked with new reference numbers, replacing the ones currently in use. Reaching the items referenced in the article will be possible through the use of concordance, as prepareed by the archivist responsible for the fonds.
19 APŁ: ZDiPU, ref. 288, p. 4.
20 Ibid., ref. 291, p. 16.

Polskiego) in Piotrków[21]. Appeals directed to men convincing them to join the ranks of the emerging Polish military can also be found in the address published by the Polish Military Organisation (Polska Organizacja Narodowa, PON)[22], Polish Legions Enlistment Commission[23] and Polish Legions officers from Zgierz[24] and the Piotrków district[25]. Ephemeral propaganda prints and leaflets were also directed at Polish women. In the proclamation by the Łódź War Alert Women's League (Liga Kobiet Pogotowia Wojennego Okręgu Łódzkiego) from 1915, the following message is aimed at female landowners: "It is your duty, too, to aid in the effort to free our homeland [...] you must advocate the cause, call others to join the ranks of the Legions and free our Country! Call your husbands, brothers and sons to fight for the sacred cause!"[26]. Women were expected to provide moral support, as well as material help. One example of this is the proclamation by the Women's Humanitarian and Educational Association (Humanitarno-Oświatowe Stowarzyszenie Kobiet) in Opatów, published in November 1915. It calls to contribute to the Christmas gift fund for Legion soldiers[27]. The Central Christmas Fund Committee (Centralny Komitet Gwiazdkowy dla Legionistów) also asked Poles for generosity in an appeal dated 1916[28]. Other preserved appeals concern the Polish Legions entering several cities in the Kingdom of Poland, such as Radomsk in 1915[29] or Warsaw in 1916[30], and the matter of commemorating fallen soldiers[31].

This fonds also includes several proclamations related to the Polish Auxiliary Corps. In this group there is a paper issued to the Legions by several dozen Polish political activists, officials and intellectuals – mainly from Warsaw – published after Józef Piłsudski's dismissal from the Polish Legions. The signatories called the soldiers to keep the faith in armed combat for Polish independence, as well as to see the imminent creation of Polish Auxiliary Corps as a sign of progress[32].

---

21 Ibid., ref. 291, p. 23.
22 Ibid., ref. 200, pp. 3–6.
23 Ibid., ref. 291, p. 79.
24 Ibid., ref. 288, p. 55.
25 Ibid., ref. 291, p. 14.
26 Ibid., ref. 299, pp. 10, 35 (duplicate).
27 Ibid., ref. 288, p. 228.
28 Ibid., ref. 288, p. 244.
29 Ibid., ref. 288, p. 52.
30 Ibid., ref. 352, p. 29 (reproduction of the address in the source publication: *Pamiątki wojenne*. Wydawnictwo Pamiątek Wojennych: Warszawa 1918).
31 Ibid., ref. 288, p. 238.
32 Ibid., ref. 288, p. 248.

The creation of a large Legions formation is also the subject of the proclamation titled "To the Officers and Soldiers of the Polish Army" (*Do oficerów i żołnierzy Wojska Polskiego*), published on 2 October 1916 by Colonels Marian Żegota Januszajtis, Zygmunt Zieliński and Józef Haller. In the proclamation, they informed the soldiers that "after two years of hard, arduous fighting, full of bloodshed and sacrifice" the first "seed of the Polish Army – the first Polish Corps" had been established. They assured their soldiers about their own unwavering will to continue on the chosen course and stay true to a Polish soldier's duty[33]. It is also worthwhile to mention another proclamation, written by Józef Haller, entitled "To the Polish Nation!" (*Do narodu Polskiego!*), published in 1918 after the Polish Auxiliary Corps troops had broken through the Austro-Hungarian front to join the Polish forces in the East[34].

An address from 9 November 1916, written by Colonel General Hans von Beseler and Governor General Karl Kuk, concerns the Polish Armed Forces formed alongside Germany. In this address they appealed to the population of Lublin and Warsaw to enlist in the ranks of the emerging Polish armed forces[35].

The Ephemeral Prints Collection features also diverse announcements and proclamations related to the Polish Auxiliary Corps. Notable among these are Regulations Concerning Voluntary Enlistment into the Polish Army (*Przepisy dotyczące dobrowolnego wstępowania do wojska polskiego*) issued by Gen. Beseler on 12 November 1916 (the regulations specify, among others, the time and place for volunteers to enlist, the required minimum age, personal documents, available weapons and appropriate uniforms)[36] and "An Instruction for Volunteers Enlisting into the Polish Army" (*Pouczenie dla ochotników do Wojska Polskiego*) published by the Polish Armed Force Enrollment Inspectorate[37] featuring, among others, the locations of enlistment posts in Łódź and Piotrków[38].

This fonds also contains ephemeral material such as songs and poems related to the Legions. A postcard print from 1915 is devoted to the memory of Rittmeister Zbigniew Dunin-Wąsowicz and a dozen other cavalry soldiers fallen in the Charge of Rokitna. The document is accompanied by a poem written by Stanisław Stwora, entitled "Of the Polish Soldier" (*Strofy o żołnierzu polskim*)[39]. Military humour

---

33 Ibid., ref. 288, p. 239.
34 Ibid., ref. 288, p. 314.
35 Ibid., ref. 293, sheet 7.
36 Ibid., ref. 293, sheet 19.
37 Ibid., ref. 293, sheet 1.
38 Ibid., ref. 293, sheet 9.
39 Ibid., ref. 288, sheet 359.

is present in an anonymous work titled "A Letter to a Girl from a Polish Legion Officer" (*List Legionisty do dziewczyny*)[40]. Among other preserved works there are two letters written in verse addressed to Józef Piłsudski, written by Zdzisław Kleszczyński[41] and Roman Musialik[42] and a flyer with a soldiers' oath (*Rota 4 p.p. W.P.*) by an unknown author[43]. Another interesting ephemeral print dates from 1915, had been published in Kraków and contains a poem by Mieczysław Smolarski entitled "To Arms" (*Pod broń*) with musical notations for a male choir, composed by Aleksander Orłowski (the title page of this print is illustrated with a drawing depicting Brigadier Józef Piłsudski)[44]. Among other notable prints is the series "Riflemen's Songs" (*Pieśni strzeleckie*), published by Military Department of the Supreme National Committee in Piotrków, containing two songbooks and musical notations for songs such as: *Hej tam pod Warszawą*[45] and *Marsz Strzelców*[46].

Furthermore, this collection contains a variety of other ephemeral material, including speeches by Bishop Władysław Bandurski (honorary Chaplain of the 1st Brigade of the Polish Legions)[47]; an open letter from Władysław Studnicki to the writer Henryk Sienkiewicz, calling the latter to use his authority to publicly support the Polish Legions[48]; an officer's letter describing the oath crisis in the 1st Infantry Regiment of the Polish Legions[49]; a postcard-image of a Legion officer given to financial contributors to the Independence Monument in Pabianice[50] and a text document containing information on the reorganisation of the enlistment system in 1917 following the creation of the Polish Armed Forces alongside Germany[51].

A separate category of materials in this fonds is formed by multi-page documents concerning the Polish Legions. Several of these are worth mentioning. A valuable publication entitled "Polish Legions 16 August 1914–16 August 1915. Documents" (*Legiony Polskie 16 sierpnia 1914–16 sierpnia 1915. Dokumenty*) was

---

40   Ibid., ref. 324, sheet 75.
41   Ibid., ref. 324, pp. 207–210, also ref. 495, pp. 60–63.
42   Ibid., ref. 495, p. 2.
43   Ibid., ref. 495, p. 110.
44   Ibid., ref. 288, pp. 214–217.
45   Ibid., ref. 288, pp. 211–213, also ref. 495, pp. 114–117.
46   Ibid., ref. 288, pp. 218–221.
47   Ibid., ref. 288, pp. 3, 226, 231–232.
48   Ibid., ref.291, sheet. 55.
49   Ibid., ref. 288, p. 280.
50   Ibid., ref. 495, p. 90.
51   Ibid., ref. 293, sheet 10.

issued in Piotrków in 1915[52]. Also preserved are six volumes of "Lists of Losses" (*Listy strat Legionów Polskich*), containing diverse data on sick, wounded or missing soldiers in 1915–1916[53]. Rich iconographic material can be found in the "Album of the 1st Regiment of the Polish Legion Brigade" (*Album I. Pułku I. Brygady Legionów Polskich*), published in Kraków in 1915[54]. Also in 1915, a small publication was issued: "The European War. Stories by Polish Soldiers" (*Wojna europejska. Krótkie opowieści żołnierzy polskich*)[55]. Texts written by Polish Legions fighters are also included in "The wounded soldier: An ephemeral collection" (*O rannym żołnierzu. Ulotne pismo zbiorowe*), printed in Warsaw in 1917[56]. Also noteworthy are two illustrated *leporella* folders from 1914 presenting uniforms (of infantry, cavalry and artillery), head gear and military rank emblems in the Polish Legions[57]. To accompany this, an instruction booklet "Allowances for Polish Legions families" (*Zasiłki dla rodzin Legionistów-Królewiaków*), published by Military Department of the Supreme National Commitee in Piotrków details the regulations concerning granting monetary allowances to families of underprivileged Legions soldiers living in the Kingdom of Poland[58]. Political issues are at the core of "The Tragedy of Polish Legions" (*Tragedia Legionów*), published in Warsaw in 1916[59] and the anonymous, and not dated, "Polish Legions: the Truth and the Gossip" (*Prawda i plotka o Legionach Polskich*)[60].

The Ephemeral Prints Collection also contains several titles of newspapers and periodicals which feature information about Polish military formations by the side of Central Powers. These are, among others: "Dekada: pismo żołnierza polskiego" – issues: 1–3, 5, 10/1917)[61], "Goniec Polowy Legionów. Dziennik rozporządzeń Komendy Legionów Polskich" (issues: 9/1915 and 13/1916) [62], "Ilustrowany Kurier Wojenny" (1/1914)[63], "Ilustrowany Tygodnik Polski" (issue 5/1915)[64], "Kronika

---

52 Ibid., ref. 288, pp. 86–206.
53 Ibid., ref. 292.
54 Ibid., ref. 289.
55 Ibid., ref. 288, sheet 229.
56 Ibid., ref. 288, sheet 222.
57 Ibid., ref. 495, pp. 74–78, 81–87.
58 Ibid., ref. 288, sheet 250.
59 Ibid., ref. 288, pp. 56–71.
60 Ibid., ref. 288, sheet 353.
61 Ibid., ref. 303.
62 Ibid., ref. 302.
63 Ibid., ref. 418.
64 Ibid., ref. 335, pp. 119–138.

Polska" (volumes: 1–3/1916)[65], "Legion Młodych" (issue 5–6–7/1934)[66], "Legionista Polski: redagowany przez Legionistów z r. 1914–1918" (issues: 3–7/1938)[67], "Legiony. Jednodniówka ilustrowana" (published in Warsaw in June 1917)[68], "Na posterunku" (a special edition published on August 6th, 1916 and the 5/1917 issue)[69], "Piłsudczycy" (3 issues from 1933–1937)[70], "Polen. Wochenschrift für Polnische Interessen" (issues: 1–14, 16, 19/1915)[71], "Polnische Legionen 1914–1915" (a single-issue publication printed in Vienna)[72], "Polska" (issue 6/1918)[73], "Rząd i Wojsko" (diverse issues from 1916–1919)[74], "Wiadomości Polskie" (several dozen issues from 1914–1917)[75], "Żołnierz legionów i POW" (seven issues from 1937–1939)[76]. Furthermore, the collection contains press cut-outs related to the events in Kielce from August 6th, 1914, from the periodicals: "Dzień" and "Łowiczanin"[77] – and an article entitled "The arrival of Polish Legions soldiers to Łódź" (*Przybycie legionistów do Łodzi*) printed in "Gazeta Łódzka" (no. 327/1916)[78].

As regards the archival material grouped in this fonds, it is also worthwhile to mention the documents which concern veteran organisations, such as the Polish Legions Veterans' Association (Związek Legionistów Polskich), the War Veterans' of the Republic of Poland Association (Związek Inwalidów Wojennych Rzeczypospolitej Polskiej) or the "Legions Family" (Rodzina Legionowa) Association. Several files contain the statutes and regulations for these veterans' and families' organisations, association activity reports, proclamations, bulletins and other material[79].

The Iconographic Collections of the State Archive in Łódź feature several publications, postcards and photographic material related to Polish Legion formations. Among these, notable are the "Polish Legions Album" (*Album Legionów Polskich*),

---

65 Ibid., ref. 298.
66 Ibid., ref. 330.
67 Ibid., ref. 331.
68 Ibid., ref. 335, pp. 24–39.
69 Ibid., ref. 300.
70 Ibid., ref. 332.
71 Ibid., ref. 428.
72 Ibid., ref. 335, pp. 1–11.
73 Ibid., ref. 335, pp. 177–188.
74 Ibid., ref. 296.
75 Ibid., ref. 294–295.
76 Ibid., ref. 333.
77 Ibid., ref. 442, pp. 52, 57.
78 Ibid., ref. 288, p. 31.
79 Ibid., ref. 323–325, 328.

printed in Kraków in 1916[80]; an album featuring photographs of bridges built in Wołyń by the soldiers of the 1st Brigade of Polish Legions[81]; several postcards adorned by satirical drawings depicting Polish Legions fighters[82]; a postcards issued by the Supreme National Committee in 1915 with a photograph of trenches near Dzierzkowice[83]; a postcard with a portrait of Józef Piłsudski by Leonard Stroynowski[84] and wartime photographs of the Brigadier[85].

Materials concerning the Polish Legions can be also found in some private archive fonds. The archives of Potocki and Ostrowski families from Małuszyn contain a manuscript of landowner Ludwika Ostrowska, in which she describes the daily life of her family in the first year of the Great War. Ostrowska mentions the Polish Legions (who had been stationed in the Małuszyn, near Noworadom-sko) on two occasions. Both fragments of her journal are revealing and illustrate the attitude of the clergy, landowners and peasantry from the Russian partition to the Polish Legions in the first year of the war. For this reason it is worthwhile to quote them in full. On 23 August 1914, Ostrowska wrote:

> [...] on Sunday, we have encountered the most painful instance of the condition affecting our miserable Country. Our politicians in Petersburg declare a brotherly alliance with Russia against a common enemy; and at the same time, our politicians in Kraków claim solidarity with the Riflemen[86]. Following meeting in three fighting armies, the volunteers are to meet on the battlefields. It is the most painful chaos. On Sunday morning, 5 armed Riflemen arrived from Kurzelów to confiscate 5 draught horses – there were no saddle horses. The mobilisation took 24 [horses – T.W.] from Małuszyn and the surroundings – that is now a total of 29. What is going to happen next? They left before the Mass – I haven't laid eyes on them. People here do not trust nor think well of them; the Russian side is who they support here[87].

---

80 APŁ: Zbiór albumów ikonograficznych 1880–1998 (Fonds of iconographic albums 1880–1998), ref. A-LXXII (Volume 1), A-LXXIII (Volume 2).

81 Ibid., ref. A-XXX.

82 APŁ: Zbiór ikonograficzny Archiwum Państwowego w Łodzi 1866–1997, 2014, (Inconographic fonds of the State Archive in Łódź 1866–1997, 2014) example signature. R/17 (*My piechota* – We, the infantry), R/20a (*A ja z N.K.N.* – I am from NKN), R/21 (*!Kawalerya!* – !Cavalry!).

83 Ibid., ref. W-I 5–103.

84 Ibid., ref. O-I P/7.

85 Ibid., ref. O-I P/21, O-I P/22.

86 In the first of the quoted memoir sections, Ludwika Ostrowska still calls the Piłsudski Legionists commonly as "shooters" – T.W.

87 APŁ: Archiwum Potockich i Ostrowskich z Maluszyna 1425–1944 (The Maluszyn Potockis and Ostrowskis Archive 1425–1944, further referred to as APiOM), ref. II/87 item 2, pp. 98–99.

The Legions entered Małuszyn for the second time on Sunday, April 25, 1915. The fighters' aim was to enlist new volunteers while there. Once again the local community approached Polish soldiers with deep mistrust. Ostrowska notes:

> Three Legions fighters from Radomsko arrived in the evening. They paid a visit to the Vicar, asking him to use the pulpit for the purpose of calling the community to arms, which he refused to do, just like all other clergymen here. After the Mass had concluded, one of the soldiers spoke to the congregation, without much success; reportedly people were leaving and paying little attention. They proceeded to visit the surrounding villages and spread the propaganda door-to-door. Apparently not many people were interested – not in the village, not in the estates. I have read the leaflets they distribute; they exude patriotism and a near-mystical religious fervour, but the feeling is of artifice and of – as they say – a cover-up, obfuscating less noble goals. It is sad to think how many young people sacrifice all, in the best of faith – and that sacrifice mostly results in an even greater sorrow for the Country.
>
> 28 [April – T.W.]: the Legions' campaigning seems to have ended. Tuesday [April 27th – T.W.] has been designated as the enlistment day. Several more officers arrived, but their effort was futile. No one volunteered, and the officers finally left for Radomsko. There had been fears of forced enlistment and the local youth have reportedly hid in the woods[88].

The archives of Potocki and Ostrowski families from Małuszyn also contain a proclamation entitled "National Government to the People of Kielce District" (*Rząd Narodowy do ogółu Obywateli Ziemi Kieleckiej*), issued in August 1914 and signed by the General Command of the Polish Armed Forces. It contains a summons to young men to "join the ranks of Riflemen", as well as an appeal to the general public to make contributions for the Polish army[89]. Information about Polish Legions is also present in the files connected to the activities of the Supreme National Committee in 1915 and collected by Count Józef Ostrowski from Małuszyn[90]. These files also contain copies of two memorials submitted by NKN to the Austro-Hungarian Ministry of Foreign Affairs in July 1915 and sent to Count Ostrowski by the Commander of the Military Department of the Supreme National Commitee, Władysław Sikorski. Another interesting document from the fonds is an invitation sent to Count Ostrowski asking him to attend "A celebration of the second anniversary of the formation of Polish Legions" (*Uroczysty obchód 2-letniej rocznicy utworzenia Legionów Polskich*), organised

---

88 Ibid., ref. II/87 item 2, pp. 210–212.
89 Ibid., ref. I/25 pp. 5–6.
90 Ibid., ref. II/30.

on 15 August in Kamieńsk by the command of a local Veterans' Hospital and Women's League[91].

In another fonds originating from an estate archive, the Walewski family from Tubądzin, documents have been found concerning the activities of Countess Maria Jehanne Wielopolska, the leader of the Legion Division in the Supreme National Committee Women's League in Lviv. These contain permission to collect money and gifts for the Polish Legions in 1915[92] and a diploma awarded to the Countess by other Women's League members in 1916[93]. The latter is decorated by a painting of a 1st Brigade soldier in a characteristic "maciejówka" cap and an eagle emblem.

A considerable amount of archival material concerning Legion formations can be found in the Bartoszewicz family archive. Among these materials are a Supreme National Committee communique dated September 1914 on moving the Eastern Legions from Lviv to Sanok and then Jasło (in order to train and equip the troops)[94]; ephemera addressed to the Polish population asking for material support[95], Legion-themed postcards[96], a memorial by Władysław Studnicki submitted to the German authorities, entitled "A Complete Solution to the Matter of Polish Armed Forces" (*Całkowite rozwiązanie sprawy polskiej siły zbrojnej*)[97]; "An Open Letter. To Brigadier Piłsudski, a Former Member of the State Council" (*Do brygadiera Piłsudskiego, byłego członka Rady Stanu*) written by Izabela Moszczeńska after the oath crisis in June 1917[98], documents concerning soldiers of Polish Auxiliary Corps[99] and materials on the internment of Polish soldiers by Central Powers in 1917 and 1918. The last of these is perhaps worth a closer look. The first document is a typescript entitled "The truth about Szczypiorno" (*Prawda o Szczypiornie*), written in October 1917 by an unnamed officer. The author explains the moral rationale behind the Polish soldiers' refusal to swear

---

91 Ibid., ref. II/82, pp. 328.
92 APŁ: Archiwum Kazimierza Walewskiego z Tubądzina (Archiwum rodziny Walewskich) 1443–1939 (Tubądzin Kazimierz Walewski Archive (Walewski family archive) 1443–1939), ref. 32, p. 501.
93 Ibid., ref. 32, pp. 502–503.
94 APŁ: Archiwum rodziny Bartoszewiczów 1552–1933 (Bartoszewicz family archive 1552–1933), ref. 582, pp. 1–2.
95 Ibid., ref. 580, sheet 1, 583, pp. 1–3.
96 Ibid., ref. 3651, pp. 220, ref. 3695, sheet 4.
97 Ibid., ref. 581, sheet not numbered.
98 Ibid., ref. 589, pp. 1–4.
99 Ibid., ref. 583, pp. 4–5.

an oath of allegiance to Germany and Austria-Hungary and sheds light on the relationships and attitudes at the Szczypiorno camp[100]. The second document is a handwritten letter penned by an anonymous Polish Auxiliary Corps soldier in March 1918 after the Battle of Rarańcza (February 15–16, 1918). Alongside his brothers-in-arms, the letter's author had been interned by the Austrian military in a prisoner camp in Bustyahaza, Hungary. He characterised the camp as follows: "the living conditions are disgraceful – dirt, filth, hunger and chaos everywhere. We are being treated not as prisoners, but as the worst sort of criminals. [...] The barracks commander – a vicious dog"[101]. This fonds also contains an album of poetry and song from 1914–1920, collected after the war had ended. Most of these relate to the Polish Legions. Among their authors are Kornel Makuszyński, Józefa Mieczysław Mączka and Edward Słoński[102]. Two poems devoted to the Legions have also been found in a separate file containing soldiers' poems from 1918[103].

An interesting item in the fonds of the Archive of Włodzimierz Pfeiffer, a well-known Łódź photographer and bookseller, is a listing of books banned by German censorship within the Government General of Warsaw in 1916–1918. The list encompasses several hundred titles, many revolving around the theme of the Polish Legions[104].

The next fonds of a private archive contains material related to the life and scientific achievements of Eugeniusz Ajnenkiel, including a typescript of his work entitled "What I've heard, seen and experienced. Memories of my life and the lives of others" (*Słyszałem, widziałem, przeżyłem. Wspomnienia z mojego i nie mojego życia*). Ajnenkiel began working on the above with his daughter, Zofia Krystyna, in mind, around late 1948. The second volume of this work concentrates on the time of the Polish Legions in Łódź in October 1914. Ajnenkiel described the following: Polish Legions entering the city on October, a cold reception from Łódź citizens, the pro-Russian attitudes of factory owners and their aversion towards both the Polish Legions and the idea of independence; a reserved approach demonstrated

---

100   Ibid., ref. 591, pp. 1–3.

101   Ibid., ref. 4–5. The text of the letter was also printed on a leaflet titled "Do społeczeństwa polskiego! Znęcanie się nad Legionistami" (To the Polish nation! Victimisation of the Legionssoldiers) cf. APŁ: ZDiPU, ref. 288, p. 292.

102   APŁ: Archiwum rodziny Bartoszewiczów (Bartoszewicz family archive), ref. 3859. The album contains a loose, unsigned photograph of a Legion soldier.

103   Ibid., ref. 3862, pp. 4–11.

104   APŁ: Archiwum Włodzimierza Pfeiffera (księgarza i fotografa łódzkiego) 1916–1939 (the archive of Włodzimierz Pfeiffer, a Łódź bookseller and photographer) 1916–1939, ref. 3, pp. 19–71.

by Łódź workers towards the soldiers; impressions made by the soldiers on the
author, who was 14 years old at the time; making a personal acquaintance with
some of the officers, including the writer Andrzej Strug; a rally at the Grand
Theatre in Łódź organised on 25 October; the author's failed attempt to enlist
due to being underage and the Legions leaving the city on 28 October[105]. Information presented in this narrative is further enriched by another publication by
the same author, entitled "The First Polish Legion Divisions in Łódź" (*Pierwsze
oddziały Legionów Polskich w Łodzi*) published in the interwar period[106]. The motif
of the Polish Legions' fight for independence is present in Ajnenkiel's work in the
wider context of the Łódź workers' movement: for example, he relates a teahouse
discussion conducted in 1915 by members of the local Polish Socialist Party –
Revolutionary Faction and the members of Social Democracy of the Kingdom
of Poland and Lithuania[107].

Researchers wishing to find valuable and practically unknown resources on the
Polish Legions might be interested in the files of the Municipal Assessment Committee in Łódź. This fonds contains over a dozen estimates concerning material
losses suffered by Łódź citizens due to requisitions enforced by the Legions. Most
of these refer to requisitioning horses and carts[108]. The case of Ludwik Wagner,
living in Łódź at ul Leszno 46, may serve as an example. Wagner lost the horses
he'd previously rented to the Konrad Reinhard's brewery at Ogrodowa Street.
Feliks Rosner, a brewery administrator, told the Commission:

> In the early days of the war, in accordance with an earlier arrangement with Mr. Kluchow –
> Mr. Wagner's business partner – Mr. Wagner's horses had been at the brewery. I had been
> feeding them and paying the carter's wages. In September 1914, I sent these horses – the
> cart was loaded with beer – to Pabianice. On the way there, Polish Legion soldiers threw
> the beer off the cart and onto the side of the road, and took the horses, cart and driver.
> The carter let me know about the incident through someone I'd never seen before; all
> I could do was to send another cart to pick up the beer[109].

---

105 APŁ: Archiwum Eugeniusza Ajnenkiela 1902–1980 (the archive of Eugeniusz Ajnen-
     kiel 1902–1980), ref. 127, pp. 105–115.
106 Ajnenkiel, Eugeniusz: op. cit.
107 APŁ: the archive of Eugeniusz Ajnenkiel, ref. 127, pp. 134–139.
108 APŁ: Komisja Szacunkowa Miejscowa w Łodzi 1914–1921 (Municipal Assessment
     Comittee in Łódź, further referred to as KSMŁ), ref. 971, 1738, 1867, 2688, 4120, 5257,
     5804.
109 Ibid., ref. 5257, sheet not numbered.

Among the goods requisitioned by the Legions were foods such as pearl barley from Dawida Toporek's shop at Nowy Rynek 12[110]. Polish soldiers were also equipped with firearms requisitioned from Łódź citizens based on the orders of German occupying forces[111]. Other documents concern the occupation of apartments in a building at ul Kościuszki 1 for the use of Polish Legions. Between 12 February 1915 and 1 April 1918 this space served as enlistment office and temporary quarters for officers; names and ranks are given in the document[112].

Material related to military formations acting alongside Austria-Hungary and Germany is also present in the fonds of the German Imperial Military Governorship Court in Łódź. Several case files have been found against persons accused of conducting illegal enlistment activities aimed at acquiring volunteers for the Polish Legions, mainly through distributing publications censored by the German authorities. The case of Stanisław Gilowski is perhaps particularly interesting. This soldier of the 2nd Brigade of the Polish Legions, born in Piotrków, had in his possession several dozen publications about the Legions (*Piosenki Legionistów, Muza Legionów Polskich, Szlakiem bojowym Legionów*, a 1916 calendar *Legionista Polski*), 50 issues of "Dziennik Narodowy", 20 issues of "Wiadomości Polskie" and several issues of "Zwierciadło Polskie". Gilowski was detained in early 1916 in Łódź and questioned at an investigation penitentiary at ul Olgińska. From there he had been sent to a prison cell on ul Długa, and later to a German camp *Kriegsgefangen Lager Bütow – Pommern – Deutschland*. From that camp, Gilowski had sent a postcard and a letter addressed to the General Austro-Hungarian Consulate in Wrocław: both are preserved in the case file. Attached also are three confiscated letters from soldiers to their families; some correspondence between the Women's League in Piotrków to the War Alert Women's League in Łęczyca; a brochure entitled "The Struggles of the Polish Legions No. 2: Fighting in Podhale" (*Boje legionów Polskich. No 2: Walki na Podhalu*), printed in Piotrków in 1915; correspondence concerning financial matters between Gilowski and the publishing administrators of Military Department of the Supreme National Committee in Piotrków – as well as a photograph of a Legion soldier, perhaps depicting Gilowski himself[113]. Other cases from 1916 include one against Kazimierz Pogodziński, of the 2nd Lancers

---

110   Ibid., ref. 5114, sheet not numbered.
111   Ibid., ref. 3407, sheet not numbered; 5180, sheet not numbered.
112   Ibid., ref. 1152, sheet not numbered.
113   APŁ: Sąd Cesarsko-Niemieckiego Gubernatorstwa Wojskowego w Łodzi 1915–1918 (The Court of the German Emperor Military Governorate in Łódź, further referred to as SCNGWŁ), ref. 1841, sheet not numbered.

Regiment of Polish Legions, for smuggling the "Znicz" magazine[114] and against Edmund Szafrański and several other people, for illegal enlistment activities and distributing the censored "Wiadomości Polskie" magazine[115]. One of the files in this fonds also contains a postcard send from a soldier of the 3rd Infantry Regiment, Emil Kaliński, to his family in Łódź[116].

Another interesting case in the one brought against two women living in Łęczyca – Józefa Sienkiewicz (aged 70) and her daughter Waleria Sienkiewicz (aged 40), investigated in August 1917 by the German Imperial Military Governorship Court. Józefa Sienkiewicz had given shelter to her grandson, Edward Ramiecki, a deserter from the Polish Armed Forces. After the German police authorities had found Raniecki, Józefa Sienkiewicz and her two daughters interfered with Raniecki's arrest. The incident is described in detail by *Feldpolizeikomissar* Bergemann. Bergmann testified that the three women had attacked him, knocked his weapon off, bit him and then pushed out into the courtyard, allowing the deserter and one of Sienkiewicz's daughters to escape. The case files also contain two prints related to the oath crisis: an anonymous brochure entitled "The Oath" (*Przysięga*), published in Warsaw in June 1917, criticising the Central Powers' Polish policy and the resulting policy of the Legions command; and a 1917 leaflet printed by the War Alert Women's League in Piotrków, confirming the League's support for Piłsudski's decision[117].

Information about the Polish Legions and Polish Auxiliary Corps are also present in some fonds of municipal institutions. A very valuable mention about the arrival of the first Polish Legions soldiers to Łódź was found in the files of the Central Citizens' Committee in Łódź. A protocol from the Committee's session on the 12th of October 1914, in a section devoted to Leon Grohman's report on Militia activities, states that on that day the Militia office had been visited by "several riflemen squads from Galicia" who arrived there to organise lodgings for a larger group of fighters. The report details the meeting between Polish Legions fighters and Tadeusz Sułowski, a Militia representative[118].

Several interesting archival units are found in the municipal fonds of Łódź from 1915–1939. The Presidential Department of the City Council files contain

---

114 Ibid., ref. 1841, sheet not numbered.
115 Ibid., ref. 1841, sheet not numbered.
116 Ibid., ref. 1838, sheet 413.
117 Ibid., ref. 1604, sheet not numbered.
118 APŁ: Główny Komitet Obywatelski m. Łodzi 1914–1915 [1916–1920, 1922] (Main Civil Committee in Łódź 1914–1915 [1916–1920, 1922]), ref. 1, p. 64.

correspondence related to enlisting volunteers to Polish Auxiliary Corps[119]; a petition to the City Council from November 1917 written by Łódź citizens and concerning an intervention to free imprisoned Legion soldiers (and Józef Piłsudski) from prisoner camps[120]; an act of the City Council from 28 November 1917 concerning assigning a sum of 5000 Mk. as financial aid for the prisoners of Szczypiorno, born or living in Łódź[121]; a protocol of the official City Council meeting on 6 August 1919, on the 5th anniversary of Piłsudski's troops entering the former Kingdom of Poland[122]; finally, letters by members of the Polish Legion Association to the Mayor of Łódź concerning the promotion of former Legion officers working in municipal structures and featuring a list of names and other personal data[123].

Additionally, singular materials related to the Polish Armed Forces can be found in a number of folders in the fonds of the municipal districts (gmina[124] districts/ gminas) of Chojny, Radogoszcz and Widzew, as well as the fonds of the city of Pabianice. These were created between November 1916 and May 1918 and are related to the issues of accommodation and provisioning of Legions soldiers who had come to the gminas with the intention of enlisting volunteers into the Polish Armed Forces, benefits paid to the families of the Legions soldiers after they had been transferred under German command, as well as organizing enlistment[125]. The final group of archival materials contains an interesting item, namely copies of letters by the Department of Polish Affairs of the Armed Forces (*Abteilung Polnische Wehrmacht*) at the Emperor-German General Governorship of Warsaw, copied to the Magistrate of the City of Pabianice by the German Imperial Police in Łódź.

---

119   APŁ: Akta miasta Łodzi 1775–1945, Zarząd Miejski w Łodzi 1915–1939 (the files of the city of Łódź 1775–1945, City Governorate of łódź 1915–1936, further referred to as AmŁ), ref. 13857.

120   Ibid., ref. 13197.

121   Ibid., ref. 13196.

122   Ibid., ref. 12223.

123   Ibid., ref. 14266, pp. 175–180; 14267, p. 482.

124   *Gmina* is the principal unit of administrative division of Poland as "commune" or "municipality."

125   APŁ: Akta gminy Chojny 1820–1940 (the files of the gmina of Chojny 1820–1940), ref. 1385; APŁ: Akta gminy Radogoszcz 1816–1940 [1941] (the files of the gmina of Radogoszcz 1816–1940 [1941]), ref. 910a; APŁ: Akta gminy Widzew z siedzibą w Ksawerowie 1823–1953 (the files of the gmina of Widzew with the seat in Ksawerów 1823–1953), ref. 1425; APŁ: Akta miasta Pabianic 1571–1944 [1945–1952] (the files of the city of Pabianice 1571–1944 [1945–1952]), ref. 47.

In the fonds of the Association of War Veterans of the Republic of Poland, Area Board in Łódź and local offices, one may find a member registry of the Association of War Veterans of the Republic of Poland in Piotrków Trybunalski from 1919–1939. It contains personal data of the First World War veterans, including the Legion soldiers[126].

The correspondence of the Voivodeship Office of Łódź has been preserved in the files of the interwar Prefect Office of Łódź; the letters concern the graves of soldiers who fought for the independence of Poland in Łódź and its surrounding area. It informs of a discovery of eleven graves of Legion soldiers at the Roman Catholic graveyard in Zarzewie, Chojny district. Names of soldiers, their ranks and membership in individual regiments are listed in the attachment to the correspondence[127].

Minor references and materials related to Polish military formations, including Polish legions, have also been found in the archives of interwar schools of Łódź. The fonds of the Private A. Zimowski Boys' Secondary School, Łódź contains a report which states that on November, "in the Dowbor, Legions, and Polish Military Organisation sections in the scouts' quarters at ul Wólczańska 27, a session started with the intention of disarming the German troops in Łódź". In this context, several Legion soldiers are named – Lieutenant Alfred Biłyk (City Commander) and Sergeant Frankowski, as well as a member of Dowbor's troops, Warrant Officer Franciszek Bereszka[128]. A few fonds additionally contain materials from Second Republic school ceremonies honouring Józef Piłsudski. Event programmes inform the reader that during such occasions, Legion songs were sung, and art and music teachers organised Legion-themed writing, arts and musical competitions[129]. During the interwar period it was also common to adorn school buildings with bronze cast bar reliefs bearing Piłsudski's image and biography. As an example, a plaque of this type was ordered in 1934 by the Father Ignacy Skorupko Secondary

---

126 APŁ: Związek Inwalidów Wojennych Rzeczypospolitej Polskiej Zarząd Okręgu w Łodzi i oddziały terenowe (The Association of Disabled Soldiers of the Republic of Poland, The Board of the Łódź Region and Field Offices). Partial fonds, ref. 122.

127 APŁ: Starostwo Powiatowe Łódzkie 1918–1939 (The Powiat Office of Łódź 1918–1939), ref. 350, pp. 117–119.

128 APŁ: Prywatne Gimnazjum Męskie A. Zimowskiego w Łodzi 1909–1939 (the A. Zimowski Private Boys' Secondary School, Łódź 1909–1939), ref. 24, sheet 78.

129 APŁ: Publiczna Szkoła Powszechna nr 25 Łódź ul. Drewnowska 88 1903–1939 (Public Common Schol No. 25, Łódź, 88 Drewnowska Street 1903–1939), ref. 69, sheet not numbered.

School for Boys in Łódź "in order to properly celebrate the 20th anniversary of the creation of the Legions by Marshal J. Piłsudski"[130].

Conspired
Polish Military Organisation

The archives of the Piotrków Main Draft Office contain some documents issued by the Chief Command Office of the Polish Military Organisation. The fonds of the Piotrków Polish Army Main Enlistment Office contains a number of documents issued by the Chief Command of the Polish Military Organisation. These are: *"Zasady organizacji POW"* (*Polish Military Organisation Rules*) – the text presents the goal behind the creation of the Polish Military Organisation, the organisational tasks, its structure and membership rules)[131]; "Przyrzeczenie wstępującego do Polskiej Organizacji Wojskowej" (*The Oath of a POW Initiate*)[132]; "*Raport w sprawie zwalczania Polskiej Organizacji Wojskowej przez Departament Wojskowy N.K.N – tzw. Krajowy Inspektorat Zaciągu",* (*The Report on fighting POW by the Supreme National Comittee – the so-called National Enlistment Inspectorate*), issued in Warsaw on 26 March, 1917)[133], and a message titled "Zamach Stanu na Radę Regencyjną na rzecz domu Hohenzollernów" (*Coup d'etat on the Regency Council, Inspired by the Hohenzollern Family*) issued on 26 June 1918[134].

The Ephemeral Prints Collection contains some PMO leaflets and posters. In an example proclamation of February 1918, the organisation called for "each within whom beats the heart of a Pole join its ranks and thus work towards reaching the Poland united, independent and based on democratic rules"[135]. In its proclamations from the last months of the war, the PMO calls its former and current members to mobilise in response to the orders of the "Chief of fighting Poland", Piłsudski, and to "build the fortress of the Republic of Poland"[136].

---

130 APŁ: Prywatne Gimnazjum Męskie im. ks. I. Skorupki w Łodzi 1915–1939 (the Private Masculineof Father I. Skorupka in Łódź 1915–1939), ref. 227, sheet not numbered.
131 APŁ: GUZWP, ref. 33, sheet 14.
132 Ibid., ref. 33, sheet 13.
133 Ibid., ref. 33, sheets 2–5.
134 Ibid., sheets 11–12. The text could also be found in the fonds of the Bartoszewicz family ref. 593, pp. 17–20.
135 APŁ: ZDiPU, ref. 288, p. 38.
136 Ibid., ref. 288, pp. 1, 302, 303.

The referenced fonds also contains PMO brochures, signed by T.H.[137] [Tadeusz Hołówko – T.W.] as well as "Do najdostojniejszej Rady Regencyjnej Królestwa Polskiego memoriał w sprawie tworzenia wojska" (*A letter on Creating an Army to the Magnificent Regency Council*) which was issued by the General Command of the PMO in November 1917[138]. The fonds also contains a few issues of the "Strzelec. Pisma Polskiej Organizacji Wojskowej" (issues: 1, 2/1916 and 3, 4–5/1917)[139], "Przełom" from 1925 describing the events of Novenber 7–11, 1918[140], and five volumes of the "Żołnierz Legionów i P.O.W." (issues: 1–4/1938 and 1–2/1939), published jointly by the Chief Command of the Legionists' Association and the Board of Polish Military Organisation Member Association[141].

As an exception to the rule, ephemera related to PMO may be found in private archive fonds. As an example, the archive of the Potocki and Ostrowski families from Małuszyn contains a leaflet issued by the PMO and Allied Parties addressed to the citizens of Lublin, referring to the expected intervention of the Polish Legions into Lublin, accompanied by Austrian and German forces in 1915. The signatories called upon Lublin to "create the same sort of suport for Piłsudski's units as the citizens of Kielce exhibited in the West"[142]. The Bartoszewicz family archive fonds contains a brochure "P.O.W. Zadania i metody" (*Polish Military Organisation. Tasks and Methods*), published in Warsaw in February 1918 and explaining the creation, activities and methods of operation of the organisation[143].

Ephemera related to the Polish Military Organisation have also been found in theatre-related fonds. Two posters announcing a "*Wieczór artystyczny z herbatką*" (*An Artistic Evening Over a Cup of Tea*) in Sunday, 11 February 1917 in the Łódź Artisan Club Hall. Tickets to the event could be purchased in the office of the Military Emergency Service Women's League; the proceeds going to the PMO, however, one of the posters refers to the "Piechur" Polish Organisation – a legal front to the conspired PMO[144]. The reverse side of the

---

137   Ibid., ref. 288, pp. 72–83.
138   Ibid., ref. 288, sheet 352.
139   Ibid., ref. 301.
140   Ibid., ref. 288, sheet 225.
141   Ibid., ref. 333.
142   APŁ: APiOM, ref. II/30, p. 38.
143   APŁ: Archiwum rodziny Bartoszewiczów (the archive of the Bartoszewicz family), ref. 593, pp. 1–16.
144   APŁ: Zbiór teatraliów łódzkich 1875–2012 (Łódź theatre publications 1875–2012), ref. 21/40, sheets 19, 20 (duplicate).

other poster announces an upcoming performance of Stanisław Wyspiański's play *Wesele* in the Polish Theatre in Łódź, on March 2nd 1917 – the proceeds also being donated to the PMO[145].

The Iconographic Collection at the State Archive in Łódź contains postcards featuring photographs of PMO members, published after the First World War by the Committee for the Restoration of the Monument for Fallen POW Soldiers. They represent the Chief Command Office of the PMO in 1914/1915[146], PMO Officer School in 1916[147], PMO Area Commanders in 1917[148], members of the Chief PMO Command with Józef Piłsudski[149] and a PMO batallion[150] during 1917 field manoeuvres in Zielonka near Warsaw, as well as members of the chapter of the Virtuti Militari Cross from the time of their duty at PMO in 1921[151].

Iconographic material at the State Archive in Łódź also includes a PMO march, in November 1917, towards the Monument of the May 3rd Constitution in Lutomiersk.[152] The photograph of PMO members in Lutomiersk can also be found in the Lutomiersk Collection of photographs. It was taken in 1916 and shows PMO fighters in the ruins of a local cloister destroyed during the First World War[153].

Files from German investigations of individuals suspected of being POW members have been found in the fonds of the German Imperial Military Governorship Court in Łódź. One of the volumes contains a list of suspects, including Peter Arndt from Zgierz, Wenzel [Wacław – T.W.] Sokolewicz from the "Piechur" organisation in Łódź and Leon Dietrich, pseudonym "Polanowicz" from the "Koło Sportowe" (Sports Club) in Łęczyca. All three individuals were interned in 1917 in the German camp at Sczypiorno, more precisely Skalmierzyce, following the

---

145 Ibid., ref. 21/26, sheet 10.
146 APŁ: Zbiór ikonograficzny… (Iconographic fonds…), ref. W-I 5/113 (duplicate: W-I 5/344).
147 Ibid., ref. W-I 5/106 (duplicate: W-I 5/343).
148 Ibid., ref. W-I 5/104.
149 Ibid., ref. W-I 5/107 (duplicate: W-I 5/341), W-I 5/108 (duplicates: W-I 5/347, W-I 5/347 D), W-I 5/110 (duplicates: W-I 5/349, W-I 5/349 D1, W-I 5/349 D2, W-I 5/349 D3).
150 Ibid., ref. W-I 5/109 (duplicate: W-I 5/342), W-I 5/111 (duplicate: W-I 5/345), W-I 5/114 (duplicates: W-I 5/346, W-I 5/346 D).
151 Ibid., ref. W-I 5/105 (duplicates: W-I 5/112, W-I 5/348, W-I 5/348 D1, W-I 5/348 D2, W-I 5/348 D3).
152 Ibid., ref. M-I L/69.
153 APŁ: Zbiór fotografii miasta Lutomierska 1916–1932 (the collection of photographs of the city of Lutomiersk), ref. 2.

official designation of the unit (*Kriegsgefangenenlager Skalmierschütz*)[154]. Another volume refers to an investigation of a 50-year-old Józef Nosek, also accused of activities within the conspired PMO and the dissemination of illegal publications. The files mention Nosek being arrested by the German police in Sieradz in March 1918. Police officers approached him wearing a Legion uniform which, as the investigation revealed, was in his illegal possession as early as the summer of 1917. The arrested individual held a rifle and forged documents. At first, he was imprisoned in a facility in Sieradz, and afterwards transported to a prison in Kalisz. The files contain attachments in the form of three photographs of Józef Nosek and orders and official attestations related to the soldiers of the 3rd Infantry Regiment of the Second Brigade of the Polish Legions[155].

PMO is also referred to in a letter to the Ministry of Religious Denominations and Public Education in Warsaw of 21 November 1918, stored in the fonds of the Boys' Secondary School of the Polish "Uczelnia" Association in Łódź. Local education authorities inform the Ministry of the fact that "in the Real School in Pabianice, Polish students and some Jews, counting 30 in all, perform militia duty in the city and its surroundings under orders from the local command of Polish army, more precise, the Polish Military Organisation"[156]. A protocol from a session of a teacher's conference of the "Uczelnia" Knowledge Association in Łódź from 27 November 1918, contains a note on collecting voluntary donations at schools, with the goal of buying a wreath for a student of the school, Stefan Linke[157], a PMO platoon commander, who died from bullet wounds on 11 November 1918 while disarming German troops in Łódź.

The Włodzimierz Pfeiffer archive contains pre-war photographs of a plaque commemorating the death of Linke, erected in 1936 on the wall of the National Bank building in Łódź[158].

Information on some former members of the PMO employed in Łódź local authority offices in the interwar period may be found in the fonds of the Łódź city files, in the section on 1915–1939 Civic Centre. As an example, The Presidial Department stores a request from The Board of the PMO member Association to the President of the City of Łódź for a promotion, and awarding a vacant post

---

154 APŁ: SCNGWŁ, ref. 1850, sheets 125–130.
155 Ibid., ref. 1501.
156 APŁ: Męskie Gimnazjum Polskiego Towarzystwa "Uczelnia" w Łodzi [1891] 1906–1920 [1924] (the Boys' Secondary School of the Polish Association "Uczelnia" in Łódź [1891] 1906–1920 [1924]), ref. 76, p. 30.
157 Ibid., ref. 26, sheet not numbered.
158 APŁ: Archiwum Włodzimierza… (the archive of Włodzimierz…), ref. 823, 824.

of a department manager in the Taxation Department to Bolesław Manikowski, who is referred to in the letter as "taking active part in fighting for Independence, currently an active member of our organisation, bearing proper certification from the Military Historical Office and is awarded with Cross for Valour and Cross of Independence"[159].

In agreement with Russia
The Puławski Legion and the First Polish Corps

The Ephemeral Prints Collection contains a leaflet and a postcard with a memorable address of Nicholas Nocholaevich Romanov from 14 August 1914. It gave rise to the creation of Polish military units allied with Russia. Addressing Poles, the chief commander of Russian military forces hoped "that the sword which had slain the enemies at Grunwald has not rusted" and promised the Reunion of Poland under the Russian sceptre as well as the rebirth of Poland free in religion, language and self-governance[160].

The fonds also contains a publication on the Puławski Legion. Unfortunately, it is incomplete; the only pages that remain are numbered 49 to 86, and the cover and title pages are missing, so the author, title and year of publication are unknown. Despite its fragmentary character, it is an item worth noticing. It contains the reminiscences of Witold Ostoja-Gorczyński, a member of the military Organizing Committee, his correspondence (orders, telegrams, letters), photographs of leaders and soldiers, poems, and press quotes[161].

The collection of ephemera contains singular material on the First Polish Corps. One example is a text of a resolution from mid-June 1917 by the First General Assembly of Polish Military Associations in Petersburg. In the resolution, the Assembly requested that the Russian government build a Polish military force that:

> ought to be formed by the way of voluntary migration and enlistment of our fellow countrymen [...], remain under the command of Polish officers and the Superior Russian Commander [...] and ought to comprise all types of weapons, have Polish officer core, own command centre, own spare parts dependent on said command centre; and own support, sanitary and supply units[162].

159　APŁ: AmŁ, ref. 14267, p. 220.
160　APŁ: ZDiPU, ref. 287.
161　Ibid., ref. 287.
162　Ibid., ref. 243, sheet 2.

An instruction titled "Program i organizacja pracy kulturalno-oświatowej w Polskiej Sile Zbrojnej" (*Programme and Organisation of Cultural and Educational Work in the Polish Military Forces*) prepared in February 1917 in Minsk by ensign Stefan Sołtyk, head of the Cultural-Educational Department in the Chief Polish Military Committee, was also discovered[163]. Also, a poem titled "*Pieśń Armii generała Muśnickiego*" (*General Muśnicki's Army Song*) was found – it was distributed in Warsaw in February 1918[164]. Posters from the first half of 1918 bear the proclamations of military administration bodies established by the command of the First Polish Corps in the occupied Belarus. The group contains the address of the commander of the Babruysk fortress, Lieutenant Colonel Bolesław Jaźwiński[165]; a few orders of the Leader of Civil Governance[166], Lieutenant Colonel Adam Aleksandrowicz[167], and an order of the Assistant Corps Leader for Civil Causes, Porębski[168]. Information on General Józef Dowbor-Muśnicki may also be found in newspapers stored in the ephemeral prints group: "Wiadomości Wojskowe" (issue 3–4/1918)[169], "Żołnierz Polski. Organ urzędowy I-go Polskiego Korpusu" (issues: 50, 51, 56/1918)[170] and "Placówka" (issues: 80 and 82/1918)[171]. Issue 80 of "Placówka" publishes the conditions of an agreement signed by General Dowbor-Muśnicki and German authorities, on the grounds of which Dowbor-Muśnicki's military formation was disarmed and disbanded.

Additionally, materials related to the I Polish Corps were found in the fonds of the Municipal Assessment Committee in Łódź: A report by a citizen of Łódź, Władysław Święcicki, a former captain of the Fifth Regiment of Polish Shooters. In mid-1918, he reported material losses during the battle of Usha on 31 January 1918, of the First Polish Corps against the Bolsheviks to the Committee. The report is supplemented by an account of a witness to the event, Włodzimierz

---

163 Ibid., ref. 288, sheet 281.

164 Ibid., ref. 288, sheet 290.

165 Ibid., ref. 441, sheet not numbered

166 Based on an agreement signed by General Dowbow-Muśnicki with the Germans on February 26, 1918, the Polish army was designated a small are in Belarus which was considered neutral. The commander of the First Polish Corps was managing it with the help of two auxiliary bodies: a headquarters and a civil governing body; cf. Lipiński, Wacław: Walka zbrojna…, pp. 265–266.

167 APŁ: ZDiPU, ref. 288, pp. 295–299.

168 Ibid., ref. 288, p. 300.

169 Ibid., ref. 335, pp. 145–176.

170 Ibid., ref. 304.

171 Ibid., ref. 305.

Nikonczow, also a citizen of Łódź, a former clerk in the Fifth Regiment of Polish Shooters, who reported:

> during the transit of the Fifth Regiment of Polish Shooters from the governorate of Zubcow in the Twersk area to the Bobrujsk governorate in the Minsk area, the Polish forces came under attack on 31 January, this year, by the Bolsheviks. The consequence of the attack was the disarmament and arrest of the whole regiment. Mr. Święcicki was arrested and sent to Minsk, to appear before a court. The Bolsheviks took all the regiment's belongings, as well as the private effects of its soldiers and officers. Mr. Święcicki's belongings as taken by the Bolsheviks are listed in a directory attached to the estimate[172].

In his account, Święcicki specified that all his property was seized by the soldiers of the First Siberian Army Corps. These were mostly the clothing items (shirts, coats, trousers, shoes, gloves, a maciejówka cap) as well as suitcases, handkerchiefs, a shaving kit, a mattress, pillow, a Browning pistol and a sabre[173].

Information on the former soldiers of the First Polish Corps in Russia who were related to Łódź because of their residence and professional activity may be found in other fonds. As an example, the fonds of the State Police in Łódź contain a personal file of a senior headsnam Leon Pabich, who served as a gunner in General Dowbor Muśnicki's army between 1 September 1917 and 31 January 1918, as evidenced by military certificates contained in the file[174].

An interesting item worthy of a mention in the iconographic fonds of the State Archive in Łódź is a photograph signed *"Legiony w wojsku rosyjskim"* (Legions in the Soviet army)[175]. It depicts peasant partisans armoured with scythes and double-barrel shotguns. This formation, archaic in the standards of the Great War, was created by Bonawentura Snarski, a teacher from Kielce, who enlisted volunteers after requesting that Russian authorities allow the formation of Polish corps with Russian support.

Among the Western powers
Polish Armed Forces in France

Established in 1917, the Blue Army is described in "Instrukcja służby łączności dla wojsk wszelkiej broni" (*Instructions for the Communication Staff for Army Units of All Types*) published by the National Printhouse in Paris in January 1919, and

---

172   APŁ: KSMŁ, ref. 5035, sheet not numbered.
173   Ibid.
174   APŁ: Komenda Policji Państwowej miasta Łodzi 1919–1939 (the Headquarters of the National Police of the City of Łódź 1919–1939), ref. 28, sheet 13.
175   APŁ: Zbiór ikonograficzny... (the iconographic fonds...), ref. W-I 5/124.

stored in the Ephemeral Prints Collection. It was translated from its 1918 French original for the Polish troops[176]. The same collection contains a poster announcing General Haller's troops passing through Łódź Kaliska railway station on 18 April 1919 at 2:40 p.m.[177].

Another iconographic resource is a photograph depicting General Haller accompanied by General Dowbor-Muśnicki (in the background)[178].

Some material related to the Polish Army is also present in the files of Łódź schools from the interwar period. The fonds of the First Private Secondary School and High School for Boys of the Merchant's Association in Łódź contains a diploma signed "Braciom Polakom Amerykanom w hołdzie VI B" (*To our Brothers, American Poles, a Tribute from Class VI B*). It was written and adorned with painted decorations by the students of the Real High School and had been intended as a sign of gratitude towards the Poles in America, fighting for Poland's independence in Haller's army. The words run as follows:

> You, our fellow compatriates, could not be scared by anything. The best of your youth and strength had come to the old lands of Europe. You arrived to fight for Poland's freedom, and the freedom of humanity [...] You shed blood on the fields of France. Poland was proud to look upon you – Haller's legions [...]. You haven't spared any means to help build Our Republic of Poland. The memory of your fallen Eagles at the fields of Meuse and Somme will live in the hearts of Poles [...][179]

The students have placed their signatures on the reverse side. Deeds of Haller's troops were also honoured by the students of the Ignacy Skorupka School for Boys in Łódź, as evidenced by an entry in the school's Visitor's Book on 20 May 1922. It mentions a school ceremony dedicated to the troops and the participation of the institution's students and teachers in a memorial service to the fallen soldiers in the Stanisław Kostka Cathedral in Łódź[180].

To summarise the above overview of archival material related to Polish military formations during the First World War: the material is extremely dispersed in the various holdings of the State Archive in Łódź. They have been found in more than twenty fonds, containing files from general and special administration offices,

---

176   APŁ: ZDiPU, ref. 334.
177   Ibid., ref. 395, sheet 30.
178   APŁ: Zbiór ikonograficzny... (the iconographic fonds...), ref. W-I 6–266.
179   APŁ: Prywatne Gimnazjum i Liceum Męskie Zgromadzenia Kupców m. Łodzi [1895] 1896–1939 [1960] (the Private School for Boys and High School of the Association of the Merchants of Łódź), ref. 3003, p. 1.
180   APŁ: Prywatne Gimnazjum Męskie im. ks. I. Skorupki... (the Private Masculine Gymnasium of Father I. Skorupka...), ref. 49, p. 23.

local authority offices on city or district levels, school and court files; private individual archives; collections of ephemera, theatre publications and iconography. The vast majority of files concern the Polish Legions; some refer to the Polish Royal Army, Polish Military Organisation and Polish Auxiliary Corps. Only a few items refer to the Puławy Legion, Polish 1st Corps in Russia and the Blue Army. The majority of resources cited in this paper are related to Łódź and its surrounding area. It might be worth adding that some material, such as combat losses appraisal reports or German court files, has been virtually unknown and so far has not been used in scientific research or publications. This makes it attractive and worthy of researchers' attention.

Kamila Pawełczyk-Dura
State Archive in Łódź

The influence of World War I on the activity of the Russian military and naval clergy

The institution of the Russian military and naval clergy had a long history. Sources concerning the official formation of church structures in the Russian army reached the beginning of the eighteenth century. In 1706 tsar Peter I issued the first decree (ukase) obliging Orthodox parish communities to the regular collection of donations for regimental chaplains and hieromonks serving in the Navy. Other Peter's laws (1716, 1720) provided a foundation for the creation of the military clergy hierarchy led by the regimental oberpriest of the active army and the oberhieromonk of the Navy. In the period of hostilities, the clergy were members of the General Staff and were subject to the commander in chief of the army and navy while remaining at the same time under the direct jurisdiction of the Most Holy Governing Synod in clerical matters. (Полное собрание законов Российской Империи с 1649 года. Типография Второго отделения Собственной Его Императорского Величества канцелярии: Санкт-Петербург 1830, т. 5, p. 240–324; Рыбаков, Николай Александрович: "Развитие правового регулирования деятельности православных священников в армии за период XVIII–XIX вв.". Молодой ученый 11, 2012, s. 339–390). The form of dependence from the Synod, as well as from the Synod field church executive bodies represented by local bishops and archbishops, without a clear definition of the scope of bishop's and oberpriest's powers, often provoked conflicts of competence relating primarily to the issue of control over military clergy and churches intended for guards regiments. The state of disorganization and mutual aversion persisted for nearly a century, complicating the military ministry of priests and depriving them of the possibility to effectively administer the property of the orthodox church entrusted to their care. (Григорьев, Анатолий Борисович: "Из истории военного духовенства". In: Галкин, Юрий Юрьевич (ed.): Религиозно-этические аспекты воспитания военнослужащих. Материалы международного семинара, состоявшегося в Международном независимом Эколого-политологическом университете (МНЭПУ) в июне 1997 года. Издательство Международного независимого эколого-политологического университета: Москва 1998, s. 37–45).

On 9 April 1800, tsar Paul I appointed the first oberpriest of army and navy in the history of the Russian Empire (Невзоров, Николай: Исторический очерк управления духовенством военного ведомства в России. Типография Ф. Г. Елеонского и А. И. Поповицкого: Санкт-Петербург 1875, p. 16). Taking the office by Paul Ozierieckovsky sealed the formal division of power between the superior military priest and the diocese military priest in the area of the troops stationing (Чимаров, Сергей Юрьевич: "Во главе военно-духовного ведомства России: П. Я. Озерецковский – первый обер-священник русской армии и флота". Военно-исторический журнал 1, 1998, s. 76–82). The oberpriest was granted authority equal to the bishop's authority. He could appoint and dismiss military clergymen from service at his own discretion, apply disciplinary sanctions, exercise Orthodox administrative and judicial power. Equipped with such substantial powers, the oberpriest was subject to the supreme authority of the Synod, which in practice was responsible only for the controlling (visiting) of the Orthodox military structures (Российский государственный исторический архив: Духовное правление при Протопресвитере Военного и Морского Духовенства, О высочащем постановлении чтобы св[ященни]ки гвардии армии и флота состояли в ведении Обер-св[ященни]ка. Zesp. 806, inw. 1, sygn. 23, k. 2).

The independence of the institution of the military and naval clergy, which was postulated for decades, proved to be only a ephemeral phenomenon. Hopes for further development of church structures in the army were dashed by the imminent death of the emperor in 1801. It stopped the process of the military clergy's becoming independent for several dozen years. Paul's project to reform this area was restored in the early fifties of the 19th century. In 1853, following the example of previous solutions, the military clergy gained autonomy expressed in terms of organizational and competence autonomy. It was confirmed by the decree of 21 December 1887, which regulated the legal and material situation of military priests. Chief chaplain's rights and wages became equal to General-lieutenant's and the position of a protoiereus was made equal to that of a colonel. (Ласкеев, Федор: Историческая записка об управлении военным и морским духовенством за минувшее столетие. Типография Товарищества художественной печати: Санкт-Петербург 1900, s. 98–103).

The process of combining the function of the army chaplain and chaplain of the fleet in a position represented by one chaplain-in-chief, occurring in this period, led to the establishment of the dignity of a Protopresbyter on 12 June 1890. He was directly responsible for the management of all temples, hospitals and educational institutions of the military located in the territory of the Empire, with the exception of the Siberian region. A Clerical Board functioned as an auxiliary and advisory body to the Protopresbyter, which coordinated the complex administrative apparatus ("Положение об управлении церквами и духовенством военного и морского ведомства". Вестник военного духовенства 13, 1890, s. 418–436; "Положение об управлении церквами и духовенством военного и морского ведомства". Вестник военного духовенства 14, 1890, s. 418–439).

The first person to become the Protopresbyter was Alexandr Alexeyevich Zhelobovsky, the founder of the "Vestnik voennogo duhovenstva" magazine (Chaplain's bulletin), the originator of the organization of parish schools in the places where the troops were stationing, skillful diplomat capable of obtaining extra financial means for salaries and pensions for the military clergymen, and for the maintenance of temples and cemeteries ("К 10-летию служебной деятельности о. Протопресвитера Александра Алексеевича Желобовского по управлению церквами и духовенствам военного и морского духовенства (1888–1898)". Вестник военного духовенства 6, 1898, s. 181–192). After Zhelobovsky's death in 1910, his former assistant, Evgeny Petrovich Akvilonov, was promoted to the rank of the Protopresbyter. He held the position very briefly because only for several months. He died in March 1911 after a short period of struggling with a progressive cancer (Богуславский, Иван: "Протопресвитер Евгений Петрович Аквилонов". Вестник военного и морского духовенства 9, 1911, s. 257–263; "Воспоминания о почившем о. Протопресвитере Евгении Петровиче Аквилонове". Вестник военного и морского духовенства 10, 1911, s. 305–308; Фирсов, Сергей Львович: "Протопресвитеры русской армии и флота (1880 – февраль 1917 гг.)". Новый часовой 1, 1994, s. 23–33). The third and at the same time the last Protopresbyter of army and navy of the Russian Empire was Georgy Ivanovich Shavelsky ("Указ Его Императорского Величества Самодержца Всероссийского из Святейшего Правительственного Синода настоятелю Суворовской Кончанской, что при Императорской Николаевской военной академии церкви, протоиерею Георгию Ивановичу Шавельскому". Вестник военного и морского духовенства 10, 1911, s. 289).

Georgy Ivanovich Shavelsky was born on 6 January 1871 in the village of Dubokraj. At the age of ten he enrolled in a clerical school in Vitebsk and continued his education at the local seminary after graduating it. In 1891 he was appointed a lecturer of the Orthodox church in one of the towns in his home province and a teacher in a village school. In 1895 Georgy was ordained. Higher Orthodox authorities appointed him a parish priest of the church of St. Nicholas in Bedriace and then of the church of the Dormition of the Virgin Mary in Azarkov. After the unexpected death of his wife, Georgy, at the instigation of the diocesan bishop, began his studies at the St. Petersburg Theological Academy. During the Russo-Japanese War he was appointed regimental chaplain, and later dean of the division. Eventually, he was appointed chief chaplain of the 1st Manchurian Army.

After the war Georgy returned to the country. He served as a priest in the church at the Imperial Military Academy of the General Staff, taught theology at the Institute of History and Philology of St. Petersburg University and was an active member of the Theological Board supporting the protopresbyter of the military and naval clergy (Дело великого строительства церковного. Воспоминания членов Священного Собора Православной Российской Церкви 1917–1918 годов. Воробьёв, Владимир Николаевич (red.). Издательство Православного Свято-Тихоновского Гуманитарного Университета: Москва 2009, s. 690–692).

On 5 May 1911 by the decision of the Most Holy Governing Synod, Georgy Shavelsky was appointed the Protopresbyter of army and navy. This is what the newly elected Orthodox chief chaplain of the Russian army wrote about his appointment:

> I was one of the youngest priests in the Ministry of the Military in St. Petersburg. I did not even think about the dignity of the Protopresbyter because I felt that I did not deserve it and I was not adequately prepared for it: I just turned 40, worked for the Ministry of the Military from the end of January 1902, and at that given moment, I was the last link, a non-permanent member of the Theological Board supporting the Protopresbyter of the military and naval clergy. My strengths were: the degree of Master of Theology (only three masters worked for the ministry), the chair of the institute of theology in college and […] my activities during the Russo-Japanese war […]. However, all these advantages did not give me a reason for thinking about the office of the Protopresbyter that should be held by those carefully prepared for it. The appointment was, therefore, a surprise to me. (Шавельский, Георгий: Воспоминания последне¬го протопресвитера русской армии и флота. Крутицкое Патриаршее Подворье: Москва 1996, v. 1, p. 19)[1].

At the moment of taking the office, Shavelsky stood at the head of an anachronistic institution, developed for almost two centuries on the basis of theoretical schemes and fragile political orders. The need for administrative reforms, aimed at activating Orthodox structures in the Russian army and improving the system of clerical management of tsarist soldiers and sailors, was highlighted by the outbreak of one of the greatest conflicts. On 28 July 1914 the Great War began. This international armed conflict involved the majority of European countries, including the tsarist Russia. Military operations put the tsarist bureaucracy in a state of emergency. Wartime military structures were organized with the Grand Duke Nicholas Nikolaevich at the head and the mobilization was announced at the end of July. By the decision of tsar Nicholas II, the Protopresbyter of army and navy became a part of the General Staff of the Russian army (Сенин, Александр Сергеевич: "Армейское

---

1   Henceforth, unless indicated otherwise, all quotations in the text have been provided by the translator.

духовенство России в Первую мировую войну". Вопросы истории 10, 1990, p. 159–165; Фирсов, Сергей Львович: "Военное духовенство накануне и в годы Первой Мировой войны". Новый часовой 3, 1995, s. 21–32).

When the hostilities began, the plans of the Orthodox Church to prepare for a military conflict were still at a preliminary stage. Protopresbyter Shavelsky was aware of the weakness and ineffectiveness of the whole system of spiritual care for soldiers and the lack of proper identification of ways and methods of pastoral service during the war and this prompted his decision to convene a gathering of the military and naval clergy from all over Russia, which would become a forum for the exchange of opinions, as well as a reformist body (Андреев, Федор: "Начало войны – начало молитв. Духовное пробуждение народа". Вестник в военного и морского духовенства Спецвыпуск, 2005, s. 23–32; Фирсов, Сергей Львович: "Военное духовенство России. К вопросу о материальном положении священно- и церковнослужителей русской армии и флота в последней четверти XIX — начала XX столетий)". Новый часовой 2, 1994, s. 19–25).

The 1st Congress of the Military and Naval Clergy took place from 1 July to 10 July 1914. It was attended by 49 representatives of military structures at all levels, sent to the Congress by the Minister of War, General Vladimir Alexandrovich Sukhomlinov. The general Congress proceeded on the basis of three principles presented by the Protopresbyter for the consideration of the participants of the meeting in his opening speech. Firstly, he drew special attention to the need to introduce changes in the operation of the institute staying under his jurisdiction, which were supposed to come from the common experience of all military and navy clergymen. Secondly, he recommended a particular concern for the spiritual development of officers and soldiers and thereby – religious and moral education of the whole nation. Thirdly, he obliged the attendees of the Congress to develop a program to raise the level of education and professional preparation of military priests and explore ways of better pastoral service in the army, aimed at ensuring complete spiritual care for all those who need it ("Из речи о. Протопресвитера Г. И. Шавельского на открытии съезда". Вестник военного и морского духовенства 15/16, 1914, № 15/16, s. 547).

These demands formed the program assumptions of the Congress and were reflected in the resolution summarizing the ten-day, sometimes stormy, debate. The final document introduced a reform of the military clergy management during armed conflicts. It was supposed to be headed by the Protopresbyter, managing and controlling it with the help of his closest associates. The second level in the hierarchy were chaplains serving on the north, west, south-west, Romanian and Caucasian fronts. Chaplains for Baltic and Black Sea fronts were also appointed in 1916 (Фирсов 1995, s. 25). The third level – subordinated to them- was the group of staff chaplains. The fourth component of the war-time Orthodox church structure was the largest group of priests serving in divisions, garrisons and military hospitals. The smooth functioning of the whole structure of management and control was ensured by conferences organized for military clergy at different levels – the Protopresbyter with army chaplains and army chaplains with staff chaplains, as well as the general congresses of the clergy held under the chairmanship of the Protopresbyter or an appointed army chaplain. This division enabled the separation of the scope and location of pastoral work of individual priests, while maintaining control by a superior (Российский государственный исторический архив: Духовное правление при Протопресвитере Военного и Морского Духовенства, Бумаги относящиеся к 1-му Всероссийск[ому] Сезду воен[ного] и Морск[ого] Духовенства в 1914г.. Zesp. 806, inw. 5, sygn. 9432, cz. 1, k. 205). It also improved the organization of the military and naval clergy that at the initial stages of the war consisted only of seven hundred and thirty priests. During the first months of the conflict the number of clergymen in the army increased to five thousand (Шавельский, Георгий: Воспоминания последне¬го протопресвитера русской армии и флота. Крутицкое Патриаршее Подворье: Москва 1996, t. 2, s. 93).

The Congress made the first attempt in the history of Russia to codify the duties of the military clergy in the form of an instruction. Protopresbyter Shavelsky summarized its contents as follows: "The instruction indicated precisely for each priest [...] where he should be, what he should do during the fighting and in the period of calmness, where and how he should celebrate a service, how to preach and what about, etc.". (Шавельский 1996b, s. 93).

The clerics, who participated in the hostilities, in addition to their normal service including the celebration of the liturgy, the sacraments and the proclamation of the Word of God in this particular time of war changing the conditions of their past life and work, were supposed to – according to the Instruction – help doctors dress the wounded, lead the retrieval of bodies from the battlefield and transport the wounded to field hospitals, maintain soldier graves and cemeteries, notify relatives about the death of their loved ones, organize support for families of war invalids and so on (Шавельский, Георгий: "Духовенству воинских частей действующей армии и госпиталей". Вестник военного и морского духовенства 20, 1914, s. 696–697; Носков, Юрий Геннадьевич: "Религия и воспитание воинов". In: Галкин, Юрий Юрьевич (ed.): Религиозно-этические аспекты воспитания военнослужащих. Материалы международного семинара, состоявшегося в Международном независимом Эколого-политологическом университете (МНЭПУ) в июне 1997 года. Издательство Международного независимого эколого-политологического университета: Москва 1998, s. 7–14). The activity of Orthodox military priests in this regard was subject to strict control by the chief chaplain of the Russian army. Many years later Shavelsky recalled:

> At the time [...] of my journey I talked with ministers in the most diverse conditions: on trains, in homes, in the open air, on a meadow, in the woods concealing us from the enemy etc. During these conversations I learned a lot, but I also had the chance to teach others and direct them. During my visits to hospitals, dressing points and trenches I could easily see if these places were often visited by my fellow clergymen, whether they properly understand and earnestly perform their duties and how the low-ranking officers and soldiers treat them. A zealous priest was well aware of the deployment and positions the company regiments, he knew the soldiers, both brave and cowardly, met them in the trenches as a frequent and peasant guest. A zealous hospital priest knew every hospital room and the status of each patient. (Шавельский 1996b, s. 97).

After the first period of the war, characterized by high efficiency of the military clergy activity, driven by feelings of patriotism and keen upon going to the front, there was a regression in the development of military pastoral activity. Its effect was the decreased number of vocations of military priests and a significant reduction in their activity in frontline areas. The atmosphere of defeat mobilized Protopresbyter Shavelsky to even stricter supervision of the fulfillment of duties by his subordinates. This is what he wrote about his obligations to the Russian soldiers:

> Almost every month I spent ten days in combat units, visiting regiments, brigades, and, sometimes under fire, trenches, stopping at every hospital, celebrating services everywhere, preaching the Word of God. These journeys were important. I appeared there not just as the Protopresbyter, but also as a representative of the Monarch, on behalf of whom I always greeted the troops and handed out crosses and icons given to me by the Empress. My greetings and visits, especially in dangerous places, raised the spirits and strengthened soldiers. (Шавельский 1996b, s. 97).

The defeatism that prevailed among priests was caused, on one hand, by external factors. These included the defeats of the Russian army in World War I, colliding with the expectations imposed on a Russian soldier and his chaplain and the enormous losses in people resulting from a bad war strategy and incompetent commanding. Among the general disintegration of the army Protopresbyter Shavelsky demanded in his circular № 3287 of 14 September 1915 that chaplains remain constantly present with the soldiers in a spiritual sense, not only during their stay in the camp, especially in the trenches and during regular fights on the front (Золотарев, Олег Валентинович: Христолюбивое воинство русское. Граница: Москва 1994, s. 74).

The complex functioning of the institutions of the Russian military and naval clergy was also influenced by internal factors such as, first and foremost, the anti-war agitation, conducted also among front troops. Priests, who were obliged by the highest authorities of the Synod to remain totally apolitical, often gave in to the wave of revolutionary propaganda. It was appealing due to the fact that the participation of the tsarist Russia in World War I exposed the country's economic inefficiency, and the consequences of the decline – high inflation, food shortages and a decrease in wages – was painfully perceptible for the Russian society, exhausted after the war (Marples, David R./Scharoch Irena: Historia ZSRR od rewolucji do rozpadu. Zakład Narodowy im. Ossolińskich: Wrocław 2006, s. 41–44; Kenez Peter/Górska, Aleksandra: Odkłamana historia Związku Radzieckiego. Bellona: Warszawa 2008, s. 28–30; Smaga, Józef: Narodziny i upadek imperium. ZSRR 1917–1991. Znak: Kraków 1992, s. 17–18; Pipes, Richard/Szafar, Tadeusz: Rewolucja rosyjska. Wydawnictwo Magnum: Warszawa 2006, s. 292–356).

The increase in social discontent led to the events of 8 March 1917. A demonstration was organized on the occasion of the International Women's Day, which quickly evolved into an anti-tsar rally. The riots triggered an uprising. An immediate effect of the "February Revolution" – this is how the Russian uprising of March 1917 is referred to in the historiography – the fall of the monarchical system in Russia. A personified autocracy was established in its place in the form of the Provisional Government. It was created on 15 March 1917 as a result of the agreement between the Provisional Committee of the Duma and the Petrograd Soviet of Workers' and Soldiers' Deputies. The first Prime Minister of the Government was Prince Georgy Lvov, who (on 21 July) was replaced by Alexander Kerensky (Kenez, s. 30–38).

Political and social changes occurring in Russia could not fail to affect the work of the military and naval clergy. The change of the situation and its implications for pastoral ministry in the army were discussed during the session of the Second All-Russian Congress of the Military and Naval Clergy. It was held in the period of 1–11 July 1917 in the Supreme High Command in Mogilev with the participation of representatives of the lower clergy and lay people interested in ecclesiastical affairs (Российский государственный исторический архив: Духовное правление при Протопресвитере Военного и Морского Духовенства, Бумаги относящиеся к 2-му Всероссийск[ому] Сезду воен[ного] и Морск[ого] Дух[овенст]ва в 1917г. Zesp. 806, inw. 5, sygn. 10140, t. 1–3). Two basic issues were raised, representing the spectrum of interest of the gathered people.

Firstly, in the new political conditions and in the atmosphere of an "Orthodox revolution" (proceeding similarly to the social and political revolution), which caused the removal of many hierarchs from their positions and promoted the slogan of the social participation in a democratic community management that should be independent from state authorities. The work on the reforms of the military and naval clergy institute was continued. It was decided, in accordance with the spirit of the times, that the function of the Protopresbyter will be filled by way of free and democratic elections, organized each time on the congress of the military and naval clergy. Candidates for this position had to meet formal requirements, which included at least five years of work in the department of military and navy and obtaining an approval from the highest authority of the Orthodox Church Synod. The Protopresbyter was supposed to be supported by a Protopresbyter Council, a supervisory and advisory body, and the Commission for Economic and Charitable Affairs (Российский государственный военно-исторический архив: Управление главного священника армий Северного фронта, О созыве съезда духовенства, о выборном начале в военном духовенстве, протоколы собрания духовенства. Zesp. 2044, inw. 1, sygn. 30, k. 35).

On 9 July by way of a ballot the Congress participants selected the Protopresbyter of the military and naval clergy. This office, this time for life, was taken again by Georgy Shavelsky (Сенин, s. 165).

The model of the functioning of the highest authorities was reflected in the organizational chart of the lower Orthodox military structures. The aspect of hierarchy and universality was strongly emphasized, treated as a counterweight for the autocracy of the church. This principle created traditional systems: collegiality and autonomy at every level of management. At the same time it was enriched by an element of modernity, expressed in the participation of society in the decision-making bodies. In practice this meant that every appointment – beginning with the division chaplain and ending with the corps chaplain – was supposed to be decided by common and democratic elections organized during the military and naval clergy congresses, the results of which were approved by the Protopresbyter. Chaplains having extensive executive, managerial and supervisory powers were supposed to cooperate with a clerical council appointed to support them when making key decisions (Российский государственный исторический архив: Духовное правление при Протопресвитере Военного и Морского Духовенства, Бумаги относящиеся к 2-му Всероссийск[ому] Сезду воен[ного] и Морск[ого] Дух[овенст]ва в 1917г. Zesp. 806, inw. 5, sygn. 10140, t. 2, k. 219–222).

Secondly, the delegates developed a proclamation to the Russian soldiers. They were urged to continue their selfless fight for their homeland, which, as it was strongly emphasized, was standing on the verge of a political disaster and at this particular time was all the more in need of help and support from its devoted citizens:

> Brothers soldiers, the best sons of Russia, its flower and hope! We, the military clergy, sharing the burdens of life in the trenches with you, washing the sacred blood of a Russian soldier, we beg you in the name of Christ and God: gain some sense, do not let the enemies of the Homeland and of our freedom, madmen and traitors make fools of you, deceive and corrupt you. Do not let Russia die. Only you can save it! Russia needs a strong authority. Recognize the full power of the Provisional Government, made up of friends of the nation, led by only one desire to save Russia, make it happy! (Бабкин, Михаил Анатольевич: Российское духовенство и свержение монархии в 1917 году. Материалы и архивные документы по истории Русской православной церкви. Индрик: Москва 2006, s. 372).

The establishment of the Provisional Government did not calm the social and political situation in the country. The proliferating economic difficulties and the increase in social discontent escalated the criticism of Alexander Kerensky's internal policy. (Williams Beryl/Tuszyńska, Agnieszka: Lenin. Zakład Narodowy im. Ossolińskich: Wrocław 2002, s. 67–78; Malia, Martin/Hułas, Magdalena/Wyzner, Elżbieta: Sowiecka tragedia. Historia komunistycznego imperium rosyjskiego 1917–1991. Wydawnictwo Philip Wilson: Warszawa 1998, pp. 120–129; Witkowicz, Andrzej: Wokół terroru białego i czerwonego. Książka i Prasa: Warszawa 2008, pp. 69–75). The growing anti-war and anti-government movement led to the outbreak of an armed uprising that shortly after turned into a civil war. On 7 November, the entire Petrograd, except the seat of government – the Winter Palace was in the hands of the rebels. Alexander Kerensky fled from the capital, and the gathered Second All-Russian Congress of Soviets of Workers' and Soldiers' Deputies announced the seizure of power by the Provisional Government of Workers and Peasants. The new leader was Vladimir Lenin (Bazylow, Ludwik: Historia Rosji. Zakład Narodowy im. Ossolińskich: Wrocław, Warszawa, Kraków, Gdańsk 1975, pp. 499–516; Smoleń, Mieczysław: Stracone dekady. Historia ZSRR 1917–1991. Wydawnictwo Naukowe PWN: Warszawa–Kraków 1994, pp. 23–35; Service, Robert/ Szczerkowska, Hanna: Towarzysze. Komunizm od początku do upadku. Historia zbrodniczej ideologii. Znak: Kraków 2008, pp. 77–89).

The policy of the Russian state created after the Bolshevik revolution by the delegates of the Second Congress and by the Vladimir Ilyich himself was oriented to achieve stability on the international arena and strengthen its position within the country. In the external sphere, the efforts to end the armed conflict as soon as possible were supposed to serve its implementation. On 8 November, the Second Congress issued a decree On peace, in which the peoples and governments of the fighting parties were called on to conclude a "just, democratic peace, [...] without annexations and contributions" (Kenez, s. 43). Following this declaration some efforts were initiated to sign a peace treaty, which initially were positively received only by Germany. Despite the difficulties in reaching a common position, which resulted in Leon Trotsky's breaking off negotiations, and Germany resuming hostilities of 18 February 1918, occupying a part of Ukraine and threatening the capital of the Empire, the peace was concluded on 3 March in Brest (Pipes, s. 596–627).

The Treaty of Brest-Litovsk was an important moment in the course of the ongoing civil war in Russia. "White" armies, led by former tsarist generals opposed to the "October Revolution" and communist dictatorship, gradually withdrew from the territory of Russia. The fate of soldiers, aristocracy and civilian population was also shared by some Russian clergymen. Protopresbyter Georgy Shavelsky, who was trying to organize a relatively normal religious life in the areas free from the Bolsheviks' power, was one of them (Поспеловский, Дмитрий Владимирович: Русская Православная Церковь в XX в. Республика: Москва 1995, s. 120; Кострюков, Андрей Александрович: "Временное Высшее Церковное управление на Юго-Востоке России как начало зарубежной церковной власти". Вестник Православного Свято-Тихоновского Гуманитарного Университета. Серия: История. История Русской Православной Церкви 3(28), 2008, s. 50–60). The previous Orthodox institutions, such as the military and naval clergy, which was led by Shavelsky, ceased to exist following the decree of the Council of People's Commissars of 16 January 1918 (Кострюков, Андрей Александрович: "Военное духовенство и развал армии в 1917 году". Церковь и время 2, 2005, s. 169), and the representatives and faithful of the Orthodox church fell victim to repressions (Емельянов, Николай Евгеньевич: "Оценка статистики гонений на Русскую Православную Церковь в XX веке". In: Воробьёв, Владимир Николаевич (red.): Ежегодная богословская конференция Православного Свято-Тихоновского Богословского Института. Издательство Православного Свято-Тихоновского Гуманитарного Университета: Москва 1997, s. 166–167).

Shavelsky's attempts to appeal to the highest national authorities and protect ecclesiastical structures from a total paralysis did not have the desired effects (Российский государственный исторический архив: Духовное правление при Протопресвитере Военного и Морского Духовенства, Об упразднении Управл[ения] Протопрезбитера и о защите прихожан принадлежащих ему капиталов, движимого и недвижимого имущества. Zesp. 806, inw. 5, sygn. 10526, k. 1, 2). In the face of defeat the army of General Anton Denikin, Shavelsky emigrated to Bulgaria. Until his death he actively participated in the life of the Bulgarian Orthodox community as a professor of pastoral theology at the University of Sofia, lecturer and director of the Russian

Gymnasium, co-organizer of the Sofia Ecclesiastical Academy. He died on 2 October 1951 (Государственный архив Российской Федерации: Шавельский Георгий Иванович, протопресбитер военного и морского духовенства (с 1911 г.), протопресбитер добровольческой армии (1918–1920 гг.), доцент богословского факультета софийского университета (с 1924 г.). Zesp. 1486).

The period of the Great Was was one of the most important moments in the biography of the last tsar's Protopresbyter of army and navy and nearly two hundred years of history of the Institute of Russian military priests. In this context, the events of the years 1914–1918 can be treated as a kind of turning point. It began in the moment of the conflict outbreak. The beginning of the warfare contributed to the flourishing of this institution, which has developed a strict, wartime organizational and institutional framework in this period. It also showed the commitment of the last tsar's Protopresbyter of army and navy, Georgy Shavelsky. The end of this chronological framework is determined by the end of the Great War. The signing of a peace treaty coincided with the collapse of the institution of the military and naval clergy, which – according to the new, Bolshevik leaders of Russia – was a relic of the old, ossified tsarist system which had to be liquidated along with the system itself.

Ionela Zaharia
Babeş-Bolyai University

Christian Religious Experiences within the Austro-Hungarian Army during the Great War

> Joy, sadness, anger, elation, jealousy, envy, despair, anguish, grief –
> all these feelings are partly social.
> They are influenced by cultural ideas and images, are refracted
> through roles and relationships.
>
> Hopkins, et al. 2009, p. 30

Over the last few years, many studies have addressed the effects that the Great War had on moral, religious and cultural matters. It is now widely acknowledged that factors such as an awareness of death, the longing to see the loved ones again, sorrow, state and church propaganda either reawakened religious feelings or intensified the already existing ones. For Christians, these feelings manifested themselves as a mixture of practices enhanced by church and superstitions. The aim of this article it is to investigate the journals and memories of former Austro-Hungarian army personnel that served during the Great War, to identify their religious experiences during the war, and discover the associated feelings and how they were adjusted to the new circumstances.

As Austria-Hungary was a multinational empire, and since studying religious feelings of all the nationalities within the army is beyond the scope of this paper, the focus of this study has been restricted to the experiences of two Austrian and two Romanian officers, one soldier and one military priest, all belonging to different donominations.

The first part of the paper will present the religious attendance in the Austro-Hungarian Army to better understand the importance of religion and the religiosity within the army and society of the time. The next part will focus on elements of the personal history that influenced the religiosity of the subjects: place of birth, in which denomination they have been baptised, social status of their family, relationship with church, their studies, and any special events that may have influenced their faith before the war. The final part will identify how the subjects portray their religious or supernatural experiences and what influenced them during the war. The paper will try to depict the differences and the similarities between the subjects, the tendency towards ecumenism, the perception of God's involvement in the war and the role of the authorities. This analysis shall cast light on other facets of the Great War, the religious experiences of individuals. It will facilitate a fuller understaning of the impact of the past and present historical events on people and their feelings, but also how these feelings influence history through their manifestations.

Religious Assistance in the Austro-Hungarian Army

Religious assistance had a long tradition in the Imperial and Royal Austrian Army. The first mention of a military chaplain, on what is today Austrian territory, dates back to the 5th century (Gröger, Ham and Sammer 2001), but only after the 30 Years War was a dedicated institution establish to provide permanent religious assistance to soldiers. In 1773, with the approval from Vatican, the Apostolic Field Vicariate of the Imperial Army was founded in the Wiener Neustadt Diocese. The institution was based on modern bureaucratic principals, as was most of the state apparatus of the monarchy, and functioned until the dissolution of the Austro-Hungarian Empire (Legler 1979, pp. 3–15).

The Apostolic Field Vicariate of the Army had under his jurisdiction only Catholic subjects, for whom it was compulsory to attend the religious services provided by the military chaplains weekly. Following the Patent of Tolerance issued in 1781, soldiers baptised in other denominations were as well allowed to publicly follow their beliefs, but only outside military establishments. During wartime the rules were changed, especially for the Border Regiments where most of the soldiers were Orthodox or Greek-Catholic. In the case of war, after 1758, an imperial decree ordered that during wartime Orthodox military chaplain had to be assigned to such regiments in order to attend the religious needs. This decision was enabled by means of an joint intercession of the Metropolitan from Karlowitz (Sremski Karlovci, Serbia), Pavle Nenadović, and the emperor Joseph II. In 1779, after another imperial decree also the first Greek-Catholic military chaplains were appointed in order to cater for the spiritual needs of soldiers who were the followers of this denomination. Situation for religious minorities improved gradually over the 19th century. In 1834 for example, it also became compulsory for soldiers belonging to other denominations to attend the Holy Liturgy in their own language at least once a year, to confess and receive the Holy Communion. Since that moment Orthodox and Greek-Catholic military chaplains were constantly present in the Army High Administration staff, both throughout time of war or peace (Bielik 1901, pp. 289–291).

The duty of the military clergy, regardless of denomination, was to assist the spiritual needs of the soldiers, officers and students within military establishments. Their responsibilities included celebrating the Holy Liturgy on Sundays and Holidays, giving military personnel the possibility to confess and receive the Holy Communion and facilitating the religious education of the students from military schools and academies (Kriegsministerium 1904, pp. 19–21).

During war time, the duties of the military chaplain included attending the wounded soldiers from the own Army in the hospitals, hold the Holy Liturgy on Sundays and Holidays, offer the possibility for confession when possible and administer the Last Rites, if possible, to moribunds. They also had to complete reports and papers concerning their activities, keep the Death Register, perform funerals, sometimes teach religion for the recruits and the students studying in the military schools and academies. Other clerical duties included work at the censorship office, translating for the authorities and wounded soldiers who did not knew German or Hungarian and attending prisoners of war (Kriegsministerium 1904, pp. 62–74). The range of tasks depended on their skills and the orders that came from the military authorities, and were divided among military chaplains belonging to all religions and denomination, according to the laws of supply and demand.

While there were around 300 military chaplains, rabbis and imams in the Religious Service of the Imperial and Royal Army before the war started, this number rose to around 3077 at the end of the war (Katholische Militärseelsorge Österreich 1999). This indicates the rising importance of the degree of religious assistance and need for priests during the war. The matter of the religious assistance was however much more complex due to several reasons. First of all, the Church still had a significant influence upon the majority of the Austro-Hungarian society. This was perhaps unsurprising as most of the population was living in rural areas and were very attached to tradition. It must be also reminded that at the same time priests represented in this areas one of the highest authorities for moral and religious matters. They gained even more importance as the promoters of national and imperial values and were guiding the manifestation of national and religious identity (Bârlea 2000, pp. 23–25, 73). Their ideas were disseminated though confessional schools, reunions, associations supported by church, sermons, and a certain cultural policy of the hierarchs and priests.

In such circumstances the state authorities regarded as very important not only giving the right to the soldiers to manifest their religious belief but also trying to use the influence of the priests to perpetuate civil loyalty, obedience and the image of a pious monarch. All the above mentioned aspects caused that the duties, policy and message of the church and military chaplains were very made the duty, policy and speech of the church and military chaplian to be very flexible and enabled them and the state to rule over good Christian civilians: obedient, brave and ready to sacrifice themselves and act as *good soldiers* on the battlefield.

Religious Feelings and their Expression

The ego-documents are one of the most important sources in the research of religious experiences and the emotions they release. This study is not only based on journals and memories, but also on pastoral reports belonging to the military priest and other documents from the War Archives in Vienna, which offer information about the religious assistance provided for the soldiers, its purpose and effects. Special attention is given to analysing the ego-documents such as journals or memoires, because in journals, feelings and experiences are described shortly after they were experienced, when they were still fresh in the memory. When it comes to memoires, here the feelings and images can be distorted and blurred by other events that took place since, they nevertheless offer valuable clues in reconstructing the historical facts and choosing the past experiences to be remembered.

The first selected ego-document were the memoirs which belonged to a general, staff officer, historian, politician and diplomat – Edmund Glaise Horstenau. He wrote his memoirs at the end of World War II, when he was in prison, and finished them shortly before he decided to kill himself in 1946. He was born in Brunau am Inn, in Tirol, to a family in which serving in the army was a tradition. It seems that as a young boy he aspired to become a priest but financial problems of the family forced him to chose a military career (Broucek 1980, pp. 7–10). After his studies at the military school in Sankt Pölten and Theresian Military Academy in Wiener Neustadt, von Horstenau attended some classes to work as an officer in the general staff of the army. This brought him close to historical writing and enabled him to work in the War Archives in Vienna.

One of the first records concerning religious practice which may have influenced the life of Horstenau and his way of feeling is the funeral of his father, who died when he was still a child. He does not mention the feelings experienced during the ceremony but mentions crying, a sign of mourning. His attachment towards the Church and his mother can be seen from this early stage of life: the former manifesting as the desire to become a priest and the latter as jealousy towards a possible stepfather (Broucek 1980, pp. 80–91). The memories are not based on inner feelings, but on facts, describing people and actions. An important mention appears on the occasion of the beginning of the war. He remembers that the whole city was filled with enthusiasm, a feeling that he did not personally embrace. What he remembers is that the news that he must serve in Lemberg, far away from his mother left in his care, triggered a great sadness. He also mentions that when he realised that the war was to be a world war he started crying, another sign of mourning (Broucek 1980, pp. 283–284).

For the whole period of the war he does not write about any other significant feelings that may have caused him to address any special prayers to God, the Saints or other intercessor Saints. However, one can sense in him the compassion during war for those who lost dear people, for the loss of a hero or terrible events that took place. He also writes about attending Holy Liturgies held by Greek-Catholic, Orthodox and Catholic military priests, and asserts that in the years before the war, religious indulgence was a distinctive characteristic of the Imperial and Royal Austrian Army. The promoter of this policy was the Emperor Franz Joseph itself (Broucek 1980, p. 290, 291, 313), which indicates the influence of the image of the Emperor upon von Horstenau.

It must be noted that that even through he does not insist on recording his feelings, it is still clear that he manifested religious indulgence, sorrow and compassion for the tragedies caused by the war. This did not suggest that he was particularly pious or pleaded more for God's intercession and this may arguably be related to at least two different aspects. Firstly, he personally admits that his memory was already suffering from oblivion, while secondly, his studies and connections indicate that he was not close to the front line for very long, and he was never on the first front line. He was working mainly for the staff of the army on the Russian Front, in an office, and then in Vienna where he had to prepare reports for the Emperor. This kept him away from the fear, anguish, longing, cold, famine and sorrow after seeing comrades killed in action; feelings that soldiers on the front line usually experienced, and caused them to be more pious and appeal to God or superstition for help.

The second experience that I selected was that of Erich Mayr. He was born in Brixen, Tirol, in a modest family. At the age of seven he became an orphan and was placed in the custody of his step mother, his aunt, and his grandmother. He attended a private Catholic gymnasium in Brixen. The loss of his parents and his studies in an environment dominated by the teachings of the Catholic Church may have influenced Mayr in being a religious person. Afterwards, he graduated from a pedagogical institute and wanted to become a teacher, but following the protests of his step mother, he chose to study Accounting and Taxation. These qualifications enabled him to be a public worker at the Finances Office of the County in Innsbruck, until his retirement in 1955. The outbreak of the war surprised Mayr as he was preparing to be engaged to a young lady who came from a modest and pious family (Brandauer 2013, pp. 11–31).

The first pages of his journal suggest that he was close to the practices of the church, attached to his step mother, passionate to his fiancé, and ready to sacrifice his life for the country, a sacrifice which he saw as a a duty, also towards God.

During the war, Mayr was a soldier in the III. Kaiserschützenregiment, and served in Galicia, the Carpathian mountains, Isonzo and Tirol. He writes in a melancholy, critical manor, which is very detailed, from the perspective of a man passionate about nature, an artist, public worker and soldier. He regards all the things that happened in the world to be decided by God for a reason, a reason that he did not question. In addition, he often thanks God for all the good things and prays for protection for him and all the beloved ones. Another sign of his piety is his eagerness to attend the Holy Liturgy and regret when the duties of a soldier hindered him from attending. For him, both the collective and individual manifestation of his faith were important and necessary to receive the intercession of God and the Holy Mother. Before he departed to the front line, he wrote that he attended the Holy Liturgy and received the Holy Communion together with his fiancé (Brandauer 2013, pp. 46–61).

Unlike Edmund Glaise von Horstenau, Mayr had to serve during the war both on and behind the front line. In the trenches, his most common manifestation of faith was thanking and praying with much passion. He also accounts collective manifestations like attending Holy Liturgy where a military priest gave a motivational sermon (Brandauer 2013, p. 62).

On the day of his departure on the train from Ampezzo he captures the farewell, the enthusiasm of the crowd and their faith in God: girls with flowers, music, the trains covered with patriotic quotes, flowers, flags, Heart of Jesus images, a cross, a rosary, portraits of the Emperor. He also writes how they were singing traditional songs that evoked memories of their brave ancestors fighting for their Emperor (Brandauer 2013, pp. 63–68).

Other important moments of intense inner experiences manifested in prayer were the important Christian Holidays. On the occasion of his first New Year during the war, while he was still far away from the front line, he thanks God for his mercy and prays for the future (Brandauer 2013, p.115). On the occasion of Easter 1915, he was already on the Russian front line. It is visible here the effect on his feelings and wishes brought by life on the front line. His praying intensifies, he asks God for the end of the slaughter (Brandauer 2013, p. 137), and to return home. Some of Mayr's remarks indicate his inner turmoil: 3 April 1915, during a night in his hiding place "[…] if only under such a peaceful sky also the people would be peaceful […]"[1] (Brandauer 2013, p.140); "[…] It is peculiar grieving to see how people treat each other with hostility. How you do to me, this is how I

---

1   These passages of Erich Mayr have been translated by the author.

do to you… Awful, how the man transforms into a wild animal during war […]"
(Brandauer 2013, p. 142).

In his journal, he also exemplifies other feelings and experiences triggered by the war. After the death of his lieutenant, he tries to fulfil the last wish of the deceased, to have a proper Christian funeral, conducted by a priest. Because the body remained between the two lines of the front, Mayr prays again to God and the Holy Mother for help. After several days of intense searching while he risked his life, and much praying, he found the body and organised the funeral (Brandauer 2013, pp. 143–145). This episode points to the importance of funeral rites and adaptbility of the human being in times of distress. Mayr, as well as his lieutenant, and others that had to serve on the front line, were aware of the possibility of premature death. To cope with this, they moved closer to the Church, its practices and what needed to be done in order to obtain salvation for the eternal life. Evidence of the rising importance of a proper funeral during the war can be found in a range of sources including memoires, journals, the press of the time, military cemeteries and museums. It is important to underline that during the war a lot of meaning was assigned not only to the funeral but to all things related to the church which could help to survive or gain the salvation: praying, praying books, icons, amulets like coins with the Heart of Jesus on them, etc.

The war was not as short as Mayr firstly imagined, and in 1916, Mayr experiences for the first time the hopelessness. (Brandauer 2013, p. 266). After he is being taken prisoner and transported to France in 1918, his hope seems to return and intensify when he finds out that the war ended (Brandauer 2013, pp. 423–425). Journals like that of Erich Mayr are a very valuable, accurate source for reconstructing the palette of emotions, spirituality and everyday life.

The third person I would like to focus on is Petru Talpeş, first prosecutor in Timiş County, which today is in Romania. He wrote his memories in 1967 as a testimony to his grandchildren. His family was a humble peasant family from Cornereva, a village in Banat. Since childhood it seems that he was close both to the Church, occult beliefs, superstition and soothsayers (Talpeş 2008, pp. 9–26). He started attending school in the nearby village, then in Orşova, and Caransebeş. In the dormitories and the host families where he lived during his studies, he learned military discipline and developed a closer connection to the Orthodox Church. This proximity to the church prompted him to embrace a monastic life and go to Holy Mount Athos; a desire that he abandoned after a while. His family did not have sufficient finances to support his studies, but because he was a diligent pupil he was able to obtain a special scholarship from the "Emanuil Gojdu" Foundation, with help from the sister of Miron Cristea, Bishop of Caransabeş at that time (Talpeş 2008, pp. 26–32).

When the war began he was still a high school student, but in 1915 he reached the legal age for being conscripted. After he attended a preparation course for officers, he was sent to the front line in Italy. The first time he had to fight on the front line, he mentions seeing a big cemetary, an image that without a doubt affected him greatly and think more about what he could do to preserve his life. On the occasion of his first battle, he remembers a magic spell that his grandfather's brother told him when he was 12 years old. This spell seems to have protected the old man when he was sent to fight at Königrätz in 1868. Fear of death, and the idea that anything that can be useful should be used, prompted Petru Talpeş to utter the spell (Talpeş 2008, pp. 39–44). The battle ended with a victory and no casualties. This strengthened his belief in magic and superstitions.

Talpeş did not remain on the battlefield for long. After a short while, he was decorated for capturing some Italian soldiers and received permission to go home. Later he was sent back to the front line, but this time to fight against Romania. He refused to fight and decided to desert. After crossing to the Romanian side, he had not very much to do with the front line, even if he volunteered to enter the Romanian Army. His religiosity and belief in God's intercession manifested until the end of the war through praying and attending the Holy Liturgy. As with Erich Mayr, Petru Talpeş thought that everything in the world is done with a purpose. An important part of his memories is his acknowledgment of being attracted to occult practices, and his belief in God, and His Son, who sacrificed for us, in the existence of destiny as well as of a protective spirit, which he described as being similar to an angel (Talpeş 2008, pp. 71–72).

Like Edmond Glaise von Horstenau, Petru Talpeş did not describe his feelings in his memories, choosingmore to focus on remembering important facts and details. What it is very conspicuous from his memories is the importance of both the cultural surroundings in which he grew up and his war experience in shaping his spirituality and way of acting for the rest of his life.

The fourth person selected for analysis is Coriolan Buracu, who left both memories and journal notes. He was born in Prigor, today in Romania, in a middle-class family with good connections to the Romanian elite from Banat. He attended school in Budapest, Viena, Blaj, and the Theological Institute in Caransebeş. After finishing his studies, he married and was ordained priest in Mehadia. Before the war started, he conducted numerous projects associated with Romanian culture in the area and so was suspected of a lack of loyalty towards the monarchy and imprisoned. His connections to the Romanian elite and the fact that he was the nephew of the first military Orthodox priest from Austria-Hungary, Pavel Boldea, helped him out of prison in order to be appointed military priest on the front line in Galicia. During the war, he performed his duty, not only on the front line but also in hospitals and a prisoner-of-war camp in Debrecen, today in Hungary (Leu și Bocşan 2012, pp. 515–518).

In his case, his belief and faith in God it is unquestionable. Since the beginning of his records, Buracu underlines that when sorrow and death become part of daily life, those who had doubts about God´s existence changed their opinion. Sorrow, death and a longing to return home were the feelings that drove the soldiers and officers to attend the Holy Liturgies that he celebrated and in which they prayed to win the war and return to their homes. Of course, Buracu shared the feelings of the soldiers, but for him the battles, the sound of explosions, death and funerals became bearable sooner. Still, from time to time, he confesses that also for him, which had a different education, bassed on seeing death as a transition event, which lead to eternal life, the situation seemed so hard that he cried at the thought that he would not survive the battle (Leu and Bocşan 2012, pp. 528–540). This highlights two important feelings that were augmented by war and shared by everybody: hoplessness and helplessness.

Another interesting record in Buracu's notes describes his admiration for the piety of the Russian prisoners-of-war he attended in Debrecen, manifested as attending the Liturgy, praying, singing religious songs, building chapels, and their possession of various religious items. In the prisoner-of-war camp, he describes how compassion was another one of the feelings that influenced people during war. In the case of father Buracu this manifested in his attempt to learn a little Russian to be able to hear the confession of prisoners and give them the Holy Communion, to provide books and newspapers for wounded and arranging cultural establishments for soldiers. All this were at the same time a part of the religious, pastoral and philanthropical duty of al military chaplains, no matter if those that thez attended were the own soldiers or those of the enemy . However, his style of writing also suggests this was a manifestation of his faith and compassion. (Leu and Bocşan 2012, pp. 544–560).

His records, especially his journal notes published in the newspaper "Drapelul" during the war, show the impact that the war had on a man of God. They are a very good third-person source, from the point of view of a specialist in religiosity, on the collective manifestation of faith.

Conclusion

Other documents, such as the reports that the military priests had to send to the War Ministry in Vienna, record also the manifestation of religious feelings (Austrian War Archives 1914–1919). They point to an increasing number of soldiers and officers that attended Holy Liturgies, and the increasing demand for prayer books. Priests encouraged and supported this behaviour, because most of them saw the war as a punishment from God (Austrian War Archives 1915). All the practices they promoted, such as Holy Liturgies and prayer, were intended to help remind humanity about love, morality, sacrifice, and the virtues of a true Christian.

Both the Austrian and Romanians whose memories and journals are analysed herein were prepared to sacrifice themselves and to go to war, some with more enthusiasm some with less. Indeed, going to war and dying for your country was considered an act of honor. But the war pushed them to their limits, which sometimes became bearable through faith in God, supernatural powers and the belief in the existence of an afterlife and Heaven.

Feelings like fear, sorrow or hope drove them to pray, attend Holy Liturgies or help those in need. The way they decided to act was influenced not only by the war but also by their past history and the cultural environment in which they grew up. The beliefs and practices that intensified during the war significantly and irreversibly influenced the spirituality of those who experienced the Great War.

Anna Caban
State Archive
in Opole

Archive traces of the drama of war. Sources for investigation into the daily life of inhabitants of cities in the Opole District in the archival fond of the State Archive in Opole

The storm which started in summer 1914 reversed the earlier arrangement of political powers, destroyed the economy of both sides of the global conflict and transformed social structure. The Great War opened the door to the formation of nation states and new political systems. The centenary of this breakthrough event represented a pretext and acted as a starting point for extensive research into the archival fond of the State Archive in Opole. The research was aimed at finding new, unknown and hitherto unstudied archival materials. Thanks to the materials, the image of the Opole District, known from historical studies as a direct military – supply base, is complemented and enriched with a panorama of the everyday life of citizens in the face of war. Archival materials presenting this event cover the period from the outbreak of war in August 1914 to the signing of the armistice in November 1918.

On the outbreak of war, the Opole District covered an area of 13 thousand square kilometers and comprised 18 village districts[1] and 8 independent municipal districts[2]. The seat of the authorities of the Opole District (Regierungsbezirk Oppeln) was established in 1815 in Opole (Oppeln)[3]. The District's authority covered 46 cities,

---

1 The village districts in the Opole district: Bytom, Gliwice, Głubczyce, Grodków, Katowice, Kluczbork, Koźle, Lubliniec, Niemodlin, Nysa, Olesno, Opole, Prudnik, Pszczyna, Racibórz, Rybnik, Tarnowskie Góry, Toszek, Zabrze. These areas were administered by "landrat" – starosts (Landratsamt) and district areas (Kreisausschuss) they ruled cf. Mendel, Edward: *Polacy na Górnym Śląsku w latach I wojny światowej. Położenie i postawa.* Wydawnictwo "Śląsk": Katowice 1971, p. 17.

2 The municipal districts of the Opole district were established through designation of areas around cities with more than 20 thousand inhabitants. These were: Opole, Gliwice, Bytom, Królewska Huta (Chorzów), Katowice, Zabrze, Nysa, Racibórz, loc. cit.

3 The Opole district was established pursuant to act of 30 April 1815 and started its operation on 7 May 1816. Throughout its existence, the district changed its scope and

1482 communes and 1102 townships (Gutsbezirk)[4]. Before the outbreak of the Great War, this area was well-developed though diversified in terms of economy and social aspects. The most industrialised and urbanised part of the district was the South-East area near to the cities of Mysłowice (Myslowitz) – Tarnowskie Góry (Tarnau) – Gliwice (Gleiwitz) – Rybnik (Ribnik), the so – called Upper Silesia Industrial Region, where the mining – metallurgy industry was located[5]. Outside this region, industrial plants were located in bigger cities. In Opole itself, the cement industry was booming[6]. However, crafts played an important part in the economy of Upper Silesia and provided employment for hundreds of thousands of people[7]. A significant part of the province was used for agriculture and forests[8]. According to the national census of 1 December 1910 (*Statistik des Deutsche Reichs. Die Volkszählung im Deutschen Reiche am 1 Dezember 1910*, Berlin 1914), the Opole District was inhabited by 2 207 981 people[9]. This number also includes 12 227[10] soldiers stationed in the area. The majority of local the population, over 53%, were Poles. According to the official statistics, there were slightly fewer Germans and the remaining part comprised other nationalities[11]. Apart from the population growth, there were no other changes in the national – social structure of the district following the outbreak of war.

---

administrative structure several times, cf. Czapliński, Marian: *Kancelaria i registratura Rejencji Opolskiej.* "Sobótka" (2/1961), pp. 179–183.

4 Mendel, Edward: *Polacy na Górnym Śląsku w latach I wojny światowej. Położenie i postawa*, Katowice 1971, p. 17.

5 Czapliński, Marek: "Dzieje Śląska od 1806 do 1945 roku". In: Czapliński, Marek/Kaszuba, Elżbieta/Wąs, Gabriela et al. (eds.): *Historia Śląska.* Wydawnictwo Uniwersytetu Wrocławskiego: Wrocław 2007, pp. 300–310; cf. Mendel, Edward, ibid., p. 18.

6 Borkowski, Maciej: "Życie codzienne w Opolu w latach Wielkiej Wojny (1914–1918)". In: Linek, Bernard/Rosenbaum, Sebastian/Struve, Kai (eds.): *Koniec starego świata – początek nowego. Społeczeństwo Górnego Śląska wobec pierwszej wojny światowej. (1914–1918) Źródła i metody.* Gliwice 20–22 June 2013, Opole 2013, [PDF.], p. 90; cf. Czapliński, Marek: "Dzieje Śląska od 1806 do 1945 roku". In: Czapliński, Marek/Kaszuba, Elżbieta/Wąs, Gabriela et al. (eds.): *Historia Śląska.* Wydawnictwo Uniwersytetu Wrocławskiego: Wrocław 2007, pp. 300–310.

7 Czapliński, Marek: *Dzieje Śląska od 1806 do 1945…*, p. 306.

8 Mendel, Edward: *Polacy na Górnym Śląsku…*, pp. 18–22.

9 Mendel, Edward: *Dzień powszedni na Śląsku Opolskim w czasie I wojny światowej.* Opole 1987, p. 7; cf. Gehrke, Roland: "Od Wiosny Ludów do I wojny światowej (1848–1918)". In: Bahlcke, Joachim/Gawrecki, Dan/Kaczmarek, Ryszard (eds.): *Historia Górnego Śląska. Polityka, gospodarka i kultura europejskiego regionu.* Dom Współpracy Polsko-Niemieckiej: Gliwice 2011, pp. 202–203.

10 Mendel, Edward: *Polacy na Górnym Śląsku…*, pp. 24–25.

11 Ibid., pp. 25–26; cf. Gehrke, Roland, ibid., pp. 202–203.

Presentation of archival materials of 1914–1918

Only part of the holdings of the State Archive in Opole relating to the period of the Great War has been preserved. An analysis of the introductions to the fond shows that only a small percentage of the archival material has been preserved, although it is difficult to determine exactly how much. Likewise, we cannot state clearly if this fact is due to World War II or to the negligence of the following years. The majority of files from municipal and district authority offices of that period has been preserved to a similar degree. World War II had a significant impact on the preservation status of the files which had been started by the Opole District. Despite the evacuation and scattering of archival files over the Upper Silesia region, many materials have been lost and it is impossible to determine how much of this fond has been preserved[12].

Currently, most of the fonds use basic inventory means that enable the identification of individual files. However, the file title does not always lead the researcher to its proper content. Almost all fonds that provided the archival materials covered by this text have been inventoried[13]. In consequence, interested persons have access to the archival materials and can use research works concerning the discussed period in the history of Silesia.

So far the archival materials concerning the Great War stored in the State Archive in Opole have received little interest from users and researchers. Available publications indicate that they are confined to political, national and military issues. Many monographs and other similar publications have been devoted to the subject of the three consecutive Silesian Uprisings[14] and the Silesian plebiscite[15]. In the said

---

12 APO, zespół nr 1191, Rejencja Opolska [Regierung Oppeln] – Wstęp do inwentarza, pp. 8–9.

13 The personal files of the fond *Rejencja Opolska (Opole District)* are an exception as they have not yet been subject to a full inventory of the archival units. The inventory works within this area are in progress. We will be able to familiarize ourselves with their final results after completion of all the works.

14 The First Silesian Uprising (16–24 August 1919) broke out in consequence of disappointment of the Polish people with the terms of the Treaty of Versailles according to which the division of the Upper Silesia region was to be decided by a plebiscite. The Second Silesian Uprising (19/20–25 August 1920) was an attempt at highlighting the presence of the Polish population in this region. It was also a revolt against the terror of the German paramilitary units. The Third Silesian Uprising (2/3 May–5 July 1921) was an aftermath of the plebiscite results and also an attempt to change the state of affairs; cf. Czapliński, Marek: *Dzieje Śląska od 1806 do 1945 roku...*, pp. 365.

15 The plebiscite in Upper Silesia (Volksabstimmung in Oberschlesien) was mandated by the Treaty of Versailles and was to determine the division of Upper Silesia between

publications, the Great War functions only as a prelude to the later events which, in Polish historiography, are depicted as the most important stages in the struggle for national independence, and in German hagiography, as a rebellion against the homeland, which was losing blood in the war. In his book, Ryszard Kaczmarek presents an interesting fragment of everyday life observed from the perspective of a trench[16]. The author devotes a lot of attention to the Poles from Upper Silesia. The life and condition of an "everyman" from the area, which during the Great War served only as the backstage of the main events, have not aroused greater interest in researchers until now. The only attempt to study the subject of the everyday life of the population of Upper Silesia of that time and to determine directions for further investigation was a scientific conference held in Gliwice on the eve of the centenary of the Great War[17]. The materials published after the conference will be a good indication of how much remains to be done in this area.

The subject matter of the preserved archival materials

Archival documents are usually silent witnesses of history. During an analysis of the preserved archival materials from the Great War period, it is easy to see that cruelty had equal effects on the whole of society and the various aspects of its life. From the announcement of mobilisation[18] by the Emperor until the signing of the armistice[19], those involved in the events of the war could not be sure of their future. The archival materials stored in the State Archive in Opole are a perfect

---

Poland and Germany. The plebiscite was conducted on 20 March 1921. Its result was unfavourable for Poland; cf. Czapliński, Marek: *Dzieje Śląska od 1806 do 1945 roku...*, p. 362; et cf. Popiołek, Kazimierz: *Historia Śląska – od pradziejów do 1945 roku.* Wydawnictwo "Śląsk": Katowice 1984, pp. 521–536.

16 Kaczmarek, Ryszard: *Polacy w armii Kajzera. Na frontach I wojny światowej.* Wydawnictwo Literackie: Kraków 2014.

17 Linek, Bernard/Rosenbaum, Sebastian/Struve, Kai (eds.): *Koniec starego świata – początek nowego. Społeczeństwo Górnego Śląska wobec pierwszej wojny światowej. (1914-1918) Źródła i metody.* Gliwice, 20–22 czerwca 2013. Opole 2013 [PDF version].

18 The mobilisation was ordered on 1 August 1914, cf. Pajewski Janusz: *Historia Powszechna 1871-1918*, pp. 324–325.

19 The terms of the armistice were signed by representatives of Germany on 11 November 1918 in a railway carriage near the Compiègne forest; Gilbert, Martin: *Pierwsza wojna światowa.* Trans. Stefan Amsterdamski. Zysk i S-ka Wydawnictwo: Poznań 1994, pp. 502–504; cf. Pajewski, Janusz: *Pierwsza wojna światowa 1914-1918.* Wydawnictwo Naukowe PWN: Warszawa 1998, pp. 759–761.

reflection of these uneasy times. Although they do not document military activities, they illustrate the importance of the supply base for warfare.

Key information concerning political – administrative issues has been preserved in the fond *Rejencja Opolska* (*Opole district, Regierung Oppeln*). The Opole District, as a superordinate body, coordinated the works of a lower – level administration in the whole of Upper Silesia, and issued or approved all decrees, announcements and other legal regulations. Additionally, the district was a control entity for lower – level administration, supervising the district authorities and the municipal authorities. The importance of this administration level increased over the discussed period. The war disturbed the economy, for example, the termination of trade contacts with Congress Poland lead to shortages of food and raw materials[20]. In this difficult situation, the local agencies within the province were charged with additional tasks resulting from the state's long – term military needs.

Of all those discovered, the best preserved and the most representative documents among have been selected for the purposes of this presentation. A large part comes from the fond of the District Authorities Office in Opole [Landratsamt Oppeln]. Apart from the political – military issues, which act as the focus of a large part of the preserved materials from this period, the archival materials that present the daily life of communities, or sometimes even individuals, are most interesting for researchers. Of these files, we will present the ones that best illustrate the more difficult aspects of everyday life during wartime.

Mobilisation of military forces

The general mobilisation declared on 1 August 1914, initially by means of telegraph, was met with enthusiasm in Upper Silesia society[21]. The information, passed by word of mouth, was confirmed the same day and complemented by the hanging of announcements and mobilisation posters in all cities[22]. Martial law was imposed in Silesia on 31 July and the power was transferred to the army[23]. With time, the crowd cheering for the volunteers leaving for the front was replaced with loyal citizens who, driven by their sense of duty, supported their fighting

---

20 Czapliński, Marek: *Dzieje Śląska od 1806 do 1945 roku...*, p. 343.
21 Reports of the local press are a good reflection of the moods of the Opole population at the announcement of mobilisation and during the first days of war; cf. Borkowski, Maciej, ibid., p. 90.
22 Kaczmarek, Ryszard, ibid., pp. 87–93.
23 Czapliński, Marek: *Dzieje Śląska od 1806 do 1945 roku...*, p. 342.

homeland. This is how a specific division of duties towards the state was constituted. The young and all those strong enough to carry arms were sent to the
trenches. The remaining citizens were fighting at the rear of the front: they worked
in armouries, chemical plants or mines, sewed clothes and worked in fields.

The preserved archival materials date back to the very beginning of the war.
What deserves our attention is the pardon of 11 August 1914 in which Emperor
Wilhelm shows favour to prisoners on the occasion of the outbreak of the war[24].
The mobilisation process is reflected in conscription announcements[25] and mobilisation summons for men who were supposed to compensate for the scarcity
of recruits during consecutive stages of warfare[26]. The lists of the names of men
summoned to join the supporting services are also preserved among these documents[27]. Re-organisation also affected transportation, procurement and medical
base. The last element is best reflected in the ordinance of 12 August1914 concerning preparation of hospitals and medical staff for the needs of the army[28].

Mobilisation concerned not only people but also animals. Mainly horses were
"recruited" and, after careful veterinary examination, equipped and sent to the
front along with the soldiers[29].

After the German troops entered the Kingdom of Poland in August 1914,
the German military authorities used a "carrot and stick" method. On the one
hand, they issued bilingual Polish-German announcements addressed to the local population and called for complete subordination to the new rule[30]. At the
same time, the German authorities in their "announcements to the Poles" presented themselves as "defenders of western civilisation" against the barbarism of

---

24 APO, zespół nr 2, Starostwo Powiatowe w Opolu [Landratsamt Oppeln], sygn. 835,
    pp. 133–135.
25 Ibid., sygn. 1777, p. 54.
26 APO, zespół nr 11, Akta miasta Grodkowa, sygn. 1109, p. 42.
27 Ibid. p. 44; The Act of the Reichstag of 5 December 1916 on the Supporting Service for
    Homeland imposed on all men aged 16–60, who could not fight on the front, a duty to
    work for the front, and mobilised them for alternative military service. The same laws
    were applied to childless women and women engaged in so-called "useless activity".
    In parallel, working time was extended, vacations were shortened; the reluctant were
    mandated to work and the work of the under-aged and the retired was formalised; cf.
    Andrzej, Chwalba: ibid., p. 531.
28 APO, zespół nr 547, starostwo Powiatowe w Koźlu [Landratsamt Cosel], sygn. 261,
    pp. 49–50.
29 Ibid., sygn. 499, p. 31.
30 APO, zespół nr 1191, Rejencja Opolska [Regierung Oppeln] – Biuro Prezydialne, sygn.
    141, pp. 30–31 (Ilustration 1).

the "Asian hordes" and appealed for full support of their military actions against Russia[31].

Finance and the war

Regardless of the times and changing circumstances, waging a war entailed the need to find funds. Governments of all the countries fighting on the fronts of the Great War secured sources of financing for the army and with time, gradually increased them[32]. Funds were acquired through the organisation of wartime loans, selling of bonds, postcards and stamps[33], additional printing of money and raising taxes[34]. In Germany, external loans represented one of the means of compensating for the financial deficit of the state. People also used, to a lesser degree, external "war credits"[35]. However, none of the steps taken by the state could prevent a serious monetary crisis[36]. Scarcity of money on the market was compensated with the issuance of substitutes: coupons and substitute money.

In Silesia, the first substitute money (Notgeld) of low and medium nominal value appeared already in August 1914. The money was issued by magistrates and municipal administration. It was withdrawn from circulation shortly after it had been issued[37]. The archival materials of the Komitet Wojewódzki Polskiej Zjednoczonej Partii Robotniczej (Voivodeship Committee of the Polish United Workers' Party) in Opole include substitute coupons for 15 Pfening and 1 German

---

31 Henceforth, unless stated otherwise all quotations in the text have been translated by the translator; ibid., p. 23 (Ilustration 2).

32 Towards the end of 1914, Germany devoted 25% of its budget for war purposes. Four years later, in 1918, these expenses constituted 52% of the total national expenditure. At the same time, Great Britain allocated as much as 80% of its budgetary funds for wartime expenses, cf. Chwalba, Andrzej: *Samobójstwo Europy. Wielka wojna 1914–1918.* Wydawnictwo Literackie: Kraków 2014, p. 526.

33 Postcards and stamps issued during World War I included images of rulers, leaders, war heroes or victorious battles. The largest number of postcards was issued during this period in Germany; cf. ibid., p. 398 and p. 526.

34 Ibid., p. 526.

35 The central powers took out loans in Swiss, Swedish and Dutch banks, cf. ibid., p. 529.

36 The outbreak of the war led to a drop of share and security prices, withdrawal of money from banks and retention of "hard money" [golden and silver coins] by society, cf. Mendel, Edward: *Dzień powszedni na Śląsku Opolskim w czasie I wojny światowej.* Instytut Śląski w Opolu: Opole 1987, p. 14.

37 Ibid., pp. 14–16.

mark issued by the magistrate of Strzelce Opolskie[38]. The same fond contains also substitute money issued in August 1914 by the German Central Bank in Berlin (Reichsbank Berlin) with a nominal value of 50 German marks. This money was in circulation to the end of the war[39].

Captivity

One of the fundamental issues closely related to war is the issue of captivity. On all fronts of the Great War, 6 to 9 million soldiers and officers, according to different estimates, were sent to prisoner-of-war camps from the beginning to the end of the war[40]. Regardless of the organisational structure and geographical latitude, the greatest problem faced by the camps was shortage of food and illnesses. Hunger and related diseases were the main cause of death, both in France and Germany, where the accommodation and sanitary conditions were most advantageous, and in camps in Russia, Italy and Turkey, where the conditions were most difficult[41]. About 2,5 million prisoners ended up in prisoner-of-war camps[42] in Germany during the Great War. Ca. 90 thousand privates, non – coms and officers, these being Russians, Romanians, Serbs, Frenchmen, Englishmen, Italians and Poles from the tsarist army, were sent to camps in Lambinowice[43] and Nysa[44]: the largest

---

38 APO, zespół nr 2579, Komitet Wojewódzki Polskiej Zjednoczonej Partii Robotniczej w Opolu, sygn. 4153, pp. 1–4.

39 Ibid., sygn. 4149, pp. 1–4 (Ilustration 3).

40 Stanek, Piotr: "Jeńcy wojenni na Górnym Śląsku w latach I wojny światowej". In: Linek, Bernard/Rosenbaum, Sebastian/Struve, Kai (eds.): *Koniec starego świata – początek nowego. Społeczeństwo Górnego Śląska wobec pierwszej wojny światowej. (1914–1918). Źródła i metody.* Gliwice, 20–22 czerwca 2013 r. Opole 2013 [PDF version], p. 36; cf., Chwalba, Andrzej, op. cit., p. 456.

41 Ibid., pp. 457–458. 175 prisoner-of-war camps supervised by the Ministry of War were established in Germany during World War I. 101 of them were intended for soldiers and non-coms – stalagi [*Stammlager für kriegsgefangene Mannschaften und Uniteroffiziere]*, 74 were intended for officers – oflagi [*Offizerslager für kriegsgefangene Offziere*] cf. Stanek, Piotr: ibid., p. 36.

42 The largest group of prisoners consisted of the Russians and the French; loc. cit.

43 The camp complex in Lambinowice was intended for privates and non-coms. From 1914 to 1918 the camp many times extended and included a few smaller camps: Popiołek Stefan, Janusz Sawczuk and Stanisław Senft (eds.): *Muzeum martyrologii jeńców wojennych w Łambinowicach. Informator.* Opole, pp. 8–10.

44 In Nysa there was a camp for officers, cf. Stanek, p. 36.

camps in Upper Silesia[45]. Already in October 1914, according to the rule "food for work", 65 thousand war prisoners were sent to work in mines, ironworks, cement plants, agricultural farms and larger factories belonging to the machine engineering, metallurgical and arms industries[46]. Accommodation, sustenance and the type of works they performed are indicated in the files of all levels of administration which was dully performing tasks defined by military authorities and resulting from military needs of the state[47]. Armed civil employees were delegated to supervise and monitor the prisoners' work in industrial plants and other forced labour facilities[48]. For the prisoners in the camps, daily life consisted of hard and exhausting work, difficult living – sanitary conditions, frequent maltreatment by the camp wardens and, with time, also growing food scarcities, which led to illnesses and death.

On the outbreak of the war, Polish seasonal labourers were kept by force in Silesia[49]. After the seizure of the Kingdom of Poland by the German army, more "volunteer" workers from occupied areas joined the group of civil prisoners (Zivil Gefangene)[50]. Their living conditions and legal status was only slightly different from those of a prisoner of war. They were low paid, isolated from the local community and contained in camps. Nevertheless, they tried to protest against their working conditions and made attempts at escaping. The archival files of the Great War stored in the fond of the State Archive in Opole preserve a lot of materials

---

45 Mendel, Edward: *Dzień powszedni na Śląsku w czasie I wojny światowej.* Instytut Śląski w Opolu: Opole 1987, p. 19; cf. Nowak, Edmund: *Obozy na Śląsku Opolskim w systemie powojennych obozów w Polsce (1945–1950). Historia i Implikacje.* Opole 2002, p. 229.

46 Czapliński, Marek: *Dzieje Śląska od 1806 do 1945 roku...*, p. 345; cf. Andrzej Chwalba, ibid., p. 459.

47 APO, zespół nr 547, Startowo Powiatowe w Koźlu [Landratsamt Cosel], sygn. 496, pp. 3–4.

48 APO, zespół nr 2, Starostowo Powiatowe w Opolu [Landratsamt Oppeln], sygn. 1601, pp. 55–56.

49 Popiołek, Kazimierz, ibid., p. 481; cf. Piotr Stanek, Ibid., p. 39.

50 Thanks an intensive conscription campaign, tens of thousands of Polish workers voluntarily moved to Upper Silesia. This did not solve the problem of the shortage of workforce for an economy that had been switched to wartime mode: Popiołek Kazimierz, loc.cit. Military authorities forced citizens from occupied areas to work. Germans specialised in recruitment through "raids" and their victims, apart from the Poles, included Belgians and French. The captives were deported to work in industry and agriculture. Between 500 and 600 thousand Poles were forced to work for the Reich during World War I. Chwalba Andrzej, ibid., pp. 534–535.

presenting the living conditions and the moods of the Polish, Russian and Jewish labourers employed in Upper Silesia[51].

In the following years, the number of wartime and civil prisoners employed in various industries was continuously increasing. Forced labourers could not fill all the positions vacated by the German citizens who had been sent to the front. Many sons, husbands and fathers found themselves in French or Russian captivity and experienced exactly the same as the hostile armies' soldiers imprisoned in Germany[52]. In particular, the soldiers imprisoned in Russia had to face all the pains of everyday camp life – hunger, disease, hard work and difficult conditions. However, from the beginning, they received support from their compatriots, who organised collections of food, clothes, medicines and money. Actions aimed at supporting German prisoners of war, whether local or nation-wide, were broadly publicised by propaganda[53]. The situation became extremely difficult after the outbreak of the Bolshevik Revolution in October 1917 and changed only after the Peace Treaty of Brest was concluded in March 1918. Pursuant to the Treaty, the exchange and gradual repatriation of captives to Germany was started[54]. Lists of war prisoners returning from Russian captivity, which have been preserved in the fond of the State Archive in Opole, are a rich and interesting source of individual and family stories[55]. The reading of the lists proves that the majority of healthy former prisoners of war were, after a short rest, returned to the front, this time in France.

---

51 APO, zespół nr 2, Starostwo Powiatowe w Opolu [Landratsamt Oppeln],sygn. 331, pp. 429–430 and pp. 496–497; cf. Miodowski, Adam: "Sytuacja jeńców wojennych z armii państw centralnych w niewoli rosyjskiej po przewrocie bolszewickim (listopad 1917–marzec 1918)". In: Grinberg Daniel/Snopko, Jan/Zackiewicz, Grzegorz (eds.): *Wielka Wojna. Poza linią frontu.* Wydawnictwo Prymat: Białystok 2013, p. 367; et cf. Chwalba Andrzej, op. cit., p. 458.

52 According to different sources from 150 to 200 thousand soldiers from the Prussian army were sent to prisoner-of-war camps in Russia. They were treated better than many of their fellow prisoners and they were granted much better living conditions, cf. Chwalba, Andrzej, op. cit., p. 458.

53 APO, zespół nr 2, Starostwo Powiatowe w Opolu [Landratsamt Oppeln], sygn. 1585, p. 798.

54 Miodowski, Adam, ibid., pp. 365–370.

55 APO, zespół nr 2, Starostwo Powiatowe w Opolu [Landratsamt Oppeln], sygn.324, pp. 9–13.

Organisation of life in areas not covered with warfare

Regular citizens living far from the front were becoming more affected by the results of a prolonged war. As the situation on the front was getting more complicated, the life of people beyond the frontline had to be carefully regulated. This concerned even such remotely related areas of life as the breeding of homing pigeons[56] to be used for military purposes. In August 1915, the president of the Opole District introduced, by means of a decree, monthly reports informing about the situation concerning housing premises, sustenance and equipment for soldiers[57]. Provisions concerning passports[58] and fire safety were strengthened[59]. All levels of administration called for strict obedience of these rules. Violation of the fire safety rules was punished with particular severity. Also, healthcare was covered with strict supervision which involved, for example, regulation of the sale of medical products[60] or determination of the procedure to be followed in case of epidemic[61].

The echoes of war did not spare school and cultural life. The introduction of "History of war" (Kriegsgeschichtsstunde)[62] as a school subject was an attempt at constraining the depraving effect of the war on youth. In addition, libraries were developed to offer titles that promoted a positive image of war[63]. One example of the disorganisation of school life was the cancellation of meetings with parents[64].

With time, as the war brought further damage, public readings, cultural events and church concerts were organised to support soldiers and war-disabled persons.

---

56 Ibid., sygn. 3474, p. 16.
57 APO, zespół nr 547, Starostwo Powiatowe w Koźlu [Landratsamt Cosel], sygn. 496, p. 3.
58 APO, zespół nr 2, Starostwo Powiatowe w Opolu [Landratsamt Oppeln], sygn. 1642, pp. 2–3.
59 Ibid., sygn. 1113, p. 65.
60 Ibid., sygn. 1413, p. 156 and p. 158.
61 Ibid., sygn. 1386, pp. 157–164 and sygn. 1395, p. 56.
62 Joanna: "Szkoła w latach I wojny światowej". In: Linek Bernard/Rosenbaum, Sebastian/ Struve, Kai (eds.): *Koniec starego świata – początek nowego. Społeczeństwo Górnego Śląska wobec pierwszej wojny światowej (1914–1918). Źródła i metody.* Gliwice, 20–22 czerwca 2013 r. Opole 2013 [PDF version], p. 103.
63 APO, zespół nr 2, Starostwo Powiatowe w Opolu [Landratsamt Oppeln], sygn. 817, pp. 1, 9–10.
64 Ibid., sygn. 742, p. 527.

The funds raised were most often donated for the organisation of nursing houses[65] and support of soldiers who had lost their sight in warfare[66].

Collections of money and valuables were organised as a reflection of a broadly understood patriotism[67]. German propaganda had a huge influence on the creation of a positive image of war[68]. A number of tricks were used to justify the calling for financial sacrifices by the state, the most convincing of which were posters containing various slogans and rhymes. It is worth quoting one of them: "Daß ich in Deutschlands schwerer Zeit/Mein Gold dem Vaterland geweiht/Zum Schutz und Schirm von Hof und Herd,/Wird offenkundig hier erklärt" (When the things were going bad for Germany/I gave my gold for my country/And wanted to protect its greatest treasures,/And now I must openly confess it)[69, 70].

Regardless of the ban on organising dancing events[71], the 500th anniversary of the Hohenzollern dynasty was celebrated pompously in 1915[72]. This event, together with similar celebrations of a propaganda nature, were the elements that sustained the atmosphere of patriotism.

Organisation of support for East Prussia after the Russian offensive in 1915

The invasion of East Prussia by the Russian army in mid-August 1914 and the helplessness of the Austrian-Hungarian army in Galicia forced Germany to

---

65 APO, zespół nr 16, Akta miasta Krapkowic, sygn. 1294, pp. 239–242.

66 APO, zespół nr 2, Starostwo Powiatowe w Opolu [Landratsamt Oppeln], sygn. 1571, pp. 17–18.

67 APO, zespół nr 22, Akta miasta Opola, sygn. 1281, pp. 234–237.

68 Military authorities introduced strict censorship of the press in the Reich with the outbreak of war. With time, the German authorities established special institutions – Zentralstelle für Auslandsdienst (05.10.1915), die Militärische Stelle des Auswärtigen Amtes (MAA) (01.07.1916), Bild – und Filmamt (BUFA) (30.01.1917) intended to manage and supervise all propaganda activity; cf. Witkowski, Michał: "Wojna Propagandowa". In: Linek, Bernard/Rosenbaum, Sebastian/Struve, Kai (eds.): *Koniec starego świata – początek nowego. Społeczeństwo Górnego Śląska wobec pierwszej wojny światowej (1914–1918). Źródła i metody.* Gliwice, 20–22 czerwca 2013 r. Opole 2013 [PDF version], pp. 115–116; et cf. Chwalba, Andrzej: ibid., pp. 390–405.

69 Henceforth, unless stated otherwise, all quotations in the text have been translated by the translator.

70 APO, zespół nr 2, Starostwo Powiatowe w Opolu [Landratsamt Oppeln], sygn. 2037, p. 122.

71 Ibid., sygn. 1762, p. 1.

72 Ibid., sygn. 686, pp. 72–73.

relocate part of its army to the eastern front[73]. The victories of Tannenberg[74] and of the Masurian Lakes stopped the Russian attack on East Prussia[75]. Owing to the victory in the winter Masurian campaign, Germany regained East Prussia[76]. Gradually, citizens began to return to their home cities and towns that had been damaged in fierce battles. They were welcomed by the sight of burnt, plundered and devastated houses. Many civilians had been killed in the fighting and a few thousands had been deported to Siberia. Completely burnt farms, destroyed crops and shortage of animals and ensuing hunger[77].

This difficult situation required immediate action. Help for East Prussia was organised on the basis of patriotic duty and solidarity with other regions of Germany[78]. The population of the Opole district, whose wartime auspices also covered the city of Elk (Lyck), took an active part[79], as demonstrated by the letters sent by the helpers along with the amounts they donated for this purpose[80]. The aid process was supervised by the President of the Opole district, for which he was awarded a certificate of honorary citizenship of Opole[81].

Spies

The first wave of spymania occurred during the early days of war. Those seen as "disloyal" or "hostile" towards the Prussian state, even before the outbreak of war, were subject to preventive arrests and retention. This group included Polish

73 Beckett, Ian F.W.: *Pierwsza wojna światowa 1914–1918*. Trans. Rafał Dymek. Książka i Wiedza: Warszawa 2009, pp. 81–82; cf. Kaczmarek, Ryszard: ibid., pp. 108–112.

74 The Battle of Tannenberg was fought between 26 and 31 August 1914, cf. Pajewski, Janusz: *Historia Powszechna 1871–1918*, Wydawnictwo Naukowe PWN: Warszawa 1996, p. 340; German propaganda attached great importance to the victory over the Russian army at Tannenberg. Tannenberg became a symbol of effective defense of the homeland and was presented on postcards, posters and in literature, cf. Chwalba, Andrzej: ibid., pp. 403–404.

75 Ibid., pp. 125–135; cf. Beckett, Ian F.W.: ibid., pp. 82–84.

76 Pajewski, Janusz: *Pierwsza wojna światowa 1914–1918*. Wydawnictwo Naukowe PWN: Warszawa 1998, pp. 253–254; cf. Łach, Bolesław W.: "Społeczeństwo Prus Wschodnich wobec agresji rosyjskiej". In: Grinberg Daniel/Snopko, Jan/Zackiewicz, Grzegorz (eds.): *Wielka Wojna. Poza linią frontu*. Wydawnictwo Prymat: Białystok 2013, p. 38.

77 Ibid., pp. 38–41.

78 Ibid., p. 42.

79 APO, zespół nr 2, Starostwo Powiatowe w Opolu [Landratsamt Oppeln], sygn. 1845, pp. 16–20.

80 Ibid., sygn. 864, pp. 545–547.

81 APO, zespół nr 22, Akta miasta Opola, sygn. 628, p. 1.

activists in Silesia[82]. A second group consisted of people who had been accidentally arrested or retained based on gossip and slander. During the days following the outbreak, anti-spy hysteria was gradually replaced by systematic and strict police supervision of all potential spies. All foreigners were under special supervision. Those who had not left of their own will on the outbreak of the war were interned or deported[83]. Both the correspondence of potential spies and the letters of soldiers and prisoners were subject to strict censorship[84].

The preserved materials reflect this particularly interesting and colourful aspect of everyday life during wartime. They include descriptions, lists of spies and people suspected of espionage who lived in the empire. Interestingly, they concern not only foreigners but also Prussian nationals. This documentation dates back to both the first and the later years of war. Announcements from the Grodków district concerning people suspected of espionage in mid-1915 are a unique example[85]. These archival materials contain short descriptions of each wanted person. Apart from names and surnames, the said materials provide also information about the age, place of residence, nationality and social group. Individual records indicate the reason for including a given person in the list of the wanted[86], together with photographs or descriptions of people suspected of espionage[87]. The above presented archival personal files list men and women, civilians and military men, foreigners and nationals, the young and the elderly, people representing all social and professional groups. The lists of people interned in Switzerland serve as an interesting case in point, even though they depict an atmosphere of increasing suspiciousness towards strangers from a different perspective. A list of civilians, German citizens, dated August 1918 includes personal data of the retained people, place and date of birth, place of retention and place of their forced stay[88].

---

82 The arrested included *inter alia*: Bronisław Koraszewski, Józef Dreyza, Konstanty Wolny, Marian Różański, Jakub Kania, and others; Czapliński, Marek: *Dzieje Śląska od 1806 do 1945 roku…*, p. 342; et cf. Mendel, Edward: *Dzień powszedni na Śląsku Opolskim w czasie I wojny światowej*. Instytut Śląski w Opolu: Opole 1987, p. 12.

83 Ibid. pp. 12–13; et. cf. Chwalba, Andrzej: ibid., pp. 378–383.

84 Ibid., p. 384.

85 APO, zespół nr 11, Akta miasta Grodkowa, sygn. 1142, p. 1.

86 APO, Ibid., p. 109.

87 APO, Ibid., pp. 261–262 (Ilustration 4).

88 APO, zespół nr 2, Starostwo Powiatowe w Opolu [Landratsamt Oppeln], sygn. 1753, p. 46.

News from the front

Reports from the front are the most emotional of the documents, with private letters from soldiers being the most personal[89]. Rare postcards are very special materials as, apart from personal messages, they contain a rich ideological-symbolic layer of a propaganda nature[90].

Lists of the fallen and of the missing in warfare[91] as well as notices of death addressed to relevant registry offices constitute official reports[92]. Victims of war were honored posthumously with the Cross of Merit[93], which in no way compensated for the bitterness and helplessness felt by the rest of society. The Prussian authorities, aware of the growing crisis, relentlessly called on the people to enlist[94] and undertake other sacrifices for the sake of the ongoing war.

Memoirs

Memoirs constitute a separate part of the archival files. And although they are not credible documents, they shed further light on how wartime was perceived and experienced by an average citizen: a soldier[95] and a labourer[96]. These archival materials include also archival files that tell us how the people who survived kept the memory of those who had fallen on the fronts of the Great War[97].

Iconographic materials

Recently, an album consisting of 44 pages with 122 photographs of various size and quality has been discovered in the fonds of the State Archive in Opole. The album conveys a unique picture of the Great War. It is possible that all the photographs were

---

89 APO, Ibid., sygn. 1826, pp. 1–3.
90 Ibid., sygn. 1636, pp. 172–173 (Ilustration 5); APO, zespół nr 22, Akta miasta Opola, sygn. 1281, p. 169.
91 Ibid., sygn. 1280, p. 74.
92 Ibid., pp. 75–76.
93 APO, zespół nr 14 Akta miasta Korfantowa, sygn. 104, pp. 5; APO, zespół nr 2, Starostwo Powiatowe w Opolu [Landratsamt Oppeln], sygn. 162, pp. 125–127.
94 Ibid., sygn. 1759, p. 132.
95 APO, zespół nr 1191, Rejencja Opolska [Regierung Oppeln] – akta osobowe, sygn. 52215, nlb.
96 APO, zespół nr 2579, Komitet Wojewódzki Polskiej Zjednoczonej Partii Robotniczej w Opolu, sygn. 3184, pp. 6–7.
97 APO, zespół nr 22, Akta miasta Opola, sygn. 2530, p. 35 and p. 137; APO, zespół nr 1550, Starostwo Powiatowe w Nysie, sygn. 309, p. 37.

taken by one person between February 1916 and May 1917. Aerial imagery, outdoor pictures and portrait photographs are a truthful illustration of the war. Burnt cities[98], destroyed buildings and machinery[99], devastated fields near the front line[100] and the nearest French forts, towns and villages of Souville, Verdun, Tavannes, Vaux and others. Aerial images presenting French forts are often accompanied by additional descriptions, which confirm that they served as supporting material for military use[101]. World War I meant also new battle techniques, new weapon types and new methods of protection against the enemy. Photos of planes, barrage balloons and zeppelins[102] belong to the foreground of the theatre of the Great War. Photographs depicting the daily life of soldiers are the most interesting part of the fond. On the one hand, soldiers are presented while performing their duties: in trenches[103], on guard[104], when marching[105] or during inspection of the chief leader[106]. On the other hand, they are presented in their free time: during meals[107], celebrations and cultural events[108] or in an officers' casino[109]. Black and white photographs halt time in order to complete a colourful picture of everyday reality.

Previously unknown and unpublished photos as well as photos already published by the press[110] tell us more about the Great War than could be said in a thousand words.

Conclusion

"Historical breakthrough" is probably the best definition of the Great War period. This was a time of turbulent events that changed both the earlier macro-scale picture of Europe and the world, as well as the micro-scale picture of local communities and individual persons.

---

98   APO, zespół nr 3211, Zbiór fotografii z I wojny światowej, sygn. 1, p. 42.
99   Ibid., p. 37.
100 Ibid., pp. 11–12, 29.
101 Ibid., p. 19 (Ilustration 6).
102 Ibid., pp. 30–31, 33–34, 43.
103 Ibid., p. 12 (Ilustration 7).
104 Ibid., p. 39.
105 Ibid., p. 11.
106 Ibid., p. 28.
107 Ibid., p. 42.
108 Ibid., pp. 14, 39–40.
109 Ibid., p. 20.
110 APO, zespół nr 2926 Związek Bojowników o Wolność i Demokrację Oddział Okręgowy w Opolu, sygn. 333, pp. 1–12.

The well-preserved materials from 1914–1918 stored mainly in the archival fonds of municipal or district authority offices, as well as in the provincial administration, enable us to carefully analyse the life of the people from the Opole district in the shadow of the main events. Although the materials the State Archive in Opole have been available for researchers for many years, they have enjoyed little interest. Earlier investigations concerning the Great War period have focused on the documentation of military-political events. It is high time they become a basis for the presentation of the social-economic changes in Upper Silesia and a canvas for illustrating the everyday reality of people who lived behind the front during the Great War.

Mobilisation decrees and lists of recruits, as well as notices and lists of fallen soldiers, document the two faces of war. New regulations of the state institutions caused changes in many spheres of civilian life. Communication, the educational system, food supply and distribution system, as well as trade in medicines were re-organised. A series of detailed regulations concerning the operation of hospitals, the work of medical personnel and the procedures preventing epidemics was introduced. Industry and agriculture were switched to "special tracks" in order to satisfy the needs of war that were growing year by year. Prisoners of war were employed in place of men fighting on the front and worked in the field and the workshop.

Prolonged war increased problems and influenced the society's attitude towards authorities which on the one hand, offered social aid for citizens but on the other, issued decrees concerning the pursuit of spies and deserters. The support for people from the war zone, which had been organised during the first years of the war on the initiative of the Opole District community, gradually disappeared.

Aversion, bitterness and a sense of helplessness grew in those who were left with only photographs of their sons, husbands or fathers wearing army uniforms. The preserved archival materials reflect each of the above mentioned spheres of life.

The question arises whether historians will be willing to familiarise themselves with the archival materials presented herein and whether they will resume the so-far neglected investigation into various aspects of the daily life of people in Upper Silesia and of the changes that took place in the socio-economic sphere during the Great War. The area of research and the resource base are extensive. It is worth assuming a new perspective on such problems as the employment of forced labour in different sectors of the provincial economy, as well as the influence of war on law and trade or social-political changes. Such matters as prisoner-of-war camps, female and under-aged labour, espionage and propaganda await a thorough analysis.

List of illustrations

Illustration 1: *Bilingual, German-Polish announcement of the Prussian authorities addressed to the Kingdom of Poland population of August 1914* – Rejencja Opolska [Regierung Oppeln] – Biuro Prezydialne, sygn. 141, pp. 30–31;

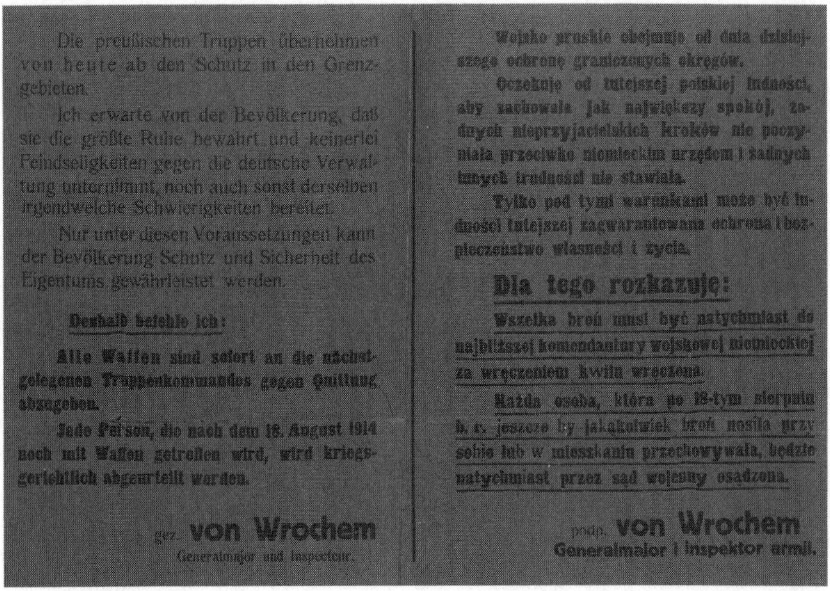

Die preußischen Truppen übernehmen von heute ab den Schutz in den Grenzgebieten.

Ich erwarte von der Bevölkerung, daß sie die größte Ruhe bewahrt und keinerlei Feindseligkeiten gegen die deutsche Verwaltung unternimmt, noch auch sonst derselben irgendwelche Schwierigkeiten bereitet.

Nur unter diesen Voraussetzungen kann der Bevölkerung Schutz und Sicherheit des Eigentums gewährleistet werden.

Deshalb befehle ich:

Alle Waffen sind sofort an die nächstgelegenen Truppenkommandos gegen Quittung abzugeben.

Jede Person, die nach dem 18. August 1914 noch mit Waffen getroffen wird, wird kriegsgerichtlich abgeurteilt werden.

gez. **von Wrochem**
Generalmajor und Inspekteur.

Wojsko pruskie obejmuje od dnia dzisiejszego ochronę granicznych okręgów.

Oczekuję od tutejszej polskiej ludności, aby zachowała jak największy spokój, żadnych nieprzyjacielskich kroków nie poczyniała przeciwko niemieckim urzędom i żadnych innych trudności nie stawiała.

Tylko pod tymi warunkami może być ludności tutejszej zagwarantowana ochrona i bezpieczeństwo własności i życia.

Dla tego rozkazuję:

Wszelka broń musi być natychmiast do najbliższej komendantury wojskowej niemieckiej za wręczeniem kwitu wręczona.

Każda osoba, która po 18-tym sierpnia b. r. jeszcze by jakąkolwiek broń nosiła przy sobie lub w mieszkaniu przechowywała, będzie natychmiast przez sąd wojenny osądzona.

podp. **von Wrochem**
Generalmajor i inspektor armii.

Illustration 2: Appeal to the Poles – *Rejencja Opolska [Regierung Oppeln] – Biuro Prezydialne, sygn. 141, p. 23;*

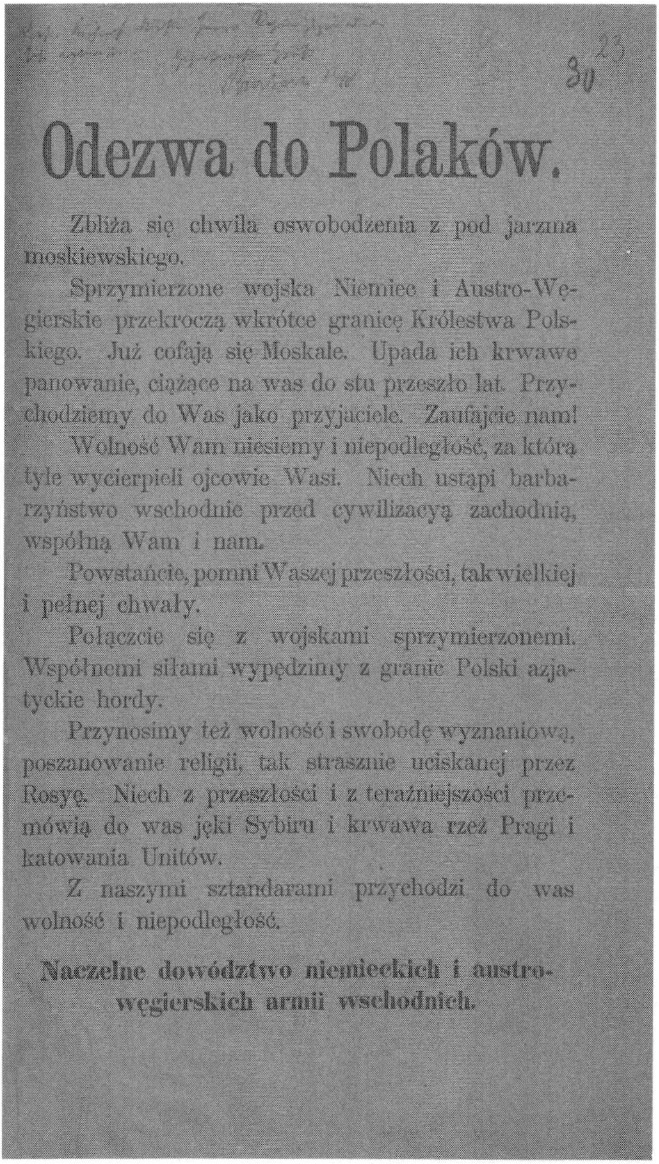

Odezwa do Polaków.

Zbliża się chwila oswobodzenia z pod jarzma moskiewskiego.

Sprzymierzone wojska Niemiec i Austro-Węgierskie przekroczą wkrótce granicę Królestwa Polskiego. Już cofają się Moskale. Upada ich krwawe panowanie, ciążące na was do stu przeszło lat. Przychodziemy do Was jako przyjaciele. Zaufajcie nam!

Wolność Wam niesiemy i niepodległość, za którą tyle wycierpieli ojcowie Wasi. Niech ustąpi barbarzyństwo wschodnie przed cywilizacyą zachodnią, wspólną Wam i nam.

Powstańcie, pomni Waszej przeszłości, tak wielkiej i pełnej chwały.

Połączcie się z wojskami sprzymierzonemi. Wspólnemi siłami wypędzimy z granic Polski azjatyckie hordy.

Przynosimy też wolność i swobodę wyznaniową, poszanowanie religii, tak strasznie uciskanej przez Rosyę. Niech z przeszłości i z teraźniejszości przemówią do was jęki Sybiru i krwawa rzeź Pragi i katowania Unitów.

Z naszymi sztandarami przychodzi do was wolność i niepodległość.

Naczelne dowództwo niemieckich i austrowęgierskich armii wschodnich.

Illustration 3: Substitute money – *4149, Komitet Wojewódzki Polskiej Zjednoczonej Partii Robotniczej w Opolu, sygn. 4149, pp. 3–4;*

Illustration 4: Photographs of people suspected of espionage that supplemented announcement of authorities – *Akta miasta Grodkowa, sygn. 1142, p. 261;*

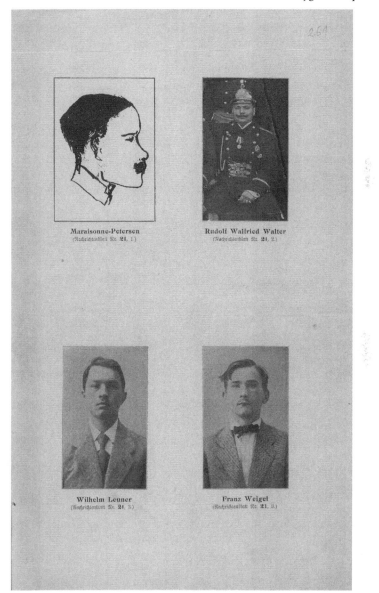

Illustration 5: Postcard sent from Opole in 1915 presenting an Austrian-Hungarian general that follows the Russian prisoners with his eyes – *Starostwo Powiatowe w Opolu [Landratsamt Oppeln], sygn. 1636, p. 173;*

Illustration 6: Army camp – Southern Verdum [Truppenlager südl. Verdun.] – *Zbiór fotografii z I wojny światowej, sygn. 1, p. 19;*

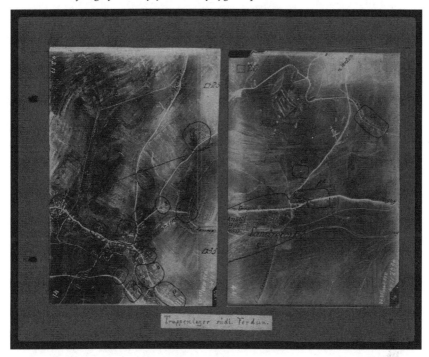

Illustration 7: Soldiers in trenches – *Zbiór fotografii z I wojny światowej, sygn. 1, p. 12.*

Marek Szczepaniak
Grażyna Tyrchan
State Archive in Poznań
Office in Gniezno

World war from a local perspective. School chronicles from the border areas of the Province of Posen (Prowincja Poznańska) as a source of information

The Gniezno region before 1914 was located on the Prussian side of the border between two mutually hostile superpowers – Germany and Russia. At that
time it comprised two *powiat*[1] districts: Gniezno and Witkowo. At the turn of
the century, the ethnic and religious structure of the local population began to
change as a result of intensive activity of the Prussian Settlement Commission
in Posen and West Prussia (Pruska Komisja Kolonizacyjna dla Prus Zachodnich
i Poznańskiego). Shortly before the outbreak of war, in 1910, 34,14% of the Gniezno
powiat population and 14,6% of the Witkowo *powiat* population declared that
they belonged to the Evangelical Church, which was basically equal to their membership of German nation (Gemeindelexikon..., pp. 76–77).

The religious division of the inhabitants of the region was reflected in the
organisation of the local schooling system. At the outbreak of the war the area
of both *powiats* encompassed 59 Catholic schools, 67 Evangelical, 2 Jewish and 7
'simultaneous' schools which could be attended by children of different religious
beliefs. Each of them, pursuant to the decree of the Prussian minister, Adalbert
Falk, of 15 October 1872, was obliged to manage a school chronicle which documented most important events in the life of the school and its neighbourhood
(Centralblatt..., p. 588). Only 12 chronicles from the area of the Gniezno and
Witkowo *powiats* have been preserved until now. They cover, among others, the
period from 1914 to 1918. The fond "Szkoły powszechne z terenu miasta Poznania i województwa poznańskiego", under reference number 265, the State Archive in Poznan, contains a chronicle of a Catholic post-Franciscan school in

---

1   *Powiat* is the second-level unit of local government and administration in Poland. The
    term "*powiat*" is most often translated into English as "county" (trans.).

Gniezno (Katholische Rectorsschule zu Gnesen [Gniezno])[2], covering the years 1854–1955. The name of the school is derived from a former Franciscan monastery building where the school was seated. The State Archive in Poznań, the Gniezno Branch, preserves chronicles of Catholic schools in Pawłowo (Katholische Schule zu Pawłowo) dated 1899–1952, in Świątniki Wielkie (Katholische Schule zu Gross Świątniki [Świątniki Wielkie]) dated 1886–1934 and in Witkowo (Katholische Schule in Witkowo) dated 1875–1917. The *gmina*[3] office in Kiszkowo owns a chronicle of a Catholic school in Sławno (Katholische Schule in Slawno [Sławno]) dated 1887–1961. The repository of Gimanzjum no 1 in Gniezno contains a chronicle of St. John's Catholic school for boys (Katholische Knabenschule zu Gnesen [Gniezno]) in Gniezno dated 1903–1949. Gimnazjum in Mieleszyno owns a chronicle of an Evangelical school in Kowalewo (Evangelische Schule zu Schoenbrunn [Kowalewo]) dated 1890–1935 and a primary school in Modliszewko (Katholische Schule in Modliszewko) is the proud owner of a chronicle of a former Catholic school dated 1871–1951. The gimnazjum no 2 in Gniezno preserves a chronicle of an Evangelical school in Jankówko (Evangelische Schule Morgenau [Jankówko]) dated 1888–1972. Private primary school in Gorzykowo owns a chronicle of an Evangelical school in Gorzykowo (Evangelische Schule in Görzhof [Gorzykowo]) dated 1899–1922 and private owners preserve chronicles of Catholic schools in Dziekanowice (Katholische Schule in Dziekanowice) dated 1896–1930 and Imielenko (Katholische Schule Johannesgarten [Imielenko]) dated 1897–1926. The Gniezno branch of the State Archive in Poznań, apart from the already mentioned originals, owns copies of all the listed chronicles.

Although school chronicles have rarely been regarded by researchers as valuable historical sources, the information they communicate deserves greater attention, especially from researchers studying the everyday life of local communities. The chronicles contain not only descriptions of events related to school life but also to the history of the people from the immediate neighbourhood. The authors of the records do not refrain from personal judgements and opinions. The substantive importance of individual chronicles as historical sources varies, and depends on the intellectual level of the chronicle author. The range of subjects covered by schoolmasters who wrote the chronicles is wide but there are some

---

2   German names of schools have been cited based on the school chronicles. The location names has been provided in its official form of the Gear War period. Square brackets indicate the earlier and current location name. If case of no changes to the location name, the square brackets have not been used (trans.)

3   *Gmina* is the principal unit of administrative division of Poland as "commune" or "municipality."

traits that often re-occur. Usually the first pages provide retrospective information concerning the circumstances of the school's construction. The chronicles
of Evangelical schools include also information about the settlement of German
settlers. After the school district had been formed and the school building had
been arranged, the records in the following years were prepared on a regular basis.
The outlook and layout of the texts changes only in wartime. In some case this
can mean that the texts were written after some time (Dziekanowice, pp. 24–26;
Jankówko, pp. 81–82).

The outbreak of war awoke a sense of uncertainty and fear in the local population of the Gniezno region. People who were adults at that time usually had no earlier personal experiences of war. Their "little homeland", in many cases "Heimat",
was located by the border of the country which was at war with Germany. The
course of this war was difficult to foresee. People feared the possible entry of the
Russians into the Poznan Province. The chronicle pages reflect nervousness in the
community behaviour and uncertainty of the authors regarding their future fate.
The authors of the Gniezno school chronicles meticulously described the last days
of peace and the first days of the war. Gniezno was located close to the Russian
border. It had convenient communication connections with the border and was
also the seat of a large garrison. For these reasons, it became an important centre
of mobilisation. Information about groups of mobilised reservists, registration
points, uniforms and arms occupies a prominent place on the chronicle pages.
as the existing two large barrack facilities could not accommodate the arriving
soldiers, it was necessary to rent private flats for them (Gniezno świętojańska,
k. 36–38v.). A lot of space is devoted to the descriptions of the community's behaviour during announcement of mobilisation, the means of supporting soldiers
leaving for the front and the organisation of field hospitals. During the first days of
the war, due to the growing number of the wounded, 11 field hospitals were organised in Gniezno, also in schools, restaurants, cafes and in the premises of various
associations (ibid., k. 39v.). In parallel the schoolmasters stress the problems with
organisation of normal school activities, which resulted from the fact that the authorities used school buildings for military purposes. The authors indicate which
rooms were used as rooms for the ill, for places where the wounds were dressed,
for guardhouses or for doctors' rooms. During the first months of the war, due to
the insufficient number of classrooms, lessons were held in the Franciscan church
and in the room rented from the Jewish school. The situation began to improve
in 1916 (ibid., k. 34–40; Gniezno pofranciszkańska, pp. 179–181).

The atmosphere of uncertainty and the loss of trust in state authorities was reflected in the outflow from the market of golden money which, in those uncertain

times, was used as for retention of profits. Local teachers expressed their due indignation at this and even organised among pupils exchanges of coins to banknotes in a local branch of Reichsbank (Gniezno pofranciszkańska, p. 185).

There is a clear difference in tone between the chronicles of Evangelical schools and the chronicles penned by headmasters of Catholic schools. The author of a chronicle of the Evangelical school in Gorzykowo, Hugo Jerschkewitz, mentioned uncertainty in the first days of the war but was much more involved in describing enthusiasm that the announcement of mobilisation evoked in the local settlers (Gorzykowo, s. 38). He observed that a profitable trade with the Poles was realized after the Germans crossed the Russian border. He also described the purchase of large quantities of crops, poultry, cattle, horses and sugar for attractive prices. The atmosphere changed for the worse only at the end of August 1914, when it was learned that the Russians had entered East Prussia. The arrival of refugees from the areas occupied by the tsarist army led to a widespread panic and initiated preparation for evacuation. The mood improved again on 29 August, when the first telegraph messages informed about Paul von Hindenburg's victory in the battle of the Masurian Lakes. Fear of the Russians revived at the end of October and at the beginning of November. Troops were located on the area of the Witkowo *powiat* to prevent the Russians from entering the border area. This improved the sense of safety in the local Germans but did not fully eliminate their sense of insecurity. The mood swings finally stopped after the general von Mackensen's defeated the Russians in the battles of Kutno and Włocławek (ibid., pp. 45–48). The pages of the chronicle from Jankówko clearly illustrate the syndrome of Germany as a besieged fortress. According to the headmaster the whole world had turned against the Hohenzollern country and intended to destroy it. He also describes in detail the mood swings which lasted practically till the end of 1914 (Jankówko, pp. 73–80).

The headmaster of the Evangelical school in Kowalewo included relatively balanced opinions in his chronicle. He writes little about events from the great European theatre of war. He discusses the formation of the Kingdom of Poland by emperors of Germany and Austria-Hungary and mentions the seizure of Bucarest by the German army. At the turn of 1916/1917 the tone of his chronicle was far from the official optimism. Instead of expected victories he writes about the peace proposals of the central powers and stated that people were generally waiting for peace (Kowalewo, pp. 61, 66–67). The message of the chronicles of Catholic schools is different. The author of the chronicle of a school in Dziekanowice describes the war as "horrible" (Dziekanowice, p. 24). Descriptions in the chronicle of the school in Imielnik reflect the insecurity experienced by the community during the last days of peace. In the subsequent years of the war the headmaster highlighted the fact that the war continued with "unflagging power" and that the number of men mobilised into the army was still growing (Imielenko, pp. 76, 87). A teacher from Modliszewko, when mentioning announcement of mobilisation and the outbreak of the war, adds that local peasants "hurried to fulfill their military duty" (Modliszewko, p. 89). In the following years he does not mention the ongoing war and returns to the subject of grand politics only towards the end of the war. At that time he writes about the outbreak of the revolution in Germany, the overthrowing of the government, the escape of Wilhelm II to the Netherlands, the establishment of Ebert's government and the formation of councils of soldiers and workers (ibid., p. 98).

Wacław Malicki, the author of the chronicle of the school in Sławno, notes that the local society was surprised by the outbreak of the war during harvest. He describes mobilisation of the first reservists from the village and requisition of horses by the military authorities (Sławno, pp. 163–164). The author of the chronicle of the school in Świątniki Wielkie, Jan Michalczyk, indicates the date of mobilisation – 2 August – and the number of 30 men from the gmina who were conscripted to the army (Świątniki Wielkie, p. 201; Imielenko, p. 71; Witkowo, p. 51). Just like other authors he describes problems caused by ongoing mobilisation.

Chroniclers from Catholic schools note first of all the tragedy of the war and all the calamities it brought about. They go on to comment about the fulfillment of "military duty" by the enlisted men, mention German victories, especially on the western front, but their enthusiasm is incomparably lower than in the chronicles of Evangelical schools. The sense of seriousness is prevailing.

A large part of all chronicles was devoted to the listing of the names of people mobilised to the army, killed in the battle or wounded on the front (Dziekanowice, pp. 24–25; Gorzykowo, pp. 41, 60–66; Imielenko, pp. 70–71, 76–77; Jankówko, pp. 74, 76–77; Modliszewko, pp. 89–92; Sławno, pp. 165–166, 169–171). Their authors focused the attention on arising economic problems caused by the shortage of labour after mobilisation. Sometimes prisoners of war were used in order to remedy the situation. The author of the chronicle of the school in Gorzykowo reported that towards the end of the war, in 1918, 14 Frenchmen and 4 Englishmen worked in his school district. In the chronicler's opinion "Englishmen were without any exception smaller and more delicate than the French" (Gorzykowo, pp. 55–57).

The German authors expressed in the chronicles their concern about the stance of the Poles in the face of military conflict. They feared the Slavic solidarity between the Russians and the Poles; information about mass meetings of the Poles in Mielżyno and Witkowo was received with concern; people gossiped about a suspected discovery of rifles in the houses of the two largest landowners in the Witkowo *powiat* (ibid., pp. 38, 40). Quite often the chroniclers complained about the reluctance of Polish society to participate in the collections of money for the war purposes. They noted that Polish children refused to be involved in these activities (Gniezno świętojańska, k. 44v; Gniezno pofranciszkańska, pp. 185, 189; Imielenko, p. 85). They accused the Poles of having no love for the emperor and their homeland, which they found not only in children but also among the elder generation (Świątniki Wielkie, p. 205). The Polish landowners did not allow pupils to collect ears on their fields after harvest. They preferred to leave the fields for their poultry rather than to join in the action organised by a Prussian school (Gniezno pofranciszkańska, p. 194).

Records from the first months of the war describe broadly the spontaneous collections of food transferred to soldiers leaving for the front. Supplies of bread, butter, sausage, bacon, fruit and other food products waited at railway stations for the passing military transports (Gorzykowo, pp. 41, 48–49; Imielenko, p. 74; Jankówko, p. 75). Prolonged war led to a gradual increase of the deficits of these goods. Already in 1915 it became necessary to register and rationally distribute agricultural produce. Local teachers were used for preparation of the registers (Świątniki Wielkie, p. 206). Gradually, substitute goods began to appear, most notably the so-called wartime bread baked of flour mixed with potatoes or pumpkin. We also know by word of mouth that fruit pits were collected and added to crops intended for bread. The main reason for collecting pits was to use them for production of oil (Imielenko, pp. 74, 80–81). Distribution of wheat flour was particularly restrictive – bun production basically ceased. Owing to a reduced production of pastry the bakeries stopped working at night. Despite these limitations on 15 March 1915 the authorities were forced to introduce food coupons in Gniezno for the purchase of flour, bread or biscuits (Gniezno świętojańska, k. 41–41v.). Distribution of the food coupons was also very often delegated to teachers (Sławno, p. 170).

The deficit of coal was a bothersome problem that had an impact not only on common citizens but also on many sectors of economy. This scarcity was partially the result of the conscription of a large number of miners for military service, and partially from the scarcity of means of transport, which were at that time used by the army. In the Gniezno and Witkowo districts, where wood and peat were scarce, people started to use dry dung as fuel (Imielenko, p. 73). From 1916 winter holidays winter holidays were prolonged due to the shortage of coal. On many occasions the number of heated classrooms was reduced and the lessons held in them were extended until late afternoon hours (Kowalewo, p. 67; Modliszewko,

p. 93; Pawłowo, pp. 36, 38). This was possible in Gniezno after some rooms got connected to electric power supply. In cities coal was supplied only to hospitals and community (Gniezno pofranciszkańska, pp. 157–158). In 1917 the Witkowo local authorities confiscated all the fuel from a local coal storage for the benefit of a local mill. Classes were completely suspended at that time (Witkowo, p. 71). Only the winter of 1917/1918 was relatively mild and in consequence the shortage of coal became less bothersome.

From the beginning of the war, the growing deficit of crude oil became a problemm and was already noticeable in autumn 1914. Better-organised villagers started to use spirit lamps to light rooms, others went to bed early (Imielenko, pp. 72–73). The ban on using English introduced in 1915 was less annoying

People tried to compensate for the deficit of some goods on the market with replacement materials and recyclables, which were typically collected by children and teenagers. In 1915, the pupils from the school in Gorzykowo collected scrap metal and old rubber, and a year later those from Gniezno collected cherry and plum pits and nettles. Through 1916 and 1917, the range of collected materials was significantly extended to tinfoil, medical herbs, pops, spikes of rye, barley and oats left by harvesters, potatoes left after digging, leaves of strawberry and blackberry and coloured scrap metals. Some collections of raw materials were organised and monitored by schools. Money from the sales of raw materials was most often paid by headmasters to the Red Cross account (Gniezno świętojańska, k. 47–47v., 53v.; Gniezno pofranciszkańska, p. 194; Gorzykowo, pp. 41, 49–50).

A deficit of available manpower caused by mobilisation was particularly problematic for agriculture. In order to address this situation, the Prussian school authorities agreed in 1915 to exempt children over 14 years old from compulsory education regardless of the planned date of their graduation. to allow them to work in the fields. From 1917 the Bydgoszcz Royal District (Regierung Bromberg [Königliche Preussische Regierung zu Bromberg]) authorities ordered volunteer pupils over 12 to be sent to work for a fixed period, mainly on farms. Children were most frequently employed in weeding, sorting potatoes, farming sugar beets, collecting stones and potatoes in fields, turning hay and grazing. The under-age workers were supposed to receive remuneration of 30 Pfenning a day for their work. The farm owners were additionally obliged to insure them and to refund possible costs of their travel (Gniezno świętojańska, k. 52v.; Gniezno pofranciszkańska, p. 202). If a large number of pupils was sent to the same place, they were to be supervised by a teacher. Most often, this youth labour was used from April to mid-November. Children from Gniezno worked mainly on the estates in Łukaszewko, Arkuszewo, Braciszewo, Jankówko, Dziekanka and Winiary.

The authors of the school chronicles provided also exact lists of working children and the number of mandays they worked (Gniezno świętojańska, k. 52–53v.; Gniezno pofranciszkańska, pp. 200–202). In order to enable employment of pupils on farms the dates of summer and autumn holidays were adjusted to the time of the harvest of crops and root vegetables (Gniezno, świętojańska, k. 47v., 48v.). At all costs, efforts were made to prevent the growth of the area of waste land.

The school authorities were forced to seek means to cope with the worsening food supply situation, especially in cities. The Gniezno Catholic school district decided that a local municipal canteen would provide free lunches for the children of widows and families of soldiers. More than half of the cost was covered with municipal money, the rest with voluntarily donations and contributions by the school community (ibid., k. 49–49v.; Gniezno pofranciszkańska, pp. 196–197). Increases in food prices forced the state authorities to provide help for widows and orphans of killed soldiers. Additional "war support" was also offered to teachers and clerks: the amount of support depending on salary and number of dependent children (Gniezno świętojańska, k. 40–41; Gniezno pofranciszkańska, p. 206)

The growing expense of industrial goods, especially of soap and oil, was particularly noticeable in the country. People started to ration food even though food shortage was not so problematic outside cities. From 1915 rye and wheat could be exported from the Gniezno *powiat* only on permission of the central German Reich authorities (Imielenko, p. 80). In order to save resources of meat, the so-called meat-free days were introduced in all Germany. On these days no meat was sold in shops and restaurants served only vegetarian dishes. Villagers usually ignored this ban. The headmaster of the school in Imielnik noted that in his village more animals had been slaughtered after the introduction of this ban than earlier. This procedure was widely employed by butchers who claimed that they were only slaughtering animals for their own use. Next, they speculated and raised prices. The chronicle author complained that for poorer people and minor clerks two meat-free days a week turned into whole meat-free weeks (ibid., p. 82). In 1915 the prices rose by 100–200% (ibid., p. 80). In subsequent months of the same year maximum prices of crude oil, rye and wheat flour were regulated. A ban on slaughtering sows was issued. Raw sheep yarn as well as cotton fabrics were confiscated. Prices of butter and milk were regulated and their consumption was rationed. On 8 December copper, brass and nickel objects were requisitioned and followed later by chrome and tungsten. Local communities were warned not to waste or damage their agricultural produce (ibid., p. 84).

Scarcities of food products on the market were noticeable also in 1917. It was assumed that the reason for this situation was a poor harvest of potatoes in the previous year. Due to the shortage of artificial fertilisers and workforce, the area intended for sugar beet cultivation was reduced. The state authorities started to intervene in the breeding of animals and ordered the slaughter of thin animals that would not bring any profit in the future. The situation worsened due to the draught of 1917, which resulted, among other things, in reduced production of butter. Farmers, who so far had produced butter themselves, were ordered by authorities to deliver butter to dairies. This decree, according to the village school chroniclers, was generally ignored (Gorzykowo, p. 56).

At the same time, a plague of caterpillars affected orchards and gardens. To prevent damage to agricultural produce, pupils collected nests of the pests from fruit trees and cabbage plants and burnt them. May of the following year saw a plague of May beetles. Children from Sławno were instructed to collect the insects, and in the case of feed shortage, dead May beetles were used to feed pigs (ibid., p. 58; Sławno, pp. 172–173).

Despite a worsening economic situation people still tried to help soldiers on the front. They started to send to the front warm clothes and woolen articles prepared by women and young girls instead of food products that prevailed during the first months of the war. Often the pages of school chronicles contain information about collections of wool, blankets and felt or money for buying them. Some of these actions were spontaneously initiated by communities, others were initiated by different authorities. Generally, local communities took part in such collections in large numbers and the German chroniclers also praise involvement of the Poles but almost solely in the actions organised by the Red Cross (Imielenko, pp. 75, 85; Jankówko, p. 76).

Another subject that was prominent in the pages of the school chronicles was a description of problems related to organisation of education. These problems resulted from the conscription of some teachers to the army and from a plague of illnesses among the teaching staff (Gniezno świętojańska, k. 39, 42–47v., 52, 54–54v.; Gniezno pofranciszkańska, pp. 181–182, 192; Jankówko, p. 81; Modliszewko, p. 94; Pawłowo, pp. 36–37; Sławno, pp. 166–170; Świątniki Wielkie, pp. 203–209). Despite difficult wartime conditions and a significant shortage of qualified staff, teachers whose health prevented them from working were sent to nursing homes. Teachers who reached a certain age were sent on retirement. In many cases the scarcities of teaching staff resulted in a reduction of the number of lessons. Although the situation was under control to some degree in Gniezno, where there were relatively many teachers, the situation was much worse in villages, where there was usually one teacher working in a small school. The authors of the chronicles often describe situations when teachers from neighbouring schools conducted classes for their absent colleagues. It happened on many occasions that classes were held only on two or three days a week in certain schools because one teacher had to work in a few locations (Dziekanowice, p. 25; Gniezno świętojańska, k. 42, 43, 44v., 46, 48–49, 52; Gniezno pofranciszkańska, pp. 178–180, 199, 210; Gorzykowo, pp. 46, 53–54; Imielenko, p. 78; Jankówko, p. 81; Witkowo, pp. 69–70). Unusual situations called for unusual measures on the part of the school authorities. From the outbreak of the war attempts were made to address the shortage of teachers caused by mobilisation, such as transferring pupils to other schools located closest to their place of residence. In 1914, the school in Witkowo was forced to accept children from Malachowo Wierzbiczany. A similar situation reoccurred in 1917 when children from Makowica were admitted to the Witkowo facility (Witkowo, pp. 60, 70). In 1915, following the conscription of a teacher called Funk from Imielnik, children from that school were taught in a school in Lednogóra for 3 weeks by the wife of a local priest, Georg Mattke, who was not a professional teacher (Imielenko, p. 78). Two years later the Royal District in Bydgoszcz allowed a crafts teacher from the post-Franciscan school in Gniezno, Lieutenant Ella Matha Schach, de domo Hausbeck, to work as a teacher even though she was married (Gniezno pofranciszkańska, p. 205). This decision might have been made easier for the district clerks by the fact that Lieutenant Schach was a daughter of Wilhelm Hausbeck, the dean of the Gniezno school for boys, which neighboured with the school for girls. In order to enable the teachers to get to work on time the beginning of lessons was moved to 7 am in many village schools (Kowalewo, p. 64).

School chronicles are, most importantly, an irreplaceable source for investigating the daily life of schools of that time. The impact of the war on the chronicles was limited to some degree. The authors of the city chronicles provided, year by year, the number of students in individual classes, the number of children attending schools, the number of organised divisions and the number of the newly-admitted pupils. Their village colleagues listed the number of children from different villages in a given school district that attended school (Gniezno świętojańska, k. 42–42v., 46v., 48v., 50v., 52, 54v.; Gniezno pofranciszkańska, pp. 186, 197, 209; Pawlowo, pp. 34–39; Świątniki Wielkie, pp. 203, 207, 210). Almost all chronicles provide dates related to the organisation of the school year. Every year, the chronicles indicated the dates of the beginning and the end of the school year as well as the dates of summer, autumn, Christmas, Easter and Pentecost holidays (Gniezno świętojańska, k. 34, 41v., 42, 45v., 47v., 48v., 49v., 54; Gniezno pofranciszkańska, pp. 181–182, 189–190, 198, 209; Kowalewo, p. 64, 67, 69, 73; Modliszewko, pp. 93–95; Pawłowo, pp. 34, 36–37; Świątniki Wielkie, pp. 203–205;

Witkowo, p. 60). However, the mentions of students held back for an extra year were very few. Although this was a frequent element of the schooling practice of the time, it was apparently not interesting enough for the authors to include it in school chronicles (Gniezno świętojańska, k. 46).

Patriotic education of the youth was one of the priorities of the authorities during a global military conflict. People continued to celebrate all the earlier commemorative events related in particular to anniversaries of important events in the history of Prussia. Almost all chronicles mention annual celebrations of the Sedan festival (anniversary of the battle with the French in 1870) and the birthday of the Emperor (Gniezno pofranciszkańska, p. 187; Pawlowo, p. 35; Świątniki Wielkie, p. 201). The Great War period covered round anniversaries of the birthday of Chancellor Otto von Bismarck, the rule of the Hohenzollern dynasty in Prussia and the declaration of Martin Luter. Descriptions of celebrations of the last anniversary are provided in the chronicles of Evangelical schools (Jankówko, p. 82). Other anniversaries were celebrated also in Catholic schools (Imielenko, pp. 86–87; Pawłowo, pp. 35, 38; Świątniki Wielkie, p. 203; Witkowo, p. 68). Events of the wartime, in particular victories of the Prussian army, became a pre-text for celebration of new festivals. On the occasion of the victories of Metz, Tannenberg, the seizure of Lodz, the end of the battles of the Masurian Lakes, the victory of Gorlice, the seizure of Lvov, Kaunas, Warsaw, Modlin, Brześć Litewski, the victory on the North Sea or the seizure of Riga official celebrations were organised and consisted also of a ceremonial speech by the teacher and a day of vacation (Gniezno świętojańska, k. 40–40v., 42–43v., 48; Gniezno pofranciszkańska, p. 183; Gorzykowo, p. 43; Jankówko, pp. 81–82; Modliszewko, p. 94; Pawłowo, pp. 34, 36, 38; Sławno, p. 16; Świątniki Wielkie, pp. 202–203, 208; Witkowo, pp. 64, 69). A cancellation of school classes on 5 March 1918 [the author wrote 1919 by mistake], on the day when the peace treaty with Russia was signed, was of a slightly different nature (Gniezno pofranciszkańska, p. 208). On the one hand, people rejoiced at the victory, on the other hand, they waited for peace treaties to be signed on all fronts.

Despite financial difficulties of wartime the local school authorities tried to keep the material assets entrusted to them in a good technical condition. The authors of school chronicles mention repairs in school buildings in Dziekanowice and Świątniki Wielkie (Dziekanowice, p. 26; Świątniki Wielkie, p. 210). They did not omit a report on the completion of the construction, the consecration and the hand-over for occupancy of a new school building in Witkowo in 1915. The school impressed with its size and outlook as well as with its modern equipment, among others, a central heating installation (Witkowo, pp. 53–55).

The school teachers did not overlook the formation on their of new associations and cooperatives on their areas. Teachers, both Polish and German ones, as representatives of a local intellectual elite, on many occasions initiated their establishment (Gorzykowo, p. 52; Sławno, pp. 171–172).

The issue of natural disasters and weather anomalies was a frequently re-occurring motif. For obvious reasons this subject appeared more often on the pages of village school chronicles. Local teachers describe draughts, long-lasting and very cold winters or rainy and chilly springs. They mention haze and violent storms that destroyed harvest, which always led to increase of food prices. They also note the good times for farmers when they could carry out field works without any problems and in a timely manner (Gniezno pofranciszkańska, pp. 197–198; Gorzykowo, pp. 52, 58; Imielenko, pp. 70–71, 79; Kowalewo, p. 68; Modliszewko, pp. 93, 96–97; Slawno, pp. 168–173). Only the author of the chronicle of a Catholic school in Świątniki Wielkie describe fires that often re-occurred in the village. The reason might have been their suspicious frequency (Świątniki Wielkie, pp. 207–210). By contrast, apart from information concerning illnesses of the pedagogical staff, information about the spread of diseases was provided rarely. An exception was the occurrence of flu epidemics which began to spread in summer 1918 and towards the end of the war led to the closing of schools in Gniezno. The chronicle author mistakenly recorded that the city schools were closed until 11 November 1919 instead of 1918 (Gniezno pofranciszkańska, pp. 210–211).

The reports of the events of 1918 are the last to be drafted in German. Polish records appeared from the turn of 1918/19 and were often prepared by different authors. In a few cases, it can be seen that some pages are missing. The time, circumstances and reasons for their removal remain unknown (Imielenko, pp. 88–89; Imielenko, from 84 to 85; Witkowo, from 73 to 74) Similarly, when a report written in German finishes at the very end of the page and the next page begins with a text in Polish, with a clear time gap between the described events, this is adequate reason for suspicion (Dziekanowice, pp. 26–27; Gniezno świętojańska, k. 54v. to 55; Gniezno pofranciszkańska, pp. 212–213). The appearance of some records concerning the time of the military conflict seems to suggest that they are retrospective and the level of detail in the narration implies that the author was using earlier prepared notes. Descriptions of events related to international politics and the course of war that are frequent in 1914 disappear from the chronicle pages in the following years. Their place is taken by descriptions of daily problems far from the front. The difference between the village and the city chronicles is visible. The former list names and surnames of men mobilised for war, soldiers killed or wounded on the front, their widows and children and often also their fathers' surnames and professions. These were the people that the chronicle author usually knew personally, in many cases they were neighbours from the same village. By contrast to these village chronicles, the city chronicles are more "anonymous". The surnames that appear on their pages are mostly teachers that the author met professionally. The records of the deans from city schools are dominated by information concerning school life. The public events outweigh the description of school problems only on the outbreak of the war. Later most records are again devoted to the daily school reality. The ongoing war is perceived by the authors from the perspective of the shortage of teaching staff and of required number of classrooms. It involves organised collections and aid actions or increasing economic problems. The village schools headmasters more often went beyond the frames of a school chronicle with their texts and eagerly depicted events of their school district and its inhabitants. The records were as much a school chronicle as a chronicle of the village community.

The majority of the pedagogues, just like the Prussian administrative clerks, were not in the habit of criticising the authorities' decisions. But it does not mean they did not have their own views. Usually they did not reveal them and sometimes they even hid them. They allowed themselves to openly criticise the Prussian system only when it collapsed (Sławno, pp. 173–174; Świątniki Wielkie, p. 212).

While not losing their official nature, some sections of the school chronicles contain personal views or records of personal experience of their authors, through which they begin to resemble diaries. On such occasions they introduce an element of subjectivity that aspires to be objective to the narrative, which is very interesting for a contemporary reader. The volume of details present on their pages can sometimes be overwhelming. However, for a historian they remain an irreplaceable source, allowing the reconstruction of the daily atmosphere of wartime. Source material included in the school chronicles of the Gniezno and the Witkowo districts remains until this day, completely unknown to researchers.

Tomasz Matuszak
*State Archive
in Piotrków Trybunalski*

The organization and the operations of the League of Women of the War Emergency Service

An example of dynamic changes happening in political and social life, for which the outbreak of World War I became a catalyst, is civil activity, which had never before been so wide-ranging. Many organizations and associations were started at that time and many of them were women organizations. One of the most interesting examples of this was the League of Women of the War Emergency Service (*Liga Kobiet Pogotowia Wojennego* – LKPW) operating in Piotrków and its surrounding area. The origins of this organization can be traced back to November 1912 when the events connected to the First Balkan War led to creation of the Temporary Commission of Confederated Independence Parties, which tried to invigorate political life and to activate Polish communities operating in the Kingdom of Poland and Galicia. In an appeal published at that time the Commission prophesied imminent outbreak of war and urged the Polish people to start organizations that would prepare the society for the armed struggle against Russia[1]. Under the influence of all that was happening during that period and the information coming from England and France that there were many social organizations with female members, a group of known educational activists and publicists with strong patriotic views, began the work aimed at starting most probably the first female social organization of this kind in the Polish lands. In April 1913, Iza Moszczeńska-Rzepecka – the Polish Socialist Party activist, Jadwiga Marcinowska, Teresa Ciszkiewiczowa and Helena Ceysingerówna who belonged to the National League and Zofia Daszyńska-Golińska, Helena Sujkowska and Leokadia Śliwińska[2], established in Warsaw the League of Women of the War Emergency Service, which in its initial phase of operating was a secret organization.

---

1 Dufrat, Joanna: *Kobiety w kręgu lewicy niepodległościowej. Od Ligi Kobiet Pogotowia Wojennego do Ochotniczej Legii Kobiet (1908–1918/1919).* Toruń 2001, p. 31
2 Dufrat, Joanna: *Powstanie Ligi Kobiet w okresie I wojny światowej.* Access 14.04.2015, http://ligakobietpolskich.pl.

All activists already had some experience in political activity because in 1905 they co-organized a strike of Polish youth in the Kingdom and before the revolution they worked together in secret educational organizations, e.g. in the Crown and Lithuania Circle (*Koło Kobiet Korony i Litwy*) and the National Education Association (*Towarzystwo Oświaty Narodowej*)[3]. The first board members of LKPW in Warsaw were Joanna Nieniewska and Helena Ceysingerówna, while Iza Moszczeńska-Rzepecka became the president. Moszczeńska-Rzepecka was a praised social and educational activist, who from 1891 ran a guest house for girls, which in fact was a secret homestay with a curriculum of a female secondary school. She collaborated actively with *The Weekly Review* ("Przegląd Tygodniowy"), *The Voice* ("Głos") and *Truth* ("Prawda") and she worked for the Working Women's Circle (*Koło Pracy Kobiet*), the Secret Crown and the Lithuania Circle (*Tajne Koło Kobiet Korony i Litwy*). Moszczeńska-Rzepecka was equally active after she moved to Poznań where she worked with the "Warta" Education Association (*Towarzystwo Oświatowe "Warta"*) and the Women's Reading Room (*"Czytelnia dla Kobiet"*)[4].

The first women's circles, which were created a few months after the circle in Warsaw started its work, began working in Kielce, Lublin, Ząbkowice and other cities. In its initial phase the organization was dispersed and worked without permanent contact with communities connected to the Riflemen's Association (*Związek Strzelecki*). In that time LKPW concentrated its operations on propaganda and educational activities[5]. The founders of LKPW, who already had some experience in working for the riflemen's movement, which was forming behind the cordon, wanted to focus their mission on "being a moral support and providing material aid in the armed struggle against Russia for Polish independence"[6]. At the same time, as an organization working for the anti-Russian irredentist movement in Galicia, it pledged itself to surrender to the legitimate authorities with the beginning of warfare and the creation of a military movement in the Kingdom. Before that, however, it was meant to be dependent on the military movement

---

3 Pająk, Jerzy Zbigniew: "Liga Kobiet Polskich Pogotowia Wojennego wobec sporów w obozie aktywistycznym (sierpień 1915–sierpień 1916)". *Kieleckie Studia Historyczne* (15), 1999, p. 79. Dufrat 2001, 78.

4 Petrozolin-Skowrońska, Barbara: "Portret publicystki i działaczki. Iza Moszczeńska-Rzepecka". *Mówią Wieki* (6), 1980, p. 26.

5 Piasta, Aleksy: *Piotrków Trybunalski w latach pierwszej wojny światowej*. Piotrków Trybunalski 2007, pp. 212–213.

6 Śliwińska, Leokadia: *Z dziejów Ligii Kobiet Polskich Pogotowia Wojennego 1913–1918* (manuscript). Archiwum Akt Nowych w Warszawie. Liga Kobiet Polskich, ref. 32, ch. 20.

which was initiated in Galicia[7]. The founders of LKPW generally disapproved of military service for women because in their opinion their work in the society was much more useful. They wanted women to take over the duties of men who had to do their military service. This also proved to be a powerful means of propaganda because in this way the members of LKPW highlighted that the men's military effort was supported beyond the front line in a concerted work effort aimed at freeing the homeland oppressed by the invaders. At the same time, members of LKPW provided material support for the military movement from Galicia and after the outbreak of war took care of wounded Polish soldiers and their families. An equally important aspect of LKPW's work was the wide-ranging propaganda in the Polish society promoting armed struggle for independence and sovereignty of Poland. Soon after the advent of LKPW Iza Moszczeńska-Rzepecka went to Cracow. Her goal was to assess the needs of the riflemen squads and to contact the leaders of the military movement in Galicia. However, it seems that the main goal that the president of LKPW had was to contact Józef Piłsudski and gain his acceptance of these kinds of operations of this women's organization. She gained such acceptance and that allowed LKPW to continue work on the formation of national awareness and patriotism among those Polish people who so far had pro-Russian views.

Since all LKPW work had to be done secretly, the board had to be very selective when choosing the new members. Hence the organization was highly elitist and consisted of very few members. A year after LKPW was founded its unique Warsaw branch had only 17 members: Helena Ceysingerówna, Teresa Ciszkiewiczowa, Maria Dąbrowska, Maria Godlewska, Helena Grotowska, Zofia Kozłowska, Jadwiga Marcinkowska, Iza Moszczeńska-Rzepecka, Halina Niemiewska, Joanna Niemierczycka, Maria Pawlikowska, Maria Przyjemska, Julia Rottermundówna, Helena Sujkowska, Leokadia Śliwińska, Ludwika Zawadzka and Jadwiga Zielińska[8]. Before the outbreak of the war, from April 1913 to August 1914, the organization was working mainly among the intelligentsia in Warsaw. The task was not easy because at that time in the Kingdom of Poland prevailed a strong political attitude similar in its overtone to the views of Roman Dmowski. Despite that the agitational campaigns for the riflemen movement in Galicia were very successful. The members of LKPW organized many debates and discussion circles where possibility of regaining independence was widely analysed. As a result LKPW began to publish its own propaganda

---

7   Pająk, p. 79.
8   Ibid., p. 80.

materials – magazines: *Outreach* (*"Wici"*), *Free Voice* (*"Głos Wolny"*), *On the Eve* (*"W Przededniu"*), *Polish Matter* (*"Sprawa Polska"*). These magazines were then distributed and promoted in different places and social communities. Because of the illegal character of LKPW operations it also had to have a network of secret premises where members of riflemen organizations could be hidden and where illegal publications and guns could be stored. All members were very careful while working, however, there were cases of women being suspected of belonging to LKPW and for this reason arrested and interrogated during an investigation. At that time, LKPW was one of the most important organizations in the anti-Russian irredentist movement and for this reason it was closely monitored by the law enforcement agencies.

The outbreak of war made the LKPW members even more active and since the society under the Russian Partition was rather reluctant to actively co-operate with Austrian authorities the members of LKPW focused on intensifying their campaigns aimed at promoting such collaboration. Since it was difficult to travel when the front line was moving in the first phase of the war the communication between the organizational units in Galicia and the Kingdom of Poland was ceased. An attempt to slink through the cordon resulted in the arrest and detention of Helena Ceysingerówna near Kalisz. As a result there was an urging need to introduce changes to the board of LKPW. From August 1914 to August 1915 the activity of LKPW was directed by Jadwiga Marcinowska (till January 1915), Helena Grotowska, Joanna Niemiewska and Leokadia Śliwińska (from January 1915)[9]. The new board quickly began the work focused on organisation. Then the subdivision was made and the following new units were created to operate in the following areas: agitation, local activities, economy, clothes, accommodation, finances and aid for the families of legionaries. LKPW also began to closely collaborate with the Polish Military Organisation, PMO (*Polska Organizacja Wojskowa, POW*). As a result some of the members of LKPW were delegated to work in a sanitary unit and a military mail unit. LKPW was also deeply committed to providing equipment for the Warsaw Battalion I of the PMO (*I. Warszawski Batalion POW*) in August 1915.

After a wide-ranging agitational campaign LKPW also increased the number of its members to one hundred. In consequence the elitist character of LKPW, which previously was enforced by the political situation of that time and the fact that all work was done in secret, was abandoned. In order to distinguish themselves other women's organisations which focused solely on education and culture, members

9   Ibid.

of LKPW always highlighted the words used in the name of the League – War Emergency Service[10]. Taking the recruitment headquarters as an example, the LKPW board decided to enroll women who represented different political groups and different social classes. The only condition of their positive verification was a declaration that they support the armed struggle against Russia to regain the independence. Additionally the candidates were asked to provide a declaration that they would not succumb to influences and pressure of other political groups or factions. Simultaneously, the members of LKPW began to promote its idea in field. It was thanks to the activists from the province unit that a close relationship was made with women's communities in Vilnius, Lublin, Radom and even in Saint Petersburg. What is more, apart from the regular secret operations LKPW began to organize very popular sanitation courses.

One of the main goals of LKPW after the outbreak of the war was to provide moral support and material aid to the legionaries and Polish soldiers serving in the Austrian army but based in the Kingdom. The League wanted to create a place that would resemble a "family home for a Polish soldier", with a kitchen, a larder, food and clothes storehouse and a clinic in which they could be treated and rehabilitated. The staff working in these "houses" was to be composed of female compatriots with hope that this would influence the patriotic attitudes of the Polish army, which had to create itself from scratch. The goal that initially was of a humanitarian importance, with time, gained political and national importance especially when the idea of military collaboration with Austria against Russia became predominant in those circles[11]. Iza Moszczeńska-Rzepecka wrote: "The woman is not serving in the army so to prove her support, she needs to show it through the work she is doing – the work for the army [...]. The fact that the soldier will be well dressed, fed and all the service will be provided to him, may impact his will and fate, however, what have a greater significance is the awareness that the country remembers about him, that he is not homeless and insignificant, that thousands of watchful eyes throwing him kind and caring glances follow his actions, take pride in his bravery, shares his sorrows and wishes him to triumph"[12]. LKPW was a freedom fighting organisation which was clearly visible in its character, operations and goals out of which the most important one was revival of the homeland. At the same time, it must not be forgotten that it was also promoting

---

10 Moszczeńska, Iza: "Liga Kobiet". *Wiadomości Polskie* (22), 1915, p. 3.
11 Archiwum Państwowe w Piotrkowie Trybunalskim, *Liga Kobiet Pogotowia Wojennego*, ref. 3, ch. 31.
12 Moszczeńska, Iza: "Liga Kobiet jako Pogotowie Wojenne". *Na Posterunku. Jednodniówka* 11 June 1916, p. 4.

ideas connected to the emancipation movement that was growing in strength in
the world. In these wartime circumstances LKPW began its more active political work and first participated in the Union of Freedom Fighting Organisations
(*Zjednoczenie Organizacji Niepodległościowych*) in Warsaw and later after it was
disbanded in November 1914, in the Union of Freedom Fighting Factions (*Unia
Stronnictw Niepodległościowych*)[13].

A complete version of the first charter of LKPW was not preserved because
only one copy of it was made because of the conspiratorial nature of operating. It
included an announcement that in case of the outbreak of the war the organisation
would surrender itself to the fighting armed force and would be at its service[14]. In
the following acts (statutes) passed during the meetings LKPW mentioned the
following tasks as the most important:

1. Taking care of the Polish Army: raising money for the fight for independence;
   providing Polish Legions or Polish Army with necessary items including: un-
   derwear, clothes, food and sanitary aid, as well as caring for the soldiers by
   opening taverns, shelters, among many others and raising the fighters' spirits
   by strengthening the faith in the victory and solidarity of the nation in their
   armed struggle;
2. Taking care of the legionaries' families and all the freedom fighters;
3. Promoting the idea of independence and moral support for the armed struggles by means of: publishing and distributing patriotic magazines and publications, organizing talks and proceedings awakening patriotic feelings and
   appreciation for the heroes of the freedom fights, raising society's awareness
   of how important and how crucial are the fights; educating in the spirit of
   freedom fights; working on cultural revival, economic growth and sanitary
   support for people as part of promotion of the idea of independence;
4. Organizing military mail for the Polish legionaries and all freedom fighters[15].

The charter also emphasized the organizational independence of this women's organisation, which could co-operate with any political organisation with the same
views, without allowing any of them to take control[16]. LKPW could create its own
circles not only in the country but also abroad, provided that they were created in
the cities with a Polish diaspora. The main institution of LKPW was the General
Assembly (*Zjazd Ogólny*), which was passing or changing the organizational acts

---

13 Pająk, p. 81.
14 Moszczeńska 1915, p. 6.
15 *Ustawa Ligi Kobiet Pogotowia Wojennego.* Lublin 1916, p. 3.
16 Archiwum Narodowe w Krakowie, *Naczelny Komitet Narodowy,* ref. 114, ch. 10–11.

and could decide on closing the organization or joining it with another one when there was a consent of two-thirds of its members. General Assembly chose the Main Board (*Zarząd Naczelny*), the Auditing Committee (*Komisję Rewizyjną*), the headquarters of the Main Board. It additionally had to deal with the proposals of the main Board and the Auditing Committee. Meetings of the Assembly were open to the deputies, all members and advisors. To facilitate communication between the circles and district branches they organized Partial Assemblies, which however did not have legislative power[17]. The highest executive power of LKPW was the Main Board, which represented the League outside and supported the growth of the District Branches and Circles. It had five members who represented all District Branches[18]. All newly created circles had to inform the Regional Committee (*Komitet Okręgowy*) about their activation and this information was later passed to the Main Board. The circles could choose their own Board consisting of three members and had full autonomy in the decision making process and acting as long as they obeyed their own regulations[19]. The circles were divided into units, which were dividing the tasks among their members and could choose their Boards as well[20]. When in the summer of 1915 the Kingdom was occupied by the Central Powers army and divided into two occupation zones, the territorial structure of LKPW already consisted of 12 district branches[21]. In the zone occupied by the Germans there were the following branches: Warsaw (sub-branches: Włocławek and Płock), Łódź, Kalisz, Siedlce and Łuków, whereas in the Austrian zone: Lublin (sub-branches: Lublin and Zwierzyniec), Kielce, Częstochowa, Radom, Olkusz, Zagłębie and Piotrków.

The importance of LKPW in propaganda grew when, in August 1915, the German army entered Warsaw. At that moment began a serious division and conflict between the supporters of Józef Piłsudski and the politicians who argued for close collaboration with the Central Powers authorities. Piłsudski, who at that time was a commander of Brigade I of the Polish Legion, believed that until Germany and Austria made a clear statement on Polish independence making further political concessions eagerly and enrolling a bigger number of recruits will endanger the national affairs. These views, however, were not shared by the politicians from the National Supreme Committee (*Naczelny Komitet Narodowy [NKN]*) from Cracow. Both conflicted sides were trying to win the support of LKPW because of

---

17 APPT, *LKPW*, ref. 6, ch. 11.
18 *Ustawa...*, p. 7.
19 Ibid., p. 10.
20 APPT, *LKPW*, ref. 3, ch. 5.
21 Dufrat 2001, p. 162.

the impact this organisation was making and the finances it had. It was especially
important for the emerging leftist political organisations, e.g, Supreme Committee
of the United Independence Factions (*Komitet Naczelny Zjednoczonych Stronnictw
Niepodległościowych*), or later the Central National Committee (*Centralny Komitet
Narodowy [CKN]*). LKPW also had a very well formed structure and useful premises, and that made it easier to recruit supporters from varying political factions,
especially from small communities. In this conflict, LKPW officially took the side
of Piłsudski and supported his decision to stop recruiting new legionaries and at
the same time engage in current politics. This attitude was visible also in the collaboration of LKPW with the Military Command (*Departamentem Wojskowym
NKN*) in Piotrków. For this reason serious conflicts were created within LKPW.
A group that was focused on the Military Command politics represented Iza
Moszczeńska-Rzepecka and Helena Ceysingerówna. Both as the heads of LKPW
decided in September 1915 to subordinate it to the Military Command. This was
strongly opposed by Leokadia Śliwińska and Joanna Niemiewska. During a ple-
nary meeting of the members they managed to stipulate the standpoint of LKPW.
Now the focus was on providing support to all brigades of the legions whereas the
decision to agitate and recruit to the Legions or cease to do that could be taken by
the members themselves. A new institution was created as well – Council of the
League of Polish Women of the War Emergency Service (*Rada Ligi Kobiet Polskich
Pogotowia Wojennego*). Despite the efforts to maintain coherence in November
1915 part of the organization, which was in Warsaw split into two circles. Circle A
gathered supporters of close collaboration with the Military Command, whereas
Circle B consisted of the members who opposed such collaboration. Another
consequence of the various activities of LKPW was that in the middle of 1916 it
also began to co-operate with the Galicia and Silesia Women's League (*Liga Kobiet
Galicji i Śląska*) created in 1915 in the Austrian Partition. When the partnership
in action started, both the organisations had more than 16 thousands members
and became the first massive organized union of women in the Polish lands[22]. The
relationship between the two Leagues was very good from the beginning and this
could be related to the fact that most members were somehow connected with
Galicia and therefore the riflemen independence movement.

On 28–29 January 1916 a ground-breaking meeting (*zjazd radomski*) of LKPW
members was held with delegates representing the League in Warsaw, Piotrków,
Kielce Voivodeship and Lublin Voivodeship. An announcement was made that a
new coherent organisation will be created for the whole Kingdom, Supreme Board

---

22 Dufrat, Internet, p. 5.

of the League of Polish Women of the War Emergency Service was chosen and three branches were created, in Kielce, in Lublin and in Piotrków[23]. This renewed the previous argument from 1915. The beginning of internal fights between the factions of LKPW led to a split which happened during the third gathering (*III Zjeździe*) in Piotrków on 24–26 August 1916. This meeting introduced to a so-far coherent community feelings of reluctance, especially in larger branches (Warsaw, Łódź, Piotrków and Lublin). The third gathering showed growing tendencies to introduce changes that will change LKPW into a political organisation (especially when the matter of the relation of the League to the Central National Committee was taken into consideration), which was clearly visible during the next meeting in Warsaw[24]. During the fourth Gathering of LKPW on 25–28 June 1917, the main goal was to heal and improve operations and the organizational structure. New following units had been created at that time:

1. The unit focusing on taking care of the soldiers and their families – its task was to coordinate and regulate the works connected to moral support and material aid for the soldiers and other victims of the freedom fights;
2. The unit focusing on organization and agitation – its task was to supervise the growth of the circles, regulate their organizational and administrative issues, facilitate communication between the circles, run a school for instructors and coordinate the agitational campaigns of the circles;
3. The unit focused on the social work – its task was to create social circles and supervise their activities and growth;
4. The unit focused on the press – its task was to collect the materials connected to the activities of LKPW and publish them in the press as well as to shape the press' attitude towards LKPW;
5. The unit focused on equal rights – ran campaigns of LKPW in order to fight for women's political rights and stayed connected to other women's organisations;
6. The unit focused on taking care of soldiers' families, children form the legionaries' families and the victims of war – these operations of LKPW were coordinated in co-operation with the Galicia and Silesia Women's League aid unit;
7. The unit focused on social and national economy – it started trading cooperatives, loan societies, supported nationalisation of industry and commerce[25].

---

23 Pająk, p. 87.
24 Piasta 2007, p. 214.
25 APPT, *LKPW*, ref. 6, ch. 8.

At that point a suite of acts was passed presenting the standpoint of LKPW on
the most important political issues of the country, including union of Polish lands
and creation of a unified country, opposition to the occupying authorities, which
sabotaged fulfilling the act issued on 5 November and organizing elections for the
Legislative Sejm. It was agreed that LKPW should be autonomous when dealing
with current Polish political situation and the role of the Central National Committee diminished. After the oath crisis in 1917 the League's Main Board took
decisions to reorganize the circles by starting new working units. Before the end
of the war the voices that LKP should be closed because of the situation were
more frequent. In the end, the two women's organisations that worked together
before united in late Autumn 1918 during a meeting of the League's Supreme
Board. On 1–2 November 1918 the League of Polish Women (*Liga Kobiet Polskich*)
was founded as an organisation, which will take active part in the public life of a
reviving country[26].

The League of Women of the War Emergency Service had a strong impact
on functioning of Piotrków city during the Great War. In the beginning of 20th
century, Piotrków, after a period of stagnation between 1904–1905, began to grow
again. In 1913 the number of citizens reached 40 thousand people. The glazier
and textile companies expanded in the city and other new companies connected
to the timber and construction industry were created[27]. Undoubtedly what influenced the growth of Piotrków city was its advantageous location in the most
industrial part of the governorate, which was a center of the administration of
that time. The largest economic growth of the city was in 1914. Because of the
city's importance military forces were garrisoned in Piotrków and in the Piotrków
governorate: one staff and two regiments – 14. Cavalry Division in Częstochowa
and Będzin (*14. Dywizja Kawalerii w Częstochowie i Będzinie*) and 2. Infantry
Brigade (*2. Brygada Piechoty*) consisting of 7. infantry regiment in Częstochowa
(*7. pułk piechoty w Częstochowie*) and 8. Płock infantry regiment in Piotrków
(*8. połocki pułk piechoty w Piotrkowie*)[28]. Units, which created the Southern Squad
of the Russian army, except the border units, in case of the outbreak of the war
were expected to form four units of 100 men of foot and four units of 100 men
of horse. They were operating on the left bank of the Vistula river and their main

---

26 Piasta 2007, p. 216.
27 Gąsior, Marcin: *Działania wojenne na obszarze byłej guberni piotrkowskiej w pierwszych
    miesiącach wojny 1914 roku*. In: Zawilski, Piotr (ed): *Drogi do niepodległości. Materiały
    z sesji naukowej*. Tomaszów Mazowiecki 1998, p. 5. Kukulski, Jerzy: "Dążenia narodowe
    i społeczne w Piotrkowskiem na początku XX wieku". *Zbliżenia* (1), 1992, pp. 17–18.
28 Gąsior, p. 6.

task was to protect the western frontiers of the empire. On 26 July 1914 General Orawnowski, the commander of the Southern Squad and 14. Cavalry Division (*14. Dywizja Kawalerii*), was informed that the enemy was preparing to declare war and four days after he began to organize the army. Although the preparations was started, Russia's strategic goals did not include protecting the western and southern lands of the Kingdom of Poland at all costs. The plan included though a possibility of evacuation of all offices and institutions from this area to the Russian hinterland in case of an outbreak of war. The first plans concerning the evacuation of administration from these areas were made in 1909[29]. Surely this was caused by the events that took place before – the annexation of Bosnia and Herzegovina by Austro-Hungary in 1908. Because Russia did not want to recognize this act, Germany entered the conflict and put a strong pressure on Russia. This political crisis showed how potential sides of the conflict would stand up against each other in case of a military intervention.

In regard to the exacerbating international situation, the Russian administrative offices began to prepare for the evacuation from the areas threatened by the military operations[30]. Not only the national administrative offices were to be evacuated but also all the workers with their families, archival materials from the registration offices and the archives of Governorate Government and Districts' Boards. The scheme for the evacuation of each governorate was the same. First, the families were taken to a safe place and later the officials supervising the evacuation of the national property. Remarkably, even though the offices and institutions were suspended at that time and did not conduct any work, the officials were still receiving their salaries and were treated as officials on duty. The evacuation of institutions and workers from the governorates threatened by war was going smoothly. After conducting the first evacuations and gaining

29 Budziński, Janusz Roman: *Polityka zagraniczna Rosji 1907–1914. Aparat decyzyjny, koncepcja, rezultaty.* Toruń 2000, p. 71.

30 Cf: Latawiec, Krzysztof: "Ewakuacja organów administracji ogólnej wyższego i niższego szczebla guberni lubelskiej w sierpniu 1914 roku". *Radzyński Rocznik Humanistyczny* (2), 2002, pp. 43–46. Latawiec, Krzysztof: "Ewakuacja cywilnej administracji ogólnej szczebla powiatowego z guberni lubelskiej latem 1915 roku". *Wschodni Rocznik Humanistyczny* (1), 2004, pp. 159–160. Malinowska, Dorota: *Ewakuacja urzędów Królestwa Polskiego w latach 1914–1915 do Rosji, ich losy i rewindykacja akt do Polski p. 1921 roku.* In: Łosowski, Janusz (ed.): *Pamiętnik III Ogólnopolskiego Zjazdu Studentów Archiwistyki w Lublinie.* Lublin 2000, pp. 189–196. Górak, Artur: *Kancelaria Gubernatora i Rząd Gubernialny Lubelski (1867–1914).* Lublin/Radzyń Podlaski 2006, pp. 144–163. Kopiczyńska, Alina: *Akta władz administracji gubernialnej Królestwa Polskiego w latach 1867–1915.* Warszawa 2004, pp. 107–109.

experience therefrom, the Russian Interior Ministry verified the regulations governing the evacuations. On 20 August/ 2 September, 1914, they were first accepted by the Council of Ministers and after this approval they were presented to the tsar[31]. The idea was to evacuate all the offices and institutions in a particular order, which, upon arrival, would allow the evacuees to immediately start the work interrupted by the military operations[32].

The citizens of Piotrków learned about the conflict between Austria and Serbia, which later turned into a world war, from the 30th issue of *Piotrków Chronicle* (*"Kroniki Piotrkowskiej"*) on 29 July 1914[33]. Mobilization of the army went very well and finished on 1 August 1914. First clashes took place at night on 1–2 August near Herby and Koziegłów. In fact, the Russian army abandoned the Piotrków governorate already on August 3 because on that day, the Russians were evacuating themselves from Częstochowa and the 8. Płock regiment garrisoned in Piotrków was transported by train to the right bank of the Vistula river. Civil authorities of the governorate's administrative offices started to prepare for the evacuation on August 1 on the grounds of an edict issued by the Piotrkow Governor – Michaił Edward Jaczewski[34], however, it was not until 11 August 1914 when they evacuated. In spite of all the previous plans and preparations, the situation on the front surprised the Russian administration. Evacuation was made hastily and chaotically. As a result, only the documents considered to be the most important and most crucial for continuing the activities were taken. The offices and their archives evacuated in such a quick manner were moved to different parts of Russia, e.g.: Kazan, Moscow, Saratov, Smolensk and Ryazan[35]. The fate of the archival materials from the offices in Piotrków illustrates what was happening then. Part of

---

31 Cf: *Przepisy czasowe o wywożeniu na koszt skarbu, wskutek okoliczności wojny majątku państwowego, instytucji rządowych, urzędników i ich rodzin. Akty prawodawcze wydane w związku z wojną 1914/1915 roku.* Warszawa 1915, pp. 259–285.

32 Matuszak, Tomasz: "Archiwalia piotrkowskie w czasie I wojny światowej". *Piotrkowskie Zeszyty Historyczne* (7/8), 2005/2006, pp. 7–8. Matuszak, Tomasz: *Archiwum Państwowe w Piotrkowie Trybunalskim 1919–1951.* Piotrków Trybunalski/Radzyń Podlaski 2009, pp. 53–54.

33 Wachowska, Barbara: *Życie społeczno-polityczne i kulturalne w latach pierwszej wojny światowej.* In: Baranowski, Bohdan (ed.): *Dzieje Piotrkowa Trybunalskiego.* Łódź 1989, p. 360. Pielużek, Anna: *Piotrków i powiat piotrkowski w świetle "Kroniki Piotrkowskiej" 1910–1914.* Piotrków Trybunalski 2005, pp. 60–61. *Kronika Piotrkowska* (30), of 29 July 1914, p. 1.

34 Kukulski, Jerzy: *Piotrkowskie u progu niepodległości.* In: *Ziemia Piotrkowska u progu niepodległości.* Piotrków Trybunalski 1988, pp. 25–26.

35 Kopiczyńska, pp. 107–108.

the documents was evacuated together with the workers and their belongings to Smolensk and Saratov. The rest of the archival materials, which were prepared for the evacuation in the beginning of August 1914 remained unsupervised. Fortunately, because they were packed into packages, wrapped with a packing paper and then stored in cases and placed in the carts, they were not destroyed[36]. Later they proved to be very interesting for the occupant – Austrian authorities, especially for the military police.

On 12 August 1914, Germans entered Radomsk and on the next day the subdivisions of the 1st Landwehr Division commanded by Gen. Wilhelm von Kluck occupied Piotrków. Lieutenant von Stallberg from the provisional cavalry regiment (*Ersatzkavalierregiment*). became the chief of the city. He immediately issued an announcement that the city was occupied, declared state of emergency and announced that contribution will be imposed on the city. German occupation lasted relatively short though, only till 27 August 1914, because the counter-offensive of the Russian troops made the German army withdraw from the northern districts of the Piotrków governorate. The Russian army held the retrieved territories for a month. In the end of September 1914 the military situation again changed on the front. On 3 October the German and Austrian army began and offensive after which the troops of Gen. Fromm corps entered Piotrków. This time Major Keller became the chief of the city and made an announcement in which he described the military situation and laid down the regulations governing the life of civilians under occupation[37]. However, the offensive of the Central Powers' army came to a standstill and on 15 October and the Russian army began its counter-offensive. The last train evacuating the German troops left the city on 30 October 1914. On 9 November the Russian army entered Piotrków again and though it was prepared to defend the city it did not manage to hold it. As a result, on 17 December 1914, the Austrian army entered Piotrków and occupied it till November 1918[38].

In 1915 already the whole Kingdom of Poland was occupied by the army of the Central Powers and divided into two occupation zones: German and Austrian. As a consequence Piotrków was governed by the Austrian military administration (O sytuacji Piotrkowa w czasie I wojny światowej, rozpatrywanej w różnych aspektach – cf Bibliography: Piasta, Aleksy). General Lublin Governorate had been created for the territories occupied by the Austrian army, with an authority structure that was similar to the one present in the

---

36 "Dokumenty niewoli". *Dziennik Narodowy* (1), 1915, p. 4.
37 Gąsior, pp. 9–11.
38 Kukulski, Jerzy: *Sto lat Rosji w Królestwie Polskim (1815–1915). Wybrane problemy*. Piotrków Trybunalski 2005, pp. 322–324.

German occupation zone before (Na temat działania władz austriackich, a w szczególności ich kancelarii i produkcji aktowej – cf. Bibliography: Gaul, Jerzy). The administrative division into governorates was no longer used and the offices of local administration were now only communal offices[39]. In February 1915, on the basis of a district functioning before the war, the Piotrków oblast was created and governed by the Reserve Command – K.u.K. Kreiskommando in Piotrków[40]. The first Reserve Commander was major von Pappe, and from 16 May 1915 to 1 January 1917 it was lieutenant colonel Juliusz Schneider. During his tenure Major Witt, who was his deputy with a strong anti-Polish mindset collaborated very closely with the chief of the military gandarmerie – Robert von Weinrichter[41]. In the beginning of 1917 the position of the commander was taken by Colonel/ General Tadeusz Wiktor. Until May 1915 there was a Citizens' Committee operating in the city and throughout the time of the occupation also the magistrate and municipality. From the first days of the occupation the new authorities were applying a depredation policy of the economy. All that had any value or significance for the army had been confiscated, the industry and agriculture were subordinated to demand-driven production for the army. Situation of the society was dramatic. The unemployment has risen and there was an increase in infectious diseases. Rationing of goods and services began. This situation gave rise to supportive social organisations like LKPW.

Since the outbreak of war Piotrków was a bastion of patriotism. Together with the legionaries came the representatives of Polish National Organization (*Polska Organizacja Narodowa*). When the situation on the front stabilized and a new administrative framework had been established, in the summer 1915 the occupied Piotrków became the headquarters of the NKN Military Command. Its main task was to recruit to the Polish Legions. Colonel Władysław Sikorski was at the head of it. This Command included: the Central Registration Office (*Centralny Urząd Ewidencyjny*), the Central Enlistment Office (*Centralne Biuro Poborowe*), Press Office (*Biuro Prasowe*), the Publishing Administration (*Administracja Wydawnictw*), the State Printing Office (*Drukarnia Państwowa*) and the Central Recruitment Office (Centralne Biuro Werbunkowe) among many others. What is more, the Polish Legions Headquarters (till November 1916), reserve centers, non-commissioned

---

39 Cf.: Lewandowski, Jan: *Królestwo Polskie pod okupacją austriacką 1914–1918*. Warszawa 1980.

40 Piasta, Aleksy: "Polityka austriackiej administracji wojskowej na terenie powiatu piotrkowskiego w latach 1915–1918". *Archiwum i Badania nad Dziejami Regionu* (1), 1995, p. 109.

41 Wachowska, p. 361.

officers schools and hospitals were also located in the city. All of them in some ways were co-operating with the Piotrków LKPW Circle. It was established in 1914 by Maria Piłsudska with a family name Koplewska. She was the first wife of Józef Piłsudski and a social and socialist activist[42]. Initially the circle had 34 members but this number increased to 65 very quickly. In the beginning the circle was operating rather secretly and for this reason its members were listed under the pseudonyms and were sworn to secrecy. The Piotrków LKPW Circle had its internal rules laid down by its Board. Obliged by these rules the members had to pay fees, which were financing operations of three subdivisions: fiscal, sewing and laundry[43]. In the beginning when the front was moving through the city the activities were limited to sewing clothes. Activation of the circle happened in the beginning of January 1915 when the Russians left the city. Then the circle was re-organized and the new chairwomen was Helena Trzcińska – pedagogical activist and a member of the National Education Association (*Towarzystwa Oświaty Narodowej* [TON]).Wanda Grabowska, also a TON activist and a participant in the strike of Polish youth in 1905, became a vice chairwoman. Other members of the board were: J. Zaleska, Maria Chelińska and Kazimiera Domańska later replaced by Zofia Rowecka. From that moment the scale of the activities of the Piotrków LKPW Circle started growing. There was also an increasing number of members. In 1916 there were 159 registered active members in the 17 units of the circle. In the time of Austrian occupation the number of active members of active units varied between 10 and 14[44].

When completing the tasks of LKPW, the Piotrków Circle and its units were focusing on helping the Polish soldier by means of creating a friendly atmosphere in a local community, providing material support, financed by money payed by the members and money earned during organized prize draws, and promoting the idea of independence. The circle's members were also sending packages to the front to help the soldiers and they were focusing on their regular work: running a profitable tea-house and a tavern, a hospital, a laundry room, a reading room, providing medical support, taking care of expelled soldiers, taking care of the families of the legionaries, agitating (agitation and distribution unit), promoting education and culture; collecting money during organized events and fundraising[45]. Piotrków was also the city where LKPW had its two aforementioned gatherings. In the first one, attended also by the delegates from Galicia and Silesia

42 APPT, *LKPW*, file no. 4, ch. 1.
43 APPT, *LKPW*, file no. 2, ch. 1.
44 APPT, *Archiwum Wandy Grabowskiej*, file no. 23, ch. 1.
45 APPT, *LKPW*, file no. 4, ch. 1.

Women's League (May 8–9, 1915), there were approximately 50 delegates from 26 circles of LKPW. During these deliberations attendees listened to 21 reports, four reports from Galicia and one from Silesia. The Piotrków Circle was eager to act, help and co-operate with other entities e.g. political formations or cultural and educational associations. Between 1915–1916 the circle closely collaborated with the NKN Military Command. These activities mainly focused on celebrating together patriotic holidays and celebrations. In exchange, the profitable ventures and celebrations of the circle were receiving artistic and technical support. The Military Command donated to LKPW in Piotrków premises where the circle could run a tea-house and for two months provided shortfall sugar and tea and for six months kerosene and carbon. The unit taking care of the soldiers, on the other hand, was given by Command (*Komenda Placu*) a venue for a soldiers' tavern and a tea-house as well as tea, sugar and wood[46]. It was a fair exchange that provided for the most urgent operational needs of the circle. After the aforementioned division which happened in LKPW, the help was vastly limited. Only the muster station continued its collaboration with the circle[47].

The Piotrków LKPW was part of the National Committee (*Komitet Narodowy [KN]*), which was constantly in touch with CKN. The Piotrków Circle collaborated with it on preparing national celebrations and events, and political speeches. The circle's delegates in KN were Wanda Grabowska and Maria Rudnicka. When the educational and cultural institution (*Polska Macierz Szkolna*) started to work again, LKPW began to collect declarations for its members (over 100 had been collected, ibid. ch. 31). When the Voice of Piotrków (*"Głos Piotrkowski"*) was being issued again the circle found 30 regular subscribers for this publication and delegated Bronisława Strużyńska to the editorial board. The premises, which belonged to the Piotrków LKPW circle, were also used by the students' choir, workers and charity organizations. Additionally, the representatives of the circle co-operated with the teachers of the primary schools in order to prepare the strike and boycott teaching in German language at schools[48]. In 1917 the League continued to work with KN and was part of the Communication Commission of the Independence Factions (*Komisja Porozumiewawcza Stronnictw Niepodległościowych*). Its representatives were also active in the military committee (*Pomocniczy Komitet Wojskowy*) and in the aid department (*Departament Opieki*). On 3 May 1917, during a session of the City Council, attended by the representation of LKPW circle,

---

46 Ibid., file no. 2, ch. 26.
47 Ibid., ch. 32.
48 Ibid., ch. 32.

the new local authorities were given a national emblem funded with the money raised by collecting fees[49].

The members of the Piotrków LKPW Circle often took part in selling occasional pads to collect the money for the State Treasury. They were also active in prisons. They were caring for the members of POW and legionaries held in prison and they were delivering warm meals to the prison five times a week. Co-operation with those institutions continued in 1918. Together with the Communication Commission of the Independence Factions, the League took part in preparing celebrations on 19 March connected to the "Chełm land" and with the prison authorities prepared an Easter table for the prisoners. All activities were financed with the money made in the tea-house, where convalescents and soldiers on leave would meet over a cup of tea, or a glass of milk, or a snack; an money earned in the laundry room where clothes and uniforms were washed[50]. The welfare unit was helping the families of the legionaries not only by providing a material aid, both financial and rendered, but also by helping to find jobs and put children in the nurseries and early kindergartens[51]. In 1915 it was taking care of 55 families, while in 1916 already 101 families[52]. Children were given warm clothes and shoes for winter and special theater shows, dance soirees and prize lotteries were organized for them[53]. The unit taking care of the soldiers was providing beds for wounded soldiers, pyjamas and bedclothes. All units worked efficiently and with a lot of passion, which revealed the devotion of the members of the Piotrków LKPW circle and the immense need of the society devastated by the war and depredation policy of the city's occupant.

All things considered, Women of the War Emergency Service, throughout the years of the Great War – a difficult time for the politics, society and economy, was for the Polish society a very important organisation. Without the help of women united in circles and units of LKPW, many families would suffer from famine and poverty while the legionaries, especially wounded ones who as convalescents were behind the front deprived of aid, would feel lonely. The patriotic and

49 Ibid., ch. 33.
50 Ibid, p. 106.
51 APPT, C. and K. Komenda Powiatowa w Piotrkowie, file no. 90.
52 APPT, *LKPW*, file no. 2, ch. 73.
53 APPT, CKKP, file no. 109.

educational aspects of the LKPW operations must not be forgotten as well since they were crucial in molding the attitudes of the future society of revived II Republic. Awaited freedom came in 1918. However, it did not put an end to the activities of the Piotrków LKPW circle[54]. Just like the structures of Polish Women's League the activities continued till 1936.

---

54 Hubka, Maciej: *Źródła do wojny polsko–rosyjskiej1919–1921 w zasobie Archiwum Państwowego w Piotrkowie Trybunalskim i Oddziału w Tomaszowie Mazowieckim.* In: Matuszak, Tomasz (ed.): *W cieniu czerwonej zarazy. W 90. rocznicę Bitwy Warszawskiej 1920 roku.* Piotrków Trybunalski – Opoczno 2012, pp. 76–77.

Sławomir Jan Maksymowicz
State Archive in Olsztyn

East Prussia as the only province of the German Empire occupied during the Great War. Wartime histories of East Prussia

The intention of the author of this study is to present East Prussia as a part of the German state during the Great War. The history of this province is strikingly different from the histories of other parts of Germany. The province area, as the only part of the Second Reich, found itself partially, during military action of 1914–1915, under Russian occupation. The author intends to outline the course of warfare and the gehenna of the German civilians as well as the scale of destruction, reconstruction process and persecution of war crimes committed by the occupant.

In August 1892 France and Russia signed a military convention. It stipulated that Russian will sent at least 800 thousand soldiers to fight with Germany[1]. The conference of 1912 decided that the Russian army would, within 15 days from the mobilisation announcement, start from the Narew River area and head for Olsztyn, provided that Germans would be defending East Prussia[2].

The assumptions of the German commandership presumed that military action should be mainly focused on the west. Their priority was to defeat France. The German commanders delegated the 8th Army to defend East Prussia. It consisted of 4 corps including a reserve one. These were the 1st Corps (Hermann von François), XVII (August von Mackensen), XX (Friedrich von Scholz) and the 1st Reserve Corps – general Otto von Below. General Maximilian von Prittwitz und Gaffron commanded the 8th Army, General Major Graf Georg von Waldersee was the chief of staff. These forces were to face a more numerous Russian army – the North–West Front – 1st Army Vilnius (General Paweł von Rennenkampf) and the 2nd Army "Warszawa" (Aleksander Wasiliewicz Samsonow), commanded by General Jakow Żyliński.

The German army had been preparing for war for a long time. The oldest file concerning mobilisation of doctors was drafted a few years before the outbreak

---

1   P. Szlanta: *Tannenberg 1914*. Warszawa 2005, p. 15.
2   Ibid., p. 15.

of the war. In 1909 a register of doctors residing in the Braniewo *powiat*[3] was established[4]. Information in this register was presented in the form of a table. It provided the degree, name and surname of a doctor, date of birth, place of residence and level of specialisation[5]. The next similar archival unit is dated 1914. By contrast to the previous one, it included also information regarding preparation of field hospitals which were planned to be staffed with supporting personnel[6]. In the face of an approaching war and in the light of enthusiasm for battle, a group of women, the members of the Women's Patriotic Association (Towarzystwo Patriotyczne Kobiet), volunteered to work in hospitals[7]. The Convent of St Catherine's Sisters delegated 25 nuns as a means of preparing for war[8]. They were expected to report for duty within 20–30 days from the announcement of mobilisation[9]. As a result of mobilisation of medical personnel a few army hospitals were established in East Prussia. A reserve field hospital was opened in Węgorzewo (Reservelazaret Rastenburg). In the Darkehmen *powiat* two hospitals were established – Vereinlazaret and Reservelazaret Gumbinnen[10].

During the last days of July 1914 a mobilisation was decreed[11] and organised according to regionalisation. East Prussia was the seat of the I Corps (Królewiec) and the XX Corps (Olsztyn) headquarters. As we can see the involvement of East Prussians in the 8th Army was significant – they constituted two corps. The fact that the corps were formed according to regionalisation suggests that ca. 70% of the corps' personnel came from Warmia and the Masurian Lake District.

East Prussia played a special role in the plans of the Russian politicians and servicemen. Some circles in the Imperial Russia proposed schemes to annex vast

---

3   *Powiat* is the second-level unit of local government and administration in Poland. The term *"powiat"* is most often translated into English as "county" (trans.).

4   Archiwum Państwowe Olsztyn (henceforth APO), Starostwo Powiatowe w Braniewie (henceforth Star. Pow. Braniewo) 10/474.

5   Ibid., for example – dr Valentin Neumann, born on 1 June 1861, residing in Wormditt, with the level II of specialisation (class II doctor).

6   APO, Star. Pow. Braniewo 10/473.

7   APO, Star. Pow. Braniewo 10/475 25 women volunteered.

8   Ibid.

9   Ibid.

10   Ibid.

11   According to the school chronicle from Biskupiec the information about mobilisation was received on 1 August 1914 ca. 5 pm – APO 2881/1. R. Juszkiewicz states that mobilisation announcements appered already on 30 July – *Działania bojowe na pograniczu północnego Mazowsza i Prus Wschodnich oraz sytuacja ludności w latach 1914–1915* in: *Nad Bałtykiem, Pregołą i Łyną XVI–XX w.* Olsztyn 2006, p. 351.

areas of Germany to the tsarist country – to incorporate East Prussia, Branden-
burg, Pomerania, the Poznań region and Silesia[12]. Such plans served a propaganda
function. Their purpose was to present Tsar Nicolas II as a defender and restorer
of a united Slavic state on the areas which had been inhabited by Slavs in the
Middle Ages. It should be noted that the priority was to incorporate Królewiec, an
extremely important southern Baltic port. The Berlin authorities had no intention
to be a passive witness in this situation. Germany also had its plans pertaining the
areas of the Kingdom of Poland located along the East Prussian border[13].

Propaganda of both sides of the conflict presented its country as the one that
was waging a defensive war. The press promoted general enthusiasm for the war
and everybody eagerly left for the battlefield. Kazimierz Jaroszyk – a participant
of the wartime actions– presented a totally different picture of the war: "the outbreak of the war was announced by ringing bells – on 2 August 1914. Fighting
spirit prevailed in the press and in restaurants, but during medical examinations
the recruits tried to show that they were unfit for the battle, ill, especially with
tuberculosis (a godsend)"[14].

The East Prussia newspaper "Allensteiner Zeitung" reported that in the vicinity of Prostek, 300m from the border, on 1 August, an exchange of fire took place
between the German and the Russian patrols. Neither side incurred any losses[15].

Ryszard Juszkiewicz discovered that the first Russian troops which crossed the
East Prussian border belonged to the 6th Cavalry Division commanded by General
Ropp. The fact that this unit consisted of a few regiments stationed in the northern
Masovia (two from Mława, one from Ciechanów, Ostrołęka and Przasnysz) could
mean that it comprised many soldiers of Polish origin[16]. On 2 August 1914, a day
after the already mentioned inconclusive exchange of fire, the more powerful Rus-
sian troops sallied forth to East Prussia. They crossed the Prussian border near
Mława but on the next day they had to withdraw under pressure from the German

---

12 Wojciech Wrzesiński, author of study *Prusy Wschodnie w polskiej myśli politycznej
    1864–1945*. Olsztyn 1994, p. 135, based on special issue of the Warsaw "Dzień" of 27
    August 1914, which provided a reprint of Oleg's article from a magazine "Gołos Russi"
    that published a programme of postulated teritorial progres of Russia to the west.
13 Ibid., p. 136.
14 K. Jaroszyk: *Wspomnienia z Prus Wschodnich*. Olsztyn 1969, p. 32. Unless indicated
    otherwise all quotations in this text have been translated from Polish by the translator
    (trans.).
15 APO, pp. 259–161.
16 R. Juszkiewicz: *Działania bojowe na pograniczu północnego Mazowsza...*, pp. 352–353.

army[17]. In another part of East Prussia, on 4 and 5 August, dragoons of the 1st Dragoon Regiment "Prince Albrecht of Prussia" clashed with the tsarist troops[18]. A frontal attack on the so-called eastern front, which covered the northern Masovia and East Prussia, began in the second half of August 1914. R. Juszkiewicz suggests the date of 19 August[19]. The first big face-off was won by the I Corps. Subordinates of General Herman von François won the battle of Stołupiany. Another battle took place nearby Gąbin and was won by Russians.

Ineffective leadership of von Prittwitz, which put the whole East Prussia at risk, led to his removal from the post of a commander. According to the German researchers the change of commandership over the 8th Army was decided during a telephone conversation between Helmuth von Moltke, Maxem von Prittwitz und Graffon on 21 August[20]. A retired general, Paul von Beneckendorff und von Hindenburg, was chosen to replace him. On 22 August at 3 pm this elderly (over 60 years old) general received a telegram from Coblence asking if he was ready to accept the said function[21]. Erich Ludendorff – a hero of the western front battles – became his chief of staff.

The troops of the 8th Army were in retreat after their defeat in the battle of Gąbin. A fear of occupants caused that many people abandoned their homes and went into exile. This was the fate of Alexander zu Dohn, a young aristocrat who, fearing a Russian invasion, fled with his five siblings to their family Darmstadt[22].

Some East Prussians refugees stopped only beyond the Oder, some at their relatives' in an unoccupied part of the province. Thousands of exiles that had been sent beyond the Vistula stopped in the province capitol – Królewiec. At the end of August 12 000 people were transported to Gdańsk via the Vistula Lagoon[23].

In case of Giżycko the authorities ordered evacuation of its population probably in order to facilitate defense of the Boyen Fortress[24]. 800 thousand out of 2 million citizens went in exile. The number of refugees from East Prussia is

---

17 Ibid, s. 353.

18 Osterroht Hermann, *Geschichte des Dragoner=Regiments PrinzAlbreht von Preußen (Litthauisches) Nr 1 1717–1919*, Berlin 1930, pp. 299–300. These battles took place by Ejdkuny – Ejdkuny-Kibarty – on 4 August and by Szirwint – 5 August 1914.

19 R. Juszkiewicz: *Działania bojowe na pograniczu północnego Mazowsza...*, p. 351.

20 D. E.: Showalter, *Tannenberg 1914, Zderzenie Imperiów*, Warszawa 2005, p. 316.

21 Ibid, p. 324.

22 A. Fürst zu Dohna: *Schlobitten Erinnerungen eines alten Ostpreussen*, Berlin 1989, p. 68.

23 J. Jasiński: *Historia Królewca*, Olsztyn 1994, s. 230.

24 M. Szostakowska: *Prasa codzienna Prus Wschodnich od XVII do połowy XX wieku. Przewodnik do dziejów wydawniczych*. Toruń 2007, p. 114.

estimated at hundreds of thousands of people[25]. Some people fled for refuge in the nearest forests. A future Polish activist in East Prussia – Jan Boenigk – recalls in his book:

> Two days after the battle the people from Tomaszów returned to their homes. Nobody suffered any losses because the Russians neither stole nor destroyed anything. Landowners found all their livestock grazing in pastures. Only cows mooed painfully as their udders were full milk[26].

In consequence of military actions numerous East Prussian locations found themselves under Russian occupation. This group included among others Olsztyn, Nidzica, Szczytno, Ełk.

Olsztyn, since 1905 the seat of district authorities, was one of the most important locations under occupation. Reinhold Herbrig, a mechanic from a municipal power plant in Olsztyn, provided some interesting information concerning occupation of the city on the Łyna. This report is preserved in the APO holdings, in a volume concerning memories of the war, which was started on request of the Olsztyn magistrate[27]. The first Russian patrols entered Olsztyn in the evening of August 26. An anonymous Olsztyn citizen reported: "I stuck my head out from some alley of the old town to see these unwanted guests"[28]. According to witnesses when Russians entered the city on Thursday, 27 August, a vast majority of citizens had left Olsztyn[29]. An account of some anonymous Olsztyn resident serves as a confirmation of Herbrig's memories. This person described the Olsztyn streets during the entrance of the Russian troops: "Along our street the tenements that usually have up to 40 residents, are empty today – we are alone!"[30]. Clerks from the district office, the post and the railway management personnel secretly left Olsztyn at the very beginning[31]. A large part of the Olsztyn power plant staff was among the runaways. The only exception was Herbrig and another worker whose identity has not been determined. Their dutiful work enabled a continuous supply of power to the city. By contrast to the district clerks that had left Olsztyn, the municipal authorities, led by the supermayor Georg Zülch, remained in the city.

---

25 *Kalendarz Pruski Ewangelicki na 1916 rok*, p. 61. Up to 350 thousand people [from East Prussia] were for months in exile, spread throughout the whole Prussia, as far as to Hannover and Westfalen.

26 J. Boenigk: *Minęły wieki a myśmy ostali* Warszawa 1971, p. 47.

27 APO, Akta miasta Olsztyna, 259/156, *Kriegserlebnisse der Beamten*, k. 4.

28 *Kalendarz Królewsko-Pruski Ewangelicki na 1917 rok*, pp. 80–81.

29 Ibid.

30 Ibid, p. 81.

31 R. Bętkowski: *Olsztyn jakiego nie znacie*, Olsztyn 2010, p. 27.

The supermayor, faced with the approaching tsarist troops, appealed to the citizens not to provoke the occupant. This proclamation was supposed to be printed on 27 August but probably it was not distributed. The draft, along with handwritten notes, has been preserved in the APO fond[32]. The people of Olsztyn varied in their attitudes towards the occupant. There was some cases of impertinence:

> Suddenly one horse reared up. What's this? A drunkard or some daredevil caught it by the bridle and blocked the way of the whole patrol. A Russian soldier aimed at him but before he fired – a senior one pulled his hand and signalled that he should turn back[33].

Other people naively believed that a piece of paper with an appeal in Russian not to break into a given apartment would protect their possessions:

> Peaceful people live here and they did not escape for fear of you, Russian soldiers, but only went to their friends in…[street] You are kindly requested not to open the flat forcibly, nor to take anything from it. Otherwise, we will be forced to complain to your commander![34]

Most people approached the existing situation with calm and humility: "plenty uncovered their heads out of fear"[35].

The fate was kind for the Olsztyn people. The occupation lasted two days: 27–28 August 1914[36]. Mieczysław Orłowicz in *Ilustrowany przewodnik po Mazurach Pruskich i Warmii* wrote that the Russians demanded provision of 120 000 kg of bread, sugar, salt, pepper, rice and tea[37]. The order to bake so much bread was difficult to obey in the city with no bakers – all the bakers had left before the occupants arrived. And so the Olsztyn women baked the requested bread[38]. Pelagia Pieniężna, a wife of an editor of "Gazeta Olsztyńska", was one of the many women who volunteered to bake bread. The Russian commandership delegated a group of soldiers to help with the baking. Kannegieser – a master – baker – was responsible for selection of flour and for baking the demanded bread[39]. The ingredients came from the tsarist army's resources or purchased based on an occupation calculator according to which one rouble cost two German mark[40].

---

32 APO 259/168.
33 *Kalendarz Królewsko-Pruski Ewangelicki na 1917 rok*, pp. 80–81.
34 Ibid., p. 81.
35 Ibid.
36 Ibid.
37 M. Orłowicz: *Ilustrowany przewodnik po Mazurach Pruskich i Warmii*, p. 151.
38 *Kalendarz Królewsko-Pruski Ewangelicki na 1917 rok*, p. 86.
39 H. Leśniowski: *W cieniu bitwy pod Grunwaldem Tannenberg 1914 fakty, mity, legendy*, Olsztyn 2014, p. 61.
40 Ibid., p. 60.

Nidzica was under Russian occupation since 22 August. Andreas Kuhn, the city mayor of the time, left the following dramatic account for future generations: "A city which was burning in undiminished flames could be compared to hell on earth. The heat was so extreme that beautiful tilias along the pavement burnt and people could not bear this heat"[41]. Also Kalendarz Królewsko-Pruski Ewangelicki mentions the shelling. According to it 300 shells hit the city in one hour[42]. After entering the city, the occupation commander of Nidzica addressed the citizens and warned them that all citizens would be executed if there was fire opened on the Russian soldiers[43]. The warning was effective – local German authorities decided to hand over all weapons to the Russians to ensure the civilians' safety[44]. There was only one casualty of the Russians' entrance. A brick factory worker who was throwing bricks at the Russian troops got shot[45]. Other reports inform that a Russian patrol was attacked by an unknown East Prussian labourer who threw stones at them.

Kalendarz Królewsko-Pruski Ewangelicki of 1916 revealed a drama of people from the Masurian Lake District city of Szczytno. In some cases residents of this city were burnt alive:

> Russians not only put houses on fire but event burnt some live people in them. Cheering and shouting hordes were looking at this horrible spectacle. The infantry was guarding doors and windows with bayonets in order to send despairing residents back to the fire when they tried to escape. Russian officers committed similar terrible deeds on a father and two sons who were summoned to the army[46].

A local priest, Reverend Sack, left a written report of the occupation of Ełk from 9 August to 10 September 1914[47]. His report presents different types of behaviour of the Russian occupants. During the occupation of Ełk three different commanders governed the city. The first of them was a cavalry general – Scheidemann[48]. According to Sack during the rule of this officer the following persons were taken hostage: the city mayor Klein, superintendent Bury, Reverend Brehm, district commissioner doctor Peters. And more than 50 thousand German mark was taken

---

41 A. Kossert, *Prusy Wschodnie Historia i mit*, Warszawa 2009, p. 183.
42 Kalendarz Królewsko-Pruski Ewangelicki z 1916 r., p. 97.
43 Ibid., p. 97.
44 Ibid.
45 Ibid., p. 98.
46 Ibid., p. 100.
47 Kalendarz Królewsko-Pruski Ewangelicki z 1917 r., p. 94.
48 Ibid., p. 100.

from the magistrate cash register[49]. Captain Wittinghoff of the 169th regiment of infantry succeeded Scheidemann. Wittinghoff was an Evangelical and probably came from a family of the near-Baltic Germans. This officer can be associated with a contribution of 30 thousand rouble imposed on Ełk. The citizens were given a strict deadline of 36 hours, until 29 August, and if this amount had not been paid, the hostages, i.e. representatives of the local elite, would have been executed. These events have a very interesting background related to the German occupation of Kalisz. The Russian authorities informed the people of Ełk that the indicated amount of 30 thousand rouble was less than the amount demanded by the Germans from the people of Kalisz. Description of the tsarist army soldiers included in Kalendarz Królewsko-Pruski Ewangelicki of 1917 illustrates mentality of some of the occupants: "in my apartment a Russ crossed himself in front of the cross, turned it back, put it aside and rushed to steal from the other part of the room"[50]. A commander of the bridge staff behaved in a totally different way. He ordered his soldiers to pay tribute to a dead child during the passage of its funerary procession. The procession had to cross the bridge occupied by the Russian troops to get to the cemetery. The lieutenant commanding the bridge staff instructed his soldiers to show due respect in the face of death – "to show respect due to the dead even in front of a child's coffin"[51].

Działdowo was undoubtedly one of the most affected municipalities in East Prussia. Jan Salm quotes L. Goldstein and states that the warfare led to destruction of 1/3 of this city including 152 residential and public utility buildings[52]. A few volumes of files in the municipal magistrate were devoted to the losses incurred by Działdowo. According to the preserved archival documents also public utility buildings including the city hall, the firehouse and the school building were

---

49 There are some doubts as to the collected amount and the date of capturing the above listing persons. According to the data provided by priest Sack 52 thousand mark was taken from the safe and the starost, mayor and two priests were taken hostage during the rule of the second commander – Ełk pod Rusami, relacja księdza Sacka in: Kalendarz Królewsko-Pruski Ewangelicki z 1917 r., p. 94. APO – APO, O.P.O., 3/I/530, p. 46 provides different information on this issue: On 19 August Landrat, mayor, two clergymen, two council members, one member of Kreisausschusu were taken hostage and they still remain in captivity, interned in Skotowo by Władywostok.

50 Ibid., p. 101.

51 Ibid.

52 J. Salm: Odbudowa miast wschodniopruskich po I wojnie światowej, Olsztyn 2006, p. 125.

ruined[53]. The damages suffered by the hospital were estimated at nearly 3 500 German mark[54].

The fact that some locations were not defended did not stop the Russian army from destroying them[55].

Withdrawal was impeded by crowds of refugees who abandoned their houses, took their most important possessions and headed for the East. For instance, the 17th corps of August von Mackensen, which earlier suffered by Gąbin, encountered problems during its passage. It should be suspected that the German soldiers who had been trained to protect East Prussia and civil population, were reluctant to force their way through the crowds of refugees, to push them aside, turn over their carriages, throw away abandoned household equipment or destroy civilian property[56]. Roads were like Dante's hell. It must have been particularly heart -breaking to see children that had been separated from their parents during their flight from the warfare area[57]. It should be stressed that among others General Martos, the commander of the 15th Corps, took care of the lost East Prussian children[58].

East Prussia was an extraordinary province. The closest circles of the Emperor and his wife as well as the staff of the Imperial Royal army included people connected to this province. For example, the family of General Paul von Beneckendorff und von Hindenburg, the commander of the 8th Army that was defending East Prussia, had an estate in the vicinity of Iława. In consequence, nobody wanted to leave the province to its fate. In particular the owner of the Ponary estate- countess von der Gröben, tried to bring the fate of the East Prussian refugees to the attention of the royal court in Berlin[59]. Reverend Hensel from Pisz requested the parliament to help the ruined province:

> I personally, via my party, submitted to the Prussian parliament in Berlin an appeal to the authorities to try and rescue the captives. And the whole Reichstag supported this motion through their eldest leaders. Besides, I also transferred a list of the captives from my parish to the charity association in Stockholm in Sweden to enable the Red Cross

---

53 APO, *Akta miasta Działdowo*, 251/780, *Kriegsschäden der Stadt Soldau* p. 1, the losses incurred by the City Office were estimated at 10 450 German mark, those of the fire brigade – 4 640 mark and by the school – 43 265 mark.

54 APO, 251/782, p. 80.

55 APO, *OPO.*, 3/I/528, pp. 317–318, according to reports – despite the fact that there were no battle in Gołdapia, the city was destroyed.

56 D. E. Showalter, op. cit., 334.

57 Ibid., p. 286.

58 Ibid., p. 351.

59 APO, OPO., 3/I/529, pp. 128–129.

to look for them in Petersburg. Once the addresses are determined, we will be able to send these people some money via the Red Cross in Copenhagen to alleviate their fate[60].

The above fragment shows that the German authorities tried to use all means to support their compatriots in their ordeal. They even asked neutral countries such as Sweden or Denmark to mediate.

In 1914, following the victory over the Russian aggressor, a parliamentary committee travelled to East Prussia to assess war losses. The committee was composed of representatives of all political groups and options from conservative MPs (von der Osten Wernitz, doctor Busse, baron Maltzahn), through central parties, to social-democrats[61]. Baron von Zedlitz und Neukirch, doctors Kewoldt and Johanssen represented the Free Conservative Party (Freikonservativen Abgeordneten)[62]. Doctor von Lampe, Fuhrmann, Hirsch, Meyer and Westermann were National Liberals[63]. The following Reichstag members represented the centre: doctor Porsch, Herold, doctor von Savigny, Fleuster, Giesberts. Wojciech Korfanty represented Polish MPs from the German parliament[64]. Hirsch from Berlin was a social-democrat. The said parliamentary committee for assessment of wartime losses included also representatives of the government – a secret governmental counsellor (Geheimer Regierungsrat) Kutscher, Schmid – a governmental assessor from the Ministry of the Interior and von Velsen – a secret financial senior counsellor (Geheimer Oberfinanzrat) from the Ministry of Finance. The Ministry of Agriculture was represented by a secret senior counsellor (Geheimer Oberregierungsrat) Eggert[65].

According to the estimates of the above mentioned delegation 24 cities, 600 villages and 300 estates were completely or partially destroyed. 34 000 buildings were destroyed and more than 100 000 apartments were plundered during the warfare[66]. Jan Salm notes that Erich Göttgen in *Der Wiederaufbau Ostpreussens* stated that 100 thousand residential buildings and service buildings had been destroyed in consequence of acts of war, which to some degree overlaps with the data gathered by the governmental-parliamentary committee[67].

---

60 Kalendarz Królewsko-Pruski Ewangelicki z 1916 r., p. 64.
61 APO 10/238, p. 20.
62 Ibid., p. 20.
63 Ibid.
64 APO 10/238, p. 20.
65 Ibid.
66 APO 10/238, p. 21.
67 J. Salm, op. cit., p. 65, za E. Göttgen, *Der Wiederaufbau Ostpreussens. Eine kulturelle*, p. IX.

Table 1: Wartime losses in East Prussia during the Great War

Damage	Parliamentary-governmental committee	Erich Göttgen	J.E. Künzel	Provincial Monuments' Conservator in East Prussia – Richard Dethlefsen
Destroyed cities	24	Not indicated, may be analogous to the committee data	35	35
Destroyed villages and estates	600 villages and 300 estates	–	1900	1900
Destroyed buildings	34 000 buildings – more than 100 thousand apartments	More than 100 thousand residential and service buildings	3100 buildings destroyed in cities, 30 900 – in the country	24 400, out of 33 533 damaged buildings, were completely destroyed

Source: APO 10/238, s. 21 and Jan Salm, *Odbudowa miast wschodniopruskich po I wojnie światowej,* Olsztyn 2006, p. 65.

Sacral buildings also suffered in wartime: 2 Catholic churches were destroyed as well as 26 Protestant chapels and 3 synagogues[68].

---

68   Ibid., p. 65, based on *Vom Kirchenbau in Ostpreussen, OB – Z 1916.*

Table 2: *Estimated losses and cost of reconstruction according to the data of the governmental-parliamentary committee*

Powiat	Losses and damages	Estimated reconstruction costs	Loss of human life
Ostróda (Osterode)	Destruction of: Olsztynek, 19 villages and 5 estates; 884 buildings, 166 residential buildings, 259 buildings and 116 residential buildings were damaged to some degree	3 981 532 M	13 persons were imprisoned, out of which 9 were released after the Battle of Tannenberg, 10 persons were killed for no apparent reason, 5 were severely wounded
Nidzica (Neidenburg)	217 residential buildings, 2 churches, 184 service buildings were destroyed in Nidzica and Działdowo; 464 residential buildings, 1278 services buildings were destroyed in 63 rural *powiat* districts and in 20 estates. All locations were plundered		Ca. 2/3 of the *powiat* population
Szczytno (Ortelsburg)	800 residential buildings and 1475 service buildings were destroyed in 57 locations. 160 residential buildings and 321 service buildings were destroyed only in Szczytno. 12 locations suffered significant damages and 6 were almost completely destroyed	6 300 000 M	
Pisz (Johannisburg)	33 residential buildings – 133 apartments were burnt		86 civilians killed, 25 wounded

Powiat	Losses and damages	Estimated reconstruction costs	Loss of human life
Ełk (Lyck)	165 houses	17 000 000 M	300 persons murdered, 1 000 persons including women and children captured and taken to Russia
Olecko	All real estates were plundered		45 civilians were killed, 500 were captured in the Olecko *powiat*. 25 women got raped.
Gołdap (Goldap)	141 residential buildings were burnt		The city was under occupation twice. On the second occasion the Siberian troops were very hostile towards the local community. While leaving in panic on 10 September, the marksmen were firing at everyone from a tower – 5 persons, including one child, were wounded. The priest's maid was raped.
Stallupönen	1 000 residential and service buildings were completely destroyed.		
Pillkallen	864 residential buildings, 1 808 service buildings were destroyed. Houses were plundered.		109 men and 13 women were murdered, 507 men, 69 women and 121 children were captured.
Insterburg			
Darkehmen	354 residential buildings and 1 178 service buildings		

Powiat	Losses and damages	Estimated reconstruction costs	Loss of human life
Gerdauen	5 estates, 239 other residential buildings, 429 stables and sheds, 5 schools and 1 church were destroyed in this *powiat*.		8 persons were murdered, 14 women and girls raped.
Wehlau	This *powiat* was partially controlled by Russians (they did not get the northern and the western part). 169 residential buildings, 101 service buildings, 71 sheds, 144 stables as well as churches in Allenburgu, Grünhayn and Gr. Elgenau were destroyed.		8 persons were killed by Russians who also captured and took to Russia 251 people. In consequence of wartime activity the *powiat* population decreased from 47 179 to 41 312.

Source: APO 10/238 and Jan Salm: *Odbudowa miast wschodniopruskich po I wojnie światowej*, Olsztyn 2006.

Table 3: Duration of military occupation in East Prussia

Powiat (location)	Occupation period
Pisz (Johannisburg)	3 weeks, 08/09 1914, 11.1914–02.1915
Ełk (Lyck)	19.08–10.09.1914 07.10.1914–13.10.1914 7.11.1914–14.02.1915. According to the preserved archival materials Ełk was occupied for the total period of 130 days.
Olecko (Oletzko)	17.08–11.09.1914
Gołdap	17.08.1914–10.09.1914 05.11.1914–12.02.1915
Stallopönnen	18.08.1914–13.09.1914 07.11.1914–10.02.1915
Pillkalen	09.1914
Insterburg	22.08–11.09.1914; 11.1914–10.02.1915
Darkehmen	22.08.1914–11.09.1914

Powiat (location)	Occupation period
Gerdauen	24.08–10.09.1914
Wehlau	25.08.1914–10.02.1914
Ostróda (Osterode)	
Nidzica (Neidenburg)	Russians entered the city on 22 August 1914, in the evening
Szczytno (Ortelsburg)	

Source: Own calculation based on APO 10/238.

The Great War entailed suffering of civilians. Some murders committed on the German civilians were justified by the occupying authorities by saying they were a means of counteracting diversion on the part of the male population of East Prussia. Using this excuse or maybe in revenge for the defeat of Tannenberg, Russians executed several persons in Sątopy. On 16 August the following inscription was installed on their grave: „*Hier ruhen Anton Fittkau – Santoppen – 24 Jahre alt Franz Gischarowski – 29 Julius Gosse – 57, Bernhard Käse – 17, Anton Neuwald – 69, Daniel Rittel – 58, Bernhard'''' – 22, Valentin Rogall, Franz Stockdreher – 40, Franz Weiss – 58, Peter Görigk – Heinrichdorf – 59, Franz Gerigk – 59, Prof. August Kallweit – Rössel – 56, Katharina'''' – 59, Barbara Lompa – Warpuhnen –52, Paul'''' – 16*. A local parish priest, Anton Werner, died in dramatic circumstances. He was executed by Russians on 28 August 1914.

Apart from the above listed crimes also other groundless murders were committed. On 31 August a Cossack patrol raided the Lengainen estate of von Oppenkowski and for no obvious reason murdered (executed) a 20-year-old worker Paul Fommerdich[69].

The outbreak of the war caused distrust, fear of strangers, especially of foreigners. Włodzimierz Borodziej and Maciej Górny write about a spymania[70]. The civilian population showed some distrust towards both the occupying army and to their own soldiers. In the face of an approaching front the commandership of the 8th German Army ordered to build watchtowers on hills. They were serviced by teenage boys – "Wooden watchtowers were located on hills. Teenage boys were equipped with bikes so that they could serve as messengers. A few German spies disguised as teenage boys or even as women were caught. When the staff of the 1st

---

69 APO 3/528, p. 43.
70 W. Borodziej and M. Górny, *Nasza Wojna*, Tom I, *Imperia 1912–1916*, Warszawa 2014, p. 115.

Army was notified about these incidents, an order was issued to "check carefully". General Gurko, irritated by the order, supposedly said to officers around him: "They went mad in the staff. I will not check what each woman in East Prussia has under her skirt"[71]. The APO holdings contain a file – *Weltkriegs 1914–1918. Sammlung von Flugblättern, Extrablättern, Behörden Bekanntmachungen*[72] which provides information about an arrest and execution of a person suspected of spying for Russians. The alleged spy supposedly sent secret data to the Russian military intelligence by means of pigeons of his own breeding[73].

By contrast to cities that suffered relatively little damage, numerous villages were completely ruined during the war. Uzdowo, which was basically blasted by the "steamroller of war", is a case in point:

> Around 11 Germans entered Uzdowo. They saw a terrible sight: earth bruised by missiles, crushed tree trunks, broken barbed wire barriers, abandoned rucksack and various weapons – from rifles and ammunition to grenades. And corpses. Stacks of dead or dying Russians. Some of them were in convulsions, others were crying for help. Among the dead soldiers- horses, also the victims of the war, with torn bellies, without legs, with crushed heads. The village buildings were still on fire. A horrible, acrid smoke was hanging low above the ground. The source of the smoke was soon determined- human bodies were burning in destroyed basements and under ruined foundations. The victorious party was in a hurry to leave the devastated village[74].

The above description can be applied to hundreds of East Prussian villages that fell victim to fire. In the Gierdawo *powiat* 50 buildings were consumed by fire in the village of Schiffus, slightly fewer – 48 – in Neuendorf, 29 in Gr. Bahohren, 23 in Doyen, 20 in Altendorf, 19 in Sutzken[75]. The already mentioned Jan Salm quotes *Der ostpreussische Provinzialkonservator über den Wiederaufbau der Provinz, OB – Z 1916* and states that 1900 rural *gminas*[76] were destroyed[77]. Reverend Link left an account of how Karwia, a village in the Pisz *powiat*, was plundered. As an eye witness of such dramatic events the priest stated: "now I have seen what is ahead

---

71 H. Leśniowski, op. cit., p. 25.
72 APO, Akta miasta Olsztyna, 259/161–167.
73 APO, Akta miasta Olsztyna, 259/161.
74 Ibid., p. 57.
75 APO, 10/238, p. 55.
76 *Gmina* is the principal unit of administrative division of Poland as "commune" or "municipality".
77 J. Salm, op. cit., p. 65.

of us. I saw from my window that they were intentionally destroying houses one by one"[78].

Another report is not a first-hand account but is based on comments of direct witnesses. A Cossack troop was ordered by their commander to put the village on fire. However, earlier they caused severe injuries (by means of spike; to breasts, back and arm) to a 76-year-old Bolesta, put fire to a house with a 90-year-old terminally ill woman (who died after 8 days of suffering – her legs and back were burnt) and injured a 14-year-old boy on the head[79].

The already mentioned Reverend Link fell victim to barbarism of the Cossack soldiers. He described his vicarage in the following way:

> This terrible mess at my place! Beyond words. Everything from the shop downstairs to the very top has been checked, destroyed. Luckily, only a few pieces of furniture have been damaged. Nobody will believe there can be such mess on the floor until they see my apartment. Bed sheets, clothes, papers, books, in short – everything – was in complete mess and marked with the stamp of the dreadful Russian offenders. The Russian stench could be smelt in the house for a long time[80].

The stories of women on the area occupied by Russians were very dramatic. Many rapes and gang rapes were committed. It can be supposed that for rapists it did not matter how old the victims were – among others a 57-year-old Joanna Capeller fell victim to a gang rape (raped 6–7 times)[81]. A testimony of August Ney related to a gang rape on his wife – three times in his apartment, once in the presence of his neighbour – proves that the rapists had no inhibitions about such crimes[82]. Many women and young girls got pregnant – among them Julia Boczkowska who provided the following account:

Since 1 November 1913 I was a chambermaid in Marggrabowa for Karl Block, a cattle trader. My employers did not live in Marggrabowa since the announcement of mobilisation. I was there alone with my employer's brother-in-law, a flour trader from Marggrabowa. At the beginning of November Russians returned to Marggrabowa. On 10 November about 6 o'clock I went to a service building and got attacked and raped by two Russians. As a result I got pregnant[83]. Children born

---

78 *Teraz wiedziałem, co nas czekało. Od okna widziałem, jak oni umyślnie dom za domem rozbili*, Kalendarz Królewsko-Pruski Ewangelicki z 1917 r., p. 105.

79 APO, *O.P.O.*, 3/I/528, p. 51.

80 Kalendarz Królewsko-Pruski Ewangelicki z 1917 r., p. 107.

81 APO, *O.P.O.*, 3/I/529, p. 278.

82 APO, O.P.O., 3/I/529, pp. 295–296.

83 APO, O.P.O., 3/I/530, p. 9.

of rape were referred to as *Russenkinder* – "Russian children"[84]. Their mothers were entitled to a monthly allowance of 20 German mark which was granted to women who placed their children for adoption as well as to women who decided to keep their children – to breastfeeding mothers[85]. After the occupying party had left, Julia Boczkowska and other girls in similar situation fled to West Germany. *In February Russians left Marggrabowa and I escaped with other servant-girls who had been raped by Russians to the Stade district in Hannover. I stayed with the wife of Stüven, a trader. On 2 July I went to a hospital for women*[86].

Also a girl who before the war had worked in an estate nearby Tylża used the allowance for mothers of the "Russian children". She was raped and got pregnant and delivered in 1915. She was eligible for the allowance which she received from a local self-government in the vicinity of Bremen where she settled after leaving East Prussia[87].

Among others an organisation called *Provinzial Verein für innere Mission* and led by Reverend Kern provided support for injured girls and women[88]. This organization (as well as other similar institutions) managed to find 300 families in Germany which were willing to take care of raped women and their children[89].

In consequence of these rapes many girls and women contracted venereal diseases. The treatment costs were covered by voluntary donations[90]. Not only Evangelical church took care of these women as not only Evangelical women fell victims to rapes. A rabbi, doctor Vogelstein, was involved in this issue as a representative of Jews[91]. The Warmia bishop, Andrzej Thiel, and the Chełmno bishop, Augustyn Rosentreter, were also engaged in supporting Catholic girls who had been raped by Russian soldiers[92]. This interest in the fate of Catholic girls, mothers of unwanted "Russian children", was an outcome of correspondence exchanged between Kern and the Warmia bishop as wells as of the communication between the Warmia and the Chełmno bishops[93].

---

84 APO, O.P.O., 3/I/530, p. 27.
85 APO, O.P.O., 3/I/529, p. 396.
86 APO, O.P.O., 3/I/530, p. 9.
87 APO, O.P.O., 3/I/529, pp. 382–383.
88 APO, O.P.O., 3/I/529, pp. 137–138, document dated 27 July 1915.
89 Ibid.
90 APO, O.P.O., 3/I/529, pp. 137–138.
91 Ibid.
92 Ibid.
93 APO, O.P.O., 3/I/529, p. 136.

This article would not be exhaustive if it did not cover the issue of education in East Prussia. The Great War period was a difficult time for East Prussian education which suffered in terms of infrastructure, the damage to the Działdowo school can serve as an example. Additionally, there was also a significant loss of human life both among active teachers and among the youth that was studying to work in education (in the interwar period a memorial plague was placed on the wall of the Olsztynek College for Teachers. The plaque listed the names of students and graduates that were killed on the fronts of the great War). When entering Flammberg, Russian soldiers shot a local teacher. The other one – William Kloss was taken to Russia. This information was provided to the committee for assessment of wartime losses in East Prussia by the wife of the captured pedagogue[94]. Teachers and people involved in education were among the unfortunates that were taken to Russia. The said William Kloss, captured on 9 September 1914, was one of them[95].

The Great War was already started on these areas during the first days of August 1914 through the invasion of the Russian army. In 1914–1915 the front travelled through East Prussia twice.

Tragic circumstances of civilian population were worsened by the fact that a vast majority of this population living in the southern regions (natives of Warmia and Masuria) was of Polish descent. The Poles were also numerous in the ranks of the tsarist army. The 2nd Army, referred to as "Warszawa", which was formed in the Kingdom of Poland and commanded by General Aleksander Samsonow, included only one fully Russian corps[96].

It can be claimed that the fate of East Prussian population depended on the nationality of occupying soldiers of the Russian army. The situation of communities under occupation of troops consisting of the Poles and Russians from the European part of the empire was better. The situation of people in locations occupied by ill-famous Cossacks or soldiers from Siberia was tragic.

Germany lost the Great War. The German state incurred huge losses in terms of its population and territory. Poland, reborn after 123 years, got access to the sea, which was only possible at the expense of Germany. A plebiscite was to determine

---

94 Ibid, p. 8.
95 Ibid.
96 D. Radziwiłłowicz: *Tradycja grunwaldzka w świadomości politycznej społeczeństwa polskiego w latach 1910–1945*, Olsztyn 2003, p. 71, based on J. Giertych: *Tysiąc lat historii polskiego narodu*, T. III, Londyn 1986, p. 13. Only one army corps by Tannenberg – XIII Smolensk corps – was composed only of Russian. Other corps consisted mainly of the Polish people, reservists conscripted on the spot.

the future of Warmia, the Masurian Lake District and Powiśle. Germany won in the plebiscite but the area of East Prussia was reduced – Poland got Działdowo with adjacent areas. The below table presents changes in the territory and population of the province in question.

Table 4: Changes in population and territory of East Prussia in 1910–1920[97].

Province area	Location (*powiat*)	Population	Year	Men	Women	Total
37002,0 km²	Olsztyn	33077	12.1910 (this data was valid till 1914)	1003340	1060835	2064175
37002,0 km²	Gąbin	14540	12.1910	–	–	–
37002,0 km²	Królewiec	245994	12.1910	–	–	–
37002,0 km²	Braniewo	13601	12.1910	–	–	–
37002,0 km²	Ostróda	14364	12.1910	–	–	–
37002,0 km²	Ełk	13428	12.1910	–	–	–
36988,3 km²	Olsztyn	34731	08.10.1919	1060796	1168491	2229290
36988,3 km²	Gąbin	17374	1921	–	–	–
36988,3 km²	Królewiec	260896	1921	–	–	–
36988,3 km²	Braniewo	13076	1921	–	–	–
36988,3 km²	Ostróda	14826	1921	–	–	–

The data in the above table is derived from yearbooks of the 1910–1920 decade.

Occupation of the discussed province lasted from August 1914 to February 1915. On 17 February 1915 Emperor Wilhelm II arrived in the destroyed Ełk[98]. In his address to the people of Ełk the Emperor described Masuria as a desert and promised to do his utmost to rebuild this area. The histories of occupied locations differ – some were occupied for a short period only (e.g. Olsztyn) while others found themselves under occupation even twice in a short term- Gołdap or Insterburg. Some of them, for instance Działdowo or Ełk, suffered huge material losses. Germany as well as some cities of the Habsburg Empire (e.g. Vienna) helped to rebuild

97 http://www.digizeitschriften.de/dms/img/?PPN=PPN5144013031913&DMDID=dm
   dlog8 and http://www.digizeitschriften.de/dms/img/?PPN=PPN514401303 1920.
98 S. Czerep: *Operacja wschodniopruska 1915 r., Wielka Wojna na Mazurach 1914–1915*.
   Giżycko 2014, p. 238.

East Prussia. Twin cities were established in order to facilitate the reconstruction process. Nidzica- Cologne can be a case in point since Cologne took patronage of the reconstruction of Nidzica. The province authorities supported by the Prussian government set and controlled the rules for the reconstruction process and its management. In case of Nidzica they established an office of a local architect whose task was to coordinate the whole process and manage the office of construction advisory. It should be added that the enthusiasm and good organisation of an architect in a given city was very important. In many cases Russian prisoners-of-war were involved in the cleaning and removal of wartime damages[99].

---

99 APO 3/I/527, p. 81.

Magdalena Żakowska
Faculty of International and Political Studies
University of Lodz

Ivan and aria for the dying world. The image of Russia in the propaganda of the central powers during the Great War

> The war in which we did not want to believe broke out, and brought –
> disappointment. It is not only bloodier and more destructive than any
> foregoing war, as a result of the tremendous development of weapons
> of attack and defense, but it is at least as cruel, bitter and merciless
> as any earlier war. It places itself above all the restrictions pledged
> in times of peace, the so-called rights of nations; [...] [and] it hurls
> down in blind rage whatever bars its way as though there were to be
> no future and no peace among men after it is over.
>
> S. Freud, *Reflections on War and Death* (1918)

It is difficult to talk about one single image of Russia in the propaganda of the central powers during the Great War, as the factors that shaped its image in each country were very complex. Firstly, the image of Russia had other characteristics central power before 1914. It was regarded by Germany as a superpower, until recently an allied one, that could still pose a military threat as an ally of France (Kissinger 1996, pp. 180–182, Ferguson 1992, p. 733). For Austria-Hungary, Russia was a long-time rival in the Balkans, which, through a panslavic ideology, had a negative impact on the Slavic subjects of a multinational empire (Kissinger 1996, pp. 223–227, Dedijer 1984, pp. 200–230). In the Ottoman Empire, Russia was perceived as a traditional aggressor and the most dangerous of the European colonial superpowers (Brummett 2000, p. 15). Bulgarian policy-makers regarded the tsarist country as an Orthodox empire which a long time ago, had helped Bulgaria to gain independence but later tried to turn the country into its protectorate (Tanty 2003, pp. 22–29).

The conviction that Russia only partially belonged to Europe and European civilisation was a common feature of the images of Russia shared by the nationals of the central powers. In their opinion, the tsarist country aspired to become "Europe", and had applied the western model during modernisation, but still many of its features made it more similar to traditional Oriental societies. The anachronistic nature of the tsarist autocracy was emphasised, as well as the Russian backwardness, oppression of peasants, drunkenness, superstitiousness and illiteracy (Wolff 1994, pp. 130–170; Łódź 1997, pp. 113–114, Łódź 2006, pp. 300–312). However, even this common conviction entailed slightly different semantic connotations in each of the said countries. In countries such as Germany or Austria-Hungary, the idea of the Russian backwardness was often accompanied by notions of the Russians' racial inferiority and of the Germans' cultural mission among the Slavs. In case of Turkey, we can say that the tsarist country was perceived as a kind of alter ego of the "sick man of the Balkans" (Brummett 2000, p. 165). Yet, the Bulgarian society positively valued a series of features distinguishing Russia from "enlighted" European countries, such as the Russian devotion to tradition and religion (Чавдарова 2000, pp. 201–203, 9, Oroschakoff 2007, pp. 264–265).

Likewise the presentation of other sides of the conflict in international propaganda was particularly important for formation of the image of Russia. In the Entente countries, the Germans were depicted as contemporary Huns: barbarians that had attacked a neutral Belgium, destroyed its cultural heritage and violated the rights of the civilian population (Jelavich 1999, pp. 42–47). Consequently, one of the main objectives of the propaganda under the Emperor Wilhelm was to attest that the Germans were waging a war in a more civilised way than their enemies (Coup. 1992, pp. 27–29). An analogous situation emerged in Turkey. An aggressive nationalistic regime, supported by Germany, created the image of the Ottoman Empire as a victim of the aggression of the European superpowers (Kiliç 2011, pp. 238–241). In turn, the Habsburg Monarchy, faced with relative military weakness and internal ethnic conflicts (Goll, Franzens 2013, pp. 91–95; Beller 1999, pp. 127–129). put particular emphasis on demonstrating examples of the military superiority and patriotism of the soldiers in the Imperial-Royal army as well as the weaknesses of its enemies. In turn, Bulgaria, which was hated by the Balkan nations, tried in its propaganda to ignore the fact that its enemies were allied with the powerful Grandpa Ivan[1] (Kelbetcheva 1999, p. 227).

The rules governing the preparation of mass media messages were another important factor affecting the creation of the wartime image of Russia in the central powers' propaganda. The Great War initiated the development of an organised, state-controlled propaganda machine. Public institutions established especially for this purpose not only participated in the production of materials to be distributed

---

1   The term "Grandpa Ivan" ("Дядо Иван") functions in the Bulgarian language as a synonym of Russia understood as a saviour – country, a mighty defender and a bastion of the Orthodox religion (Aretov 2011, p. 69).

through posters, press or film tape, but also exerted censorship on private media, in particular on the press market. This phenomenon concerned all central powers but Germany to the greatest extent. Moreover, especially at the beginning of the conflict, they were accompanied by auto-censorship. At that time, in a burst of wartime enthusiasm, even the editors of magazines which had been so far regarded as critical towards the government started to propagate pro-war slogans driven by their opportunism (Coup. 1992, pp. 23–24; Jelavich 1999, pp. 32–34; cf. Dimitrova 2005, pp. 183–184).

Finally, the ranking of the Russian Empire in the hierarchy of enemies was also significant. For Germany and Austria-Hungary, Russia was, just like France and Great Britain, a deadly enemy with which both central powers were in conflict from the outbreak of the war to the separatist peace treaty of 3 March 1918. Turkey battled the tsarist country, first by the Black Sea, next in the Caucasus, from October 1914 to the outbreak of the October Revolution. Bulgaria, in turn, found itself in a state of war with Russia in October 1915. In practice though, the Bulgarian armies fought the Russian forces only in the second half of 1916 during the Bulgarian-Romanian war for Dobruja (Tanty 2003, p. 133; Dąbrowski 1937c, pp. 105–117).

My thesis will analyse the main metaphors and visual motifs accompanying the mass media communication concerning Russia in the following, most representative satirical magazines published in Germany, Austria, Turkey and Bulgaria during the Great War.

Germany	*Der Wahre Jacob* – a magazine representing social-democratic views[2] *Simplicissimus* – a liberal periodical[3] *Kladderadatsch* – a magazine with a rightish-conservative attitude[4]
Austria	*Kikeriki* – a magazine with a conservative profile, representing antisemitic views[5]
Turkey	*Karagöz* – a leftish-liberal magazine
Bulgaria	*Baraban* – a liberal periodical[6]

---

2   Published in Hamburg and then in Stuttgart from 1879 to 1933. During World War I it reached a circulation of over 160 000 copies.

3   Published in Munich from 1896 to 1967 with a break from 1944 to 1954. At the beginning of the 20th century it reached a circulation of ca. 85 000 copies.

4   Published in Berlin from 1848 to 1944. During World War I it reached a circulation of over 40 000 copies.

5   Published in Vienna from 1861 to 1933. At the height of its popularity it reached a circulation of 25 000 copies.

6   Established in Sofia in 1909.

What changes did the Great War cause in the European satirical discourse? What changes in the vision of the tsarist empire – a hostile empire – were reflected in the above mentioned newspapers?

The Great War firstly fostered patriotic enthusiasm, then a trauma which had a great impact on all aspects of life of the societies caught in its stream. Undoubtedly, it also influenced hyperbolisation of satirical media. In the satirical discourse which developed in the second half of the 19th century, Russia was visualised by means of three main images: "Ivan", a ruling Tsar and "a Russian bear". The figure of "Ivan" alluded to a stereotypical image of a Russian peasant: bearded, muscular and wearing a peasant's homespun coat; and to a firmly rooted image of a Cossack: with slanting eyes, wearing a fur cap and waving a knout. As such it was partly a variation on the theme of the Russian auto-stereotype. Caricatures of individual tsars reflected, usually in a truthful but also humorous way, their posture, facial features and even personal characteristics: Their clothing was stylised as a Cossack's clothes and the Russian rulers held knouts in their hands. On the other hand, "the Russian bear" was usually a large and dangerous animal which was cast in three main roles: as a predator lounging on the world map, as a trained chained animal, or most often, simply as a member of the European bestiary of countries. What is important is the fact that the figure of "the Russian bear", by contrast to popular symbols of other countries such as John Bull, the British lion, Marianne or the Gallic rooster, was not imported to the European repertoire of images of Russia as a symbol with which the Russians themselves would identify, but was an invention of Western Europe (de Lazari, Riabow, Żakowska 2013, p. 11, 109).

What changes in the images did the war cause? On the outbreak of the war, the world of well-known images was coloured with an unprecedented pathos and venom within the messages, which were intended to disparage and kill the enemy. Later, the trauma of a never-ending war led to an unprecedented public cry for peace and to the accusation that the enemies were scuttling the peace reinstatement (Coup. 1992, p. 27). All the above phenomena were reflected in the central powers' satirical discourse concerning Russia.

In order to systematise the multitude of narrative threads and metaphors present in the said discourse, four dominant visions of the tsarist country were identified. In addition, the analysis also presents the degree to which they were reflected in the press of the individual countries of the coalition against the Entente.

The conclusions are presented in the table below:

		Visible presence in .... satirical discourse			
		German	**Turkish**	**Austrian**	**Bulgarian**
Type of image / **Motifs:**	**Aggressor**	Ivan / Russian bear			
		Asian horde			
	Giant with feet of clay	Russian bear / Ivan			
		Two-headed eagle / Nicolas II		Two-headed eagle	
		Submotif: Rasputin			
				Father Frost	
	Country of tyrants	Nicolas II / Ivan the Cossack / Submotifs: / A peasant in shackles / Orthodox church / Winter Palace / Mother Russia / Rasputin			
	Grandpa Ivan	Ivan			Grandpa Ivan
		Good revolutionists			

The following part of the paper discusses the four key characteristics in greater detail.

Aggressor

The image of Russia as an aggressor, or one of the aggressors, was a leading motif in the German and Turkish propaganda, especially at the beginning of the war. The motif of a barbarian beast attacking the defenseless inhabitants of a peaceful land is clearly reflected in the titles of the caricatures: "Tamerlan" (ill. 1), "Testament of Peter the Great" ("Das Testament…" 1915, p. 8341) or "Hell on the Balkans" ("Das Inferno…" 1914).

The engraving entitled "Tamerlan" published in the German magazine *Der Wahre Jacob* on 3 September 1915 aims at convincing the addressee that the Russian forces are a destructive power. Although the enemy army is not visible, we can see fire and a column of smoke resembling a whirlwind that is swirling over the river and a burnt-down, abandoned city. German and Austrian soldiers standing on the other side of the river are silent witnesses of this destruction. The caption under the illustration says that "according to the order given to the Russian army, the scorched earth tactics is applied while the army withdraws"[7]. We can assume that the drawing refers to the end of August 1915 when the German and Austrian armies crossed the River Bug, and, in particular, to 26 August when they took the Brest fortress, abandoned by the Russians, and set the town on fire. The author is clearly juxtaposing two worlds in the engraving. On the one side, we can see calm soldiers on bikes, on the other – an invisible enemy who, like a leader of an Asian horde, does not hesitate to use cruel attacks against civilians.

The cartoonist's ideas cannot be questioned as they refer to the summer of 1915, when the Russian military authorities announced the relocation of the local population and the destruction of houses and crops within the area of military activity in order to impede the passage of foreign troops. In consequence, although "there were attempts to [...] confine this destruction programme to incidents of "wartime necessity", it was implemented on a large scale" so that "whole spreads of land were consumed by fires of villages and crops or even standing crops, [and] thousands of people were driven to forced exile" (Dąbrowski 1937b, p. 113). Yet one cannot overlook the signs of hypocrisy in the above described German propaganda. Firstly, in 1914, German public opinion reacted with enthusiasm to the acts of destruction by the German armies on enemy territory, including the burning of the Belgian city of Louvain, which also included its 15th century university library. Secondly, the author of the drawing omitted the fact that he was commenting on the course of a victorious passage of his own country's army through the territory of Russia, which they were conquering.

The exuberant ambitions of the tsarist country were in turn stigmatised, among others, in a caricature entitled "Testament of Peter the Great". The caricature depicts Nicolas II and a Russian clergyman with a cross who are rushing a monstrous polar bear stamping over dead bodies: "Here lies Constantinople, my teddy bear; we must have it even if thousands should to die for it". The main character of a drawing entitled "Hell on the Balkans" is Ivan, a Cossack, who, by waving a curved sabre, forces the Balkan rulers to withdraw in the bloody whirl of the conflict.

Russia as an embodiment of evil appears also in caricatures that present it in the company of other Entente superpowers. This can be seen, for instance, on a poster-like drawing "Through" (Heine 1914, p. 1), where the German Michel acts as Saint George fighting, among others, the Russian bear. The motif of the three

---

7   Henceforth, all quotations in the text have been translated by the translator unless indicated otherwise.

attackers was used also for example in a Turkish caricature "Theme of the day" of 1914, showing the Entente countries as a band of criminals flinging with knives at the map of the world. However, their plan fails because of a German soldier who chases them away with his clenched fist. The figure of the Russian particularly attracts the reader's attention since he is in the central part of the drawing, between the Englishman and the Frenchman. Besides, he is the largest and the most threatening of all the attackers. His Russian uniform and the beard make him resemble "Ivan" – an image of a Russian deeply rooted in the European caricature of that time. The Russian is more rapacious thanks to the knife (dagger?) in his hand and the peak of his cap, which covers one eye and lends him the appearance of a pirate. Also, his name, Ayikoff ["Beardov"], appears as the first word in the caption under the drawing.

It is also worth noting that the narratives with the participation of the Russian aggressor were generally composed according to the rule of contrast. Figures juxtaposed against him were always innocent: defenseless victims, brave defenders, neutral soldiers or witnesses condemning the criminals. Additionally, the narrative style accompanying the said drawings should also be emphasised as it was often epic and gave the presented reality the rank of a historical tale or even a religious aspect.

A giant with feet of clay

However, it was the image of Russia as a giant with feet of clay that became a leitmotif of satirical discourse concerning the tsarist country, which was construed in the press of the central powers. This image, present in the propaganda of all states fighting against the Entente countries, was arguably, best reflected in the Austrian satire. Russia, shown directly or implicitly as a giant on feet of clay, was to be a superpower "only for show". It appeared powerful but in reality it was losing against seemingly weaker opponents. The reason for Russia's failure was first of all the lack of heart for the fight, demoralisation and detachment from reality of the army leaders and the Russian political elite, as well as a social relaxation caused by the revolutionary fever. How was this emphasised in the content and symbolic meaning of individual caricatures?

The drawing of the "Giant with feet of clay" published at the beginning of the war in the Austrian magazine *Kikeriki*, suggests that the contemporary weapons of the Russian army would not suffice in the face of the anachronistic, rigid structure of the state and poor logic preventing fast military manoeuvres (ill. 2). The size and population of the Russian empire are its advantages but the "fragile" economic potential and poor infrastructure are its weaknesses. Large, old Ivan, presented in the caricature, groans under the weight of badly chosen equipment and orders coming from all directions, and, in consequence, cannot defend himself from seemingly weaker enemies. A six-pointed star, resembling the Star of David, is an interesting artefact placed on the Russian's cap. It is not easy to interpret the meaning it has in the drawing. Maybe the cartoonist wanted to make reference to the fact that Russia's accession to war was accompanied by declarations of support for the government from all political and ethnic groups in the empire, including the Jews, who were strongly discriminated by the tsardom (cf. *Documents…*). Therefore, the Star of David could serve as a mocking metaphor of a miraculous nation-wide unity of the Russian society[8].

Another drawing, published in *Kikeriki* at the beginning of war, juxtaposed an authentic baptism of fire of the Archduke Charles, a young successor to the throne, against the conduct of Tsar Nicolas II. The tsar, instead of going to the front, only posed for a leader and the father of the nation and in reality was only fighting with stress related to the war and stayed in his bed covered with pillows, like in the Princess and the Pea. There were also some allusions made to the poor morale and drunkenness in the Russian army. For instance, a drawing entitled "An illustrated Serbian proverb: We are not alone!" suggests that overconsumption of vodka was the only impressive trait of a Russian soldier during the war ("Illustriertes Schlagwort…" 1914).

The external causes of Russia's weakness were also indicated. On the one hand, it was suggested that the other Entente countries were exploiting their Eastern ally in terms of its military potential. This was, among others, reflected in a caricature depicting a lying, extremely exhausted Russian bear which the allied countries try to awaken by forcing money into its muzzle and by brutal attempts to roll the bear over onto its feet ("Die russische Offensive" 1917). On the other hand, the cartoonists emphasise the military superiority of their own army as well as those of the allied armies. This can be seen in the drawing where the German and Austrian eagles are savaging the two-headed eagle of the Romanov empire. The two-headed eagle holds a knout in its paw, has the image of Saint George on its breast and is chained to the ball- a symbol of the revolution ("Der europäische Krieg" 1914). Since the main objective of the described messages was to humiliate the enemy, its presentation is dominated by a humoristic (at least supposedly) narrative style which is full of irony.

---

8   It should be stressed that *Kikeriki* was a magazine with a visible anti-semitic profile and, among others, with a critical attitude towards assimilation of Jews with the Austrian society.

The question concerning the political context surrounding creation of such messages remains to be answered. Undoubtedly, the messages were intended to convince fellow countrymen that the enemy was much more dangerous than it might seem. Such communication is justified when it is necessary to improve the self-confidence of the people and their faith in victory. The said context is clearly perceivable during analysis of the content of the above quoted caricatures. Allusions to the weakness of the Russian leadership and to the morale in the army were probably intended to perform a compensating function in a country such as Austria-Hungary. This country, at the verge of war, possessed a well-equipped army that was often wrongly commanded and had poor morale related to the anti-militaristic attitude of the Czechs, "undermining of the trust in monarchy in the Croats and Slovenians, explicit antipathy of the Italians from Istria and Damatia, [or] obvious hostility of the Bosnians" (Grodziski 1983, pp. 174–175). Likewise, the accentuation of the bravery of the Austrian leaders was, arguably intended to charm the reality. As Stanislaw Grodziski observes, what the elderly Emperor Franc Josef valued most in Archduke Charles was his obedience, and so the Emperor did everything he could to prevent him from being independent. Although at the beginning of the war he assigned him to the main headquarters, he soon requested his return to Schönbrunn.

Country of tyrants

Another motif – Russia as a bastion of global tyranny – was publicised in the German socialist press. Cartoonists of *Der Wahre Jacob* stressed, with emphasis and pathos, the tragic fate of the Russian nation which continues to live as in the pagan days, of the Jewish people haunted with slaughters, of the Poles and Fins tormented with the policy of Russification. The gap between the Tsar and the nation was emphasised as well as the gap between the Tsar's imperial policy and the slogans about freedom that were used to justify it. Finally, people expressed their hopes that the war will destroy the Russian *ancient regime* and lead to introduction of a democratic system in Russia.

It should be noted that the press was equally critical of the role that representatives of the Orthodox church and, generally, the Orthodox religion, played in Russia. It was suggested that a direct connection existed between the deep religiousness of Nicolas II and his alienation from his own nation, as well as his incapability to assume a rational view of reality. An illustration published on 4 September 1914 on the title page of *Der Wahre Jacob* (ill. 3) is a suggestive example of a caricature referring to the image of the monarch as a bloody tyrant, an image which, as we must add, was formed already during the revolution of 1905. It depicted Nicolas Romanov as a contemporary incorporation of Richard III, haunted by ghosts of the Jews whose slaughters he did not prevent and of the Poles crying over the independence they lost through the fault of his predecessors. The title: "Dear Jews and Poles of the Tsar") – a quotation from the wartime speeches of Nicolas II addressed to the empire nations (cf. Dąbrowski 1937a, p. 147) – is contrasted to the macabre content of the illustration. Moreover, the Tsar turns his eyes away from both the apparitions that are tormenting him and from the bloody hands. And the Orthodox cross he desperately clutches in his hand seems to be his only comfort.

It would be fair to include the drawings depicting Grigorij Rasputin published in *Der Wahre Jacob* in this category of caricatures. His presence beside the tsar was supposed to make the monarch, staring at the phantasmagoria of a monk, overlook the anger of the revolutionists and the bombs aimed at him ("Hofvergnügen..." 1916).

Was this humanistic discourse. based on empathy towards "the injured and the humiliated". fully selfless considering that it concerned problems tormenting a hostile superpower? Without a doubt, there is no denying it was authentic if only for the reason that the description of the plagues affecting Russia was not accompanied by the motif of *Schedenfreude*, but by rhetorics of pathos alluding to the Biblical trait[9] and the Shakespearean tragedy.

It is difficult to talk about a premeditated message of the picture "War for Peace in Russia" ("Der Kampf..." 1917) of December 1917, which condemns the cruelty of the Russian civil war and accompanies the following commentary:

> Warum ist der Haß der Brüder soviel stärker in der Schlacht?
> Warum ist das Volk nicht einig, wenn es im Besitz der Macht?
> Nach dem **einen** soll der Frieden auferglühn aus finstrer Nacht,
> Nach dem **andern** mag verderben, was höchstselbst er nicht erdacht![10]

On the other hand, we should also note that this humanistic and anti-clerical discourse surprisingly rarely appeared in the press published in other countries fighting against the tsarist empire or in the press in general, other than the socialist press. How to explain the reasons for keeping silent on the subject of the "country of tyrants"? Probably it was due to conservative views of the publishers and readers of the said magazines, which led to the omission or the need for tabooisation of socially and politically sensitive issues that could evoke even very loose associations with the situation in their own countries.

---

9   For instance, the motif of Samson.

10 Why is the hatred between the brothers growing as the battle continues? / Why aren't the people united when they are finally in power? / Now, when peace should build our future heaven, / Why is this country again on its road to perdition! [trans. Z. Piwowarska].

Grandpa Ivan or about the country of hope

The final motif I have chosen refers to the image of Russia as a superpower that represents a political adversary rather than an enemy. This discourse was, for obvious reasons, the least popular of the discussed topoi. It was visible among others in the Bulgarian press in connection to the Bulgarian-Romanian war in which Russia reluctantly supported the military weak Romania. A series of caricatures describing the course of war on the Balkan front presents "Grandpa Ivan" who speaks about his ally with contempt and who is reluctant to help him (ill. 4).

The motif of Russia as a superpower which does not want to be involved in war was also present in the German press when the Bolsheviks who ruled the country expressed their readiness to make a separatist peace. An illustration published in *Der Wahre Jacob* in January 1918 is an interesting visualisation of a new, soviet Russia. Two figures represent the soviet country in the illustration: Lenin, stylised as a good-mannered and hospitable man from the Orient, and a cheerful Russian soldier attending a peace concert together with representatives of the central powers (ill. 5).

A positive message of the discussed image is enhanced by the fact that it was inscribed on the vision of a magical Christmas Eve night. Its atmosphere consists of the falling snow, three guests (representing the Entente countries) standing by the door, just like the Three Magi suite, and of an illuminated room where the residents who, just like a good German family, engage in music-making by the fireplace. However, this vision involves a dissonance. Could not the image of Lenin, with his slanting eyes and wearing the robes of a respectful host, awake in a German reader, unintentional associations with the infamous Tamerland? Did not the fact that the image of Lenin did not convey any positive cultural connotations demonstrate the helplessness of the author? Was not the author forced to accept the role of a "politically correct" illustrator instead of a courageous satirist?

In conclusion, I would like to highlight the fact that the image of Russia in the propaganda of the central powers' practically throughout the whole Great War was inspired by linguistic and visual schemes which had solidified a long time before 1914. Their strength lied in their recognizability and their capacity to refer to the topoi of the tsarist country, which were deeply rooted in the collective imagination. But there was also a serious weakness hidden in them. It was difficult to use metaphors as a frame of a new, uncertain and unknown reality, which was exactly what the world arising from autocracy meant. The Bolsheviks, the representatives of a new world and its positive protagonists, initially appeared as faces that did not cover any coherent, symbolic narrative, any specific "grand story". This fact demonstrates that a nascent reality cannot be defined, it can only be recognised "from a distance". However, it also confirms another rule governing the world of satire and propaganda, in that the main focus is on enemies, and little attention is devoted to neutral actors.

List of illustrations

Illustration 1: "Tamerlan". Der Wahre Jacob (760) 3.09.1915, p. 8773. Caption under the illustration: "According to the order given to the Russian army, the scorched earth tactics is applied while the army withdraws".

Illustration 2: "Der Koloß auf tönernen Füßen". Kikeriki (34) 1914. Caption under the illustration: "Frenchman and Englishman: Turn back and fire! Russian: My legs are too weak!".

Kikeriki.

Der Koloß auf tönernen Füßen.

Franzos' und Engländer: Dreh' di' um und schieß'!
Russ': I bin zu schwach auf die Füß!

Illustration 3: *"Die'lieben Juden und Polen' des Zaren". Der Wahre Jacob (734) 4.09.1914, title page. Caption under the illustration: "Dream on, dream on, of bloody deeds and death. Faiting. depair; despairing, yield thy breath" Richard III.*

Die „lieben Juden und Polen" des Zaren.

Illustration 4: Paspalew, P.: untitled. Baraban *17.09.1916, p. 8. Caption under the illustration: "You son of a bitch, why should I need such an ally?"*

Отъ П. Паспалевъ,

Дѣдо Иванъ. Тфу, собачи синъ, отъ кждѣ те намѣрихъ за съюзникъ.

Illustration 5: *"Ein kritischer Moment"*. Der Wahre Jacob *(822) 01.1918, title page.*

Ein kritischer Moment.

Wenn das Friedenskonzert auch ab und zu eine Störung erleiden sollte, seine Aufgabe wird es dennoch erfüllen, — die Völker wollen es.

Frank M. Schuster
University of Łódź, Poland

Between paralysis, crisis and renewal: The effects of the war on the polyhedral industrial city of Łódź (1914–1918)

The city of Łódź was the centre of the textile industry in the Kingdom of Poland, the Russian part of Poland. It was shaped by German, Jewish and Polish immigrants, who had attempted since the 1820s, to make their fortunes there. Therefore, it is equally appropriate to say or write Łódź, Lodz, לאָדזש, or Лодзь.

In summer of 1914 nobody in Łódź, which was at that time inhabited by over half a million people, knew what the Great War would mean for the city and its inhabitants[1]. But one did know that the city would not continue as before – if only because the raw materials – especially cotton – were imported and the main market was the Russian Empire[2].

---

1 Cf. on Łódź during the Great War: Hertz, Mieczysław: *Łódź w czasie wielkiej wojny.* Łódź 1933; Hofmann, Andreas R.: "Die vergessene Okkupation. Lodz im Ersten Welt-krieg". In: Löw, Andrea/Robusch, Kerstin/Walter, Stefanie (eds.): *Deutsche – Juden – Polen. Geschichte einer wechselvollen Beziehung im 20. Jahrhundert. Festschrift für Hubert Schneider.* Frankfurt a. M.: 2004, pp. 59–78; Schuster, Frank M.: "Zwischen Paralyse, Krise und Aufbruch. Die zentralpolnische Industriestadt Lodz im Übergang 1914–1918". In: *Fejtová, Olga/ Ledvinka, Václav/ Pešek, Jiří (eds.): Unermessliche Verluste und ihre Bewältigung: die Bevölkerung der Europäischen Großstädte und der Erste Welt-krieg/Nezměrné ztráty a jejich zvládání. Obyvatelstvo evropských velkoměst a I. světová válka. Prag/Praha:* 2015, in print; id.: "Zwischen Identitätskrise und Herausforderung: Polen, Juden, Deutsche während des Ersten Weltkrieges in der Textilmetropole Lodz". In: Lasatowicz, Maria Katarzyna (ed.): *Der städtische Raum als kulturelle Identitätsstruktur.* Berlin: 2007, pp. 95–109; Radziszewska, Krystyna/Zawilski, Piotr (eds.): *Łódź i region łódzki w czasie I wojny światowej. Między wielką historią a codziennością.* Łódź: 2012; Daszyńska, Jolanta (ed.): *Operacja łódzka. Zapomniany fakt I wojny światowej.* Łódź 2011; Daszyńska, Jolanta (ed.): *Łódź w czasie wielkiej wojny.* Łódź 2012.

2 Cf. Hertz: Łódź, p. 3.

Already on 1 August 1914 Adolf Eichler (1877–1945)[3], a *Łódź German*[4], who worked as a corporate representative for *reichsdeutsche* firms, noted that: "anywhere […] in the city, it was discussed whether the factories next Monday would continue operating, or should be closed, with regard to the impending shortage of coal"[5]. Everybody ran out of money because the banks had also closed. "The whole of Łódź was without money; the incredible was happening!"[6]. Public authorities, police and military prepared to leave the city, part of the civilian population would also follow them.

During the war the Łódź population dropped sharply by almost half, from around 630 000 to around 342 000[7]. The ethnic and religious composition of the population changed, too[8].

The small Russian population of Łódź, mostly people employed in administration, left the city in 1914. Many of the predominantly Polish factory workers, who had come into the boomtown decades earlier in hope of finding work, returned to the countryside during the war[9]. There was a decline in the number of immigrants, mainly from Germany, who had come to the city between 1820 and 1880 as skilled textiles workers and artisans. They were predominantly from Protestant families. They had for a long time seen themselves as Łódź German and usually had little to do with the Reich Germans. As many had since become Russian subjects, they were not interned as 'enemy aliens', except for those, who had kept their original citizenship[10].

With the collapse of the economy and the occupation of the city by the German army Łódź Germans travelled to Germany, too, mostly for employment. Just like

3 Cf. for Eichlers biography: id.: *Deutschtum im Schatten des Ostens*. Dresden: 1942. The reader should keep in mind that book was published during the Nazi period in Germany.

4 The term *Łódź German* refers to an inhabitant of Łódź, whose family had immigrated in into the city from German lands in the 19th century. It shall be used in this text as distinct from a Reichsdeutschen – a citizen of the German Empire, who lived there also.

5 Eichler, Adolf: *Zwischen den Fronten. Kriegsaufzeichnungen eines Lodzer Deutschen*. Lodz 1918. p. 11.

6 Ibid. p. 8. Cf. Hertz: *Łódź*. pp. 9, 24.

7 Cf. Hofmann: Okkupation. p. 67; Karwacki, Władysław Lech: "Włókniarze Łodzi w latach I wojny światowej 1914–1918. Łódzka Rada Delegatów Robotniczych". In: Rosset, Edward (ed.): *Włókniarze łódzcy. Monografia*. Łódź 1966. pp. 90–102, especially: p. 93.

8 Cf. For indicative statistics of January 1918: Goerne, Antoni: "Z zakresu statystyki ludności". In: *Informator miasta Łodzi na rok 1919*. Łódź 1919, pp. 25–37, here p. 25, table 1.

9 Cf. Karwacki: *Włókniarzem* p. 98; Eichler: *Fronten*, pp. 20, 28.

10 Cf. in general: Lohr, Eric: *Nationalizing the Russian Empire. The Campaign against Enemy Aliens during World War I*. Cambridge/MA, London: 2003. pp. 122–128.

in other areas the Jewish population, suspected of conspiracy with the enemy[11], was to be deported to various regions of Russia[12]. However, those in Łódź were lucky: The planned deportation of the Jews from Łódź away from the front did not happen and so they stayed in the city. This was fortunate because most of these people had nowhere to go. They had no land and were unable to work in Germany. Due to the widespread anti-Semitic prejudice no-one wanted them there[13].

As late as 1916, after the introduction of forced labor, the German occupation administration noted: "The employment of Jews still accounts for difficulties because they are seriously reluctant to go about any hard work"[14]. However, the majority of the Jewish population had no choice but to stay in the city, anyway[15].

Only a few manufacturers, merchants and traders fled in time from the city, less out of fear of the German troops, but rather in the hope of moving their businesses in time to the east to continue being economically successful there[16]. The remaining representatives of various ethnic groups from the Łódź ruling elite, including entrepreneurs, merchants and clerics, founded a citizen committee (Główny

---

11 For the reasons not only Rusia's German subjects were blamed for the Russian military failure and declared scapegoats, but the Jews, too cf. Lohr: Enemy, especially pp. 155–161, and Schuster, Frank M.: *Zwischen allen Fronten. Osteuropäische Juden während des Ersten Weltkrieges (1914–1919)*. Köln, Weimar, Wien 2004, pp. 164–168.

12 Cf. Lohr: Nationalizing; id.: "The Russian Army and the Jews. Mass Deportation, Hostages, and Violence During World War I". In: *The Russian Review* 60 (2001), pp. 404–419; Goldin, Semion: "Deportation of Jews by the Russian Military Command 1914–1915". In: *Jews in Eastern Europe* (Spring 2000), pp. 40–73; id.: "Russkoe komandovanie i evrei vo vremja Pervoj mirovoj vojny: Pričiny formirovanija negativnogo stereotipa". In: Budnickij O.V. et al. (eds.): *Mirovoj krizis 1914–1920 godov i sud'ba vostočnoevropejskogo evrejstva/The World Crisis of 1914–1920 and the Fate of the East European Jewry. History and Culture of Russian and East European Jewry: New Sources, New Approaches. Proceedings of the International Conference. St. Petersburg, November 7–9, 2004*. Moskva/Moscow: 2005, pp. 29–46 and Schuster: Fronten. pp. 161–233.

13 Cf. Archiwum Główne Akt Dawnych w Warszawie (AGAD), Niemieckie władze okupacyjne na terenie byłego Królestwa Polskiego 1914–1918 (NwotbKP), Kaiserlich Deutsches Generalgouvernement Warschau 1915–1918 (GGW), Verwaltungschef beim Generalgouvernement Warschau 1915–1918 (GGW VCh) 6, Bericht des Verwaltungschefs Nr. 6. p. 42.

14 AGAD NwotbKP GGW VCh 7. Bericht Nr. 7. p. 41.

15 Ca. 5.000 Łódź Jews were deported for forced labor, and had to work in the occupied territories. Cf. Hertz, Mieczysław: *Łódzki bataljon robotniczy. Z.A.B. 23*. Łódź: 1918.

16 Cf. Eichler: Fronten. p. 67.

Komitet Obywatelski miasta Lodzi (GKO) to fill the resulting power vacuum and prevent anarchy as the Russian administration left the city[17].

As a result of his experience as a Łódź textile entrepreneur[18] Dr. Alfred Biedermann (1866-1936)[19] became in 1914 the chairerson of the Citizens Committee. Having grown up in the multiethnic, multilingual environment of Łódź entrepreneurial families, like others from his social circles, he was opposed to the growing nationalism. For him it was all about keeping Łódź economically and socially functional. But supplying the city was difficult. According to official statistics already by September 1, 1914, 135 733 people were unable to support themselves financially – a number that rose to over 250 000 people by May 1915[20].

Since this concerned, in particular, the already suspicious Jewish population, Stanisław Silberstein[21], another leading industrialist of Łódź, and the Deputy Chairman of the Citizen committee, took it upon himself, to keep the Jewish community factional.[22] The former Jewish community board, the *Dozór Bóżniczy*[23], had left Łódź with the city administration. The community was therefore leaderless.

---

17 Cf. for the GKO: Hertz: Łódź. p. 61–70; Bąkowicz, Stanisław/Nowak, Edward: "Z problemów działalności Głównego Komitetu Obywatelskiego miasta Łodzi". In: *Acta Universitatis Lodziensis*. Seria 1, 41 (1979), pp. 181–187; Skarżyński, Mieczysław: "Akcja pomocy społecznej w Łodzi w okresie działania Głównego Komitetu Obywatelskiego (3 VIII 1914–1 VII 1915 r.)". In: *Rocznik Łódzki* 20 (1975), pp. 265–283, id.: "Polityka niemieckich władz okupacyjnych w Łodzi w okresie działania Głównego Komitetu Obywatelskiego 6 XII 1914–1 VII 1915". In: *Zeszyty Naukowe Politechniki Łódzkiej. Nauki Społeczno-Ekonomiczne* 4 (1977), pp. 91–106; id.: *Główny Komitet Obywatelski w Łodzi i jego działalność w latach 1914–1915*. Łódź 1986; *Skład Komitetów Obywatelskich w dniu 1. Maja 1915 r.* s. l.: s. a. [Łódź: 1915], p. l.

18 On image, self-image and self-understanding pf the population of Łódź cf. Frank M. Schuster: "Die Stadt der vielen Kulturen – Die Stadt der Lodzermenschen: Komplexe lokale Identitäten bei den Bewohnern der Industriestadt Lodz 1820–1939/1945". In: Lewandowska-Tomaszczyk, Barbara/Pulaczewska, Hanna (ed.): *Intercultural Europe. Arenas of Difference, Communication and Mediation*. Stuttgart 2010. pp. 33–60.

19 Cf. on the Biedermann family: Archiwum Państwowe w Łodzi (APŁ), *Archiwum rodziny Biedermannów* (ARB) 1 and 3; Wanda Kuźko: *Biedermannowie. Dzieje rodziny i fortuny 1730–1945*. Łódź: 2000; ead.: *Metamorfozy: image trzech pokoleń Biedermannów*. In: Kołodziejczyk, Ryszard (ed.): *Image przedsiębiorcy gospodarczego w Polsce w XIX i XX wieku*. Warszawa: 1993. pp. 131–150.

20 Cf. Nowy Kurier Łódzki, 1.9. 1914 and 22.5. 1915; Hertz: Łódź. p. 9f.

21 Cf. Kempa, Andzej/Szukalak, Marek: *Żydzi dawnej Łodzi. Słownik biograficzny. Żydów Łódzkich oraz z Łodzią związanych*. Vol. 1. Łódź: 2001. pp. 142–243.

22 Cf. Schuster: Fronten, pp. 261–263, 265–267, 267–270, 276–277.

23 Cf. APŁ, Główny Komitet Obywatelski miasta Łodzi (GKO) 1, p. 71.

In this situation Silberstein organized together with the Łódź Chief Rabbi, Leib Lejszar Trajstman (1862-1920)[24], the election of an interim Board in November 1914[25]. Among the respected community members elected were orthodox representatives of various factions: Chasidim and Midnagdim were represented as well as liberal reformers, Maskilim[26], but Zionists and Socialists were missing[27]. So unlike in other cities, in Łódź, the Jewish community resumed its activity relatively quickly and so was able to face most urgent problems such as social welfare and public security. Impoverished Jews could again turn to the community for help with the community attempting to provide even more.

The Citizens Committee, consisting predominantly of Poles, established a militia to maintain law and order. This was urgently needed in a heavily fought over city that was repeatedly bombarded by heavy artillery, as Anna Violet (Violetta) Thurstan (1879-1978), a British Red Cross nurse in the Russian service, noticed during her brief stay in Łódź:

> The shelling […] was terrific; crash, crash, over our heads the whole time. […] The shells were bursting everywhere in the street, and civilians were being brought in to us severely wounded[28].

The city was under German control on 20-24 August and 8-26 October 1914. After the re-conquest by the Russian army, a real spy hysteria spread throughout the city. "Denunciation blooms"[29], Adolf Eichler writes in his diary and on 2 November continues: "Despite the assurance of senior officers not to allow a pogrom to happen, excesses against Jews took place[30]". Nevertheless, the militia prevented major looting and pogroms in Łódź. But equally important might have been that the transitional period was short, because on 6 December Łódź again found itself under German occupation and this time it was for good.

With the Germans taking over, the situation for the population of Łódź changed fundamentally again. Everybody had different expectations, hopes and fears. They therefore responded differently and often hesitantly to the German conquest[31].

---

24 Cf. Kempa, Szukalak: *Żydzi*. p. 149.
25 Cf. APŁ Łódzka Gmina Wyznaniowa Żydowska (ŁGWŻ) 418.
26 On the Jewish religious spectrum cf. Mendelsohn, Ezra: *On Modern Jewish Politics.* New York: 1993, pp. 3-36.
27 Cf. APŁ, Akta miasta Łodzi (AmŁ) 1567. pp. 49-54.
28 Thurstan, Violetta: *Field Hospital and Flying Column. Being the Journal of an English Nursing Sister in Belgium and Russia.* London 1915. p. 135.
29 Eichler: Fronten. p. 37.
30 Ibid. p. 94.
31 Ibid. p. 130.

Count Bogdan von Hutten-Czapski (1851–1937), a high-rank German official, noted that, when the Germans captured Łódź, Jews were "crowded together on the streets and welcomed the incoming troops with obvious relief and joy[32]". This joy was not entirely unfounded, as the Central Powers had actually promised the Jews relief from the uncultured Russians and an end to the pogroms[33].

Similarly, the Russian commander in chief, the Grand Duke Nikolai Nikolaevič (1856–1929) tried, through a promise of autonomy, to win the Poles over to the Russian side in 1914[34]. Therefore, the reluctance of many Poles is understandable. The hopes set often into the German cultural nation by local Jews and Germans, would not be fulfilled in Łódź. This was largely because the Germans behaved not as liberators but as occupiers. Their interest was not to rebuild, but to rigorously exploit the war-torn country, both in terms of raw materials and food as well as labor.

Just eight days after the conquest of the city it was officially announced that raw materials, such as wool, fabrics, metals, leather, etc. are to be delivered to the Germans, or otherwise would be confiscated[35]. This led to violent protests of Łódź manufacturers and merchants, not only with the Łódź police chief Matthias v. Oppenheimer (1873–1924), who was heading the entire civil administration of the city, but when they achieved nothing there, directly with the Head of German administration in Poland, Governor-General Hans Hartwig v. Beseler (1850–1921) in Warsaw[36].

But that did not help at all, because the Germans still confiscated metals and even dismantled whole production facilities[37]. They were not willing to put the Łódź spinning looms and machines back in operation to combat unemployment

---

32 Hutten-Czapski, Bogdan v.: *Sechzig Jahre Politik und Gesellschaft*. 2 Vols. Berlin: 1936, here Vol. 2. p. 173.

33 Cf. Schuster: Fronten, pp. 236–239.

34 Published in: Kumaniecki, Kazimierz W. (ed.): *Odbudowa państwowości polskiej. Najważniejsze dokumenty 1912–1924*. Warszawa, Kraków 1924. p. 12.

35 Cf. APŁ, Związek Przemysłu Włókienniczego w Państwie Polskim (ZPW), 151, p. 27.

36 Cf. for instance the letters to Beseler, 25. 2. 1916 and September 1916. APŁ, ZPW 151, pp. 28–30; 42–46 and Radziszewska, Krystyna: "Korespondencja Związku Przemysłowców Królestwa Polskiego z szefem zarządu Generalnego Gubernatorstwa Warszawskiego 1915–1916. Prezentacja źródła archiwalnego". In: Radziszewska, Krystyna/ Zawilski, Piotr (eds.): *Łódźi region łódzki w czasie I wojny światowej. Między wielką historią a codziennością*. Łódź: 2012. pp. 37–48.

37 Cf. Hertz: Łódź. pp. 187–191.

and hunger. Poland should no longer be economically independent[38]. Instead, the unemployed should report for work in Germany[39].

Subsequently in late autumn 1914 a number of Łódź German entrepreneurs, including Alfred Biedermann, gave up any hope of being economically success-ful under German rule and left the city. The Polish merchant and trader Antoni Stamirowski (1863–1938)[40] in January 1915 thus became chair of the Citizen Committee until its dissolution by the German occupiers six months later.

For the Łódź upper class, the welfare of their city was the most important thing after their economic success, while their ethnic origin or religious assignment played only a minor role. This pragmatism and lack of patriotism was often met with incomprehension by Poles in Warsaw and German occupiers alike[41]. Both were defaming the Polish or Jewish entrepreneurs as "ruble patriots," while the manufacturer's loyalties lay – in my view at least – not entirely but clearly on the Russian side[42].

But Russian administration enabled them to embody, against all odds, the American myth of a career "from rags to riches". Furthermore according to their religious understanding both the Lutheran and Jewish immigrants saw, unlike the Poles, the Russian administration as legitimate rulers and thus as God-given. With the change of power, lower middle-class Łódź Germans became more and more patriotic and some became outspoken German nationalists. People like

---

38 Cf. Basler, Werner: *Deutschlands Annexionspolitik in Polen und im Baltikum 1914–1918.* (East) Berlin: 1962 p. 139.

39 Cf. Heid, Ludger: *Maloche – nicht Mildtätigkeit. Ostjüdische Arbeiter in Deutschland 1914–1923.* Hildesheim, Zürich, New York: 1993, p. 363; APŁ, AmŁ 13752, p. 90f.

40 Cf. Jaskulski, Mirosław: *Władze administracyjne Łodzi do 1939 r.* Łódź: 2001. p. 99–100.

41 Cf. *Rozwój,* Nr. 189/1901. p. 3 or Althaus, Paul: *Ihr und wir.* In: *Deutsche Post* Nr. 18, 24.10.1915, p. 1, id.: *Lodzer Kriegsbüchlein.* Göttingen 1916.

42 Here I disagree with Andreas R. Hofmann, who states the Citizens Committees in Congress Poland "consisted either of Pols, who sympathized with the different political groups of the Polish national movement and were striving for national independence of their country, or of people who made no secret of their Russian imperial loyalty, which in practice was in Łódź invariably true of the members of the German or Jew-ish industrial bourgeoisie". Hofmann: Okkupation. p. 63. Arkadiusz Stempin cannot be agreed with either since he in my opinion adopts position of the German Imperial administration in Warsaw and does not distance himself enough from their pejora-tive imperialist terminology. Cf. id.: *Próba 'moralnego podboju' Polski przez Cesarstwo Niemieckie w latach I wojny swiatowej.* Warszawa: 2014. p. 428f, 447, 458.

Adolf Eichler were under the impression that "the city should be deprived of their German countenance"[43].

A Protestant theologian Paul Althaus (1888–1966), who was from 1915 to 1917, a military chaplain in Łódź, and who later became very famous, stood by the Protestants in the fight for their faith and the recognition of their Germanness. He did not even notice Poles and Jews[44]. Officially the German occupiers did not favor any ethnic group. But until then, compared with the Polish and certainly the majority of the Jewish population the Łódź Germans had been a privileged minority. Therefore, some of them now felt discriminated against. The growing nationalism intensified the inter-ethnic tension.

Also the conflicts among other ethnic groups intensified. In the working-class and poor neighborhood of Bałuty, according to the report of the German Field Rabbi Dr. Arthur Levy (1881–1961)[45], at least in one outlet set up by the Citizens Committee to aid the poor Jews, they were told: "To Jews we do not sell!"[46].

As regards everyday life, coexistence between Poles, Jews and Germans was not smooth. The difficult situation was exacerbated by the fact, that the German occupiers not only requisitioned goods and restricted travel possibilities drastically[47], but also tried to control the trade and commerce, on which most of Łódź Jewry relied for living[48]. As a result, the occupying power, for which the supply of the civilian population was no priority[49], fostered unintentionally the black market, smuggling[50] and even prostitution[51], although they did everything else to fight it.

The Germans did not see, or did not want to see, that they themselves contributed to the spreading of filth and disease, by the requisitioning for the metal, of

---

43 Eichler, Adolf: *Das Deutschtum in Lodz*. In: *Deutsches Leben in Rußland* 3 (1925) Nr. 3/4. p. 39–41, here p. 41.

44 Cf. Fischer, André: *Zwischen Zeugnis und Zeitgeist: Die politische Theologie von Paul Althaus in der Weimarer Republik*. Göttingen 2012; Hetzer, Tanja: "Deutsche Stunde". *Volksgemeinschaft und Antisemitismus in der politischen Theologie bei Paul Althaus*. München: 2009.

45 Letter by Arthur Levys 5.1.1915 APŁ ŁGWŻ 20. Cf. also Levys open letters published in Jewish newspapers on the Situation of the Polish Jewry for example in *Jüdische Rundschau* Nr. 2, 8. 1. 1915, p. 10, Nr. 6, 5.2.1915. p. 45f, Nr. 22, 28. 5. 173f.

46 Ibid. p. 1. APŁ ŁGWŻ 20.

47 Cf. Schuster: Fronten. pp. 320–328.

48 Cf. on the situation of craftmen in Łódź see the report about their situation after 2 ½ years of war, in: Central Zionist Archives (CZA), Jerusalem, Z3 149.

49 Cf. APŁ AmŁ Sgn. 13720, pp. 192–198; APŁ ŁGWŻ 81.

50 Cf. Schuster: Fronten. pp. 316–320.

51 Cf. APŁ ŁGWż 45; Schuster: Zwischen allen Fronten. pp. 349–356.

water pipes, taps and bath tubs meant for the Jewish ritual baths[52]. Instead, they saw their anti-Semitic prejudices of dirty Jews confirmed. They complained even in official administrative reports about

[t]he population, that is not steepened in preference and understanding for the purification of body, clothing and housing, especially the Jewish part of it (Lice had been found even with rabbis!) [...][53]

First one has to treat the Jew with soap, before political and cultural measures could even be considered – as was generally believed by the German officers[54].

As strange as it may sound, when considering the economic and social situation, German occupation offered many possibilities for the different ethnic groups to engage in a wide range of not only social but also cultural and even political activities. In addition to various charities and Łódź clubs, the singing and multilingual music groups began working again[55] and by 1915 the Łódź stages were again hosting performances[56].

A Berlin actor, director, and later also a well-known screenwriter Walter Wassermann (1883–1944) directed plays by Frank Wedekind, Hermann Sudermann, Gerhard Hauptmann and Arthur Schnitzler on the German stage with actresses and actors from Germany and the German army[57]. In 1916/1917 the renowned Polish poet Bolesław Leśmian (1877?–1937) staged among others, plays of Oscar Wilde, Henrik Ibsen, Maksim Gorky Nikolai Gogol in Polish, and in 1918 even the work of Stanisław Wyspiański (1869–1907), the famous Polish play 'Wesele' (The Wedding)[58]. With Morris D. Wachsman (1874–19??)[59], Herman Sierocki

---

52 Cf. APŁ ŁGWź 127; 64 p. 12.

53 AGAD NwotbKP GGW VCh 10, 10. Bericht. p. 32.

54 Cf. "Protokoll der Unterredung mit Major Simon in Warschau", 13.2.1916, CZA A 15. VIII. 9c.

55 Cf. Pelowski, Alfons: *Kultura muzyczna Łodzi*. Łódź 1994.

56 Cf. *Neue Lodzer Zeitung* (NLZ) Nr. 192/1915. p. 2.

57 Prykowska-Michalak, Karolina: *Teatr niemiecki w Łodzi. Sceny, Wykonawcy, Repertuar (1867–1939)*. Łódź 2005. p. 112–124: ead.: 'Łódzkie teatry w okresie I wojny światowej'. In: Radziszewska, Krystyna/Zawilski, Piotr (eds.): *Łódź i region łódzki w czasie I wojny światowej: Między wielką historią a codziennością*. Łódź: 2012. pp. 119–133.

58 Cf. Kuligowska-Korzeniewska, Anna: *Scena obiecana. Teatr polski w Łodzi 1844–1918*. Łódź 1995. pp. 224–227, 242.

59 Cf. Zilbertsweig, Zalman: *Leksikon fun yidishn Teater*. Vol. 1. New York 1931, col. 660–661.

(1880–194?)[60] and Jacob Adler (1855–1926)[61], there were three prominent Jewish artists, all natives of the city of Łódź, who presented Yiddish operettas. In addition, Abraham Goldfaden (1840–1908)[62] brought classic plays and the works of August Strindberg and Ibsen onto stage.

In Łódź the cinema was even more popular than the theatre[63], also during the war, as everyone could afford it. Despite the German censorship the cabaret was equally popular as it offered an ironic comment on hard times. For exmaple Julian Tuwim(1894–1953)[64], who during the war staged for the first time, his poems or sketches in Łódź[65]. But not only the young Polish avant-garde was formed in the generally open-minded city, but also the Artist's Association 'yung-yidish' was founded in Łódź by some young Jewish artists like the writer Moyshe Broderzon (1890–1956)[66] and the painters Jankel Adler (1895–1949)[67] and Marek Szwarc (1892–1958)[68] in 1918[69].

Although the time under German occupation offered several cultural possibilities, politically the German occupiers tried to stay in control. After the dissolution of the Citizens Committee on 1 June 1915, a city council was appointed[70]. Heading

60 Cf. Zilbertsweig, Zalman: *Leksikon fun yidishn Teater*. Vol. 2. Varshe 1934, col. 1496–1497.
61 Cf. Adler, Jacob: *A Life on the Stage. A Memoir*. Ed. by Lulla Rosenfeld. New York: 1999; Rosenfeld, Lulla: *Bright star of exile. Jacob Adler and the Yiddish theatre*. New York 1977.
62 Cf. Sandrow, Nahma: *Vagabond Stars: A World History of Yiddish Theater*. Syracuse/NY 1995. pp. 40–69.
63 Cf. Krajewska, Hanna: *Życie filmowe Łodzi w latach 1896–1939*. Warszawa, Łódź: 1992; Biskupski, Łukasz: *Miasto Atrakcji. Narodziny kultury masowej na przełomie XIX i XX wieku. Kino w systemie rozrywkowym Łodzi*. Warszawa: 2013.
64 Cf. Matywiecki, Piotr: *Twarz Tuwima*. Warszawa: 2007.
65 Cf. For instance Tuwim, Julian: *Łodzianie*. In: *Estrada* Nr. 2 1918, pp. 11–20.
66 Cf. Rozier, Gilles: *Mojżesz Broderson od Jung Idysz do Araratu*. Łódź 1999; Zilbertsweig: *Leksikon*. Vol. 1. Sp. 215–216.
67 Cf. *Adler, Jankel 1895–1949. Katalog anlässlich der Wanderausstellung 1985: Städtische Kunsthalle Düsseldorf, The Tel Aviv Museum, Muzeum Sztuki w Łodzi*. Köln 1985.
68 Cf. Kempa, Andrzej/Szukalak, Marek: *Żydzi dawnej Łodzi. Słownik biograficzny Żydów łódzkich oraz z Łodzią związanych*. Vol. 3. Łódź: 2003. pp. 123–124.
69 Cf. Malinowski, Jerzy: *Grupa "Jung Idysz" i żydowskie środowisko 'nowej sztuki' w Polsce, 1918–1923*. Warszawa: 1987; id.: The 'Yung Yiddish' (Young Yiddish) Group and Jewish Modern Art in Poland, 1918–1923. In: *Polin* 6 (1991). pp. 223–230.
70 Cf. Verordnungsblatt für das General-Gouvernement Warschau. Nr. 5 (1915). Pos. 25; "Einstweilige Geschäftsordnung für die Stadtverordneten" 14.8.1915. APŁ AmŁ 13583, pp. 31–39.

it until 1917 was the *reichsdeutscher* mayor Heinrich von Schoppen[71], the former mayor of Gnesen (Gniezno). The Łódź German factory owner Ernst Leonhardt (1849–1917)[72], who had already before the war, unlike other manufacturers, explicitly argued for the German language and culture in Łódź, was appointed the deputy mayor, because the city could not completely forego the local notables. He was one of several entrepreneurs in the city council[73], which consisted of twelve Łódź Germans, twelve Poles and twelve Jews, who all enjoyed a certain prestige in the city. They appeared, to the occupying power, to be suitable to take over the administration of the city[74]. However, the clear ethnic tripartite division would not remain for long, as some Jewish councilors joined the Polish, while others tended to German side[75]. In spite of all ideological, ethnic and cultural differences and heated debates in the council pragmatism usually prevailed. At least until the end of the 1920s local issues formed the primary focus of activity.

The objective of the occupying power to treat the various ethnic groups alike in the course of its policy of *divide et impera* was clearly missed, not only because a mismatch between the complex reality of occupied Poland, and the occupiers' own schematic way of thinking. According to the plans of the Governor-General in Warsaw and the German government in Berlin there should be "no Germanization"[76], and no benefits "for one or the other group of the [local] population"[77].

Several Łódź Germans had, however, expected to be given preferential treatment by the Imperial German rulers, and were now disappointed. In 1916 an

---

71 Cf. Podolska, Joanna/Waingertner, Przemysław: *Prezydenci miasta Łodzi.* Łódź 2008. 28–29; Jaskulski: *Władze.* p. 100.

72 Cf. Heike, Otto: "Ernst Leonhardt 1849–1917. Ein Industrieller und Förderer des deutschen Bildungswesens in Lodz". In: Weigelt, Fritz (ed.): *Von unserer Art. Vom Leben und Wirken deutscher Menschen im Raume von Weichsel und Warthe.* Wuppertal: 1963. pp. 85–88; Skrzydło, Leszek: *Rody nie tylko fabrykanckie.* Łódź 2007. pp. 23–31.

73 Cf. Hertz: Łódź, pp. 132–133.

74 Cf. Silber, Marcos: "Ruling Practiced and Multiple Cultures. Jews, Poles and Germans during World War I". In: *Simon Dubnow Institute Yearbook* V (2006). pp. 189–208, here p. 193; Hertz: Łódź. p. 120.

75 Cf. Silber: Ruling. pp. 194–195.

76 Beseler in a letter to Reichs-Chancenlos Theobald von Bethmann-Hollweg (1856–1921), 2.8.1916, Cf. Bundesarchiv/Militärarchiv (BA/MA) Freiburg, N 30/12.

77 Beseler in instructions for officers and higher administration, 10.3.1916, Archiwum Państwowe w Lublinie (APL), Kreisamt Lukow 6. Cf. also BA/MA Freiburg N 30/54, p. 30.

independent Polish state, at least on paper, was proclaimed[78], and Łódź Germans such as Adolf Eichler, saw their fears confirmed. They had been already of the opinion that the German occupying power saw only second-class citizens in them. Therefore they had on 5 March 1916 founded the "Deutscher Verein für Lodz und Umgebung" (German Association for Łódź and region)[79], seeking to resist such tendencies[80].

In response to the proclamation of the Polish state, association representatives sent a memorandum to the German Reichs-Chancellor in December 1916[81]. They declared the Poles to be the "hereditary enemy of all Germanness"[82] and demanded the incorporation "of the momentarily adjacent parts of Russian Poland to the German Reich [that] already has a strong German population"[83]. However, in Łódź, the German share in the total population lay somewhere between 11% and 15%[84]. The memorandum neither found a broad support in Łódź nor did the German government respond. In view of such claims Governor General Beseler in Warsaw remained reserved[85], even after he saw an opportunity to create a counterweight to the more openly displayed Polish nationalism in cautious support of the association[86]. Its Chairman, Adolf Eichler, tried to limit the damage. After 1917 he became involved mainly in ensuring minority rights for Germans in the future Polish state. This brought him into conflict with the Protestant Church in Łódź.

---

78   Cf. Conze, Werner: *Polnische Nation und deutsche Politik im Ersten Weltkrieg*. Köln, Graz 1958, pp. 206–226.

79   Flierl, Friedrich: ,Der Deutsche Verein für Lodz und Umgegend. Seine Entstehung und Entwicklung. In: *Jahrbuch des Deutschen Vereins für Lodz und Umgegend*. Lodz 1917. pp. 5–30.

80   The association had in Łódź little more than 200 followers, thus has not been based on the majority of Łódź Germans. Cf. Hofmann: Okkupation. pp. 71–73.

81   Cf. Kulak, Zbigniew: "Memorandum of the Germans form Łódź Concerning the Annexation of Polish Territories to the Reich at the Time of World War I". In: *Polish Western Affairs* 7/2 (1966), p. 388–403, die Denkschrift ibid. pp. 396–403.

82   Ibid. p. 401.

83   Ibid. p. 402.

84   Ibid.

85   Cf. Beselers letter tot he Chairman of the ,Verein für das Deutschtum im Ausland' Franz v. Reichenau (1857–1940), March 1916, BA/MA Freiburg N 30/25.

86   Beseler's Speach is quoted in: Eichler, Adolf: "Der Deutsche Verein im zweiten Jahr seines Bestehens". In: *Jahrbuch des Deutschen Vereins, Hauptsitz in Lodz*. Lodz: 1918. pp. 70–86, hier pp. 80–81. Cf. Protokoll der Sitzung am 3. November 1917 im Auswärtigen Amt. BA/MA Freiburg N 30/15.

Pastor Rudolf Gundlach (1850–1922)[87], the head of the Łódź Protestants, who saw himself language wise and culturally more as Polish than German, was deeply rooted in the Lutheran German tradition. He therefore tried to bring about a convergence of the different ethnic, linguistic and religious groups, by way of proselytizing and acculturation. He wanted to overcome the widespread notion Protestant = German, Pole = Catholic. That's why he turned in face of increasingly nationalistic tones during the Great War demonstratively towards the Polish side, especially as he feared that the German occupying power saw in the Łódź Protestants a means of Germanization. This led in 1917 to conflict with Eichler and the majority of the lay faithful present at a Synod meeting in Łódź[88], because they saw Guntlach's actions as an attempt to polonaise the Lutheran Church in Poland.

Despite the heated debate, the following year in view of the changed situation in the new Polish state, Gundlach took the side of those who still held on to the German language and tradition. He argued for minority rights and protection because he was convinced that their violent polonization would lead to nothing. Everybody should be granted the same rights. Gundlach's position standing always on the side of the weak, was not dissimilar to Beseler's, who finally had to leave Warsaw on 11 November 1918 with the end of the war.

At least in Łódź, the transition of power in 1918 would take place relatively peacefully, which was the result of the negotiating skills of the Polish pharmacist and chemist Leopold Skulski (1877–1940?)[89], who was the city's elected mayor since September 1917. Although in Łódź, Polish and German socialists formed socialist "workers and soldiers councils", too, the Mayor succeeded in ensuring the orderly withdrawal of the German troops. He achieved control of the inhabitants of the city, so there were no riots and no violent conflict occurred between ethnic and religious groups[90].

The Great War brought down the textile industry city of Łódź due to an economic crisis, from which it would never fully recover in the interwar period. The measures taken by the German occupiers to economically exploit the city,

---

87 Cf. Schedler, Gustav: *Eben-Ezer, eine Jahrhundertgeschichte der evangelischen St. Trinitatisgemeinde zu Lodz.* Lodz 1929. pp. 47–50.

88 Cf. *Protokoll über die Evangelisch-Augsburgische Synode am 18. und 19. Oktober 1917 in Lodz.* Lodz 1917.

89 Cf. Podolska, Waingertner: *Prezydenci.* p. 30–31; Jaskulski: *Władze.* p. 103.

90 Cf. Bogalecki, Tadeusz: *11 listopada 1918 roku w Łodzi. Geneza, przebieg i rezultaty akcji rozbrajania Niemców w Łodzi.* Łódź 1988; Karwacki, Wacław Lech: *Walka o władzę w Łodzi 1918–1919.* Łódź: 1962; Daszyńska, Jolanta (ed.): *Łódź w drodze do niepodległości.* Łódź: 2013.

paralyzed it completely. Ultimately, the occupiers would solve none of the urgent problems with which they were confronted during the occupation of the city, neither the problem of food supplies, nor that of spreading diseases, nor labor and unemployment. The reasons for this failure can be seen in the conditional stereotypical views of the occupiers which led to misunderstanding of the situation in the occupied territories. Instead of seeing the causes of their problems in the way they themselves contributed to the catastrophic situation of the civilian population, many German officers, soldiers and officials maintained a general sense of cultural and moral superiority which saw just their xenophobic, anti-Slavic or anti-Semitic stereotypes confirmed. They did not see that their policy of treating all citizens alike, was perceived differently by the different ethnic and religious groups. These, I think are the main reasons for the increase in tensions within and between the various population groups. They were forced in paradoxical circumstances to become aware of their own self-understanding and had to newly position themselves in a rapidly changing world, but they knew how to use the many cultural and political opportunities. The fragile inter-ethnic balance that has long been determined life in the city was not entirely lost during the war. This is probably due to the Łódź pragmatism that ultimately prevailed. Local interests were immediately after the war – at least in Łódź – still more important than ideological positions.

Marcos Silber
Department of Jewish History, University of Haifa, Israel

Jews, Poles, and Germans in Łódź during the Great War: Hegemony via Acknowledgment and/or Negation of Multiple Cultures*

Introduction

How was the multi-ethnic and multi-cultural space shaped and reshaped during the Great War? How its contested characteristic was expressed in ruling practices and policies in a period of a continuous change? This paper will explore these questions focusing on ruling practices in Łódź during the Great War. It will argue that both the German direct rule and the subsequent Polish administration accepted the city's ethno-national and linguistic-cultural mosaic while de-legitimizing it for political purposes. It will follow the occupiers' policy and that of the new Polish authorities shaped under the occupational rule. Specifically, the article will compare German and Polish governmental practices and attitudes toward multilingualism and ethno-national representation in the Łódź local government.

In the first section this paper will explore the effects of the German occupational regime's practices that enabled the imagination of the urban space of Łódź as multilingual and multinational, i.e. as composed of three equal ethno-national segments (Jews, Poles and Germans). The German occupation regime asked to emphasize the triple facade of Łódź, thus providing legitimization of the German dominance.

The second section will investigate the ruling practices carried out by the elected municipal council under the hegemony of the Polish national movement. It presented the minority claims of language and cultural recognition as "separatist" and therefore illegitimate, undermining a society that promotes its independence and marches "together" towards an autonomous state.

---

*   This article is a revised and updated version of my article: "Ruling Practices and Multiple Cultures – Jews, Poles, and Germans in Łódź during WWI". In: *Simon Dubnow Institute Yearbook 5*, 2006, pp. 189–208.

My main claim is that legitimizing or negating a sense of multiculturalism in Łódź was a strategy of the specific hegemonic force to reach its political objectives to appropriate the city space.

My claim will thus challenge a well-known thesis regarding German policy towards local ethno-national groups and will emphasize the importance of looking at the policy not only from the center's perspective but also from the peripheries to get a more nuanced picture of this complex period.

Łódź, had for over a century been the centre of the textile industry in Poland. Especially during the last quarter of the 19th century, still under the aegis of the tsars, the city experienced years of rapid industrial development, a dynamic increase of the population as well as fast and chaotic urbanization. Industry remained the most important factor in its development, but also those trades and crafts concerned with it were important. In a relatively short time it became the second largest city in Poland, growing from 32500 inhabitants (in the 60s of the 19th century) to 314,000 residents according to the census of 1897[1]. The exceptionally dynamic development of Łódź was the outcome of a number of factors such as the beneficial economic policy of the Government, the immigration to the town of German weavers and entrepreneurs, the absorptive Russian markets (particularly during the three decades before the outbreak of the Great War), as well as the initiative of its socially heterogeneous inhabitants.

Of 314,000 residents of Łódź in 1897 about 48% (150 720) of the population were Catholic; 32% (98 700), Jewish; 18% (56 500), Protestant; and 2% (6 000), Orthodox. Ca. 46% spoke Polish as their mother tongue while 21% spoke German; 29% Yiddish; and 3% Russian and other languages[2]. The city's Jewish population was particularly complex. Besides Yiddish, 4 084 (4.1%) cited Polish as their mother tongue; 1 228 (1.2%), Russian; and 1 034 (1.1%), German. In addition, many Jews employed what Itamar Even-Zohar calls a "multilingual system," speaking different languages in different circumstances[3]. Likewise, the core of other

---

1 Janczak, Julian: *Ludność Łodzi przemisłowej 1820–1914* [The population of the industrialized Łódź]. Uniwersytet Łódzki: Łódź 1982; Puś, Wiesław: *Żydzi w Łodzi w latach zabiorów 1793–1914*. Wydawnictwo Uniwersytetu Łódzkiego: Łódź 2000, pp. 26–27.

2 Janczak, Julian: "Struktura Narodowościowa Łodzi w latach 1820–1939". In: Puś, Wiesław/Liszewski, Stanisław (eds.): *Dzieje Żydów w Łodzi 1820–1944, Wybrane problemy*. Wydawnictwo Uniwersytetu Łódzkiego: Łódź 1991, pp. 42–44, here 48; Janczak, Julian: "The National Structure of the Population in Łódź in the Years 1820–1939", *Polin* 6, 1991, pp. 20–26, here 25.

3 Bartal, Israel: "Mi-Du-Leshoniut Mesoratit le-Had-Leshoniut Leumit" *Shvut* 15, 1992, pp. 183–194; Even-Zohar, Itamar: "Aspects of the Hebrew-Yiddish Polysystem. A Case

religious groups shared a mother tongue (Polish or German), but the peripheries were fluid[4].

On the eve of the Great War, the population of Łódź approximated half a million, and its multi-ethnic, multi-religious, multilingual, and multicultural character was undimmed. Approaching 1915, Due to immigration and acculturation, hybridization increased, with "Poles of Mosaic faith", Polish Evangelists, German Catholics, Russian Jews (so called "Litvaks"), etc. Traditional, cohesive society collapsed amid the rise of exclusionary Polish, Jewish, and German nationalism. National principle became one of vision and division, a category that helped to reimagining the changing urban society, boundaries and characteristics of a region, the political domain and the principle that demanded its reorganization. By the turn of the century, and especially during the decade preceding the Great War, relations between ethnic groups were strained. The Polish national movement grew more organized, aggressive, and overtly antagonistic to Jews. As for the Jewish national movement (in all its variants, from the workers' Bund and Poalei

---

of a Multilingual Polysystem". *Poetics Today* 11, 1990, pp. 121–130. Shmeruk refered to this aspect of Jewish life in interwar Poland and emphasized the connections between the different languages in this multilingual polysystem. Shmeruk, Chone: "Hebrew-Yiddish-Polish. A Trilingual Jewish Culture". In: Gutman, Yisrael et al. (eds.): *The Jews of Poland between Two World Wars*. University Press of New England: Hanover/London, 1989, pp. 285–311. See also Batsheva Ben-Amos' insightful analysis of the multilingual diary of a young man from the Łódź ghetto, probably born immediately after the end of World War I: Ben-Amos, Batsheva: "A Multilingual Diary from the Ghetto". *Galed* 19, 2004, pp. 51–74. The bilingualism so widespread in Jewish life was present in some measure also in non-Jewish society, see Radziszewska, Krystyna/ Woźniak, and Krzysztof (eds.): *Pod Jednym dachem. Niemcy oraz ich polscy i żydowscy sąsiedzi w Łodzi w XIX i XX wieku/Unter einem Dach. Die Deutschen und ihre polnischen und jüdischen Nachbarn in Lodz im 19. und 20. Jahrhundert*, Literatura: Łódź, 2000, pp. 127, 138. On social interaction between Jews and non-Jews in nineteenth-century Łódź, see: Guesnet, François: *Lodzer Juden im 19. Jahrhundert. Ihr Ort in einer multikulturellen Stadtgesellschaft*, Simon-Dubnow-Institut für Jüdische Geschichte und Kultur: Leipzig, 1997.

4   Janczak, "Struktura Narodowościowa Łodzi", 1991, p. 49. Almost 6% of all Protestants (i.e., more than 3 000 persons) claimed Polish as their mother tongue; 8% of all Catholics (13,000) claimed German. Janczak, "The National Structure of the Population in Łódź", 1991, p. 22. See also: Budziarek, Marek: "Konfessionelle Koexistenz in Lodz im 19. und 20. Jahrhundert". In: Jürgen Hensel, Jürgen (ed.): *Polen, Deutsche und Juden in Lodz 182–1939, eine schwierige Nachbarschaft*. Fibre: Osnabrück, 1999, pp. 269–282, especially 270–272.

Tzion to the Zionists progressively enamored of autonomist ideas), which was more and more in evidence, its clear, firm demands were impossible to ignore[5].

1. German Rule

Germany's capture of Łódź from tsarist Russia on 6 December 1914, launched a new era for both the country and the city[6]. From the economic point of view, the outbreak of the First World War and the four years of German occupation put an end to the dynamic development of Łódź. After Łódź was captured by the German army, factory production practically ceased. The disconnection from the Russian market was a severe stroke for the Łódź industry. Large losses were suffered from unfulfilled trade contracts with partners beyond the front and from the loss of assets in Russian banks.

Moreover, in the first months of the occupation there was a lack of coal deliveries. That was the first reason for production ceasing. Later on, the German policy of requisitions, expropriations and confiscations of raw material, products and machinery paralyzed the production. Consequently, the collapse of industry produced massive unemployment. Gradually until May 1915 the inhabitants of the city remained with no means to live[7]. During the war the city was devastated. Its industry was destroyed. The city experienced depopulation. At the beginning of 1918 its population numbered 342000, i.e. about 260000 (43 percent) less compared to the position before the war.[8] The ethno-religious composition changes too: The Russian population was mostly evacuated, Polish speaking Catholics

---

5   For an excellent introduction to the rise of anti-Semitism and ethno-national tension in this period, see: Golczewski, Frank: *Polnisch-jüdische Beziehungen 1881–1922. Eine Studie zur Geschichtes des Antisemitismus in Ost-Europa*. Steiner: Wiesbaden, 1981. The literature on the growth of Polish and Jewish nationalism is vast. On the rise of Polish xenophobic nationalism, see: Porter, Brian: *When Nationalism Began to Hate. Imagining Modern Politics in Nineteenth-Century Poland*. Oxford University Press: New York/ Oxford 2000. As an introduction to the rise of Jewish nationalism, see Frankel, Jonathan: *Prophecy and Politics. Socialism, Nationalism and the Russian Jews, 1862–1917*. Cambridge University Press: Cambridge, 1981; Mendelsohn, Ezra: *On Modern Jewish Politics*. Oxford University Press: New York/Oxford 1993.

6   On the beginning of the German rule in Łódź regarding the Jewish population see: Schuster, Frank M: *Zwischen allen Fronten. Osteuropäische Juden während des Ersten Weltkrieges (1914–1919)*. Böhlau: Köln/ Weimar/Wien 2004, pp. 265–269.

7   Puś, Wiesław: "The Development of the City of Łódź (1820–1939)", *Polin* 6, 1991, pp. 4–19, here 13.

8   Janczak: "The National Structure of the Population in Łódź", 1991, p. 24.

abandoned the city to places with more chances to survive the hunger the German occupation brought. Most of the Jewish population remained in the city in spite of a number of Jewish refugees who looked for shelter in the city.

The German occupation was a political turning point, too. The German regime was more permissive to political life than the previous Russian regime. In the middle of 1915, the Germans worked toward convening independent municipal councils in Łódź. They did it for two reasons, one practical and one propagandistic. The practical was to relieve German personnel of local responsibility. The propagandistic was to win over the local population to a Wilhelmine empire supposedly more attentive and considerate to political claims than the czarist conqueror[9]. This strategy sought to promote German political aims, including control over western territories of Congress Poland and its main city, Łódź[10].

Closed forums as well as local newspapers debated the expedient ethnic composition of the local councils. Placing ethno-national subjects on the discussion agenda for the composition of the local councils wasn't news in these territories now conquered from Russia. Shortly before the German occupation, the Russian regime had already divided the population into ethno-national groups for council elections[11]. Increasing legitimization of ethno-cultural differences, thanks to the emergence of ethno-cultural bodies engaged in the politics of identity (such as the Jewish and Polish national movements), justified this division even more. No strangers to such rhetoric, the German occupation forces themselves classified the population along these lines viewing ethno-national divisions as natural[12]. The German Jewish, mostly Zionist leaders of the KfdO (Komitee für den Osten)

9   Pajewski, Janusz: *Odbudowa państwa Polskiego, 1914–1918.* Państwowe Wydawnictwo Naukowe: Warsaw 1985, p. 106.

10 Silber, Marcos: "Hukei Behirot be-Folin ha-Kongresait be-Milhemet ha-Olam ha-Rishona ve-Yitzug ha-Yehudim ba-Mosdot ha-Nivharim". *Michael* 16, 2004, pp. 144–164.

11 Engel, David: "Ha-She'ela ha-Polanit ve-ha-Tenua ha-Tzionit. Ha-Vikuah al ha-Shilton ha-Atzmi be-Arei Folin ha-Kongresait". *Galed* 12, 1993, pp. 66–69; Weeks, Theodore: "Nationality and Municipality. Reforming City Government in the Kingdom of Poland, 1904–1915". *Russian History* 21, 1994, pp. 23–48; "Di Takones fun der zelbst-Fervaltung in Poiln". In: *Lodzer Folksblat*, 24.6.1916.

12 On German policy regarding this territory and its population in the beginning of the German occupation, see: Conze, Werner: *Polnische Nation und Deutsche Politik im Ersten Weltkrieg.* Böhlau: Köln/ Graz 1958, pp. 46–105; Geiss, Imanuel: *Der polnische Grenzstreifen 1914–1918. Ein Beitrag zur deutschen Kriegszielpolitik im Ersten Weltkrieg,* Matthiesen Verlag: Lübeck/Hamburg 1960, pp. 70–90; Knebel, Jerzy: *Rząd Pruski wobec sprawy polskiej w latach 1914–1918* . Wydawn. Poznańskie: Poznań 1963, pp. 7–33. On such policy in the Oberost region, see: Liulevicius, Vejas Gabriel: *War, Land on*

proposed that ethno-national categories be reflected in the government institutions of the occupied territories and championed Jewish national rights and representation in local politics[13]. The Polish leadership, for its part, demanded implementation of the national principle regarding the Polish nation. In exchange for full recognition of Polish rights to Congress Poland, the austrophile NKN (Naczelny Komitet Narodowy, or Supreme National Committee) – which represented Polish parties in Galicia and fervently supported the Central Powers – was prepared to accept German minority rights in Łódź[14]. As a result of this particular constellation, the occupation forces adopted ethno-national categorization in the public discourse.

Discussions revolved around the question of ethnically designated election districts (*curiae*). The city's German and Jewish press emphasized that this system would avert the tyranny of the majority and equip minorities with the legal tools to prevent discrimination and represent their national interests[15]. After a well-orchestrated public debate[16], a council was appointed in Łódź on July, comprising twelve Poles (members of the Catholic, Polish-speaking elite), twelve Germans (from the Protestant, German-speaking elite), and twelve Jews (regardless of

---

the Eastern Front, Culture. National Identity and German Occupation in World War I, Cambridge University Press: Cambridge 2000.

13 On the KfdO during this stage of events, see Zechlin, Egmont: *Die deutsche Politik und die Juden im Ersten Weltkrieg.* Vandenhoeck & Ruprecht: Göttingen 1969, 126–143; Ticker, Jay: "Max I. Bodenheimer. Advocate of Pro-German Zionism at the Beginning of World War I". *Jewish Social Studies* 43, 1981, pp. 11–30; Silber, Marcos: *She-Polin Ha-Hadasha Tihie Em Tova le-Hol Yaldeha: Ha-Maamatz be-Merkaz Eropa le-Hasagat Otonomia le-Yehudei Folin ha-Kongresait be-Milkhemet ha-Olam ha-Rishona* (Doctoral Thesis) Tel Aviv University: Tel Aviv 2001, pp. 36–89, 121–137.

14 Lemke, Heinz: *Allianz und Rivalität. Die Mittelmächte und Polen im Ersten Weltkrieg (bis zur Februarrevolution).* Akademie-Verlag: Wien, /Köln/Graz, 1977, pp. 38–99, 113–156, (in particular 154–155); Sibora, Janusz: *Narodziny Polskiej Dyplomacji u Progu Niepodległości .* Wydawn. Sejmowe: Warsaw 1998, pp. 11–24, 61–65.

15 See, for example, "Jüdische Angelegenheiten – Jüdische Wahlkurien". *Deutsche Lodzer Zeitung,* 18.6.1915.

16 Central Zionist Archives [henceforth CZA], A15/VIII/2a, Max Bodenheimer to Franz Oppenheimer, June 1, 1915. On German control of the local press, see: Hertz, Mieczysław: *Łódź w czasie wielkiej wojny* [Łódź in the time of the great war]. Skł. gł. Księg. S. Seipelt: Łódź, 1933, pp. 171–178; Uger, Yeshaya: "Hindenburg Kegn 'Haint'" [Hindenburg vs. "Haynt"]. Haynt Yubilei Bukh [Haynt's Jubilee Book], Haynt Farlag: Warsaw 1928, pp. 11–12; Archiwum Państwowe w Krakowie [National Archive in Cracow, henceforth APwK], NKN 87, "Die deutsche Zensur in Łódź."

language)[17]. This appointment affirmed the equality of all three groups, their rights to representation in city institutions, and their say in municipal decision-making. The determination of parity representation for the three segments was presented as equal inclusion of the three ethno-national groups. With no "majority" and "minorities," each group's special needs would be equally protected.

This peculiar policy wasn't applied in Congress Poland's areas occupied by the Germans in summer 1915, i.e. Warsaw and the left bank of the Vistula. Moreover, while in Łódź they emphasized the parity of the ethnic composition of the city, while relating to Warsaw they emphasized its Polish character. Two days after the occupation of Warsaw, the *Deutsche lodzer Zeitung* explained to its readers that "Warsaw is a Polish city" because "Warsaw is not charged with national questions as Łódź"[18].

This last point is important to understand the German policy not only examining it from the center (Warsaw and the central occupation authorities in Poland), but looking from the peripheries (in this case, Łódź) to the center (Warsaw and the policy implemented there). This perspective gives us the possibility to comprehend the nuances of the German occupation policy, creating a more complexed picture.

Regarding multilingualism, the occupation forces allowed each ethno-national group to found or revive its own newspaper. Two papers were published in Yiddish: *Lodzer Togbalt* and *Lodzer Volksblat*; two in Polish: *Gazeta Łódzka* and *Nowy Kurier Łódzki*; and two in German: *Deutsche Lodzer Zeitung* and the weekly *Deutsche Post*[19]. These practices emphasized the equality of the groups in the common municipal domain, their equality of representation in the institutions that dealt with the daily concerns of the common public sphere while the press was granted legitimacy to serve as a formal public sphere exclusive for each one of the ethno-national segments. In other words, they formally created a common public sphere apparently attentive to the ethno-cultural complexity while permitting the existence of a separated particular public sphere.

---

17 CZA, A15/VIII/2a, Arthur Levi to Oppenheimer bureau, July 9, 1915; CZA, A15/VIII/7, Paritätische Behandlung der Juden in der neuen städtischen Selbstverwaltung Russisch-Polens; Hertz, 1933, p. 120; "Di zelbstfervaltung in okupirtn Poyln" [The self-government in occupied Poland]. *Lodzer Folksblat*, 2.7.1915.
18 "Warschau". *Deutsche Lodzer Zeitung*, 6.8.1915. A similar policy to that applied to Łódź was implemented in Oberost, shortly after its occupation. See: Liulievicius. 2000, p. 115–116, 118.
19 On the press in Łódź, see: Hertz, 1933, pp. 170–178.

As opposed to the discriminatory Russian rule, the new German administration professed formal neutrality toward ethnic groups and seemed to improve their political condition, at least nominally and relatively. Jewish national circles interpreted German liberalism as a triumph of their politics of identity. However, a study of these policies shows that they in fact delegitimized the multiple cultures they purportedly condoned.

The appointment of a local council on an ethno-national basis gave the city a semblance of a public domain composed of three segments, each segment was perceived as uniform, different from and even inimical to the others in spite of the hybridization process described above. The German acknowledgment of multiple cultures was thus predicated as rigid and essentialist regarding group identities.

The occupation forces appointed thirty-six prominent residents of Łódź to the council, divided evenly among the city's three main ethno-national groups[20]. This parity conferred on the Jews, hitherto victims of discrimination, representation almost commensurate with their percentage of the population – approximately one-third. Yet the German element gained disproportionate political power, arousing the Polish community's wrath[21]. The occupation authorities had apparently expected the Jewish and German council members to form a coalition of minorities against the Polish relative majority.

However, this reductionist Procrustean bed, which reinforced the differences *between* ethno-national segments while flattening the differences *within* them, did not stand the test of reality. Religion (so important to German-occupation concepts of national identity) did not completely define nationality: Though the occupation forces had scrupulously selected council members from each ethno-national group, seven of the Jews "defected" to the Polish faction, and the remaining five (including three Zionists) joined the Germans[22]. Despite overwhelming Jewish support from Jewish representatives for Polish national claims in the appointed council, Polish national circles accused "foreign" Jews of conspiring against Poland with Jewish national aspirations alien to Łódź Jewry spirit[23]. There was even talk of a "Litvak" conspiracy led by progressive Galician rabbi and preacher Mordechai

---

20 CZA, A15/VIII/7, Paritätische Behandlung der Juden in der neuen städtischen Selbstverwaltung Russisch-Polens; Hertz, 1933, p. 120.

21 APwK, NKN 88, "Z życia społeczno-publicznego miasta Łodzi" ["About the social and public life of the city of Łódź"].

22 CZA, A15/VIII/2a, Arthur Levi to Oppenheimer bureau, July 9, 1915; APwK, NKN 88, "Z życia społeczno-publicznego miasta Łodzi"; Hertz, 1933, p. 120.

23 "W sprawie stosunków Żydów do Polaków w Łodzi". In: *Wiedeński Kurier*, 22.7.1915; APwK, NKN 88, "Sprawozdanie z Łodzi." September 25, 1915.

Ze'ev Broide[24]. Such propaganda sought to invalidate the increasingly assertive demand for collective Jewish rights, which seemed to negate collective Polish ones. From the very beginning of the German occupation, the linguistic question was central. Various regulations erased the Russian language from the public sphere: Russian was banned in all municipal institutions. It was forbidden to study in or learn the language, and school use of books in Russian was illegal. Even posting an announcement on a billboard in Russian risked a fine of 5,000 ruble, a fortune in such arduous times[25]. This linguistic molding of the municipal domain was intended principally to uproot the language of the previous regime as a means of legitimizing the introduction of German.

The German occupation authorities decreed that each segment of the population would study separately. Even before the war, there had been separate (though not exclusive) municipal schools for Catholics, Jews, Protestants, the Orthodox, and Mariavites[26]. Russian was to have been the language of instruction. Facing resistance to this regulation, however, the government permitted Polish in Catholic schools and German in Protestant ones. On the eve of the war, Polish was introduced in Jewish schools, where Hebrew was taught too. In all cases, Russian was at least a language of study[27]. Non-municipal schools were often bilingual or multilingual, such as the Angelica Rothert Gymnasium (German and Polish) and the Handweker Talmud Toire (Russian, Polish, Hebrew, and German)[28].

---

24 APwK, NKN 88, "Z życia społeczno-publicznego miasta Łodzi." Mordechai Ze'ev Broide (1869–1950) was born in Brest Litowsk, however, at the age of three moved to Galicia, where he grew up; was educated there and became an active Zionist. At the age of forty, in 1909, he moved to Łódź. Sadan, Dov (ed.): *Zikhron Mordekhai Ze'ev Broda: kovets le-zekher ha-doktor Mordekhai Ze'ev Broda*, Hasifirah hatzionit: Jerusalem 1960 (Remembrance of Mordekhai Ze'ev Broda: collection in memoriam of Mordekhai Ze'ev Broda).

25 "Russisch – verboten. Die Strassenschilder in Lodz". *Die Zeit* (Wien), 3.9.1915; "Verordnung betreffend Regelung des Schulwesens". *Deutsche Lodzer Zeitung*, 10.9. 1915.

26 Podgórska, Eugenia: *Szkolnictwo elementarne w Łodzi w latach 1808–1914* . Łódzkie Towarzystwo Naukowe: Łódź, 1966, pp. 142, 149.

27 Regarding the development of the language question in the municipal system during the early twentieth century, see, for example, Lewin, Sabina: *Prakim be-Toldot ha-Hinuch ha-Yehudi be-Folin ba-Mea ha-Tesha-Esre u-ve-Reshit ha-Mea ha-Esrim*. Tel Aviv University: Tel Aviv, 1997, pp. 217–219; CZA, A15VIII 9a, Bericht über das jüdische Schulwesen in Lodz, May 21, 1915; Hertz, 1933, pp.183–184; APwK, NKN 86, "Sprawa szkolna w Łodzi", October 21, 1915.

28 Radziszewska and Woźniak: 2000, p. 127; CZA, A15VIII 9a, Bericht über das jüdische Schulwesen in Lodz, 21 May 1915.

Initially, the municipal council maintained the previous school system, eliminating Russian and fortifying Polis[29]. Yet the occupation forces prohibited Polish in Jewish schools[30], based on essentialist arguments ("Jews in Poland need not be Poles, nor can they be")[31] as well as instrumental ones ("only 200 Jews use the Polish language")[32]. Rather, Jews would study in German in its own selective schools[33]. This was an expression of the policy of selective Germanization of the Jews aimed to reinforce German in the public sphere even as the population adopting it remained outside the German ethno-national segment[34]. This policy of selective and limited Germanization was a tool to deepen German dominance of the city and region while alienating its population.

Jewish and Polish teachers protested that it was impossible to teach in a language students did not understand and that they should be taught in their mother tongue (Yiddish or Polish) – lively arguments attended this topic[35]. The German superintendent of Jewish schools countered that the solution was to improve Jewish children's German: "If under normal circumstances there are twenty-four hours in a day, and in wartime there are twenty-eight, Jews must study German twenty-three hours a day"[36]. Such blatant Germanization irked the council's Polish faction – Jews and Catholics alike – as well as Jewish nationalist leaders[37].

In September 1915, left-wing Jewish activists clamored for Yiddish-language schools for the Jewish population[38]; a petition to this effect was signed by 30,000

---

29 APwK, NKN 86, "Sprawa szkolna w Łodzi."
30 CZA, A15/VIII/9a, Notizen über die Tätigkeit des Herrn Justizrat Dr. Bodenheimer in Lodz (Zum Protokoll über die Sitzung vom 11.6.15.); "Verordnung betreffend Regelung des Schulwesens". *Deutsche Lodzer Zeitung*, 7.9.1915. See also: Schuster, 2004, pp. 360f.
31 APwK, NKN 86, "Sprawa szkolna w Łodzi."
32 APwK, NKN 88, "Sprawozdanie z Łodzi." September 25, 1915.
33 CZA, A15/VIII/2c, Moritz Sobernheim to Max Bodenheimer, September 2, 1915; "Verordnung betreffend Regelung des Schulwesens". *Deutsche Lodzer Zeitung*, 7.9.1915.
34 See: Schuster, Frank M. "Zwischen Paralyse, Kriese und Aufbruch: Die zentralpolnische Industrienstadt Łódź im Übergand 1914–1918", unpublished article. I thank Frank Schuster who graciously provided me a copy of his article.
35 "Dos Lodzer Lebn. A farzamlung vegn der yidisher folks-shul". *Lodzer Folksblat*, 9.9.1915; Hertz, 1933, p.183; APwK, NKN 86, "Sprawa szkolna w Łodzi."
36 APwK, NKN 88, "Sprawozdanie z Łodzi." September 25, 1915.
37 APwK, NKN 86, "Sprawa szkolna w Łodzi"; APwK, NKN 88, "Sprawozdanie z Łodzi." September 25, 1915.
38 "Dos Lodzer Lebn. A farzamlung vegn der yidisher folks-shul". *Lodzer Folksblat*, 9.9.1915.

Jews[39]. Jewish parents also urged that Polish be taught in Jewish schools,[40] and in a contra-petition 3,000 Jews signed demanding schools in Polish for their children[41]. Though the Germans had to accept cultural-linguistic differences *within* ethno-national groups, they consecrated the boundaries *between* these groups and clung to segregated education. They preferred schools in Polish for each ethnonationality rather than one integrative school united by language. Just before the 1916–1917 academic year, the occupation authorities promised municipal schools in Yiddish and Polish, exclusively for Jews[42]. This step was understood in the Yiddish daily press as part of a broader policy confirming that "the Jews are a different people with a peculiar, independent culture, with a particular language, or with two languages. Based on this acknowledgment, the German power in Poland recognized the Jewish nationality and strives not only to set equally civil rights but also national rights, like the Poles"[43].

In summation, the German occupying forces implemented a dualistic policy vis-à-vis ethno-national groups:

On the one hand, the Germans acknowledged ethnic-national differences and reinforced the construction of closed societies, making movement between them difficult and even suspect. This step determined the essential and static definitions of the community and its culture, strengthening rigid, deterministic perceptions of the individual. It facilitated selective Germanization, which had increased the need for German without absorbing all its speakers into the German ethno-national segment. This educational process ultimately produced distinct (though internally

---

39 APwK, NKN 86, "Sprawa szkolna w Łodzi"; Ch. Kazdan, Di Geshichte fun yidishn shulvezn in umophengikn poiln. Mexico City 1947, 52–54; Hertz, Yankl Sholem: *Di Geshichte fun Bund in Łodz*. Unzr Tzayt: New York, 1958, p. 256.

40 Hertz, 1933, p. 166.

41 YIVO Archive in New York [henceforth YIVO], RG 1400, Bund, MG2, Box 15, folder 145, Protokoł posiedzenia 37-go Rady Miejskiej z dn. 29 Października 1917 r.

42 "Dos lodzer lebn. Di unterrichts-shprach in di yidishe folksshuln. *Lodzer Folksblat*, 10.8.1916; "Dos lodzer lebn. Tog notitsen: Ofn shvel fun nayem shul-yor". *Lodzer Folksblat*, 28.8.1916. The Yiddish schools were to be run by the municipal school board, composed mainly of Polish Catholics or polonized Jews seeking to polonize the Jewish school system despite German regulations. The Folks-Bildung Farain tried unsuccessfully to enlist some of its members in the municipal commission on Jewish schools to help open Yiddish schools. "Di Farzamlung fun yidishn shul farain". *Lodzer Folksblat*, 28.8.1916. See also: Bałaban, Majer: "Raport o żydowskich instytuciach oświatowych i religijnich na terenach Królestwa Polskiego okupowanych przez Austro-Węgry". *Kwartalnik historii Żydów* 1, 2001, pp. 35–68, here p. 54.

43 "Der bankrot fun der yiudish-poylisher asimilatsye". *Lodzer Folksblat*, 23.5.1916.

heterogeneous) ethnic blocs accustomed to German dominance within a German framework.

On the other hand, the occupation authorities had to accept lingual and/or cultural complexity within each ethno-national population, allowing it to develop a separate and particular public sphere. By emphasizing a triad of languages and ethno-national equivalent groups with definite boundaries, the German regime sought to de-Polonize Łódź and thereby promote German rule in the region, either directly – by annexing the area (with or without its residents) to Germany – or by preserving it as a colonial or semi-colonial territory[44]. Selective Germanization thus helped place Greater Łódź under the aegis of the Reich without necessarily including the region's non-German population. The division of the city and its inhabitants into three rigidly defined, apparently equal sections aimed at delegitimizing its attachment to any Polish political entity likely to arise.

By its co-optive conduct of municipal affairs, its apparent tolerance of cultural pluralism, and its separation of ethno-national segments within an atmosphere of increasing nationalism and aggravation of inter-ethno-national relations, the German occupation generated relative calm and acceptance among the locals. This despite its predatory subjugation[45], expropriation of goods and means of production[46], and discriminatory budget allocation, which spread economic deprivation, hunger, crime and disease[47], resulting in an alarming increase in mortality rate [48].

2. New, Elected Local Authorities

The war lasted longer than expected. It demanded more resources than estimated and an adjustment of the economic policy within the Reich as well as in occupied lands. The long war reality of the late 1915 and 1916 with no clear definition

---

44 On the annexation tendencies of the German Reich toward Poland see Geiss, 1960. German speaking population in Łódź petitioned for the annexation of western parts of Congress Poland (including the city of Łódź) to Germany. See: Kulak, Zbigniew: "Memorandum of the Germans from Łódź concerning the annexation of Polish Territories to the Reich at the Time of World War I". *Polish Western Affairs* 7, 1966, pp. 388–403.

45 Hertz, 1933, pp. 200–213.

46 Ibid., 187–191; Schuster, 2004, pp. 305–309.

47 Hertz, 1933, pp. 200–221; Schuster, 2004, pp. 309–323, 349f.

48 APwK, NKN 88, "Sprawozdanie z Łodzi". September 25, 1915; APwK, NKN 89, "Śmiertelność w Łodzi, według danych Wydziału zdrowotności publicznej" (apparently May 1916).

in the eastern front[49], attrition of the population in the German hinterland and its weariness[50], the plunder of the civil population in occupied Poland and its exhaustion[51], manpower difficulties[52], and lack of raw materials[53] led to a crisis in the occupation regime[54]. Its rehabilitation necessitated negotiations between occupiers and occupied.

The joint decisions of politicians and military men, Austrian and Germans alike, during the fall of 1916 gave a green light for the establishment of an "independent" Polish buffer state. Consequently the act of Two Emperors restituting the Polish state, was published on 5 November 1916. Its aim was to gain the Polish national movement's heart and to take advantage of its manpower. It was, as Titus Komarnicki characterized in his classical work "an attempt to 'buy the Polish business cheaply.'"[55] The occupational regime co-opted branches of the Polish national movement guaranteeing them ostensible progress toward an autonomous Polish political entity. Manipulatively, they created new governmental institutions, like the Interim Council of State, that were intended to promote the restoration of a Polish state[56].

---

49 Stone, Norman: *The Eastern Front, 1914–1917.* Hodder & Stoughton, New York, 1975, pp. 219–231, 245–263.

50 Vincent, Paul: *The Politics of Hunger: The Allied Blockade of Germany, 1915–1919,* Ohio University Press: Athens OH 1985; Herwig, Holger: The First World War, Germany and Austria-Hungary 1914–1918. Arnold: London, 1997, pp. 283–301; Bonzon, Thierry and Davis, Belinda: "Feeding the cities". In: Winter, Jay and Robert, Jean Louis (eds.): *Capital Cities at War, Paris, London, Berlin 1914–1918,* Cambridge University Press: Cambridge UK 1997, pp. 305–341, especially pp. 333–338.

51 Molenda, Jan: "Królestwo Polskie i Galicja, sierpień 1915–luty 1917". In: Kormanowa, Żanna and Najdus, Walentyna (eds.): *Historia Polski,* Vol III, part III. Państwowe Wydawnictwo Naukowe: Warsaw 1974, pp. 172–236, here pp. 172–175, 177–179, 184–194.

52 Feldman, Gerald: *Army, Industry and Labor, in Germany 1914–1918,* Oxford University Press: Oxford 1992, pp. 45–52, 150–168, 273–283.

53 Herwig, 1997, pp. 254–256, 259–264.

54 See for example the seminal work of Fritz Fischer: *Germany's aims in the First world War,* Chatto & Windus: London 1967, 327 (first Published in 1961).

55 Komarnicki, Titus: *Rebirth of the Polish Republic, A Study in the Diplomatic History of Europe, 1914–1920.* W. Heinemann: Melbourne-London-Toronto 1957, p. 115.

56 On the Proclamation of the 5th November and its practical aftermath see: Grosfeld, Leon: "La Pologne dans les Plans impérialistes allemands pendant la grande guerre 1914–1918 et l'acte du 5 Novembre 1916". In: *La Pologne au X Congrès international des Sciences Historiques à Rome,* Académie Polonaise des Sciences, Institut d'Histoire: Warszawa 1955, pp. 334–340, 34–354; Conze, 1958, pp. 106–226; Grosfeld, Leon:

This political development produced a serie of results in Łódź, such for instance a reaction of the *Deutsche Verein für Lodz un Umgebung* to annex the region to Germany, or at least, to secure German dominance over it[57]. In such political context Łódź elected a new municipal council in early 1917, following a process begun with the election of the Warsaw city council in spring 1916[58]. In Łódź the German regime sought to preserve the *curia* formula, which benefited the German minority and could ensure it a cardinal role in the city's political life. Von Oppen, who headed the German occupation forces in the city asked: "In Łódź, which differs from nationally homogeneous Warsaw [!], would it not be appropriate [to establish] national districts that guarantee reasonable representation of the Germans and a reasonable degree [of representation] for the Jews?" [59].

Polityka państw centralnych wobec sprawy polskiej w latach pierwszej wojny światowej. Państwowe Wydawnictwo Naukowe: Warszawa 1962, pp. 155–186; Lemke, Heinz: "Die Politik der Mittelmächte in Polen von der Novemberproklamation 1916 bis zum Zusamentritt des Provisorischen Staatsrats". *Jahrbuch für Geschichte der UdSSR und der volksdemokratischen Länder Europas* 6, 1962, pp. 69–136; Kozłowski, Czesław: *Działalność Polityczna Koła Międzypartyjnego w latach 1915–1918.* Książka i Wiedza: Warsaw 1967, pp. 115–127; Jarausch, Konrad: *The Enigmatic Chancellor, Bethmann Hollweg and the Hubris of Imperial Germany.* Yale University Press: New Haven and London 1973, 416–420; Jerzy Holzer – Jan Molenda, *Polska w pierwszej wojnie światowej.* Wiedza Powszechna: Warsaw 1973, pp. 146–244; Lemke, 1977, pp. 321–374; Pajewski, 1985, pp. 116–138; Sukiennicki, Wiktor: *East Central Europe during World War I: From Foreign Domination to National Independence.* East European monographs: Boulder 1984, pp. 241–295.

57 Schuster, "Zwischen Paralyse, Kriese und Aufbruch".

58 A huge literature exists on the municipal elections in Warsaw. Basically see the classic book written by Paul Roth: *Die politische Entwicklung in Kongreßpolen während der deutschen Okkupation,* K. F. Koehler: Leipzig 1919, pp. 35f.; see also the chapter written by Wilhelm Stein, "Die politische Entwicklung im polnischen Judentum während der Zeit der deutschen Okkupation", in the same book, 161–163. More recent works refer to the municipal elections: Silber, 2001, 185–209; Weiser, Keith: *The Politics of Yiddish. Noiekh Prilutski and the Folkspartey in Poland, 1900–1926.* (doctoral thesis) Columbia University, New York 2001, pp. 222–252; Gilinski-Meller, Chaya: *Mifleget ha-Folkisitim [Folks-partei] be-Folin, 1915–1939.* (doctoral thesis) Bar-Ilan University, Ramat Gan 2004, pp. 71–96; Schuster, 2004, pp. 401–405. Specifically, on the elections in Łódź see Silber, 2001, 283–285; Schuster, 2004, p. 403.

59 APwK, NKN 86, "Radę miejską wybieraną w Łodzi".

As Frank Schuster pointed it out, the German authorities sought in Łódź to search for a counterweight to the new Polish state in formation[60]. However, the Germans' new allies from the Polish national movement argued that proportional elections would accomplish the same, assuming that the Poles would gain the majority of council seats. The occupation regime agreed to partisan proportional elections similar to those in Warsaw.

The electoral system divided the 32,127 voters into six socioeconomic categories (*curia*), each electing ten representatives. The number of voters in each *curia* was unequal. For example, the sixth, general workers' *curia* registered 17,656 voters (more than half the electorate), while the second – for major industrialists, merchants, and entrepreneurs – admitted only 568[61].

Głos Żydowski, a Jewish weekly published in Piotrków, just south of Łódź but in the Austrian occupation zone and free of German censorship, characterized the elections as "on the one hand, a struggle between three ethnic groups; on the other, a political party's electoral struggle"[62]. The description was accurate. On the one hand, candidates were almost completely listed ethno-nationally, following the patterns developed previously in other cities in Congress Poland, reflecting growing tension between Jews and Poles as well as the magnitude of the ethno-national agenda. On the other hand, each list indicated a partisan, ideological, or class inclination within each ethno-national group[63].

Only the German parties and political factions in Łódź formed a united electoral front, stressing internal cohesion and downplaying differences. Ironically, leaders of the "Poles of Mosaic faith" preached integration into Polish society but organized their own roster of candidates, separate from both the Polish and Jewish national lists. The deepening abyss between ethno-national groups – despite ideological and political proximity – reduced their chances of incorporation into

---

60 Schuster, "Zwischen Paralyse, Kriese und Aufbruch". The ordinance was a tool used by the German authorities to limit the Polish sovereignty over the Jewish population. See: Silber, Marcos: "The German 'Ordinance Regarding the Organization of the Religious Jewish Community' (November 1916–1918)". *Studia Judaica* 18(1), 2015, pp. 35–55.

61 Hertz, 1933, pp.129–130; Walicki, Jacek: "Juden und Deutsche in der Lodzer Selbstverwaltung". In: Hensel. Jürgen (ed.): *Polen, Deutsche und Juden in Lodz 1820–1939. Eine schwierige Nachbarschaft*. Fibre: Osnabrück 1999, pp. 215–236, here 216; Hertz, 1958, p. 246.

62 "Wybory w Łodzi". In: Głos Żydowski, January 21, 1917.

63 See, for example, YIVO, RG 28, box 12, Lodz 19, Platform fun yidishn sotzial demokratishn arbiter vahl komitet (P.Tz.); ibid., Dos Platform fun yidishn sotzialdemokratishn vahl komitet.

the Polish electoral lists. It was a symptom of the extreme process of ethnification of the local politics during the war years which worked against the integration of Jews and Catholics into the same electoral organization. The electoral regulations deepended the divisions between ethno-national segments and emphasized internal ethno-national heterogeneity[64]. The electoral process expanded the public spheres – the one common to all ethno-national segments as well as those particular to each.

Lists championing an ethno-national agenda succeeded in imposing it on the municipal agenda and captured the vast majority of votes, regardless of the social composition of the *curia*. The few votes for the list of the "Poles of Mosaic faith" show the failure of assimilation as a viable political option as well as the failure of the minor integrative lists of Jews and non-Jews. These called for cooperation on a purely economic base, ostensibly blind to ethno-national differences[65]. As a result of the electoral law, no ethnic segment achieved an absolute majority in the city council[66]. Nevertheless, the Polish parties grouped in the Polish Circle attained a relative majority (twenty-six out of sixty seats, including four "Poles of Mosaic faith"). The twenty-one Jewish representatives of the Yiddishe Tzentrale Wahl Komitet shaped the main opposition group, mostly supported by the eight German representatives[67].

How did the new municipal authority reconcile Łódź's multiple languages, cultures, including the existence of particular public spheres with its own vision of Polish national hegemony? Before the first meeting of the council, Polish council members demanded exclusive recognition of the Polish language[68]. Because of the pressure of German local authorities, Polish council members applied to the Interim Council of State for assistance and submitted a memorandum declaring that:

> 1) In so far as the issue of the Polish language as the only official language will not be favorably and conclusively arranged before the first [City] Council's meeting, 2) In so far

---

64 "Polen". *Neue Jüdische Monatshefte* 1, 1916, p. 207; "Der rezultat fun di vahlen in Lodz". In: *Haynt*, 21.1. 1917; Hertz, 1933, pp. 130–133.

65 Compare the call of the list 21 of the industrialists: "Do wyborców II kuryi". *Lodzer Togblat*, 8.1.1917 with their poor results – 123 votes from a total of 518. "Di vahl campanie in Lodz". *Lodzer Togblat*, 17.1.1917. All the remainder votes were received by other three lists, each one representing a different ethno-national segment.

66 Hertz, 1933, pp. 132f.; "Wybory w Łodzi". *Głos Żydowski*, 21.1.1917; "Der rezultat fun di vahlen in Lodz". *Haynt*, 21.1.1917.

67 Hertz, 1933, p.134. The Jewish circle was very often supported by the two representatives of the Poalei Tzion (Zionist Socialists).

68 Ibid., p. 135f.

as the mayor and its deputy will not be nominated from among the polish citizens, 3) In so far the [city] chairman [...] will not be nominated from among the polish citizens – then the Polish council city member will consider their labor as impossible[69].

The dispute was characterized as "a controversy on a vital, crucial issue, on the Polishness [Polskość] of the municipal council"[70]. The Polish Circle members of the municipal council looked for stressing the "Polish" character of the municipal council. They did that by stressing the Polish language's status and by keeping the most prestigious and influential functions in the "Polish" (i.e. ethnically Polish) hands, regardless of their political stance. The polish character of the city was presented as a "zero-sum game", in which simple recognition of another official language besides Polish or keeping central functions in "non-Polish" hands were presented as a menace of the city's "Polishness". The proposition presented by the Polish circle aimed at a total elimination of "non-Poles" from the city's new public arena. The Polish council faction then endeavored to exclude German and Yiddish, now constituted as minority languages, from the public sphere as a tool to enhance the Polonization of Łódź.

However, the political circumstances dictated a compromise. The Interim Council of State understood that total exclusion of German minority and language from the political arena of a city as important as Łódź will not be accepted by the occupation regime. At the same time, the occupation regime was alarmed by the strong opposition and compromised, while declaring German as the language of communication with the occupation authorities, recognized Polish as the official language. In addition, German Council members were authorized to deliver speeches in German[71].

The exclusion of minority languages and their public spheres implied the waiver of council authority over said minorities. However, this waiver undermined not only the legitimacy of municipal institutions but their relations with non-Polish-speakers. Thus, it was shortlived. For example, despite Jewish council members' objections, the municipality initially refused to publish information and announcements in the Yiddish press, ignoring such a language, based on instrumental arguments ("all the Jews with no exception know the Polish language")[72] as well as formalistic arguments (It is not native language but the language of

---

69   Suleja, Włodzimierz: *Tymczasowa Rada Stanu*. Wydawn. Sejmowe: Warsaw 1998, p. 159.
70   APwK, NKN 88, "Sprawozdanie z Łodzi"[Report from Łódź], April 17, 1917.
71   Hertz, 1933, p.136; Suleja, 1998, pp. 159–161; Archiwum Akt Nowych , T.R.S., Sygn. 7, "Sprawy Samorządowe, Posiedzenia Wydziału Wykonawczego w d. 16.2.17, 5.3.17".
72   YIVO, RG 1400, Bund, MG2, Box 15, folder 145, Protokoł posiedzenia 62-go Rady Miejskiej z dnia 23 Stycznia 1918 r.

"newcomers")[73] in order to exclude it from the public sphere. A group of Jewish members of the city council asked for the meaning of such behavior and demanded that it should be changed[74]. In this context argued Israel Lichtenstein, the Bundist representative in the municipal council, that "since there are people who speak such a language and since it is a press in such a language with its readers, then it is the obligation of the municipal authorities to serve these citizens […] and to find out this way to publish the municipal announcement"[75]. Eventually, though, rather than relinquish its influence over tens of thousands of Yiddish readers, the council recanted. The council accepted a proposal to publish announcement in the Yiddish press – although in Polish and not in Yiddish[76]. It was a sophisticated way of compelling council authority over the Yiddish speaking minority and influence it, without legitimating the use of the Yiddish language.

A new occasion to discuss the status of the different languages appeared when the responsibility for Polish educational system was transmitted in September 1917 to the Interim Council of State by the German occupational forces, who retransmitted part of the responsibilities to the local councils[77]. The question of the status of the minority languages aroused again. The effort of the Polish Circle to de-legitimize the minority languages' presence in the public sphere continued. Language and ethno-cultural issues were increasingly paramount. Claims for recognition of German and Yiddish culture were labeled nationalist, anti-Polish, anti-state, and separatist[78]. The Polish Circle sought to favor the Polish language and culture, empowering the Polish ethno-cultural group and eliminating minority cultures from the public sphere. The Polish Circle insisted that independence and the construction of a Polish state required the assimilation of "backward

---

73 Ibid.
74 "Polin" *Hatzfira*, 31.1.1918.
75 YIVO, RG 1400, Bund, MG2, Box 15, folder 145, Protokoł posiedzenia 62-go Rady Miejskiej z dnia 23 Stycznia 1918 r.
76 Zieliński, Konrad: "Stosunki polsko–żydowskie w Królestwie Polskim w czasie I wojny światowej (na przykładzie rad miejskich)". *Kwartalnik Historii Żydów* 206, 2003, pp. 164–194, here: 181–182; Zieliński, Konrad: *Stosunku polsko–żydowskie na ziemiach Królestwa Polskiego w czasie pierwszej wojny światowej*. Wydawnictwo Uniwersytetu Marii Curie-Skłodowskiej: Lublin 2005, 283.
77 Konarski, Kazimierz: *Dzieje szkolnictwa w b. Królestwie Kongresowym 1915–1918*. Skł. gł. w Ksiaznicy Polskiej w Warszawie: Warsaw 1923 pp. 1–56; Ogonowski, Jerzy: *Uprawnienia Językowe mniejszości narodowych w Rzeczypospolitej Polskiej 1918–1939*. Wydawn. Sejmowe: Warsaw 2000, pp. 22–23.
78 YIVO, RG 1400, Bund, MG2, Box 15, folder 145, Protokoł posiedzenia 37-go Rady Miejskiej z dnia 29 Października 1917 r.

minorities" into the constituted Polish majority. In contraposition, Lichtenstein considered that "the use of the mother tongue belongs to the rights usually called holy, [...] together with other most basic human rights. In this case it is about the equality of the languages. About the right of everyone to use his own language"[79]. He stressed the connection between equal citizenship and minority languages' recognition in the different public spheres, be it the municipal council; the school system or the press[80]. He was strongly attacked by his opponents because he explicitly pointed to such a nexus[81].

Regarding Łódź's Yiddish speakers, Israel Lichtenstein demanded the complete recognition of Yiddish spheres (whether press or schools) as a condition to achieve complete equality for the different citizens. That is because, he stressed, the limitation of such recognition means limiting their equal rights: "Above all it is about being a citizen". In order to enjoy its basic rights [...] "no characteristic, no other demand should be required from any citizen"[82]. He objected to the creation of a civic hierarchy based on linguistic or national adscription. He asserted that "Poland will be fortunate only when all inhabitants of this land will be such. General prosperity can be built on complete equality for all citizens, regardless of nationality and language"[83].

Likewise, a Protestant clergyman, August Gerhardt, denounced the Polonization of the public sphere and the de-legitimization of the minority's separate particular spheres, when discussing the issue of schooling, its budgeting and its character:

The German faction [in the Łódź city council] protests the innuendo and claims against individual council members and specific social groups as though the Germans in Łódź had anti-Polish and anti-state, separatist aspirations. [We] the German population [...], who will loyally fulfill our civic duty, do so while maintaining our right to linguistic and religious distinction. We are of the opinion that the Polish language is without doubt the national language and must be compulsory for all citizens. Knowing that a country gains strength, grows, and becomes independent only when all its citizens – regardless of belief, nationality, or status – feel free and happy, [we] the German faction will support all aspirations to preserve equal rights for all citizens of the country, without distinction of

---

79 YIVO, RG 1400, Bund, MG2, Box 15, folder 145, Protokół posiedzenia 62-go Rady Miejskiej z dnia 23 Stycznia 1918 r.
80 Ibid.
81 Ibid.
82 Ibid.
83 Ibid.

nationality and religion, [and] the attainment of religious freedom, freedom of conscience, personal freedom, and freedom of expression[84].

Discussing the local schools, Gerhardt presented language and culture as central to both individual freedom and political community. Moreover, like Lichtenstein, he clearly pointed out that the public expression and institutionalization of ethnocultural diversity was a precondition for a stable, independent, and just state.

Backed by the German occupying forces, members of the council's German faction could subtly threaten without fear. They knew how to phrase their desire shifting from simple toleration of different cultures and languages' existence to a multinational and multilingual society inclusive for of all its citizens, i.e. demanding not only a superficial acceptance of the differences as necessary evil but real, profound respect of the different citizens and their equal inclusion in the citizen's corpus regardless of their language and culture[85].

Some of the research regarding the German policy in Poland during the Great War which analyses the German policy from a Warsaw's perspective, claims that after November 1916, it rejected Jewish national claims[86]. But again, the perspective from Łódź shows a more nuanced reality. The attempts to marginalise minority cultures and languages in Łódź led to a renewed German-National Jewish alliance in local politics. Jerzy Rozenblatt, a leader of the Jewish faction, gave Gerhardt his full support. Rozenblatt demanded autonomy in issues concerning education and demanded the creation of autonomous municipal educational committees for Germans and Jews. Each population, he argued, was entitled to a school that spoke its language[87]. He defined the situation this way:

> The population of Poland is not homogeneous. Alongside the Polish are other nationalities, which constitute 30% of all inhabitants. [...] The Jewish nation wants to live in harmony with the Poles. *Politically, we are Polish. In our internal life, we are Jews* [...]. We demand national, cultural autonomy, that is to say, the right to self-determination in all

---

84 Hertz, 1933, pp. 167f.
85 Hertz, 1933, pp. 167f.
86 See, for instance, Stempin, Arkadiusz: *Próba 'moralnego podboju' Polski przez Cesarstwo Niemieckie w latach I wojny światowej*. Neriton: Warsaw 2013, pp. 553–580. For a different perspective see: Silber, Marcos: Leumiut shona, ezrkhut shava! ha-mamatz le-asagat otonomia le-yehudey polin be-milkhemet ha-olam ha-rishona. The Zalman Shazar Center for Jewish History and Tel Aviv University Press: Tel Aviv 2014.
87 Ibid., p. 168.

internal matters [...] we seek not separatism but mutual understanding, working for the common good and prosperity[88].

The only way to build the Polish state, argued Lichtenstein, Gerhardt and Rozenblatt, was with the voluntary participation of all citizens, including those identified as minorities. Deferring minority rights in the name of national consolidation would likely be counterproductive. Instead, Gerhardt, Rozenblatt, Lichtenstein and their followers proposed recognition of the cultural particularity of the groups constituted as minorities. These three fraction's spokesmen demanded recognition of their separate public spheres. They sought reinforcement of separate public spheres and public measures. These aimed at protecting or even promoting ethnocultural identities, (by means of a just budgeting of their cultural necessities, or constructing recognized school councils for every minority[89]) in order "to give every one the possibility of a free development"[90].

In an renewed coalition they proposed to refer to the common public sphere as bringing groups together to express their differences but within common institutions and a shared commitment to the larger political order, loyal to the nascent Polish state. Indeed, they envisaged a political culture common to all ethno-national-linguistic-cultural segments but only if it guaranteed the basic interests of the non-dominant groups, which Łódź encountered formal and informal discrimination as a result of their cultural differences. Their model attempted to accommodate cultural differences while encouraging interdependence.

Polish reactions ranged from open aversion to empathy for the cultural minorities disenfranchised by monolithic nation-building. Some demanded segregationist schooling for each religious group, in Polish (like J. Wolczyński, of the Chrześciańska Demokracja), regardless of student body and regardless of any empathetic attitude to one who would probably be discriminated against in this situation. Others (like A. Rzewski of the Polska Partia Socjalistyczna) sought a uniform, nonsectarian school, also in Polish (regardless of the language or culture of the child who attended it)[91], lest separate schooling – and minority rights in general – arouse ethnic conflict[92]. For the sake of national consolidation, minorities were

---

88   "Mowa d-ra Rozenblata, prezesa frakcji żydowskiej w Łódzkiej Radzie Miejskiej". In: *Głos Żydowski*, 1.11.1917. Emphasis in the original.

89   YIVO Archive [henceforth YIVO], RG 1400, Bund, MG2, Box 15, folder 145, Protokoł posiedzenia 37-go Rady Miejskiej z dn. 29 Października 1917 r."Fun lodzer shtotrat". *Lebensfragen*, 15.12.1917.

90   "Debatn in Lodzer shtotrat vegn di yiddisher natzionale recht". *Haynt*, 16.11.1917.

91   Hertz, 1933, p.168.

92   "Debatn in lodzer shtodt-rat vegn di yiddishe natzionale recht". *Haynt*, 16.11.1917.

asked to renounce their claims to "minority rights" (already formulated before the outbreak of the war), which were perceived as competing with the Polish ones[93].

I. Gralak of the Polska Partia Socjalistyczna – Lewica, a party supporting minority rights, expressed empathy for the situation of the deprived cultural minorities in a monolithic nation-building process and agreed that small children should be taught in their mother tongue, although the school system should be standardized to prevent nationalism, and education should be in Polish from the youngest possible age[94]. Free of chauvinism, Gralak sincerely wished to neutralize attributive variables in order to achieve equality within the state. He recognized only the class struggle for political and economic equality, which was to represent supra-cultural and supra-ethno-national interests and culminate in assimilation into one united cultural collective. Gralak dismissed minority claims that these interests were abstract and rhetorical and served the majority. He didn't realize his approach was not the only way to an equitable division of resources[95].

Even sympathizers viewed the Jewish and German politics of identity as "separatist" and therefore illegitimate, undermining society's "united" advancement toward independence. Any group's campaign for recognition of its particularity and separate public sphere implied lack of commitment to – and even alienation from – the common public sphere. This interpretation reflected fear of the fragmentation that was, prima facie, endemic to the politics of identity, with "the other" endangering civil solidarity and nation-building.

The German and Jewish representatives passed resolutions demanding budgetary equality and education councils for each minority. They defended separate public spheres without forgoing the common one[96]. In short, the minority groups partially advanced their agenda.

However, despite its multiple cultures, identities, and boundaries and its increasing number of particular, minority-reinforced public spheres, Łódź was not

---

93   Hertz, 1933, p.168; "Debatn in lodzer shtodt-rat vegn di yiddishe natzionale recht". *Haynt*, 16.11.1917. The Bibliography regarding the formulation of minority rights is huge. The monograph by Janowsky, Oscar: *The Jews and the Minority Rights (1898–1919)*. AMS Press: New York 1966, is still the basic introduction to the topic.

94   Hertz, 1933, p.168. On the attitude of the PPS Lewica to the Jewish question and minority rights, see: Zimmerman, Joshua: *Poles, Jews and the Politics of Nationality. The Bund and the Polish Socialist Party in Late Tsarist Russia*. The University of Wisconsin Press: Madison 2004, pp. 267–270.

95   Protokoł posiedzenia 62-go Rady Miejskiej z dnia 23 Stycznia 1918 r.

96   "Fun Lodzer shtotrat" [From Łódź's city council]. *Lebensfragen*, 14.12.1917; "Polin". *HaTzfira*, 29.12.1917.

"multicultural". Institutional acceptance of such spheres derived not from ideological accord acknowledging their benefit to society, but from political pressure. It
was considered in some way a necessary evil. Furthermore, the city didn't promote
informal norms of power sharing or cultural tolerance.

Ostensibly, the recognition of multiple cultures empowered Jews and Germans
(the most prominent minorities) to help negotiate the future of the municipal
domain. Yet, these negotiations were conducted within the context of an unequal
system that divided the ethno-national and cultural-linguistic segments of the
population into two groups: those intended to define the essence and objectives
of an ever more firmly established political entity, and those that had to adapt to
these aims.

The forced recognition of a minority school system was accompanied by budgetary deprivation of Yiddish and German educational and cultural institutions,
philological discussions of the jargonistic nature of Yiddish and, even more important, arguments about the linguistic future of the Jewish community supposedly marching toward Polonization. Homogeneity advocates pointed to Yiddish
speakers' the fluid cultural identity as reason to deny them minority rights as well
as a separate public sphere[97]. However this call, that actually was raised against
essentialisation of these identities saw in these groups, that were calling for their
own recognition, basically, their fluidity, and did not recall an equivalent process
within itself. The hegemonic group emphasized minority groups' fluid identity
and self-definition in order to de-legitimate it and make room for a standard,
all-embracing Polish national-cultural identity, with an essential status of its own.

Conclusions

German and Polish authorities both legitimised and negated cultural multiplicity
in Łódź in order to strengthen those in power. While the German occupying
forces emphasized the tri-cultural nature of Łódź in order to promote de-Polo-
nization, the Polish national movement regarded these politics as "separatist" in
order to affirm the "Polish" character of Łódź. The movement perceived multiple
cultures as sabotaging national solidarity and the formation of a Polish political
entity. However, given the minorities' massive ethno-national segments, the Polish
Circle was forced to tolerate linguistically or culturally particular public spheres

---

97 YIVO, RG 1400, Bund, MG2, Box 15, folder 145, Protokoł posiedzenia 37-go Rady
    Miejskiej z dn. 29 Paźddziernika 1917 r. YIVO, RG 1400, Bund, MG2, Box 15, folder
    145, Protokoł posiedzenia 46-go Rady Miejskiej z dnia 22 Listopada 1917 r. Protokoł
    posiedzenia 62-go Rady Miejskiej z dnia 23 Stycznia 1918 r.

exclusively pertinent to the relevant linguistic or cultural minority and was also forced to relate to it as part of the general public domain. Nevertheless, since the minorities were regarded as a necessary evil, the Polish national movement de-legitimized the minorities' presence in the common public sphere as well as their separate and particular spheres and their symbolic significance – cultural pluralism and civic equality.

Krzysztof Paweł Woźniak
University of Łódź,
Department of Polish History of the 19th century

Betrayed twice. The German community in the Kingdom of Poland during the Great War

Shortly before the outbreak of World War I the Kingdom of Poland was inhabited by about 500 thousand Germans who accounted for approximately 5% of the total population of the Kingdom. Three-quarters of this population lived in the countryside with the largest concentrations in the provinces of Piotrków, Kalisz, Warsaw and Płock[1]. The largest number of Germans living in the cities inhabited Łódź and Warsaw as well as industrial centers of the Łódź and Częstochowa – Sosnowiec districts. In many cases, after living together with the Polish population for over a century, the German national consciousness was limited to a sense of community regarding the language and religion. Gradually the process of acculturation deepened, which was visible mainly in the cities, especially in

---

1 Around 1910, the percentage of German population in the total population of the Kingdom of Poland fluctuated, according to various estimates, from 3.6% to 5.6% (compare: Chrapowicki, Włodzimierz: *Krótki opis topograficzny i statystyczny Królestwa Polskiego.* Zakłady Graficzne Braci Wierzbickich: Warszawa 1912; Krzyżanowski, Adam/ Kumaniecki, Kazimierz: *Statystyka Polska.* Polskie Towarzystwo Statystyczne: Kraków 1915; Romer, Eugeniusz/ Weinfeld Ignacy: *Rocznik polski. Tablice statystyczne.* Nakładem Księgarni G. Gebethnera,: Kraków 1917; Wakar, Włodzimierz: *Rozwój terytorialny narodowości polskiej.* St. Święcicki: Kielce 1917; Strasburger, Edward (ed.): *Rocznik statystyczny Królestwa Polskiego z uwzględnieniem innych ziem polskich. Rok 1915.* Gebethner i Wolff: Warszawa 1916). In 1913 it was assumed that the Kingdom was inhabited by 719 thousand Germans, who made up 5.5% of the total population (Pruss, Witold: *Społeczeństwo Królestwa Polskiego w XIX i początkach XX wieku. Cz. I: Narodowości, wyznania, sekty, organizacje kościelne,* "Przegląd Historyczny", t. 68, 1977, z. 2, p. 276). In January 1915, the Russian Ministry of Internal Affairs referred to the data from 1908, showing the number of 552,895 Germans, with a note that this figure "increased significantly" in the period 1908–1914 (Российский Государственный Исторический Архив, Санкт Петербург (RGIA), fond 821, opis 10, sygn. 1169, k. 68). The overwhelming majority of Germans lived in the countryside, making up, according to various estimates, from 62% to 75% of the total German population in the Kingdom of Poland.

Warsaw[2]. The state of national consciousness was also heavily influenced by Russian public institutions, especially educational. For the youngest generation of Germans in the Kingdom, that is the people born in the last decades of the 19th and early 20th century, the Russian character of the country where they lived was absolutely natural. Similar to their Polish and Jewish neighbors, Germans felt subjects of the country in which Russian was the official language, the Orthodox religion the privileged denomination and military service under Russian command an undisputed duty of young men. Not without reason, a German geographer and historian, Eugen Oskar Kossmann, coming from Rudy Bugaj near Aleksandrów Łódzki wrote about "the late national awakening"[3] of his compatriots[4]. In many cases, this happened only under the influence of wartime events[5].

For more than 400 thousand German peasants often funning their farms in the territory of the Kingdom of Poland for several generations, the outbreak of the Great War carried a threat much more serious than for Polish peasants and reached much further than the fear for one's own life and the entire family fortune. The first months of the conflict between Russia and Germany brought an end to speculations that have appeared in the press in the Kingdom and Empire since the end of the Russian-Japanese war, raising the question who the Germans living within the borders of Russia really were. They suddenly became a threat to the

---

2   See: Stegner, Tadeusz: *Ewangelicy warszawscy 1815–1918*. Semper: Warszawa 1993. Even the traditionally German environment of the congregation of the Lutheran Church in Warsaw was very diverse. In 1906 it consisted of 9257 Germans and 9145 Poles (Merczyng, Henryk: "Ilu jest ewangelików Polaków?". *Zwiastun Ewangeliczny*: 1906, nr 5, p. 17).

3   All quotations in the text have been prepared by the translator.

4   Kossmann, Oskar: *Es begann in Polen. Erinnerungen eines Diplomaten und Ostforschers*. Verlag J. A. Koch, Marburg 1995, pp. 19–20. Compare: Krebs, Bernd: *Nationale Identität und kirchliche Selbstbehauptung. Julius Bursche und die Auseinandersetzung um Auftrag und Weg des Protestantismus in Polen 1917–1939*. Neukirchener Verlagsgesellschaft: Neukirchen-Vluyn 1993, pp. 15–18; Wegener, Tadeusz: *Juliusz Bursche – biskup w dobie przełomów*. Augustana: Bielsko-Biała 2003, p. 60.

5   This process is well documented in the memories of Paul Althaus, a military chaplain from Łódź in the years 1915–1917 (Althaus, Paul: *Lodzer Kriegsbüchlein. Deutsch-evangelische Betrachtungen*. Vandenhoeck & Ruprecht: Göttingen 1916; idem: *Um Glauben und Vaterland. Neues Lodzer Kriegsbüchlein*. Vandenhoeck & Ruprecht: Göttingen 1917). See also: Kucner, Monika: *I wojna światowa w świetle badań literaturoznawczych: kazania pastora Paula Althausa z lat 1915–1917*. In: Radziszewska, Krystyna/ Zawilski Piotr: *Między wielką historią a codziennością. Łódź i region łódzki w okresie I wojny światowej*. Archiwum Państwowe: Łódź 2011, pp. 111–127.

most vital interests of the state. It was stated with trepidation that the weakness of the Romanov monarchy, disclosed during fights with Japan, contributed to the development of a pan-germanic idea among the German-speaking subjects of the tsar. The Russian press also informed about the increasing number of Germans in the Kingdom of Poland and the growing area of land they owned[6].

The propaganda campaign directed against the colonists started in the first decade of the 20th century raised two types of allegations. Firstly, the Polish press sounded the alarm because of Germans purchasing land. Then, in the years just before the outbreak of the war and in its first months, colonists were accused of spying for the German army. In light of the sources known today it can be stated with full confidence that the allegation of espionage was invented in Moscow and St. Petersburg, and was taken up and maintained by some of the press in the Kingdom.

Tracing the main themes present in the journalism shows the creation of a specific topos of a colonist – a spy and a traitor[7]. Repeated display of often identical motifs proves that the action was directed, but also reveals the limited ingenuity in creating this vision of danger[8]. Even before the war, during the maneuvers of Russian troops at the Narew River near Modlin, elements of a bridge "of a strategic importance" were allegedly discovered in a mill belonging to a German colonist[9]. In November 1914, so already in the course of the war, Vasily Nemirovich-Danchenko reported on a similar mill near Sochaczew (Niemirowicz-Danczenko 1914, p. 7). This extremely unreliable correspondent of "Russkoe Slovo" ("Русское Слово") left many descriptions of the treacherous attitude of the colonists. His

---

6   "Утро России" dated 11.01.1915, p. 3 (correspondence from Warsaw). According to Russian estimates, in 1908 German colonists in the Kingdom of Poland owned 11 716 diesiatin (12 770 hectares) of land (RGIA, fond 821, opis 10, sygn. 1169, k. 68). In the light of the available random data, this figure seems to be underestimated (Archiwum Państwowe w Kielcach (APK), Kancelaria Gubernatora Kieleckiego (KGK), sygn. 98, p. 41, 47.

7   Hensel, Jürgen: *Ewakuacja kolonistów niemieckiego pochodzenia z Królestwa Polskiego "w głąb Rosji" w latach 1914–1915*. In: Borodziej, Włodzimierz/ Wieczorkiewicz, Paweł (ed.): *Polska między Niemcami a Rosją. Studia ofiarowane Marianowi Wojciechowskiemu w 70. rocznicę urodzin*. Wydawnictwo Instytutu Historii Polskiej Akademii Nauk: Warszawa 1997, p. 47 footnote. 33.

8   RGIA, fond 821, opis 10, sygn. 1169, k. 66, 78; Niemirowicz-Danczenko, Wasilij: "По крестам боев. Под Лодзиою". *Русское Слово* dated 21.11.1914.; *Rys historyczny Kościoła Ewangelickiego w Radomiu*, vol. 1: 1826–1926, k. 43–45 (a copy in the German Historical Institute in Warsaw).

9   "Kronika miesięczna". In: *Biblioteka Warszawska* 1908, t. 2, p. 424.

reports, and the ones repeated later, were swarming with exposed spies, agents enlisting in the German army and following the Russian command at the front. "When we were passing through the colonies, especially at night, piles of grain, haystacks, barns and stables were burning. Bells were ringing on weekdays" and colonists supposedly transmitted signals using mirrors. It was also believed that German farmers used carrier pigeons to communicate with Wilhelm's troops[10]. German colonists were perceived as "an intelligence office collecting information about the movements of Russian troops"[11]. It was they who led Germans to the resting units of Russian troops, lured Russians into ambushes, served as guides, hid German prisoners who escaped, provided them with food and forage, while refusing it to Russians[12]. Soon, it turned out that creating and maintaining such a psychosis of threat allegedly posed by colonists served a specific purpose. At the turn of 1914 and 1915, neither colonists nor the administrative authorities, especially military, could have expected that the fate of German farmers in the Kingdom of Poland was already sealed.

On 19 December 1914, commander in chief, the Grand Duke Nikolai Nikolaevich gave an order with a clause "to carry out promptly", demanding rapid evacuation of all male German farmers above 15 years of age, living less than 15 versts away from railways and resettling them deeper into the empire[13]. The term "evacuation" itself was not understood as sinister because while the difficult situation of Russian troops at the front developed, state institutions together with the employed staff were transferred from the Kingdom of Poland to Russia. Equipment of industrial plants was taken away as well.

With regard to German peasants, "evacuation" meant in practice displacement and deportation, which spared only the sick who would not have survived the travel. The evacuation included also family members, because, as it was justified:

10 RGIA, fond 821, opis 10, sygn. 534, k. 6.
11 Ibidem; Compare: Septimus: "Szpiegostwo niemieckie w byłym zaborze rosyjskim w czasie wojny światowej". In: *Kurier Warszawski* dated 29.12.1925, p. 2.
12 Revelations published by the Russian correspondent were in contradiction with the reports of the Russian military authorities from areas of hostilities and their direct supply areas (APK, KGK, sygn. 2987, k. nlb. See also: Stegner, Tadeusz: "Protestanci na terenie guberni radomskiej i kieleckiej w XIX i na początku XX wieku". In: *Studia Kieleckie. Seria Historyczna* 1, 1995, p. 19).
13 Archiwum miasta stołecznego Warszawy Oddział w Grodzisku Mazowieckim, Pełnomocnik Gubernatora Warszawskiego w Twierdzy Modlin, sygn, 20, k. 142–143; APK, KGK, sygn. 2987, k. nlb.

"military authorities complain of female espionage."[14] Warsaw Governor-General repeatedly admonished to consider these deportations a "national necessity" (государственная необходимость) and carry them out without severity, but persistently[15]. In practice, families were separated, women and children were not taken to the same places, to which their husbands and fathers were deported[16]. Local administrative authorities were supposed to protect abandoned households. Still, "terrible things happened" in the left villages. First of all, all belongings of the colonists were sold to Polish peasants and Jews for next to nothing. In front of colonists' very eyes peasants looted and stole anything they could and anywhere they could. Only very, very few showed some compassion and mercy. "It serves Germans right, let them go, everything will be ours", their Polish neighbors said. After the colonists disappeared, everything they left behind was plundered: fences, barns, whole houses.[17] By suggesting the alleged threat posed by colonists, Russian authorities succeeded in instilling a belief that Germans were being punished for treason. The words of a pastor from Lublin, Adolf Tochtermann are important evidence of how strong this belief was: "Many otherwise noble and good people did not see the great injustice done to these people. This was only seen as revenge for the wrongs done in Poznań and considered as a historical nemesis" (Rys historyczny, k. 47). In the course of the colonists deportations, Russian authorities used a stereotype equating Germans with Evangelicals, which meant that Polish evangelical peasants were also displaced (e.g. in the Suwałki and Lublin provinces). "They demanded a list of parishioners from the pastor and are sending all of them orders to leave. Many people with German names live in fear" – noted Reverend Józef Rokoszny in his diary under the date of 28 February 1915[18]. "Russian Protestant subjects, must leave. There are also such situations: the husband went to the war as a Russian soldier and his wife, a Protestant, is now being sent to Russia [...]" (Caban/Przeniosło 1998, p. 224). This unplanned institutionalization of the

14 APK, KGK, sygn. 2987, k. nlb. – cyrkularz gubernatora kieleckiego do naczelników powiatów z 12.02.1915 r.

15 Ibidem, k. nlb. – a telegram dated 12.02.1915

16 APK, KGK, sygn. 2769, k. 17–18.

17 *Kronika Zboru Ewangelickiego Lubelskiego*, t. 1 (1888–1932), k. 183, 185, 186 (a copy in the German Historical Institute in Warsaw).

18 Caban, Wiesław/Przeniosło, Marek (ed.): Rokoszny, Józef ks.: *Diariusz Wielkiej Wojny 1914–1918*. Wyższa Szkoła Pedagogiczna im. Jana Kochanowskiego: Kielce 1998, vol. 1, p. 224.

deportees made it easier in the future to estimate losses that Germany suffered in the Kingdom of Poland during the Great War[19].

The term "evacuation" used with regard to German colonists was a euphemism concealing the real purpose of the operation. Its true meaning was revealed in a telegram of the Warsaw Governor-General dated 20 February 1915: "Dislocation concerns only German colonists, i.e. farmers of German descent, owning land, wherever they may be, but not all persons bearing German names"[20]. The legal basis for this decision was included in the decrees of liquidation issued five days earlier. They were published in the form of highest ukases, which means they were extraordinary ordinances confirmed by the tsar without the Duma. They introduced the purchase of land owned by the colonists, which in fact meant expropriation[21]. Upon entering the war, Russia did not take into account that it might take an unfavorable course for this very country. Expropriation of German farmers, to be carried out in 26 provinces and the Grand Duchy of Finland, was to protect the great Russian land property against expropriation and parceling as well as to ensure the gratitude of the Russian and Polish peasantry, who was offered to buy the expropriated land. The course of war prevented the implementation of these plans[22].

---

19 According to the balance drawn up by the Consistory of the Lutheran Church at the end of 1916, the Church as an institution has suffered such enormous material losses that "a million rubles would probably not be enough to restore 5 destroyed and 18 damaged churches, 15 presbyteries, 7 parish houses, 79 houses of worship and 78 schools" (Holtz, Edmund: *Der Krieg und die Evangelisch-Lutherische Kirche in Polen. Erweiterter Konferenzbericht verfaßt auf Grund von amtlichem Material im Auftrage des Warschauer Evangelisch-Ausgburgischen Konsistoriums. Deutsche Staatsdruckerei.* Łódź 1916, p. 11). This estimate did not take into account further losses resulting from requisitions of the church property taking place until the last months of the war. In October 1917, the German authorities took away bells and tin and lead organ pipes from St. John's Lutheran Church in Łódź.

20 APK, KGK, sygn. 2987, k. nlb.

21 "Gesetze über die Ländereien der deutschen Kolonisten. Landbesitz feindlicher Ausländer und der Kolonisten". In: Hummel, Theodor: *100 Jahre Erbhofrecht der deutschen Kolonisten in Rußland.* Reichsnährstand Verlags-Gesellschaft m b. H., Berlin 1936; Anhang 2. Teil: Enteignungs- und Liquidationsgesetze, pp. 223–253.

22 The deportations were accompanied by various guesses as to their consequences: "Newspapers write that colonists form Russia, who have so far been deported to Siberia, will be brought in place of German colonists" (Caban / Przenioslo 1998, p. 226). Centrally managed and administratively regulated resettlement of peasants in Russia had a tradition dating back to at least the third quarter of the 18th century. In 1894 an ukase of 1889 permitting resettlement of peasants settled on government land was

The scale of displacement of the German inhabitants from the Kingdom of Poland was huge. Some idea of the loss of population may be given by the information provided by Eduard Kneifel, which is, however, by no means exhaustive[23]. In the area of the Diocese of Warsaw, almost all the faithful from the parishes in Przasnysz, Paproć Duża and Pilica were deported to Russia. The same happened with the Lutherans belonging to the parish branch of Stara Iwiczna in Błędów. 3.6 thousand out of 4 thousand Lutherans from the parish in Radzymin were deported. In the Diocese of Płock, only in the period of 15–17 January 1915, 2,806 Evangelicals from the parish in Płock were deported to Russia. Only 40 people out of 1,200 parishioners of the parish branch in Płońsk stayed in their homes. All people were deported from the cantorate in Boryszew and the house of prayer and many farms ware razed to the ground[24].

The progress of the war provided more time for the displacement of German farmers from the eastern regions of the Kingdom of Poland. 15 thousand out of 17 thousand faithful of the parish in Chełm were deported to the area near Samara, Orenburg and even further east. Out of 8.8 thousand evangelicals from Lublin, only 519 people avoided deportation. Parishes in Kielce, Kamień and Radom lost almost all their faithful. The parish branch in Kozienice, a part of the Radom parish, lost 600 people, only 80 of whom returned after the war. Only the dioceses of Kalisz and Piotrków did not suffer such severe population losses due to the rapid seizure of the western parts of the Kingdom by the German army. However, Russian authorities managed to start the "evacuation" there as well[25]. They deported, among others, about 30 families from the parish in Kleszczów. In the diocese of Łódź Russians displaced the majority of evangelical inhabitants from the parish of Nowosolna. 150 peasant homesteads in the village of Nowosolna were completely destroyed and another 50 only partially. During the fighting 18 parishioners were

---

extended to the territory of the Kingdom of Poland. It was assumed that at least a part of about 850 thousand landless peasants in the Kingdom would move to Russia. An ukase of 1904 facilitated the resettlement of farmers and farming townspeople to the other side of the Urals (APK, KGK, sygn. 1554, passim). War time allowed hiding the real purpose of evictions of German peasants from the Kingdom – expropriation.

23 Kneifel, Eduard: *Die evangelisch-augsburgischen Gemeinden in Polen 1555–1939.* Selbstverlag des Verfassers: Vierkirchen 1971, pp. 30–172.

24 Lackner, Franz: *Chronik der Gemeinde und Volksschule Tiefenbach (Nowe Boryszewo, kr. Plock, Polen).* Ostdeutsche Forschungsstelle im Lande Nordrhein-Westfalen: Dortmund 1959, p. 32.

25 Archiwum Państwowe w Łodzi, Kancelaria Gubernatora Piotrkowskiego, sygn. 2863 passim.

killed, other 4 were shot or hanged by Russians (Kneifel 1971, p. 172). It is difficult
to find a larger paradox in history: during the November Uprising the residents of
Nowosolna ostentatiously showed loyalty to the Russian monarch[26]. In the nearby
Łaznowska Wola, inhabited in 1802 by immigrants from Swabia, a local cantor
and teacher, Emil Froelich, was shot by the Russians after being falsely accused
of espionage (Kneifel 1971, p. 150). Estimates prepared by the authorities of the
Lutheran Church state that approx. 140 thousand of their faithful, i.e. about 37%
of the Evangelicals living in the Kingdom of Poland in 1914 were deported to
Russia (Holtz 1916, p. 2).

The fate of the people deported to Russia who were transported to almost all
western provinces of the European part of the country, was extremely tough,
especially for women who in most cases did not speak Russian. "They unloaded
these poor people in any town and left them there in the hands of God's mercy"[27].
In larger cities that they passed on the way, e.g. in Kharkiv, they could count on
help of local Evangelical parishes. The situation in Kharkiv was particularly difficult because 6 thousand Evangelicals from the Kingdom of Poland were transported there until July 1915. Most of them had no money and needed material
help. Poor conditions during the long journey caused that many deportees failed
in health, and the mortality rate was growing, especially among children. There
were cases of death from infectious diseases[28]. The scope of the necessary help
for the needy exceeded the capabilities of the Kharkiv Evangelical parish. It is
worth noting that Evangelical clergymen were not subject to deportations, being
quite rightly regarded as spiritual leaders of the local communities of colonists[29].
Russian administration launched vigorous steps against those of them whose
statements or manifested attitude were recognized as contrary to the Russian
reason of state. Such allegations were made against Juliusz Bursche, the superintendent of the Warsaw Lutheran Consistory, accusing him of "close relationships
with persons accused of collaborating with the enemy" (Krebs 1993, p. 17). This
absolutely unfounded accusation was a reaction to the efforts undertaken by the
superintendent to organize help for the displaced people, which were supported
by all Lutheran clergy in the Kingdom of Poland. On 13 March 1915 the College
of The Church of the Warsaw Luteran parish wrote to the Grand Duke Nicholas

---

26 Woźniak, Krzysztof Paweł: *Niemieckie osadnictwo wiejskie między Prosną a Pilicą
    i Wisłą od lat 70. XVIII w. do 1866 r. Proces i jego interpretacje.* Wydawnictwo Uniwer-
    sytetu Łódzkiego: Łódź 2013, p. 232.
27 Archiwum Państwowe w Poznaniu, Spuścizna Alberta Breyera, sygn. 30, k. 2.
28 RGIA, fond 821, opis 133, sygn. 1068, k. 31–31v.
29 APK, KGK, sygn. 2987, k. nlb.

Nikolaevich a memorial expressing a protest against equating Evangelicals with Germans and against their deportations. The memorial did not bring any positive effects and additionally J. Bursche was removed from all his duties by the highest order dated 8 July 1915 (Wegener 2003, pp. 32–33). The Russian interior ministry prepared draft regulations that allowed removing pastors from their offices by way of administrative proceedings[30]. Julius Bursche spent the time of German occupation outside the Kingdom, returning in February 1918. In turn, pastor Rudolf Buse from Grodziec in the province of Kalisz was accused of informing Germans about the location of Russian troops and organizing resistance among the colonists in his parish. The charges against him were supported by an argument that Poles were also convinced that Buse was a German spy. He was exiled to Ufa and died in 1917[31].

German inhabitants of the Kingdom of Poland treated deportations, expropriation, requisition, finally, persecution and repressions of the Russian authorities as providences caused by the war, but also as an expression of undeserved injustice that they suffered only because they came from a different culture and went to different temples than their non-Evangelical neighbors. This forced them to look differently at the German occupant, to seek brotherhood, awaken memories and sentiment to the homeland of their ancestors. The disappointment with the people thinking like this was equal to the feelings of rejection and stigmatization by the Russian authorities. Rapid offensive of the German army in August 1914 prevented the deportation of the colonists from the provinces of Kalisz and Piotrków. And that is the area where we find numerous examples proving there was no cooperation between colonists and the German army. What's more, there were numerous cases of prosecuting German farmers for active cooperation with Russians. Common origin, language and religion were not a factor mitigating suspicions of the German military and occupation authorities. German command only rarely treated the indigenous compatriots as potential allies, ready to welcome Wilhelm's troops with joy, offer help, provide intelligence information.

It has to be taken for granted that the German occupation authorities perceived Germans in the Kingdom of Poland as subjects of the tsar, other (meaning "worse") Germans who had to be treated with reserve. They were often suspected of special servility to Russians. Gustav Friedenberg, a pastor in Prażuchy in the Diocese of Kalisz, was arrested already in 1914. He was charged with admonishing reservists from the pulpit to do their duties as Russian subjects. During the hearing

---

30   RGIA, fond 821, opis 133, sygn. 1114, k. 35v.
31   Ibidem, k. 17.

before a court-martial Friedenberg said that he said only what he was required to say as a pastor, "dass sie ihrem Lande zu unwandelbarer Treue verpflichtet sind" (you owe unwavering loyalty to your country)[32]. Saying that he was convinced that any possible sign of disloyalty of German reservists would give an excuse to blame them for desertion. The court did not believe these explanations and sentenced the pastor to 10 years imprisonment. However, Friedenberg directed a request for clemency to the emperor, which was supported by opinions of pastors Eduard Wende from Kalisz and Sigismund Michelis from Lipno. This resulted in a change of the sentence for 10 years in a fortress. For almost two years Friedenberg was imprisoned in Berlin and in Strzelce Wielkie near Opole. In April 1917 through the intercession of the General-Superintendent, pastor Rudolf Gundlach, and with the support of the consistory, he was released[33] But he was prohibited from returning to his parish in Prażuchy. He was entrusted with the duties of a parish administrator in Kleszczów. It was not until the end of 1917, after obtaining a permission from the Governor-General, Hans von Beseler, that he returned to Prażuchy. The allegations of cooperation with the enemy, i.e. Russians, were raised also against pastor Ryszard Paschke from Koło, who was consequently removed from the parish, and against Aleksander Paschke from Chodecz, who was interned for 9 months (Kneifel 1964, p. 189; 1971, p. 88).

Military requisitions carried out on a large scale also left no illusions about Berlin's perception of Germans in the Kingdom. German workers in the cities responded to recruiting them to work in the Reich with great reluctance. As a form of pressure the occupation German administration refused to pay unemployment benefit to persons who did not decide to leave[34]. All these circumstances caused that Germans in the Kingdom of Poland found themselves in the proverbial position: "caught between a rock and a hard place"[35].

---

32 Kneifel, Eduard: *Geschichte der Evangelisch-Augsburgischen Kirche in Polen. Ein biographisches Pfarrerbuch.* Selbstverlag des Verfassers, Niedermarschacht 1964, pp. 88–89, 189; idem, *Die evangelisch-augsburgischen...*, p. 83.

33 R. Gundlach also exposed himself to the occupation administration and in 1916 he was tried "for dissidence, hostile attitude and hostile acts" (Kopczyńska-Jaworska, Bronisława/Woźniak, Krzysztof: *Łódzcy luteranie. Społeczność i jej organizacja.* Polskie Towarzystwo Ludoznwacze: Łódź 2002, p. 143).

34 Hertz, Mieczysław: *Łódź w czasach wielkiej wojny.* Izba Przemysłowo-Handlowa w Łodzi: Łódź 1933, p. 113.

35 Numerous examples of various attitudes are presented in: *Zwischen den Fronten. Kriegsaufzeichnungen eines Lodzer Deutschen.* Lodz 1918.

This atmosphere caused that the German national idea began to awaken. It came to the fore most vividly in the ethnically diverse urban environments of the Łódź area. People were aware of the fact that the situation of the German population in this area was fundamentally different from that of the Germans living in western and northern reaches of the Kingdom of Poland bordering with the Reich. It was feared that the "German island of Łódź", surrounded by the "Slavic sea" will be forgotten and no-one could help it. It was decided that Germans in the central Poland were left to their own resources, therefore, they must form a unity, fostering their language and culture. Hence the special activity of German activists who from the very beginning more or less firmly emphasized the need to preserve the national identity.

In the opinion of Eugen Fröhr, a well-informed editor of the occupation newspaper "Lodzer Deutsche Zeitung", the German community in the district of Łódź in the first period of the occupation was divided into three groups. The first one consisted of "activists" who felt responsible for all Germans in the Kingdom of Poland. The second group consisted of German workers and representatives of the petty-bourgeois. They were ready to manifest their Germanness, but put economic interest in the first place and felt aggrieved by the unfulfilled promises of the German management of factories. They perceived requisitions of raw materials and machinery as machinations of their economic competitors from the Reich. The third group consisted of factory owners who achieved prosperity under Russian rule. They did not get engaged in national issues, were quite cosmopolitan and even considered the possibility of transferring their factories to Russia, which was prevented by the outbreak of the revolution[36]. With the benefit of hindsight, Otto Heike, saw this problem a bit differently. In his opinion, after the ultimate entrance of German troops to Łódź, its German inhabitants were torn between the loyalty to the Russian state, whose citizens the believed to be, and the national sense of community with the Germans from the Reich and its soldiers[37]. Many signs suggest that this feeling was shared by wide circles of the German community in the Kingdom of Poland[38]. War events, especially the lack of German military successes,

---

36 Eichler, Adolf: *Deutschtum im Schatten des Ostens*. Meinhold Verlag: Dresden 1942, p. 253.

37 Heike, Otto: *Deutsche Minderheit in Polen bis 1939. Ihr Leben und Wirken, kulturell, gesellschaftlich, politisch. Eine historisch-dokumentarische Analyse*. Selbstverlag des Verfassers: Leverkusen 1985, pp. 41–42.

38 More detail in: Woźniak, Krzysztof Paweł: "Niemcy w Królestwie Polskim wobec odrodzenia państwa polskiego w 1918 r.". *Studia z historii społeczno-gospodarczej XIX i XX w.* 9, 2011, pp. 331–342.

left no illusions as to the possibility of extending the territory over the Polish land. In 1917 it became clear that thinking about the future Germans from the Kingdom of Poland must take into account the emergence of an independent Polish state.

Already in 1915 the "activists" attempted to organize the German community[39]. In July they began issuing their own publication, the weekly "Deutsche Post", by definition competitive, also ideologically, to the widely read daily "Neue Lodzer Zeitung"[40]. "Deutsche Post", edited by Adolf Eichler and appearing from October 1918, set itself the goal of strengthening social bonds in the environment of Germans living in the central Poland, by referencing to the community of language, national identity ("von deutscher Art") and memory of the achievements of their ancestors. It fulfilled its objective by encouraging to form associations and reporting on the effects of common achievements, especially in the sphere of organizing national education.

In December of 1915, the circle of "activists" formulated a memorandum which was submitted through official channels via the chief of police in Lodz, Matthias von Oppen, and the Governor-General Hans von Beseler, to the Chancellor of the Reich – Theobald Bethmann-Holweg[41]. The most important part of the document was a fragment, in which the authors postulated, justifying it extensively, to incorporate into Germany the following provinces of the Russian occupation: Kalisz, Piotrków and Płock. The memorial was issued under a euphemistic title "Die Deutschen in Russisch-Polen" and sent to influential, nationalist-minded German politicians, who, as the authors of the memorial expected, should support their demands. The anti-Polish character of this document was reflected primarily in blaming the Poles for deportations of German-Evangelicals to Russia conducted by the Russian authorities. According to the signatories of the memorandum, Russian authorities had no doubts about the loyalty of their German subjects until the war. The deportations were a result of the Polish anti-German propaganda. The postulated annexation of parts of the Kingdom was presented as a kind of punishment for the injustice done to Germans by the Poles. The memorandum did not bring the effects that were expected by its authors. The policy of Berlin was evolving in the direction that found its expression in the Act of 5 November

---

39 Eichler, Adolf: "Die Lodzer deutsche Aktivisten und ihre Gegner". *Deutsche Wissenschaftliche Zeitschrift im Wartheland* 3-4, 1941, pp. 283–327.

40 Kucner, Monika: *Prasa niemiecka w Łodzi 1863–1939.* In: Kuczyński, Krzysztof/Ratecka, Barbara (ed.): *Niemcy w dziejach Łodzi do 1945 r. Zagadnienia wybrane.* Wydawnictwo Uniwersytetu Łódzkiego: Łódź 2001, pp. 216–217.

41 Kulak, Zbigniew: "Memoriał Niemców łódzkich w sprawie aneksji ziem polskich do Rzeszy w okresie I wojny światowej". *Przegląd Zachodni* 6, 1966, pp. 338–353.

1916. The noisy activities of the "activists" from Łódź were not always accepted by the German civilian administration in Warsaw (Kulak 1966, p. 343).

In this situation the "activists" have attempted to gather all Germans living in the area of the Russian partition within one organization. At the beginning of 1916 they began to create institutions of the "Bund der Deutschen in Polen". However, neither the German civil administration, nor the authorities in Berlin agreed to its establishment, fearing it would be seen as a manifestation of a Germanization policy. These fears were not unfounded, because the union leadership secretly remained in contact with a prominent activist of Hakata (Ostmarkenverein), George Cleinow (Eichler 1942, p. 201). In March 1916, the local authorities agreed to register the organization under the name of "Deutscher Verein für Lodz und Umgegend". The organization focused on practical activities: they germanized names of the streets, developed the education system and socio-economic organizations, especially savings and loan funds, influenced the make up of police personnel and rogatory offices. They obtained funds from the Reich to achieve these goals (Eichler 1942, pp. 423–424). In February 1917 the name of the association was changed for "Deutscher Verein", which should be seen as another, this time successful attempt to create an organization covering the entire area under Russian rule. "Deutscher Verein" quickly became the largest and the most influential German organization in the Kingdom of Poland. In February 1918 it had around 20 thousand members, and in October of the same year already more than 30 thousand, grouped in more than 200 local branches. The Association dissociated itself from political purposes, while it strongly emphasized the need to guarantee Germans' right to cultural identity.

> Germans in Poland love the country whose industry, commerce and crafts they enliven with their minds and hands. They care about the future of the country with the same seriousness as their Polish compatriots. They want to loyally fulfill all the obligations which the state requires from its citizens. They want to be self-sacrificing and helpful in everything that enriches their homeland and the welfare of the state. For this unlimited devotion they expect only one thing: a full recognition of their German mother tongue and their individuality (Eigenart) and everything that results from this individuality – the freedom to develop the German education system, associations and cultural life. Germans living in the Kingdom associate only in order to protect and develop these things (Dinge) that are dearest to them (Eichler 1942, p. 242).

The German circles paid special attention to the issue of education. It welcomed provisions issued by the Regency Council at the end of 1917 relating to addressing school needs of national minorities in the Kingdom od Poland. They were seen as a signal of a guarantee for minority education given by the emerging Polish state[42]. Already in June 1917, "Deutsch-Evangelischer Landesschulverband" was established, which declared cooperation with the Polish authorities and the society for the good of the entire state[43]. In February of 1918 the "Verband deutscher Lehrkräfte Polens" was created. Its management included teachers of German elementary schools (Volksschule) and secondary schools[44]. Two months later "Deutscher Lehrerverband in Polen" begans its activity[45]. As the years of war have relaxed the discipline at school, the German environment began promoting the idea of quick introduction of compulsory education[46].

In addition to the national education, the second most important element of preserving national identity was the Lutheran Church. The occupation authorities in Warsaw governorate-general sought to impose a new law in place of the one being in force since 1849, which would increase the participation of Germans in the authorities of the Church. They made a lot of effort to push through three demands: 1) to make German the official language of the Church; 2) to make a rule that only those candidates who have studied theology at a German university could become pastors; 3) to move the consistory from Warsaw to Łódź, in which the German nationalist environment had a much stronger influence. The meeting of the Synod ended in a fiasco, because 32 out of the total of 44 pastors demonstratively left the meeting to express their protest against the planned changes[47]. The friction connected with national issues ("Kirchenkampf") within the Lutheran Church was reflected in the 16-year-efforts to develop and adopt the Ecclesiastical Law and the Essential Inner Law[48].

The ethnic problem, including the definition of the relationship to the emerging Polish state, did not apply to German Catholics. Among all Germans in the Kingdom of Poland they represented a small percentage. Their organizational

---

42 *Deutsche Post* Jg 4, 1918, issue 4, p. 1.

43 *Deutsche Post* Jg 4, 1918, issue 40, p. 1.

44 *Deutsche Post* Jg 4, 1918, issue 7, p. 2.

45 *Deutsche Post* Jg 4, 1918, issue 11, p. 2.

46 *Deutsche Post* Jg 4, 1918, issue 40, p. 1.

47 From extensive literature see: Krebs, Bernd: op. cit.; Kneifel, Eduard: *Bischof Dr. Julius Bursche. Sein Leben und seine Tätigkeit (1862–1942)*. Selbstverlag des Verfassers, Vierkirchen über München [1980]; Kossert, Andreas: *"Nieprzejednane sprzeczności?" Napięcia narodowe w protestantyzmie łódzkim w latach 1918–1939*. In: Milerski, Bogusław ks / Woźniak, Krzysztof (ed.): *Przeszłość przyszłości. Z dziejów luteranizmu w Łodzi i regionie. Praca zbiorowa*. Wydawnictwo Ewangelickie św. Mateusza: Łódź 1998, pp. 151–174.

48 *Entwurf eines Staatsgesetzes betreffend Evangelisch-Augsburgischen Kirche im Königreich Polen*, "Deutsche Post", Jg 4, 1918, issue 18, p. 2; Wegener, Tadeusz: op. cit., p. 34.

resilience was also lower than in the case of the Evangelical community. It was only at the turn of 1917 and 1918 when "Verein der deutschen Katholiken in Polen" was founded, which was chaired by father Sigismund Brettle from Konstantynów. One could formulate a thesis that the politically conscious part of the German community in the Kingdom of Poland tended towards conservative, nationalist attitudes. The group was visible thanks to its activity, which resulted in the creation of numerous professional associations and organizations with the very influential "Deutscher Verein" at the helm. "Deutsch-Evangelischer Landesschulverband" gathered approx. 500 schools, in which German was the official language[49] and "Deutschen Genossenschaftsverband" founded in March 1917 was formed by 150 savings and loan funds[50]. The "Activists" were also the prime mover causing ethnic rifts in the church. Germans in the Kingdom of Poland generally accepted the attitude of waiting to see what the political consequences of the war will be. Extremely harsh conditions of existence and the effort to survive exhausted virtually all their energy.

On the eve of the Polish independence a huge part of the Germans who settled in the Kingdom three, four generations ago, did not feel a significant distance from Polishness. Such attitudes were aptly characterized on 7 March 1919 by Józef Spickermann from Łódź, a Member of the Legislative Sejm and the Sejm of the first term, later a senator, when he said in the Sejm:

We, the citizens of German origin, consider Poland as our homeland, because we were born here, we spent our youth here, we are bound with the local land by all our thoughts; our entire psyche is completely different than the psyche of the Germans abroad, all our moral strength comes from this land, our native land; nowhere but here we can feel at home, nowhere but here we are completely at ease, therefore we gladly make every sacrifice for the good of the state. We are ready to give up our property and life to contribute to the creation of a strong and powerful Poland. We only have one request: we want to be able to use our native language at school, at home and in church. The language which we use from the day we are born, and which we want to keep until we die, because our moral strength is related to the homeland as much as to our mother tongue, which we consider a sacred inheritance from our fathers and grandfathers[51].

---

49 *Deutsche Post*, Jg 4, 1918, issue 40, p. 1.
50 *Deutsche Post*, Jg 4, 1918, issue 20, p. 1; issue 40, p. 1.
51 Quoted after: Krasuski, Jerzy: *Stosunki polsko-niemieckie 1919–1932.* Instytut Zachodni, Poznań 1975, p. 176. See also a slightly idealized biographical note on J. Spickermanna (Brehmer, Ursula: *Verantwortung als Aufgabe und Lebensgesetz. Josef Alexander Spickermann zum 50. Todestag,* "Jahrbuch Weichsel-Warthe", Jg 43, 1997, pp. 68–72.

The voice of the same deputy sounded very differently when in a discussion on the Sejm expose of Prime Minister Wincenty Witos, the head of the Government of National Defence, delivered on 24 July 1920, he said on behalf of the Club of German Unification:

> The German Union expresses its confidence in the new government and will support it in all its positions. We hope that the new government will manage to quickly bring us to an honorable peace. As a German national minority we expect that the new government will enter the path of true tolerance and complete equality to concentrate all forces on the work for the reconstruction of the whole country and our common Homeland[52].

Although this short speech was interrupted with applause three times, it revealed the feeling of the German community in Poland of "incomplete" tolerance the lack of "real" equality. In subsequent years, the awkwardness of the Polish policy towards national minorities inhabiting the area of the Second Republic collided with the increasingly stressed nationalistic attitudes in the German circles[53]. No consensus could be reached.

---

52 http://kronika.sejm.gov.pl/kronika.97.3/text/pl/an-6.htm (access on: 17.10.2014).

53 Compare: Matelski, Dariusz: "Za i przeciw Polsce. Niemcy polscy w Wehrmachcie i Wojsku Polskim w kampanii wrześniowej 1939 r.". In: Nijakowski, Lech M. (ed.): *Udział mniejszości narodowych w różnych formacjach wojskowych w czasie kampanii wrześniowej 1939 r.* Wydawnictwo Sejmowa: Warszawa 2009, pp. 33–70.

Andrea Brait

War museums at the former frontline between Austria-Hungary and Italy during World War I

1. On the significance of World War I 100 years after the beginning of the fights

In view of Jan and Aleida Assmann's definition of a communicative or social memory, which indicates a life span of about 80 to 100 years[1], a 100-year-anniversary is a particularly interesting point in time for taking a look at a historical event. Contemporary historians are currently discussing the boundaries of their own subject, which for a long time had been defined, in Rothfels' words, as an "epoch of contemporaries"[2] and thus based on the communicative memory. The enormous attention paid to World War I in 2014, however, raises the question of whether it might be more appropriate to speak of an "epoch of empathy"[3].

With regard to World War I, however, numerous other facts besides the time span have had an influence on the way this event is perceived today: the collective and cultural memory regarding the war was shaped especially by later decisive events of the 20th century. Consequently, in many states the memory of World War II and National Socialism, as well as of the Cold War, has to a large degree superimposed that of World War I[4]. This is, for instance, reflected in the fact that World War I has not been included in various volumes on national lieux

---

1   Cf.: Assmann, Jan: *Das kulturelle Gedächtnis. Schrift, Erinnerung und politische Kultur in frühen Hochkulturen*, München 1997, p. 56; Assmann, Aleida: "Vier Formen des Gedächtnisses". In: *Erwägen Wissen Ethik. Deliberation Knowledge Ethics* 1/13 (2002), pp. 183–190.

2   Cf.: Rothfels, Hans: "Zeitgeschichte als Aufgabe". In: Vierteljahreshefte für Zeitgeschichte 1/1953, pp. 1–8.

3   Cf.: Tagungsbericht: "Quo vadis Zeitgeschichte? / L'histoire du temps présent et ses défis au XXIe siècle". 01.10.2014–02.10.2014 Paris. In: *H-Soz-Kult*. 21.02.2015, http://www.hsozkult.de/conferencereport/id/tagungsberichte – 5841 (28.02.2015).

4   Cf.: Hirschfeld, Gerhard: "Der Erste Weltkrieg in der deutschen und internationalen Geschichtsschreibung". In: Aus Politik und Zeitgeschichte B 29–30 (2004), pp. 3–12, p. 3.

de mémoire[5]. The editors of the volume on the European lieux de mémoire, too, failed to dedicate an article to World War I, whilst including one on "Verdun"[6]. In the Italian volume on lieux de mémoire titled "I luoghi della memoria", however, a text entitled "La Grande Guerra" can be found[7].

This intended omission can also be noted in museum presentations. In Germany and Austria, for example, the presentation of the Second World War by far exceeds that of World War I. Nowadays, however, regions that were immediately affected by the armed conflicts offer enormous open air museums presenting the military events. The numerous memorials and theatres of war preserved for future generations have led to a kind of "World War tourism". Thus, the war is "not seen as the primal catastrophe of the 20th century, but occasionally as a nostalgic spectacle", according to Manfried Rauchensteiner[8]. The journeys, however, also encourage a critical debate about the war. This is, for example, the guiding principle for the Park of Peace on Mt. Sabotin north of Gorizia, where part of the system of caverns has been reconstructed[9]. Further examples include the Walk of Peace, a route of about 100 kilometres through the upper Soča valley established in 2007, which connects numerous open-air museums and the most important remnants and plaques in memory of the Isonzo Front[10].

The following analysis, however, shall focus on museums, which face particular challenges with respect to the representation of war:

---

5   Cf.: Brix, Emil/ Bruckmüller, Ernst/ Stekl, Hannes (eds.): *Memoria Austriae I–III.* Wien 2004/2005; François, Ettiene/ Schulze, Hagen (eds.): *Deutsche Erinnerungsorte, volume 1–3.* München 2001.

6   Krumeich, Gerd: "Verdun". In: Boer, Pim de/ Duchhardt, Heinz/ Kreis, Georg/ Schmale, Wolfgang (eds.): *Europäische Erinnerungsorte 2. Das Haus Europa.* München 2012, pp. 437–444.

7   Isnenghi, Mario: "La Grande Guerra". In: Isnenghi, Mario (ed.): *I luoghi della memoria. Strutture ed eventi dell'Italia unita.* Roma/Bari 1997, pp. 273–309.

8   Rauchensteiner, Manfried: *Geschichte der Erinnerung. Die Transformation des Ersten Weltkriegs (Vortrag im Rahmen der Tagung Isonzofront 1915–1917: Die Kultur des Erinnerns 29. September 2005 bis 01. Oktober 2005 in Bovec/Slowenien)* [Lecture at the conference Isonzofront 1915–1917: Die Kultur des Erinnerns (29 September, 2005 to 01 October, 2005 in Bovec/Slovenia].

9   Cf.: Mazohl-Wallnig, Brigitte/ Barth-Scalmani, Gunda/ Kuprian, Hermann J. W./ Bösche, Andreas: "Einleitung". In: Mazohl-Wallnig, Brigitte/ Barth-Scalmani, Gunda/ Kuprian, Hermann J. W. (eds.), *Ein Krieg – zwei Schützengräben. Österreich – Italien und der Erste Weltkrieg in den Dolomiten 1915–1918* (Bolzano 2005) 9–21.

10 Cf.: http://www.potmiru.si/deu/ (05.07.2014).

The representation of violence and war situations in showcases and dioramas [...] remains extremely risky. The various informative and explanatory texts make clear that there is an unbridgeable gab between the *real* past and the *reconstructed* past as it is presented in a museum. [...] Bringing *war* to *life* in a museum [...] implies striking a fragile balance between aesthetics and historically accurate representations[11].

Museums, especially historical ones, cannot only be described as a mirror of the cultural memory; in the words of Aleida Assmann, the exhibitions show the functional memory[12]. Therefore, the question arises of whether museum representations react to changes in society and, in particular, to new findings and emphases in research. In recent years, experts have repeatedly emphasised a shift in paradigm from so-called "classical war history" towards a "cultural history of war" which "has valorised the role of the individual in the war, thus individualising the representation of war. The acting, feeling and suffering of the (plain) combatant, his subjective impressions and experiences form a substantial part, at times even the centre of the historical analysis,"[13] as Thomas Thiemeyer points out, and thus these aspects are also increasingly taken into account in exhibitions.

The question to what extent such a perspective is realised in exhibitions shall subsequently be examined more closely on the basis of three permanent exhibitions which are located along the former Isonzo Front Line: The museum in Casa III. Armata in Redipuglia, the Museo della Grande Guerra in Borgo Castello in Gorizia, and the Kobariški Muzej.

2. Permanent exhibitions: overview

2.1 Casa III. Armata in Redipuglia

In Redipuglia one can find probably the most extraordinary memorial site of the region, which was inaugurated in 1938 by Mussolini[14]. At the foot of the memorial

---

11 Gryse, Piet de: "Introduction". In: Muchitsch, Wolfgang (ed.): *Does War Belong in Museums? The Representation if Violence in Exhibitions.* Bielefeld 2013, pp. 13–17, here p. 16.

12 Assmann, Aleida: "Funktions- und Speichergedächtnis. Zwei Modi der Erinnerung". In: Platt, Kristin/ Dabag, Mihran (eds.): *Generation und Gedächtnis. Erinnerungen und kollektive Identitäten, herausgegeben unter Mitwirkung von Susanne Heil.* Opladen 1995, pp. 169–185.

13 Thiemeyer, Thomas: *Fortsetzung des Krieges mit anderen Mitteln. Die beiden Weltkriege im Museum.* Paderborn/Vienna 2010, p. 243.

14 For more details hereto, cf. i.a. Wörsdorfer, Rolf: *Krisenherd Adria 1915–1955. Konstruktion und Artikulation des Nationalen im italienisch-jugoslawischen Grenzraum.* Paderborn 2004, p. 109 f.

site, there is a small exhibition in Casa III. Armata (House of the Third Army), which dates back to the year 1974[15], but has been modified in certain areas in recent years[16].

The exhibition is split into three rooms: Sala "3^A Armata" offers an overview of the First World War, with the main focus on the Isonzo Front. The course of the war is extensively explained in text, albeit only available in Italian language, as well as in pictures and on a large map. Various items of equipment used by the soldiers, as well as letters and postcards from the war are displayed in showcases.

In Sala "Duca D'Aosta" the visitor first finds a recreation of an Italian entrenchment from the front line on Monte Sei Busi. In this room, the focus is put on the Italian Navy and Air Force, as well as the memories of this war, while the history of the memorial site in Redipuglia itself is also accounted for. Finally, as the room's title already suggests, the exhibition also refers to the Duke of Aosta.

Sala "Grande Guerra" is the museum's largest showroom. There, the exhibition is dominated by an arrangement placed in the centre of the room and manifesting the Italian triumph. Placed on the wall at the far end of the showroom, the exhibition's focal point is the Italian flag (naval ensign of 1851–1946), which was hoisted on 9 August, 1916 in Gorizia (i.e. one day after it had been conquered by the Italian Army during the Sixth Battle of the Isonzo), and – placed beneath the flag in the centre of the room – a display with all kinds of war waste and a variety of weapons. Displays on the walls of the large room are dedicated to various special themes, such as life in Gorizia and the city's capture, the trenches, war letters, storm troops, and the war industry. The crammed showcases alongside the walls show a variety of equipment, such as medical aids or various models of gas masks.

---

15 Verbal information to the author by the museum staff on 22.03.2014.
16 Verbal information to the author by a member of staff at Kobariski Muzej on 23.03.2014. Changes can also be seen on the basis of the German-language brochure of the museum, which shows room views that are not (no longer) existent.

Illustration 1: View of the "Grande Guerra" showroom.

The majority of objects displayed in this exhibition are of Italian provenance. One of the few exceptions is an Austro-Hungarian "Schwarzlose" 8mm machine gun, pointed at the visitors left of the entrance to Sala "3^A Armata". In addition, the texts in the exhibition are only in Italian. Thus, the museum offers a rather one-sided Italian view of World War I and particularly the Battles of the Isonzo.

2.2 Museo della Grande Guerra in Gorizia

An entirely different approach can be found at Museo della Grande Guerra, which is accommodated in Borgo Castello in Gorizia, in a building in the town's castle district. Kept in black, the showcases already make clear that the museum has no intention of presenting war in a heroic way. The exhibition is kept extremely modest. According to the museum's leaflet, it is the goal of the exhibition to "convey a transparent and effective illustration of the war with all its human and social impacts". In this regard, the text continues, "emphasis is put on an impartial portrayal of the events which shall be a message of peace". The fact that the exhibition aims to reach an audience of different nations is reflected in the German, English and Slovenian translations of the Italian exhibition texts in all showrooms in the form of sheets that can be taken from the exhibition. The museum is evidently aware of the fact that there can be no final answer to the question of how war shall be displayed, which becomes apparent at the end of the exhibition from the look into the past of the museum through various photographs and explanatory texts, as well as the exhibition of numerous donated items which played a central part in the establishment of the museum.

The current exhibition stands out through its specific selection of objects that clearly contradicts the large accumulation of military equipment found in Redipuglia. In addition, the objects in Gorizia are contextualised and explained in detail – with other objects and texts in four languages. This is illustrated, for example, in a showcase with an Italian gas mask, which has a photograph showing soldiers with the same kind of gas masks attached in the background, and which is accompanied by an instruction manual in Italian.

Illustration 2: Italian gas mask (Polivalente model), Italian instruction manual and photographs.

Besides the above-mentioned modest presentation, two larger orchestrations can be found: Right at the beginning of the exhibition, the visitor is presented with a staged field of corpses, or more precisely a reconstruction of a destroyed trench with two dead soldiers wearing different uniforms. According to the exhibition's caption, the two soldiers killed in action "symbolise the awful blood toll of the war"[17].

The second orchestration is considerably larger: The museum has re-enacted a life-size trench modelled on the Austro-Hungarian layout, which was, however, partly equipped with Italian objects, too. It features smaller caverns equal to those inhabited by soldiers, as well as a number of simulated weapons. As visitors pass through, they experience light and sound effects simulating the shelling of the trench. Although it has been apparent for many years that the "idea of the museum as a classical temple of muses and dusty place of learning [...] has changed"[18] and these institutions are increasingly trying to assimilate to the leisure society[19], the question of to what extent such reconstructions are capable of conveying a "feeling" for past living conditions – in this case the life of the soldiers in the drench – still remains controversial, particularly as the visitors do not expose themselves to any danger. The spatial dimensions of a trench and the resources available to the soldiers, however, do become apparent.

17 Transcribed in the exhibition on 22.03.2014.
18 Schäfer, Hermann: "Zwischen Disneyland und Musentempel: Zeitgeschichte im Museum". In: *Museumskunde* 60 (1995), pp. 27–32, here p. 29 f.
19 Cf. Lord, Gail Dexter: "Function & Form: Museums in Response to a Changing Social, Cultural and Economic Climate". In: Matt, Gerald/ KUNSTHALLE wien (edd.): *Jetzt oder nie. 5 Jahre Kunsthalle Wien. Elfenbein und Disneyland. Kooperationen, Internationalisierung, Globalisierung. Kunstinstitutionen im nächsten Jahrtausend (Schriftenreihe der KUNSTHALLE wien 3)*. Klagenfurt 1997, pp. 191–200.

Illustration 3: View of the re-enacted trench.

The remaining exhibition offers a chronological overview of the First World War with a special focus on the South-West Front, where both opposing armies are presented and particular attention is given to the Battle of Caporetto, the ensuing dismissal of General Cadorna from his post of Chief of Staff, and the fights along the Piave River. Besides, there are a number of thematic focal points, such as the one found in the 3rd showroom, which sheds a light on the situation in Gorizia. The main focus here is an extensive list of the fallen volunteers from Gorizia with a detonated warhead of a large calibre shell placed in front – the presentation is reminiscent of a memorial. After the 8th showroom, which is dedicated to the history of the museum, visitors finally reach the Diaz hall, dedicated to Armando Diaz, Chief of Staff of the Italian Army, at the end of the exhibition. The room forms a contrast to the otherwise critical examination of the war and its consequences, particularly as it presents classical souvenirs of a commander, from his war memoirs to school essays and children's drawings which were created on the occasion of the general's death in the year 1928. A particularly positive feature, however, is the large didactic room that offers plenty of space to convey the exhibition and its subject matter to school classes or other groups – apart from the numerous decorations Diaz received in the course of his military career, which are also displayed in this room.

Although the narration in this exhibition was developed from the Italian side of the front, most of the objects are of Italian provenience and a focus is put on the regional history, the museum stands out with its large degree of critical distance from the events. The museum also avoids creating a victory pose as it can be found in Redipuglia, emphasising instead the enormous losses also suffered on the Italian side (whereby emphasis is placed on human suffering and the destruction of cultural heritage alike). Thus, Museo della Grande Guerra in Gorizia manages to meet many of the expectations set for a modern war museum. It is neither possible, nor necessary for all museums to attempt to create an overall presentation of the First World War, an attempt that must be doomed to failure anyway. The only regrettable point is that the name of the museum does not express the particular cultural-historical and regional focal points by which the exhibition distinguishes itself.

2.3 Kobariški Muzej

Kobariški Muzej, which is located right in the old town centre of Kobarid, regards itself as a mirror of the keen public interest in World War I and the Isonzo Front Line[20] and is based on a collection put together by the local population. Since its opening in 1990 it has drawn much attention in Slovenia and beyond. In 1993 the exhibition was awarded the Council of Europe Museum Prize. At the award ceremony in Strasbourg, Friedrich Waidacher explained:

> In the course of my professional career I visited hundreds of museums, among them war museums. Kobarid was the first one where I could not find the slightest trace of chauvinism, bias, or glorification. Its display is deeply touching. It takes its visitors by their hearts and souls and conveys a message which cannot be disseminated too often and too loud: war is insanity, crime, it only generates victims[21].

The museum seems to be incredibly proud of the praise it has received from various sides, which is reflected in an own room especially dedicated to awards and prizes, as well as the many "notable persons" that have visited the museum.

The exhibition is mainly dedicated to the Isonzo Front and is spread over two floors. The entrance foyer on the ground floor features a variety of symbols: Flags refer to the nations that were involved in the war at the Isonzo River. Coming in through the entrance, to the right one finds 36 photographs of soldiers and, placed

---

20 Cf. Museum von Kobarid. Führer. 1. Weltkrieg – Isonzofront. 1914–1918, [Kobarid 1993], p. 5.

21 http://www.kobariski-muzej.si/museum/awards/ (24.08. 2014).

below, various grenades, while on the opposite side of the foyer, 18 crosses and five gravestones can be seen. The museum's focus on the "blood toll that was paid by the soldiers on this part of Slovenian soil, regardless of their origin"[22], already becomes apparent at this stage.

The exhibition begins on the ground floor with a 20-minute film offering an overview of World War I and, in particular, the Isonzo Front, followed by a number of showrooms on the two upper floors, which are thematically arranged. For most objects, short captions in four languages (German, English, Slovenian and Italian) are available. In addition, there are a few short summaries offering an overview of the course of the war, as well as some quotes by contemporary witnesses.

The showrooms on the first floor, the Krn Room, the White Room, the Room of the Rear, and the Black Room are all characterised by the fact that none of the opposing armies is paid more attention to, and that the main focus is put on the human suffering, albeit visitors can follow changes in the front lines on various maps. The Black Room resembles an oratory for the fallen soldiers, which becomes particularly apparent through the staging of a cross and, placed before it, the sculpture of a soldier mourning at a grave. In addition, photographs of seriously injured soldiers and the gate of the Italian military prison in Smast near Kobarid, where numerous accounts of prisoners are written, are very present.

Illustration 4: View of the Black Room.

The entire museum not only stands out with a flood of photographs, but also with various showcases which, similar to Redipuglia, have been filled with equipment of different types and provenance, such as a showcase with different picks and spades of Italian, Austro-Hungarian and German origin, or one with Austro-Hungarian as well as Italian wire cutters found in the White Room.

On the second floor, two rooms are particularly dedicated to the battle for Kobarid. A large ground relief of the upper Isonzo Valley not only illustrates the military situation before the Twelfth Isonzo Battle, but also sheds light on the geographic conditions. The recreation of the mountainous landscape from Bovec to Tolmin and from the Krn mountain range to the Friulian Plain indicates the exact distribution of units, weapons and equipment on 23 October, 1917, the day before the 12th Isonzo Battle began.

At the end of this room, attention is drawn once more to the suffering of the soldiers at the front: the visitors can enter a recreated cavern that shows an Italian soldier writing a letter, the lines of which can be heard through an audio installation. The text expresses the soldiers' life in the high mountains and the deprivations they had to suffer.

Besides the permanent exhibition on World War I, the ground floor offers rooms for special exhibitions, and the first floor has three rooms dedicated to Kobarid that offer a short outline of the township's historical development from Iron Age to the 1990s, with a special focus on the changing powers ruling over the area.

3. Representations of war by comparison

For a long time, the representations of wars in museums were places of hero worship and glorification of war, serving war propaganda: In all the nations involved in World War I, for instance, exhibitions of spoils of war were shown[23]. Weapons and other militaria therefore dominated the presentation of the war in the museum[24]. The guiding principles, however, have shifted: War museums are increasingly

---

23 Cf. Krumeich, Gerd: "Der Erste Weltkrieg im Museum. Das *Historial de la Grande Guerre* in Pérronne und neuere Entwicklungen in der musealen Präsentation des Ersten Weltkrieges". In: Korte, Barbara/ Paletschek, Sylvia/ Hochbruck, Wolfgang (eds.): *Der Erste Weltkrieg in der populären Erinnerungskultur (Schriften der Bibliothek für Zeitgeschichte 22).* Essen 2008, pp. 59–71, here p. 59.

24 Cf. Thiemeyer, Thomas: "Waffen und Weltkriege im Museum. Wie sich die museale Darstellung der beiden Weltkriege und der Umgang mit Militaria gewandelt haben". In: *Militärgeschichtliche Zeitschrift 1/69* (2010), pp. 1–16, here p. 2.

becoming institutions of peace and commemoration of the victims[25]. Despite the fact that since the 1990s many new museums and exhibitions on World War I have been established and many of them pursue the above-mentioned objective – the Kobariški Muzej is a striking example here, but the same motif can also be seen in Museo della Grande Guerra in Gorizia, it must be stated that not all museums arrange their exhibitions in this spirit. The small exhibition in Redipuglia shows a narration that places the heroisation of the war, the technical advances and the glorification of the heroes in its centre.

Along with this, war exhibitions of the present tend to abandon a national-historical interpretation of the war. This is facilitated by renouncing the look at the offenders, and adapting a look at the victims (on both sides of the front), as accusations are avoided and war appears as a "jointly endured disaster". Such a transnational point of view is evidently aspired by the exhibition in Kobarid and, with some limitations, also the one in Gorizia, whereas the exhibition in Redipuglia presents a classical Italian viewpoint. This not only becomes evident through the display of objects that are largely of Italian provenience and the use of texts only available in Italian language, but particularly through the orchestra-tion in the museum's Sala "Grande Guerra", where the Italian capture of Gorizia is celebrated as a heroic victory.

Besides the central messages of war exhibitions, the forms of representation have also seen major changes since the first war exhibitions. Once it was no longer the objective to glorify spoils of war and a nation's own powerful weapons, mu-seums began trying to find ways of conveying a realistic image of the war to the soldiers' relatives and descendants. In response to the strongly text-laden exhibi-tions that had been seen for many years, museums began to show more and more staged exhibitions, particularly from the late 1970s and the 1980s. In the course of the 1970s and 1980s, more and more exhibitions were arranged by designers, who took over the curators' and museum directors' work of assembling the showcases; ever more exhibitions showed orchestrated showrooms[26]. Since that point, as the historian Martin Große Burlange argues, a certain event character can be assumed in exhibitions that are received as a social event[27]. Many modern museums of con-temporary history, however, are currently going one step further: "[T]he primacy

---

25 Cf. Thiemeyer, T. 2010, p. 1.

26 Cf.: Klein, Hans-Joachim/Wüsthoff-Schäfer, Barbara: *Inszenierungen an Museen und ihre Wirkung auf Besucher (Materialien aus dem Institut für Museumskunde 32)*. Berlin 1990, p. 5.

27 Große Burlange, Martin: *Große historische Ausstellungen in der Bundesrepublik Deutschland 1960–2000 (Zeitgeschichte – Zeitverständnis 15)*. Münster 2005, p. 176.

of the museum experience has shifted from object to performance"[28], as Valerie Casey points out. This, at least, is the claim often made to date. The museum in Gorizia, in particular, presents the war in this spirit: The recreated trench with various light and audio effects shows that the museum's intention is not merely to convey knowledge, but to provide a "historical experience" to the visitors.

Often, orchestrations in exhibitions are accompanied by a reduction of the number of original objects, consequently upgrading individual objects. The museums in Redipuglia, in Gorizia and in Kobarid show, however, that this does not necessarily have to be the case. While the staged parts of the exhibitions do indeed only show very few objects (and in Kobarid it remains unclear if any of the objects are originals), the showcases in the remaining parts of the museums are used to show a host of objects, in particular photographs and equipment used by the soldiers.

Orchestrations always imply structuring the perception of the visitor, the facilitation of certain understandings, but also the hindrance or prevention of others[29]. The replicas of the trenches and caverns attempt to direct the visitors' perspective to daily life at the front and the suffering of the soldiers. Thus, the exhibitions in Gorizia and Kobarid already show various elements of a cultural-historical perspective on war, albeit both museums had already been inaugurated before the change of paradigm in military history, which John Keegan introduced in his work "A history of warfare"[30] in 1993[31]. The focus is not on the subjects of major military policy and operational history, but on the daily life of the soldiers at the front and on killing and being killed.

Unless otherwise indicated, illustrations were made by the author.

---

28 Casey, Valerie: The museum effect. Gazing from object to performance in contemporary cultural-history museum, www.archimuse.com/publishing/ichim03/095C.pdf (28.02.2015), p. 4.

29 Cf.: Hoffmann, Detlev: "Laßt Objekte sprechen! „Bemerkungen zu einem verhängnisvollen Irrtum. In: Spickernagel, Ellen/ Walbe, Brigitte (eds.): *Das Museum. Lernort contra Musentempel (special volume of the journal "Kritische Berichte").* Gießen 1979, pp. 101–120, here p. 101.

30 Keegan, John: A history of warfare, London 1993.

31 Cf. Nowosadtko, Jutta: "Gewalt – Gesellschaft – Kultur": Ein Ersatz für "Krieg – Staat – Politik?". In: *Zeithistorische Forschungen/Studies in Contemporary History, Online-Ausgabe, 1/2 (2005),* http://www.zeithistorische-forschungen.de/1-2005/id=4619 (27.02.2015).

Hassan A. Jamsheer
Chair of International Relations
Warsaw Management University

The Middle East and the Centenary of the Great War[1]

During the decades prior to the Great War, leading European powers consolidated their positions by expanding the spheres of influence: i.e., their colonial/imperial possessions. Great Britain was interested mainly in securing the route to India, meaning with respect to the Middle East, annexing Aden (1839), and controlling Bahrain (1880), Muscat (1891) and Kuwait (1899). The French began the foundation of their Empire by the conquest of Algeria (1830), followed later by the occupation of Tunisia (1881) and the incorporation of Morocco (1912). Russia was building a vast Asian Empire, also at the cost of the Ottoman Empire. All of the Middle East – including Egypt, Persia (Iran) and the Sudan – was drawn into great powers' politics.

With the beginning of the 20th century, both the Ottoman Empire and Persia had every cause to feel insecure: hence, the reform movements and revolts of 1908 and 1911 in Turkey, and the constitutional movement in Iran of 1906–1911. Turkey established close relations with Germany[2].

The Entente Cordiale, triple Entente, or in short, the Entente, was formed in two stages: in 1904 (8 April) by the conclusion of a British – French agreement, and in 1907 by the access of Russia. According to the major clauses of the 1904 agreement, France resigned from all objections to British occupation of Egypt (the French resigned from insisting on fixing a time for its termination), while Britain acknowledged the right of France to interfere in Moroccan affairs, together with

---

1 The Middle East is understood in this paper as the Arab North African and South West Asian countries in addition to Turkey, Iran, Afghanistan and (after its establishment) Israel. See: Owen, Roger: *State, Power and Politics in the Making of the Modern Middle East.* Routledge, London – New York 1994, pp. 8 ff. (map on page 12, including North African and Asian countries of the region, but excluding Afghanistan). Also: Chapter 1 of Part I of: Corme, George: *Le Proche-Oriente eclate. 1956–2000.* Editions La Decouverte: Paris 2003.

2 Cleveland, William I.,: *A History of the Modern Middle East.* Westview Press, Boulder – San Francisco –Oxford 1994, pp. 99 – cf.

the introduction of so-called reforms on condition of respecting the hitherto-acquired rights of British citizens. French recognition of British rights in Egypt (and understandably, also in the Sudan) did not have any practical significance, particularly as they were forced to leave Fashoda (in Southern Sudan) in 1898. The French, however, gained a great boost to their empire by being granted a free hand in Morocco. Furthermore, the British monarch Edward VII (1901–1910), in recognition of British isolation on the international arena, was ready to go as far as possible to satisfy the French (and later Russians) and attract them into a British sponsored political-military alliance.

The British-Russian Convention (signed on 31 August 1907) covered three matters, which were of interest to both sides: Tibet, Afghanistan and Persia. Russia and Britain resigned from interference in the affairs of Tibet. Russia guaranteed the security of Afghanistan. Both sides agreed to the partition of Persia into their own spheres of influence. Britain allowed the northern and richer part of Persia to enter the Russian sphere of influence, while retaining the southern part of the country within its own. The two sides were separated by a "neutral" central part that included the capital Tehran[3].

So, the Entente Cordiale had obviously a Middle Eastern moment at its core: firstly, in 1904, when it was convened between Great Britain and France. The two world powers solved at least some of the problems of their so-far rivalry in Egypt (unilateral occupation of the country in 1882, earlier attainment of controlling shares over the Suez Canal Company in 1875), the Sudan (the Mahdist uprising and the Mahdist state of mid-1880's and 1890's conquered by the British in 1898 by Kitchener) and North Africa (accepting the primacy of French interests explicitly in Morocco and implicitly in Tunisia and Algeria). Hence, each side accepted the other's sphere of influence and their attainments in the Middle East, granting them freedom of action on the particular terrain.

The expansion of the Entente Cordiale by the access of Russia in 1907 to the club, through a British initiative, again took place at the cost of Middle Eastern nations. This time, Persia (since 1935, Iran) was at stake, not to mention Afghanistan. The division of Persia into a northern – Russian – sphere of influence, and southern – British – sphere of influence proved a strategically vital moment during World War II and the battle for the Middle East with the Axis states: i.e., the occupation of northern Iran by the USSR and southern Iran by Britain.

---

3   Armand, Collin: *L'orient arabe, Arabisme et islamisme de 1798 a 1945*. Paris 1993; text of Entente Cordiale of 1904 as annex [in:] Carpetier, Jean/Lebrun Francois (eds.): *Histoire de la Mediterranee*. Editions du Seuil: Paris 1998.

Following the chronological sequence of the Great War events, the penetration of the Ottoman Empire by Germany led to its involvement on the side of Central Powers and entry to the Great War. Although the majority of the leading political force in Ottoman Turkey, namely the Committee of Union and Progress (*Jamiyyat al-Ittihad wal-Taraqqi*), were in favour of neutrality, a small decision-making group within the Committee (rather a triumvir) led by Enver Pasha were determined to align the Ottoman Empire with Germany by signing on 2 August 1914 a secret bilateral alliance directed against Russia[4]. The accord was put into effect on 29 October, when the Ottoman fleet bombarded the Russian Black Sea ports of Odessa and Sevastopol. On 11 November, the Ottoman state declared war against the Entente powers and simultaneously announced a Holy War (*Jihad*) on them.

The war theatre of the extensive borders of the Ottoman Empire covered the eastern front with Russia, as well as the operational theatres of Greater Syria, the Suez Canal, Iraq (Mesopotamia) and Arabia. Hence, in the regions of eastern Anatolia and Caucasus, war campaigns continued until 1917[5]. Despite starting with some successes, the 1914–1915 offensive was generally poorly led by Enver Pasha, leading to high casualties. Moreover, under the impact of the Russian offensive, the Ottoman army had to retreat from Erzurum. From then onwards, the Ottomans adopted defensive tactics until the Russians withdrew in 1917 in the aftermath of the Bolshevik Revolution. In these new circumstances, the Ottomans were able to regain most of the territories lost earlier.

Here we should mention the Armenian question. Most Armenians were loyal to the Ottoman state, but Armenian nationalist organisations in both Russia and the Ottoman Empire were acting for the establishment of an independent Armenia. With some Armenians collaborating with Russia, this was treated as a danger to the Ottoman forces behind the lines. Subsequently Armenian villages were evacuated and Armenians were pushed south towards the Syrian Desert, resulting in massive death tolls, while others were killed before leaving Anatolia.

Returning to the war, it should be added that at the time of the Russian advances, the Allies were fighting on two further fronts: the first in the direction of Istanbul, the second towards Mesopotamia. In both cases, the Ottomans were able to repulse the offensives. The first case, the Gallipoli campaign, was launched in February 1915 and aimed at seizing the Dardanelles together with Istanbul. Having ended with success, it would have separated the Ottomans from Germany and simultaneously opened supply lines between Russia and other Entente states

---

4 Cleveland W.I., op. cit., p. 140.
5 Ibid., pp. 141–160.

through the Black Sea. The plan collapsed even after the intervention of 200,000 British-French force that landed at the Gallipoli peninsula. Ottoman artillery and defences inflicted heavy losses on the expeditionary formation, ultimately forcing them to evacuate in January 1916.

At the southern stretches of the Ottoman Empire, the British were ready to implement their military goals. One of them had been shaped a long time earlier, intended for the defence of the imperial land route to India. The second goal was aimed at defending the Iranian oil field, in addition to gaining the potentially oil rich area of northern Mesopotamia. The conversion of fuel for the navy from coal to oil initiated before the war greatly enhanced the importance of the Persian Gulf and Mesopotamian battle front. Therefore, the British landed at Al-Fau on 6 November 1914, while the port town of Basra was occupied by the Anglo-Indian army on 22 November. The road to Baghdad seemed to be open, but at Kut al-Amara, the forces headed by General Charles Townshend were surrounded, and after suffering a long siege they decided to surrender on 29 April 1916. However, this front was so highly significant for the British that within a year, another expedition under the command of General Frederick Stanley Maude was organised, which on 11 March 1917, conquered Baghdad, bringing the southern provinces of Basra and Baghdad under British rule. After the capitulation of Baghdad, British forces were directed towards the east in order to join the Russian forces. The two met at Qizil Rabat on 2 April. The Russians, however, withdrew from the war gradually after the February and October revolutions of 1917. When the war was approaching its end, British forces were on the outskirts of Mosul. The town, together with the province was taken afterwards on the basis of Article X of the Armistice Agreement signed at Mudros on 31 October 1918. The article gave the allied powers the right to demand the withdrawal of Turkish troops from chosen territories on grounds of security.

The next battle grounds of the Middle East during the Great War were areas of Syria, British occupied Egypt (especially the Suez Canal) and the Arabian Peninsula. At the time of the eastern Anatolian campaign of early 1915, Jamal Pasha, another leading figure of CUP, one of the triumvir, led a force of 80 000 soldiers through the Sinai Peninsula with the object of performing a quick strike at the unprepared British defences of Egypt and the Suez Canal, with the latter intended for capture by the Ottomans.

In the aftermath of the assault, the British introduced rather major changes to their war plans. Early in 1917, the British amassing their own army in Egypt, launched their own offensive in the direction of Palestine under the command of General Edmund Allenby. The Arab Revolt against the Ottomans was yet another factor rendering assistance to the British war effort. Jerusalem was captured in December 1917, while, in the face of stiff Ottoman resistance, the war in Syria continued. On 1 October 1918 Damascus was captured by the Arab Revolt forces; a few days later French forces captured Beirut. As mentioned above, on 31 October 1918 at Mudros, the Istanbul government signed an unconditional surrender agreement, the Mudros Armistice, a document that emerged to seal the end of the Ottoman Empire.

During the war, the Ottoman administration bodies treated the non-Turkish population of the Empire in an extremely harsh and brutal manner. In Greater Syria, setbacks on the battle fronts were accompanied by repressive measures, including the public execution of Arab leading figures (eleven persons in Beirut in August 1915; another twenty-one in Beirut and Damascus in May 1916). These martyrs, as they became in the Arab historical mind, were not advocating independence from the Ottoman state, but merely decentralisation: an idea advocated by CUP at its initial stage.

Hence, the circumstances were ripe for an Arab uprising. However, the initiative was to come from the British. Whereas the Ottoman sultan (bearing simultaneously the title of Caliph of Muslims) had declared *jihad* against the infidels, it was conceived that there had to be a significant counterweight. The Hashimite custodian of Islam's holy cities of Mecca and Medina, Husayn Ibn Ali was persuaded step by step to stand at the head of an uprising against the Turkish rulers of the Ottoman Empire. The allied price for that Arab support in the war effort was a pledge to support the establishment of a post-war Arab state. Husayn came from a family claiming decent from the Prophet, and thus having the title of sheriff. The plan was consulted, and apparently for the Arab side elaborated, through correspondence between Husayn and the British high commissioner in Egypt, Sir Henry McMahon. Sharif Husayn claimed to represent all Arabs, in whose name he requested British recognition of an Arab state covering the Arabian Peninsula, Greater Syria (including Lebanon and Palestine) and Iraq. To that effect, Husayn sent a letter in July 1915 to McMahon, setting a starting moment for the widely known Husayn-McMahon correspondence lasting from July 1915 until March 1916. After receiving the first letter, the British government instructed the high commissioner to continue the exchange with Husayn. Later controversy surrounded the question whether Britain promised to support the establishment of the Arab state and later opposed the idea. Meanwhile Britain, during the war, supplied the Arab rebellion with funds, weapons and ammunition. The revolt, commanded by Husayn's elder son Faisal, was formed of Arabian tribal forces, assisted by Iraqi ex-Ottoman army officers in addition to a small number of British army advisers, among them Captain T.E. Lawrence. These forces proceeded from Hijaz province in Arabia, through the port of Aqaba (1917), Palestine and Damascus (reached on 1 October 1918). At Damascus, Faisal started to establish his administration, in the hope of implementing earlier agreements.

However, the agreements with the Arabs, although being vague, opposed the allied Anglo-French-Russian accords during the war, namely the Sykes – Picot agreement. First, in March 1915, concerned with continued Russian participation in the war, France and Britain signed the Constantinople Agreement with Russia, granting Russia the right to annex the Turkish Straights together with Constantinople – an agreement that was never implemented due to the events of 1917 in Russia, which drew it out of the war, as well as wartime agreements. The Arabs came to know about allied secret agreements after their publication by the Bolshevik government of Russia. The British-French Sykes-Picot Agreement, negotiated since 1915 and signed in May 1916 covered the following:

- France and Britain were prepared to recognize and protect an independent Arab state in areas 'A' and 'B' marked on an annexed map, under the suzerainty of an Arab chief. France in area 'A' and Britain in area 'B' shall have priority of enterprises and nomination of officials at the request of the Arab State or Confederation of Arab States.
- France in the blue area and Britain in the red area shall have the right of establishing direct or indirect administration after agreement with the mentioned Arab State or Confederation.
- The brown area (Sanjaq, Province, of Jerusalem) shall be established, after consultation with Russia and other allies, as an international administration pending agreement with the Sherriff of Mecca.

Another pledge of far reaching implications was made to the Zionists in a British declaration. It was contained in a letter from Arthur James Balfour, British Foreign Secretary, to Lord Rothschild, the British Zionist leader dated 2 November 1917, which stated:

His Majesty's Government view with favour the establishment in Palestine of a national home for the Jewish people, and will use their best endeavours to facilitate the achievement of this object, is being clearly understood that nothing shall be done which may prejudice the existing civil and religious rights of existing non-Jewish communities in Palestine, or the rights and political status of Jews in other countries. I should be grateful, if you would bring this declaration to the knowledge of the Zionist Federation. Yours sincerely, Arthur James Balfour[6].

The downfall of the Ottoman Empire as a consequence of the Great War ensured the British and French supremacy in the Middle East, or rather, European supremacy. The system of mandates meant the establishment of new nation states in the region modelled on French and British patterns. During the inter-war period, the area included an independent Turkey, Iran, an Italian, French and British occupied Eritrea and Somalia.

British-French supremacy in the area during the post-World War I period was legalised within the framework of the League of Nations. Hence, article 22 of the League of Nations Covenant referred to colonies and dependent territories, whose inhabitants were not yet capable of ruling themselves in difficult international circumstances. The prosperity and development of those people is a sacred civilisational mission (The White Man's Burden) which could only be carried out by developed nations whose resources, experience and geographical location could best undertake such a responsibility as League mandatory powers. Particular reference was made to some communities of the former Ottoman Empire whose development allowed their existence as independent nations to be temporarily acknowledged, on condition of receiving the advice and assistance of a mandatory until they become capable of independent government. However, the will of particular nations should be taken into consideration in the choice of the mandatory. This was the case of A-type mandates (there were also B and C). Hence, Iraq, Palestine and Transjordania were assigned to Great Britain, and Syria and Lebanon to France[7].

The inter-war period[8] in the Middle East was marked by the struggle for independence. The main efforts of Arabs during the period were directed towards ending foreign rule and gaining independence. Social, economic and political reforms were pushed into the background (e.g.: Iraq, whom formal independence was granted in 1932, and Egypt – in 1936; both as kingdoms; the question of Palestine; the Balfour Declaration of 2 November 1917; Jewish mass immigration into mandatory Palestine; Fascist/III Reich menace; inconsistent British policies in Palestine). In that period and during World War II, the situation in the Middle

---

6   *The Middle East and North Africa 1974–1975*. Europa Publications: London 1974, pp. 49–50, 396.

7   Gelberg, Ludwik: *Prawo międzynarodowe i historia dyplomacji. Wybór dokumentów (International Law and History of Diplomacy. Selected Documents)*. Warszawa 1958, vol. II, p. 39.

8   For a detailed view of the Middle East during these times, see: Roger Owen, op. cit.

East was highly complicated both strategically (in the context of great powers politics) and regionally (with respect to inter-state and local politics).

With the liquidation of the Ottoman Empire, after the Great War, the stage was set for Great Britain and France as the new dominant powers of the Middle Eastern region to achieve their goals. Their status was, on the one hand, defined by the League of Nations, which, as mentioned, formally granted them mandatory powers in accordance with article 22 of the League Covenant. On the other hand, due to popular opposition to the mandatory system, relations had to be regulated by bilateral treaties, such as the 1930 British – Iraqi treaty, becoming the basis for Iraqi formal independence as a constitutional monarchy and access to the League of Nations in 1932. Egypt also achieved formal independence from the British in 1936, also becoming transformed into a constitutional monarchy. None the less, the British continued to maintain military bases in the area, while the French continued a direct presence in the mentioned mandatory areas and North Africa (Morocco, Algeria and Tunisia).

The strategic importance of the Middle East, particularly for British and, to a lesser extent, French imperial interests, later for the Allies' war efforts, and naturally for the rival Axis powers[9], was crucial in connection with substantial oil riches of the region, as well as its importance for sea and land communication lines between Europe and the United States on the one hand, and Central Asia and the Far East on the other.

With the outbreak of World War II, the area became directly threatened by Italy and Germany, to the effect of weakening British positions throughout the area, including Iraq, Egypt and Iran. Hence, after the defeat of France by Germany in May–June 1940, Syria and the Lebanon became an Axis sphere of domination through the Vichy authorities. These Levantine territories were used by Germans to render assistance to the anti-British coup of May 1941 in Iraq headed by Rashid Ali al-Kailani. In June–July 1941 British forces together with Free French defeated Vichy forces, who were given the choice of leaving to France or joining gen. De Gaulle's forces. The majority joined De Gaulle's Free French.

---

9 See: Hirszowicz, Łukasz: *The Third Reich and the Arab East*. Routledge and Kegan Paul: London 1966; (Polish original edition: Hirszowicz, Łukasz: *III Rzesza a Arabski Wschód*. Waszawa 1963); Hart, Liddell: *1953. The Rommel Papers*. Collins: London 1963; *The Memoirs of Field-Marshall The Viscount Montegomery of Alamein, K.G*. Collins: London 1958; Cleveland, William L., op. cit.; Mansfield, Peter: *A Modern History of the Middle East*. Penguin: London 1992; *The Middle East and North Africa 2000*. Europa Publications: London 2000.

As for Iraq, the mentioned serious development came, when in April/May 1941 Al-Kailani, a pro-Axis politician, with the support of the army headed by nationalist elements, seized power in Iraq, forcing the pro-British regent Abdel-Ilah to leave the country. German propaganda and Arab nationalists accused the British of conspiring to get rid of King Ghazi I (1933–1939; killed in car accident), who polarized national anti-British sentiments, and appointing his uncle as regent while the heir to the throne – king Faisal II would be under age. By deciding upon prompt military intervention against the Kailani government (May 1941), the British launched a period called by historians the second British occupation of the country.

Combat operations in the Balkans (operation "Marita"), particularly the seizure of the Crete (May–June 1941), coupled with the mentioned Vichy menace in Syria and the Lebanon, and the Iraqi coup, constituted a valuable opportunity for the Germans to take over the entire Middle East.

Somewhat earlier, in spite of many unfavorable circumstances, the Middle East seemed secure until Italy joined the war in June 1940 on the side of Germany. On 10 June 1941 Italy declared war on Great Britain and France, which meant the extension of military operations to the Mediterranean and Africa. At the same time, British forces were forced to wage battles against Italian forces in Libya and Eritrea. Egypt came within striking range of the Italian air force operating from Libya. On 18 September 1940 the Italians started their offensive against Egypt, advancing by 18 September to Sidi Barrani. The loss of Egypt would have given the enemy control over the Suez Canal, in addition to access to the routes towards the oil-rich Persian Gulf and strategically important Indian Ocean. However, Italian forces had to withdraw into Libya after losing the battle against the British at the end of the same year (Operation "Compass" under the command of gen. O'Connor). Within only a few days, the Italian forces of Marshall Graziani were destroyed. The British continued their march on Libyan soil controlling Bardia (5 January 1941), fortified Tobruk (23 January), and Benghazi (6 February).

Heavy losses induced Mussolini to accept the German offer of participation in the defense of Tripolitania on 10 February, and within a few days, the first formations of what was later called the Deutsche Afrika Korps (DAK), under the command of gen. Erwin Rommel, landed in Libyan Tripoli.

In the meantime, the British became involved in the defense of Greece (attacked by Italy on 28 October 1940), while certain British forces were engaged in battles waged in Ethiopia, Somalia and Eritrea. Gen. Rommel took advantage of the occasion by attacking weakened British positions, conquering successively: Benghazi (4 April 1941), Derna (7 April), Bardia (9 April), and the important port of Tobruk (20 June). The fall of Tobruk was for the Allies a heavy loss, which opened the way for the enemy to Alexandria. On 30 June, Axis forces reached Alamein. The main battle of Alamein was decided by the British counter-offensive initiated on 23 October 1942 under the command of Field Marshall Montgomery, which proved to be a surprise for Axis forces and successful in breaking the German-Italian front (4–5 November). Consequently, the battle of Alamein ended with a long retreat by Rommel forces, chased by the VIII Army of Montgomery. The battle marked the end of the Axis presence in North Africa.

Simultaneously, the American-British Operation "Torch", Allied landing on the North African shore (November 1942) did the rest by liquidating both the Vichy presence and the remnants of the Axis presence in Libya. In brief, the battle of Alamein was a major victory in the fight for the Middle East. Seven months later, the entire North Africa was cleared of Axis forces. The British-American Middle East Supply Center then became the coordinating body of Allied war efforts in that region.

As to the impact of events on the Egyptian scene, it should be mentioned that when the German-Italian forces accelerated their march in the direction of Alexandria at the end of 1940, many Egyptians in their hatred of the occupants attached their hopes for liberation with the defeat of Great Britain in the Middle East and North Africa. Aziz Ali al-Misri, Egyptian army chief of staff (later dismissed), was active in this respect, Colonel Anwar al-Sadat (later jailed) was organizing secret anti-British military actions, and the pro-Fascist para-military organization of *Jam'iat Misr al-Fatat* (*Green Shirts' Society*) were hoping for such change. Fearing for his own eventual position, king Farouk started to hesitate and distance himself from the British, by nominating Ali Maher, then unsympathetic to the British, as Prime Minister.

The balance of power on the Egyptian internal scene started to shift away from the British, who in this critical moment undertook a decisive action. On 4 February 1942, the British ambassador Sir Miles Lampson forced king Farouk, by means of British tanks surrounding the royal palace, to dismiss Maher and nominate the leader of the Wafd party, Mustafa al-Nahhas as Prime Minister instead of him. The action shocked the country deeply and discredited the Wafd among the Egyptian population and army. At the time, this insult to the monarch was viewed as tantamount to an insult of the Egyptian nation. General Muhammad Nagib submitted his resignation from the army (rejected by the monarch), while lieutenant Gamal Abdel Naser with a group of young officers, thought about ways to rid the country of the British.

Equally important as Egypt for the Allies was Iran. Its strategic significance (also naturally in connection with Iranian rich oil fields) became enhanced after Germany's attack on the USSR in June 1941, followed by serious German successes on the Soviet fronts. Besides, German industrial and trade interests were well established in that country at an earlier stage. Nazi propaganda was actively stirring up anti-Ally (particularly, anti-British) national sentiments, while Reza Shah and Iranian elites (including the army) were generally displaying a pro-German attitude.

With the access of the USSR to the war on the side of Allies, there arose (in August) the question of Allied arms deliveries to that country through Iran. Reza Shah's rejection of this idea, which had been supported by the US within the Lend – Lease Act of 1941, caused the Soviet Union and Great Britain to undertake action. On 25 August 1941, Iran was invaded by the Soviet Union from the north and Britain from the south, meeting insignificant resistance on the part of Iranian troops. King Reza abdicated, being replaced by his son Muhammad Reza. A treaty was signed between Iran, Britain and the Soviet Union to the effect of respecting the territorial integrity of Iran, its independence, defense against aggression, and the pledge of leaving the country by foreign forces within six months after the end of the war.

After the Second World War, during the Cold War period, the fight of Middle Eastern nations for independence from European domination became more forceful, especially in the aftermath of the Palestinian *An-Nakba*: The Catastrophe, connected with the establishment of the state of Israel in mid-May 1948 and the resulting defeat in the war. The ensuing unrest took the shape of mass movements as well as military coups d'etat (Egypt, Syria, Iraq, Yemen), successively removing British and French positions from the region[10].

During the Cold War and the prevalence of the bi-polar world order, the Middle Eastern countries joined different sides of the international fence, becoming client states of one of the superpowers. Military-political pacts became commonplace. In the Middle East, the British-sponsored Baghdad Pact covered Turkey, Iraq, Iran and Pakistan. The organisation was renamed the Central Pact in 1959 after the withdrawal of Iraq. This tendency was opposed in the Arab world by Egypt of the Free Officers, who seized power in July 1952 and were headed by Gamal Abdel Naser[11]. Naser was one of the first advocates of a nationalist pan-Arab policy,

---

10 See: Calvocoressi, Peter: *World Politics since 1945, VII edition*. Longman: London – New York 1996, (on the Middle East, particularly) Part III.

11 On Naser's ideas and life, see: Nasser, Gamal A.: *Falsafat al-Thawra (The Philosophy of the Revolution), Cairo 1954*; Nasser, Gamal A.: *Egypt's Liberation: The Philosophy of the*

with the Palestine question being one of the major issues on the Egyptian agenda. With the passage of time, a radical-populist (branded officially as socialist) socio-political programme evolved in Egypt, republican Iraq (after 1958), Libya (since Qadhafi's seizure of power in 1969) and Algeria (after independence in 1962). These governments all shared close ties with the USSR, which, coupled by the requirements of the fight against Israel, drew them into an anti-Western position. On the regional Middle Eastern level, it meant the aggravation of the Arab-Israeli conflict. Lack of victory in the wars against Israel and on the Palestinian front, in addition to the costs of armaments and the militarisation of the particular countries, together with the inadequacy of the theoretical and practical proposals of so-called Arab socialism, created the circumstances for the rise in activities and the domination of the political scene by existing rival ideological-political options, above all, by Islamic radicalism, often called fundamentalism.

Revolution. Government Publishing House: Cairo 1954; Al-Sadat, Anwar: *Revolt on the Nile*. London 1957; Nutting, Anthony: *Nasser*. London 1973; Kerr, Malcolm H.: *The Arab Cold War: Gamal Abd al-Nasir and His Rivals 1958–1970*. London 1971; Hofstader D., (ed.): *Egypt and Nasser*, vol. I–III, New York 1973.

Bibliography

The Łódź War Losses Assessment Committees (Łódzkie komisje szacunkowe strat wojennych) – an undervalued source for research of the Great War in the Łódź region

Piotr Zawilski

References

Archival sources

Archiwum Państwowe w Łodzi, Komisja Szacunkowa Miejscowa w Łodzi.
Archiwum Państwowe w Łodzi, Komisja Szacunkowa Strat Wojennych Powiatu Łódzkiego.

Published works

Radziszewska, Krystyna/Zawilski, Piotr (eds.): *Między wielką historią a codziennością*. Archiwum Państwowe w Łodzi/Wydawnictwo Uniwersytetu Łódzkiego: 2011.

Unpublished works

Pietras, Tomasz: *Zniszczenia wojenne z okresu I wojny światowej w okolicach Łodzi* – a paper on conference *Łódź w drodze do niepodległości*.
Rynkowska, Anna: Komisja Szacunkowa Miejscowa w Łodzi. (wstęp do inwentarza) Archiwum Państwowe w Łodzi: 1970.

Polish military formations of the First World War in documents preserved at the State Archive in Łódź

Tomasz Walkiewicz

References

(Wykaz zespołów archiwalnych z zasobu APŁ)

Akta gminy Chojny 1820–1940.

Akta gminy Radogoszcz 1816–1940 [1941].

Akta gminy Widzew z siedzibą w Ksawerowie 1823–1953.

Akta miasta Łodzi 1775–1945, Zarząd Miejski w Łodzi 1915–1939.

Akta miasta Pabianic 1571–1944 [1945–1952].

Archiwum Eugeniusza Ajnenkiela 1902–1980.

Archiwum Kazimierza Walewskiego z Tubądzina (Archiwum rodziny Walewskich) 1443–1939.

Archiwum Potockich i Ostrowskich z Maluszyna 1425–1944.

Archiwum rodziny Bartoszewiczów 1552–1933.

Archiwum Włodzimierza Pfeiffera (księgarza i fotografa łódzkiego) 1916–1939.

Główny Komitet Obywatelski m. Łodzi 1914–1915 [1916–1920, 1922].

Główny Urząd Zaciągu do Wojska Polskiego w Piotrkowie 1914–1920.

Komenda Policji Państwowej miasta Łodzi 1919–1939.

Komisja Szacunkowa Miejscowa w Łodzi 1914–1921.

Męskie Gimnazjum Polskiego Towarzystwa "Uczelnia" w Łodzi [1891] 1906–1920 [1924].

Prywatne Gimnazjum i Liceum Męskie Zgromadzenia Kupców m. Łodzi [1895] 1896–1939 [1960].

Prywatne Gimnazjum Męskie A. Zimowskiego w Łodzi 1909–1939.

Prywatne Gimnazjum Męskie im. ks. I. Skorupki w Łodzi 1915–1939.

Publiczna Szkoła Powszechna nr 25 Łódź ul. Drewnowska 88 1903–1939.

Sąd Cesarsko-Niemieckiego Gubernatorstwa Wojskowego w Łodzi 1915–1918.

Starostwo Powiatowe Łódzkie 1918–1939.

Zbiór albumów ikonograficznych 1880–1998.

Zbiór druków i pism ulotnych 1882–2007.

Zbiór fotografii miasta Lutomierska 1916–1932.

Zbiór ikonograficzny Archiwum Państwowego w Łodzi 1866–1997, 2014.

Zbiór teatraliów łódzkich 1875–2012.

Związek Inwalidów Wojennych Rzeczypospolitej Polskiej Zarząd Okręgu w Łodzi i oddziały terenowe. Zbiór szczątków zespołów [1919–1939] 1945–1951.

The influence of World War I on the activity of the Russian military and naval clergy

Kamila Pawełczyk-Dura

References

Bazylow, Ludwik: *Historia Rosji*. Zakład Narodowy im. Ossolińskich: Wrocław, Warszawa, Kraków, Gdańsk 1975.

Kenez Peter/Górska, Aleksandra: *Odkłamana historia Związku Radzieckiego*. Bellona: Warszawa 2008.

Malia, Martin/Hułas, Magdalena/Wyzner, Elżbieta: *Sowiecka tragedia. Historia komunistycznego imperium rosyjskiego 1917–1991*. Wydawnictwo Philip Wilson: Warszawa 1998.

Marples, David R./Scharoch Irena: *Historia ZSRR od rewolucji do rozpadu*. Zakład Narodowy im. Ossolińskich: Wrocław 2006.

Pipes, Richard/Szafar, Tadeusz: *Rewolucja rosyjska*. Wydawnictwo Magnum: Warszawa 2006.

Service, Robert/Szczerkowska, Hanna: *Towarzysze. Komunizm od początku do upadku. Historia zbrodniczej ideologii*. Znak: Kraków 2008.

Smaga, Józef: *Narodziny i upadek imperium. ZSRR 1917–1991*. Znak: Kraków 1992.

Smoleń, Mieczysław: *Stracone dekady. Historia ZSRR 1917–1991*. Wydawnictwo Naukowe PWN: Warszawa–Kraków 1994.

Williams Beryl/Tuszyńska, Agnieszka: *Lenin*. Zakład Narodowy im. Ossolińskich: Wrocław 2002.

Witkowicz, Andrzej: *Wokół terroru białego i czerwonego*. Książka i Prasa: Warszawa 2008.

Андреев, Федор: "Начало войны – начало молитв. Духовное пробуждение народа". Вестник в военного и морского духовенства Спецвыпуск, 2005, s. 23–32.

Бабкин, Михаил Анатольевич: Российское духовенство и свержение монархии в 1917 году. Материалы и архивные документы по истории Русской православной церкви. Индрик: Москва 2006.

Богуславский, Иван: "Протопресвитер Евгений Петрович Аквилонов". Вестник военного и морского духовенства 9, 1911, s. 257–263.

"Воспоминания о почившем о. Протопресвитере Евгении Петровиче Аквилонове". Вестник военного и морского духовенства 10, 1911, s. 305–308.

Государственный архив Российской Федерации: Шавельский Георгий Иванович, протопресбитер военного и морского духовенства (с 1911 г.), протопресбитер добровольческой армии (1918–1920 гг.), доцент богословского факультета софийского университета (с 1924 г.). Zesp. 1486.

Григорьев, Анатолий Борисович: "Из истории военного духовенства". In: Галкин, Юрий Юрьевич (ed.): Религиозно-этические аспекты воспитания военнослужащих. Материалы международного семинара, состоявшегося в Международном независимом Эколого-политологическом университете (МНЭПУ) в июне 1997 года. Издательство Международного независимого эколого-политологического университета: Москва 1998, s. 37–45.

Дело великого строительства церковного. Воспоминания членов Священного Собора Православной Российской Церкви 1917–1918 годов. Воробьёв, Владимир Николаевич (red.). Издательство Православного Свято-Тихоновского Гуманитарного Университета: Москва 2009.

Емельянов, Николай Евгеньевич: "Оценка статистики гонений на Русскую Православную Церковь в XX веке". In: Воробьёв, Владимир Николаевич (red.): Ежегодная богословская конференция Православного Свято-Тихоновского Богословского Института. Издательство Православного Свято-Тихоновского Гуманитарного Университета: Москва 1997, s. 166–169.

Золотарев, Олег Валентинович: Христолюбивое воинство русское. Граница: Москва 1994.

"Из речи о. Протопресвитера Г. И. Шавельского на открытии съезда". Вестник военного и морского духовенства 15/16, 1914, № 15/16, s. 547.

"К 10-летию служебной деятельности о. Протопресвитера Александра Алексеевича Желобовского по управлению церквами и духовенствам военного и морского духовенства (1888–1898)". Вестник военного духовенства 6, 1898, s. 181–192.

Кострюков, Андрей Александрович: "Военное духовенство и развал армии в 1917 году". Церковь и время 2, 2005, s. 143–198.

Кострюков, Андрей Александрович: "Временное Высшее Церковное управление на Юго-Востоке России как начало зарубежной церковной власти". Вестник Православного Свято-Тихоновского Гуманитарного Университета. Серия: История. История Русской Православной Церкви 3(28), 2008, s. 50–60.

Ласкеев, Федор: Историческая записка об управлении военным и морским духовенством за минувшее столетие. Типография Товарищества художественной печати: Санкт-Петербург 1900.

Невзоров, Николай: Исторический очерк управления духовенством военного ведомства в России. Типография Ф. Г. Елеонского и А. И. Поповицкого: Санкт-Петербург 1875.

Носков, Юрий Геннадьевич: "Религия и воспитание воинов". In: Галкин, Юрий Юрьевич (ed.): Религиозно-этические аспекты воспитания военнослужащих. Материалы международного семинара, состоявшегося в Международном независимом Эколого-политологическом университете (МНЭПУ) в июне 1997 года. Издательство Международного независимого эколого-политологического университета: Москва 1998, s. 7–14.

Полное собрание законов Российской Империи с 1649 года. Типография Второго отделения Собственной Его Императорского Величества канцелярии: Санкт-Петербург 1830, t. 5.

"Положение об управлении церквами и духовенством военного и морского ведомства". Вестник военного духовенства 13, 1890, s. 418–436.

"Положение об управлении церквами и духовенством военного и морского ведомства". Вестник военного духовенства 14, 1890, s. 418–439.

Поспеловский, Дмитрий Владимирович: Русская Православная Церковь в ХХ в. Республика: Москва 1995.

Российский государственный военно-исторический архив: Управление главного священника армий Северного фронта, О созыве съезда духовенства, о выборном начале в военном духовенстве, протоколы собрания духовенства. Zesp. 2044, inw. 1, sygn. 30.

Российский государственный исторический архив: Духовное правление при Протопресвитере Военного и Морского Духовенства, Бумаги относящиеся к 1-му Всероссийск[ому] Сезду воен[ного] и Морск[ого] Духовенства в 1914г. Zesp. 806, inw. 5, sygn. 9432, cz. 1.

Российский государственный исторический архив: Духовное правление при Протопресвитере Военного и Морского Духовенства, Бумаги относящиеся к 2-му Всероссийск[ому] Сезду воен[ного] и Морск[ого] Дух[овенст]ва в 1917г. Zesp. 806, inw. 5, sygn. 10140, t. 1–3.

Российский государственный исторический архив: Духовное правление при Протопресвитере Военного и Морского Духовенства, Бумаги относящиеся к 2-му Всероссийск[ому] Сезду воен[ного] и Морск[ого] Дух[овенст]ва в 1917г. Zesp. 806, inw. 5, sygn. 10140, t. 2.

Российский государственный исторический архив: Духовное правление при Протопресвитере Военного и Морского Духовенства, Об упраздниении Управл[ения] Протопрезбитера и о защите прихожан принадлежащих ему капиталов, движимого и недвижимого имущества. Zesp. 806, inw. 5, sygn. 10526.

Российский государственный исторический архив: Духовное правление при Протопресвитере Военного и Морского Духовенства, О высочащем постановлении чтобы св[ященни]ки гвардии армии и флота состояли в ведении Обер-св[ященни]ка. Ф. 806, оп. 1, sygn. 23.

Рыбаков, Николай Александрович: "Развитие правового регулирования деятельности православных священников в армии за период XVIII–XIX вв.". Молодой ученый 11, 2012, s. 339–343.

Сенин, Александр Сергеевич: "Армейское духовенство России в Первую мировую войну". Вопросы истории 10, 1990, s. 159–165.

"Указ Его Императорского Величества Самодержца Всероссийского из Святейшего Правительственного Синода настоятелю Суворовской Кончанской, что при Императорской Николаевской военной академии церкви, протоиерею Георгию Ивановичу Шавельскому". Вестник военного и морского духовенства 10, 1911, s. 289.

Фирсов, Сергей Львович: "Протопресвитеры русской армии и флота (1880 – февраль 1917 гг.)". Новый часовой 1, 1994, s. 23–33.

Фирсов, Сергей Львович: "Военное духовенство России. К вопросу о материальном положении священно- и церковнослужителей русской армии и флота в последней четверти XIX – начала XX столетий)". Новый часовой 2, 1994, s. 19–45.

Фирсов, Сергей Львович: "Военное духовенство накануне и в годы Первой Мировой войны". Новый часовой 3, 1995, s. 21–32.

Чимаров, Сергей Юрьевич: "Во главе военно-духовного ведомства России: П. Я. Озерецковский – первый обер-священник русской армии и флота". Военно-исторический журнал 1, 1998, s. 76–82.

Шавельский, Георгий: "Духовенству воинских частей действующей армии и госпиталей". Вестник военного и морского духовенства 20, 1914, s. 696–697.

Шавельский, Георгий: Воспоминания последне¬го протопресвитера русской армии и флота. Крутицкое Патриаршее Подворье: Москва 1996a, v. 1.

Шавельский, Георгий: Воспоминания последне¬го протопресвитера русской армии и флота. Крутицкое Патриаршее Подворье: Москва 1996b, v. 2.

Christian Religious Experiences within the Austro-Hungarian Army during the Great War

Ionela Zaharia

References

"Austrian War Archives". *OeStA, KA, MBeh, AFV, Pastoralberichte.* Vienna, 1914–1919.

"Austrian War Archives". *OeStA, KA,ZSt, KM, HR, Akten 8244 (neu 767), 9. Abteilung 11.3–11.35.* Vienna, 1915.

Bârlea, Eugenia: *PhD Thesis: Perspectiva lumii rurale asupra Primului Război Mondial.* Cluj Napoca: Universitatea Babeş-Bolyai, 2000.

Bielik, Emerich: *Geschichte der k.u.k. Militärseelsorge und des Apostolischen Feldvicariates.* Wien: Verlag des Apostolischen Feldvikariat, 1901.

Brandauer, Isabelle: "Der Krieg kennt keine Erbarmen". In: *Die Tagebücher des Kaiserschützen Erich Mayr (1913–1920).* Innsbruck: Universitätsverlag Wagner, 2013.

Broucek, Peter: *Ein General im Zwieliecht. Die erinnerungen Edmund Glaises von Horstenau k.u.k. Generalstaboffizier und Historiker.* Vol. 1. Wien, Köln, Graz: Herman Böhlau Verlag, 1980.

Gröger, Roman Hans/ Ham, Claudia/ Sammer, Alfred: *Zwischen Himmel und Erde. Militärseelsorge in Österreich.* Graz: Styria Verlag, 2001.

Hopkins, Debra et al.: *Theorizing Emotions. Sociological Explanation and Application.* Frankfurt–New York: Campus Verlag, 2009.

Katholische Militärseelsorge Österreich. 1999. http://www.mildioz.at/index.php?option=com_content&task=view&id=57&Itemid=8 (accessed 3.08.2013).

Kriegsministerium, k.u.k. *Dienstvorschrieft für die Militärgeistlichkeit.* Wien: kaiserlich-königliche Hof- und Staatsdruckerei, 1904.

Legler, Johannes: *Dissertation: Militärseelsorge in der Österreichisch-Ungarischen Armee von 1867 bis 1918.* Wien: Wiener Katholische Akademie, 1979.

Leu, Valeriu/ Bocşan, Nicolae: *Marele Război în memoria bănăţeană 1914–1919.* Cluj-Napoca: Presa Universitară Clujeană, 2012.

Talpeş, Petru: *Amintiri.* Edited by Vasile Dudaş and Vali Corduneanu. Timişoara: Editura Mirton, 2008.

Archive traces of the drama of war. Sources for investigation into the daily life of inhabitants of cities in the Opole District in the archival fond of the State Archive in Opole

Anna Caban

References

Źródła archiwalne z zasobu Archiwum Państwowego w Opolu

Akta miasta Grodkowa (1407–1944).

Akta miasta Korfantowa (1800, 1831–1941).

Akta miasta Krapkowic (1582–1944).

Akta miasta Opola (1322–1945).

Komitet Wojewódzki Polskiej Zjednoczonej Partii Robotniczej w Opolu [1944] (1950–1990).

Rejencja Opolska [Regierung Oppeln] [1704–1815] (1816–1945).

Starostwo Powiatowe w Grodkowie [Landratsamt Grottkau] (1742–1942).

Starostwo Powiatowe w Koźlu [Landratsamt Cosel] (1803–1944).

Starostwo Powiatowe w Nysie (1945–1950).

Starostwo Powiatowe w Opolu [Landratsamt Oppeln] [1735, 1742] (1743–1942).

Zbiór fotografii z I wojny światowej (1916–1917).

Związek Bojowników o Wolność i Demokrację Zarząd Okręgu w Opolu (1946–1973, 1989).

References

Beckett, Ian F. W: *Pierwsza wojna światowa 1914–1918*, z angielskiego przełożył Rafał Dymek. Książka i Wiedza: Warszawa 2009.

Borkowski, Maciej: *Życie codzienne w Opolu w latach Wielkiej Wojny (1914–1918)*. In: *Koniec starego świata – początek nowego. Społeczeństwo Górnego Śląska wobec pierwszej wojny światowej. (1914–1918) Źródła i metody.* Gliwice, 20–22 czerwca 2013 r., pod red. Linek Bernard, Rosenbaum Sebastian, Struve Kai. Opole 2013 [wersja elektroniczna w PDF.], pp. 90–98.

Chwalba, Andrzej: *Samobójstwo Europy. Wielka wojna 1914–1918*. Wydawnictwo Literackie: Kraków 2014.

Czapliński, Marek: *Dzieje Śląska od 1806 do 1918 r.* In: *Historia Śląska*, pod red. Czapliński Marek, Kaszuba Elżbieta, Wąs Gabriela, i in. Wydawnictwo Uniwersytetu Wrocławskiego: Wrocław 2007.

Czapliński, Marian: *Kancelaria i registratura Rejencji Opolskiej "Sobótka"* Nr 2/1961, pp. 176–199.

Gilbert, Martin: *Pierwsza wojna światowa*, z angielskiego przełożył Stefan Amsterdamski. Zysk i S-ka Wydawnictwo: Poznań 2003.

Historia Górnego Śląska. Polityka, gospodarka i kultura europejskiego regionu, red. Bahlcke, Joachim, Gawrecki Dan, Kaczmarek Ryszard. Dom Współpracy Polsko-Niemieckiej: Gliwice 2011.

Kaczmarek, Ryszard: *Polacy w Armii Kajzera. Na frontach I wojny światowej*. Wydawnictwo Literackie: Kraków 2014.

Krasuski, Jerzy: *Historia Niemiec*. Zakład Narodowy im. Ossolińskich: Wrocław 2008.

Lusek, Joanna: *Szkoła w latach I wojny światowej*. In: *Koniec starego świata – początek nowego. Społeczeństwo Górnego Śląska wobec pierwszej wojny światowej (1914–1918). Źródła i metody*. Gliwice, 20–22 czerwca 2013 r., pod red. Linek Bernard, Rosenbaum Sebastian, Struve Kai. Opole 2013 [wersja elektroniczna w PDF.], pp. 99–104.

Łach, Bolesław W.: *Społeczeństwo Prus Wschodnich wobec agresji rosyjskiej*. In: *Wielka Wojna. Poza linią frontu*, red. Grinberg Daniel, Snopko Jan, Zackiewicz Grzegorz. Wydawnictwo Prymat: Białystok 2013, pp. 31–43.

Mendel, Edward: *Dzień powszedni na Śląsku Opolskim w czasie I wojny światowej*. Instytut Śląski w Opolu: Opole 1987.

Mendel Edward, *Polacy na Górnym Śląsku w latach I wojny światowej. Położenie i postawa*, Wydawnictwo "Śląsk" Katowice 1971.

Mendel, Edward: *Z zagadnień udziału Ślązaków na frontach pierwszej wojny światowej 1914–1918*. Instytut Śląski w Opolu: Opole 1965.

Miodowski, Adam: *Sytuacja jeńców wojennych z armii państw centralnych w niewoli rosyjskiej po przewrocie bolszewickim (listopad 1917–marzec 1918)*. In: *Wielka Wojna. Poza linią frontu*, red. Grinberg Daniel, Snopko Jan, Zackiewicz Grzegorz. Wydawnictwo Prymat: Białystok 2013, pp. 363–372.

Muzeum martyrologii jeńców wojennych w Łambinowicach. Informator, oprac. Popiołek Stefan, Sawczuk Janusz, Senft Stanisław, Opole.

Nowak, Edmund: *Obozy na Śląsku Opolskim w systemie powojennych obozów w Polsce (1945–1950). Historia i Implikacje*. Opole 2002.

Pajewski, Janusz: *Historia Powszechna 1871–1918*. Wydawnictwo Naukowe PWN: Warszawa 1996.

Pajewski, Janusz: *Pierwsza wojna światowa 1914–1918*. Wydawnictwo Naukowe PWN: Warszawa 1998.

Popiołek, Kazimierz: *Historia Śląska: od pradziejów do 1945 roku*. Wydawnictwo "Śląsk": Katowice 1984.

Stanek, Piotr: *Jeńcy wojenni na Górnym Śląsku w latach I wojny światowej*. In: *Koniec starego świata – początek nowego. Społeczeństwo Górnego Śląska wobec pierwszej wojny światowej. (1914–1918) Źródła i metody*. Gliwice, 20–22 czerwca 2013 r., pod red. Linek Bernard, Rosenbaum Sebastian, Struve Kai. Opole 2013 [wersja elektroniczna w PDF.], pp. 36–41.

Witkowski, Michał: *Wojna Propagandowa*. In: *Koniec starego świata – początek nowego. Społeczeństwo Górnego Śląska wobec pierwszej wojny światowej. (1914–1918) Źródła i metody*. Gliwice, 20–22 czerwca 2013 r., pod red. Linek Bernard, Rosenbaum Sebastian, Struve Kai. Opole 2013 [wersja elektroniczna w PDF.], pp. 115–118.

List of illustrations

World war from a local perspective. School chronicles from the border areas of the Province of Posen (Prowincja Poznańska) as a source of information

Marek Szczepaniak
Grażyna Tyrchan

References

Archiwum Państwowe w Poznaniu Oddział w Gnieźnie, Szkoła Podstawowa w Pawłowie, sygn. 1: Kronika szkoły w Pawłowie 1899–1952.

Archiwum Państwowe w Poznaniu Oddział w Gnieźnie, Szkoła Podstawowa nr 1 w Witkowie, sygn. 1: Kronika szkoły w Witkowie 1875–1917.

Archiwum Państwowe w Poznaniu Oddział w Gnieźnie, Szkoła w Świątnikach Wielkich, sygn. 1: Kronika szkoły w Świątnikach Wielkich 1886–1934.

Archiwum Państwowe w Poznaniu, Szkoły Powszechne z terenu miasta Poznania i województwa poznańskiego, sygn. 265: Kronika szkoły pofranciszkańskiej w Gnieźnie 1854–1955.

Archiwum zakładowe Urzędu Gminy w Kiszkowie, Kronika szkoły w Sławnie 1887–1961.

Centralblatt für die gesammte Unterrichts Verwaltung in Preussen, issue 10, 31 X 1872.

Gemeindelexikon für die Regierungsbezirke Allenstein, Danzig, Marienwerder, Posen, Bromberg und Oppeln, Heft V, Regierungsbezirke Bromberg. Berlin 1912, pp. 76–77.

Kronika szkoły w Dziekanowicach 1896–1930 (w zbiorach prywatnych).

Kronika szkoły w Imielenku 1897–1926 (w zbiorach prywatnych).

Składnica akt Gimnazjum nr 1 w Gnieźnie, Kronika Szkoły Podstawowej nr 1 w Gnieźnie 1903–1949.

Składnica akt Gimnazjum nr 2 w Gnieźnie, Kronika szkoły w Jankówku 1888–1972.

Składnica akt Gimnazjum w Mieleszynie, Kronika szkoły w Kowalewie 1890–1935.

Składnica akt Niepublicznej Szkoły Podstawowej w Gorzykowie, Kronika szkoły w Gorzykowie 1899–1922.

Składnica akt Szkoły Podstawowej w Modliszewku, Kronika szkoły w Modliszewku 1871–1951.

The organization and the operations of the League of Women of the War Emergency Service

Tomasz Matuszak

References

Archival sources

Archiwum Akt Nowych w Warszawie (AAN)
    Liga Kobiet Polskich (LKP)
Archiwum Narodowe w Krakowie (ANK)
    Naczelny Komitet Narodowy (NKN)
Archiwum Państwowe w Piotrkowie Trybunalskim (APPT)
    Archiwum Wandy Grabowskiej (AWG)
    C. i K. Komenda Powiatowa w Piotrkowie (CKKP)
    Liga Kobiet Pogotowia Wojennego (LKPW)

Literature

Budziński, Janusz Roman: *Polityka zagraniczna Rosji 1907–1914. Aparat decyzyjny, koncepcja, rezultaty*. Toruń 2000.

"Dokumenty niewoli". *Dziennik Narodowy* (1), 1915.

Dufrat, Joanna: *Kobiety w kręgu lewicy niepodległościowej. Od Ligi Kobiet Pogotowia Wojennego do Ochotniczej Legii Kobiet (1908–1918/1919)*. Toruń 2001.

Dufrat, Joanna: *Powstanie Ligi Kobiet w okresie I wojny Światowej*. Access 14.04.2015, http://ligakobietpolskich.pl/.

Gaul, Jerzy: "Organizacja pracy w kancelarii Generalnego Gubernatorstwa Wojskowego w Lublinie w latach 1915–1918". *Krakowski Rocznik Archiwalny* (2), 1996.

Gaul, Jerzy: *Kancelaria Generalnego Gubernatorstwa Wojskowego w Lublinie 1915–1918*. Warszawa 1998.

Gąsior, Marcin: *Działania wojenne na obszarze byłej guberni piotrkowskiej w pierwszych miesiącach wojny 1914 roku*. In: Zawilski, Piotr (ed.): *Drogi do niepodległości. Materiały z sesji naukowej*. Tomaszów Mazowiecki 1998.

Górak, Artur: *Kancelaria Gubernatora i Rząd Gubernialny Lubelski (1867–1914)*. Lublin/Radzyń Podlaski 2006.

Hubka, Maciej: *Źródła do wojny polsko-rosyjskiej 1919–1921 w zasobie Archiwum Państwowego w Piotrkowie Trybunalskim i Oddziału w Tomaszowie Mazowieckim.* In: Matuszak, Tomasz (ed.): *W cieniu czerwonej zarazy. W 90. rocznicę Bitwy Warszawskiej 1920 roku.* Piotrków Trybunalski – Opoczno 2012.

Kopiczyńska, Alina: *Akta władz administracji gubernialnej Królestwa Polskiego w latach 1867–1915.* Warszawa 2004.

Kronika Piotrkowska (30), from June 29, 1914.

Kukulski, Jerzy: "Dążenia narodowe i społeczne w Piotrkowskiem na początku XX wieku". *Zbliżenia* (1), 1992.

Kukulski, Jerzy: *Piotrkowskie u progu niepodległości.* In: *Ziemia Piotrkowska u progu niepodległości.* Piotrków Trybunalski 1988.

Kukulski, Jerzy: *Sto lat Rosji w Królestwie Polskim (1815–1915). Wybrane problemy.* Piotrków Trybunalski 2005.

Latawiec, Krzysztof: "Ewakuacja cywilnej administracji ogólnej szczebla powiatowego z guberni lubelskiej latem 1915 roku". *Wschodni Rocznik Humanistyczny* (1), 2004.

Latawiec, Krzysztof: "Ewakuacja organów administracji ogólnej wyższego i niższego szczebla guberni lubelskiej w sierpniu 1914 roku". *Radzyński Rocznik Humanistyczny* (2), 2002.

Lewandowski, Jan: *Królestwo Polskie pod okupacją austriacką 1914–1918.* Warszawa 1980.

Malinowska, Dorota: *Ewakuacja urzędów Królestwa Polskiego w latach 1914–1915 do Rosji, ich losy i rewindykacja akt do Polski p. 1921 roku.* In: Łosowski, Janusz (ed.): *Pamiętnik III Ogólnopolskiego Zjazdu Studentów Archiwistyki w Lublinie.* Lublin 2000.

Matuszak, Tomasz: "Archiwalia piotrkowskie w czasie I wojny światowej". *Piotrkowskie Zeszyty Historyczne* (7/8), 2005/2006.

Matuszak, Tomasz: *Archiwum Państwowe w Piotrkowie Trybunalskim 1919–1951.* Piotrków Trybunalski/ Radzyń Podlaski 2009.

Moszczeńska, I.: "Liga Kobiet jako Pogotowie Wojenne". *Na Posterunku.* Jednodniówka from June 11, 1916.

Moszczeńska, I.: "Liga Kobiet". *Wiadomości Polskie* (22), 1915.

Pająk, Jerzy Zbigniew: "Liga Kobiet Polskich Pogotowia Wojennego wobec sporów w obozie aktywistycznym (sierpień 1915–sierpień 1916)". *Kieleckie Studia Historyczne* (15), 1999.

Petrozolin-Skowrońska, Barbara: "Portret publicystki i działaczki. Iza Moszczeńska-Rzepecka". *Mówią Wieki* (6), 1980.

Piasta, Aleksy: "Administracja miejska Piotrkowa Trybunalskiego w okresie pierwszej wojny światowej 1914–1918". *Badania nad Dziejami Regionu Piotrkowskiego* (3), 2002.

Piasta, Aleksy: "Organizacja austriackich władz okupacyjnych szczebla powiatowego i ich pozostałość aktowa na przykładzie K.u.K. Kreiskommando in Piotrków i K.u.K. Kreiskommando in Noworadomsk (1915–1918)". *Archeion* (105), 2003.

Piasta, Aleksy: "Polityka austriackiej administracji wojskowej na terenie powiatu piotrkowskiego w latach 1915–1918". *Archiwum i Badania nad Dziejami Regionu* (1), 1995.

Piasta, Aleksy: *Piotrków – życie pod okupacją 1914–1918.* In: Zawilski, Piotr (ed.): *Drogi do niepodległości. Materiały z sesji naukowej.* Tomaszów Mazowiecki 1998.

Piasta, Aleksy: *Piotrków Trybunalski w latach pierwszej wojny światowej.* Piotrków Trybunalski 2007.

Pielużek, Anna: *Piotrków i powiat piotrkowski w świetle "Kroniki Piotrkowskiej" 1910–1914.* Piotrków Trybunalski 2005.

Przepisy czasowe o wywożeniu na koszt skarbu, wskutek okoliczności wojny majątku państwowego, instytucji rządowych, urzędników i ich rodzin. Akty prawodawcze wydane w związku z wojną 1914/1915 roku. Warszawa 1915.

Śliwińska, Leokadia: *Z dziejów Ligi Kobiet Polskich Pogotowia Wojennego 1913–1918* (manuscript).

Ustawa Ligi Kobiet Pogotowia Wojennego. Lublin 1916.

Wachowska, Barbara: *Życie społeczno-polityczne i kulturalne w latach pierwszej wojny światowej.* In: Baranowski, Bohdan (ed.): *Dzieje Piotrkowa Trybunalskiego.* Łódź 1989.

East Prussia as the only province of the German Empire occupied during the Great War. Wartime histories of East Prussia

Sławomir Jan Maksymowicz

References

Primary sources

Archiwum Państwowe Olsztyn:
   Oberpräsidium Ostpreussen – 3/I/ 527, 528, 529, 530.
   Starostwo Powiatowe w Braniewie – 10/I/ 238, 473, 474, 475.
   Akta miasta Działdowo – 251/I/ 780, 782.
   Akta miasta Olsztyn – 259/ 156, 168, 161.
   APO 2881/1.
Ośrodek Badań Naukowych im Wojciecha Kętrzyńskiego w Olsztynie:
   Kalendarz Pruski Ewangelicki – 1916.
   Kalendarz Pruski Ewangelicki – 1917.

Secondary sources

Bętkowski, Rafał: *Olsztyn jakiego nie znacie.* Olsztyn 2010.

Boenigk, Jan: *Minęły wieki a myśmy ostali.* Warszawa 1971.

Borodziej, Włodzimierz/Górny Maciej: *Nasza Wojna,* Tom I, *Imperia 1912–1916.* Warszawa 2014.

Czerep, Stanisław: *Operacja wschodniopruska 1915 r.* In: Kempa, Robert (ed.): *Wielka Wojna na Mazurach 1914–1915.* Giżycko 2014.

Fürst zu Dohna Alexander: *Schlobitten Erinnerungen eines alten Ostpreussen,* Berlin 1989.

Jaroszyk, Kazimierz: *Wspomnienia z Prus Wschodnich.* Olsztyn 1969.

Jasiński, Janusz: *Historia Królewca.* Olsztyn 1994.

Juszkiewicz, Ryszard: *Działania bojowe na pograniczu północnego Mazowsza i Prus Wschodnich oraz sytuacja ludności w latach 1914–1915.* In: Rondomańska, Zenona (ed.): *Nad Bałtykiem, Pregołą i Łyną XVI–XX w.* Olsztyn 2006.

Kossert, Andreas: *Prusy Wschodnie Historia i mit.* Warszawa 2009.

Leśniowski, Henryk: *W cieniu bitwy pod Grunwaldem Tannenberg 1914 fakty, mity, legendy.* Olsztyn 2014.

Orłowicz, Mieczysław: *Ilustrowany przewodnik po Mazurach Pruskich i Warmii*. Olsztyn 1991.

Osterroht Hermann: *Geschichte des Dragoner=Regiments PrinzAlbreht von Preußen (Litthauisches) Nr 1 1717–1919*. Berlin 1930.

Radziwiłłowicz, Dariusz: *Tradycja grunwaldzka w świadomości politycznej społeczeństwa polskiego w latach 1910–1945*. Olsztyn 2003.

Salm, Jan: *Odbudowa miast wschodniopruskich po I wojnie światowej*. Olsztyn 2006.

Showalter Denis E.: *Tannenberg 1914, Zderzenie Imperiów*. Warszawa 2005.

Szlanta, Piotr: *Tannenberg 1914*, Warszawa 2005.

Szostakowska, Małgorzata: *Prasa codzienna Prus Wschodnich od XVII do połowy XX wieku. Przewodnik do dziejów wydawniczych*. Toruń 2007.

Wrzesiński, Wojciech: *Prusy Wschodnie w polskiej myśli politycznej 1864–1945*. Olsztyn 1994.

Ivan and aria for the dying world. The image of Russia in the
propaganda of the central powers during the Great War

Magdalena Żakowska

References

Aretov, Nicolai: "Forging the myth about Russia: Rayna, Bulgarian Princess". In: Sujecka, Jolanta (ed.): *Semantyka Rosji na Bałkanach*. Wydawnictwo DiG: Warszawa 2011.

Bazylow, Ludwik: *Historia Rosji*. Zakład Naukowy im. Ossolińskich: Wrocław, Warszawa, Kraków 2005.

Beller, Steven: "The tragic carnival: Austrian culture in the First World War". In: Roshwald Aviel/ Stites, Richard (eds.): *European culture in the Great War. The arts, entertainment, and propaganda, 1914–1918*. Cambridge University Press: Cambridge 1999, pp. 127–161.

Brudek, Paweł: *Rosja w propagandize niemieckiej podczas I wojny światowej w świetle "Deutsche Warschauer Zeitung"*. Wydawnictwo Neriton, Instytut Historii PAN: Warszawa 2010.

Brummett, Palmira: *Image and Imperialism in the Ottoman Revolutionary Press, 1908–1911*. State University of New York Press: Albany 2000.

Coupe, William: "German cartoons of the First World War". *History Today* (42) August 1992, pp. 23–31.

Dąbrowski, Jan: *Wielka Wojna 1914–1918*, vol. 1. Księgarnia Trzaski, Everta i Michalskiego: Warszawa 1937a [reprint: Poznań 2000].

Dąbrowski, Jan: *Wielka Wojna 1914–1918*, vol. 2. Księgarnia Trzaski, Everta i Michalskiego: Warszawa 1937b [reprint: Poznań 2000].

Dąbrowski, Jan: *Wielka Wojna 1914–1918*, vol. 3. Księgarnia Trzaski, Everta i Michalskiego: Warszawa 1937c [reprint: Poznań 2000].

"Das Inferno auf dem Balkan". *Der Wahre Jacob* (732) 08.08.1914, title page. Caption: "Zanurzać się – inaczej przetnę was na pół".

"Das Testament Peters des Großen". *Der Wahre Jacob* (741) 12.12.1915, p. 8341.

De Lazari, Andrzej/Riabow, Oleg/Żakowska, Magdalena: *Europa i niedźwiedź*. Centrum Polsko-Rosyjskiego Dialogu i Porozumienia: Warszawa 2013.

Dedijer, Vladimir: *Sarajevo 1914*, vol. 2. Wydawnictwo Łódzkie: Łódź 1984.

"Der europäische Krieg". *Kikeriki* (35) 30.08.1914.

"Der Kampf um den Frieden in Rußland". *Der Wahre Jacob* (819) 12.1917,

"Die russische Offensive erfordert erst noch eine Umwälzung". *Kikeriki* (22) 1917.

Dimitrova, Snezhana: "'Taming the death': the culture of death (1915–18) and its remembering and commemorating through First World War soldier monuments in Bulgaria (1917–44)". *Social History* 30 (2), May 2005, pp. 175–194.

Dmitrów, Edmund: *Obraz Rosji i Rosjan w propagandzie narodowych socjalistów 193–1945. Stare i nowe stereotypy*. Instytut Studiów Politycznych PAN: Warszawa 1997.

Documents of Russian History 1914–1917, retrieved 20.02.2015, from http://archive.org/stream/documentsofrussi027937mbp/documentsofrussi027937mbp_djvu.txt.

Ferguson, Niall: "Germany and the Origins of the First World War: New Perspectives". *The Historical Journal* 35 (3) Sept., 1992, pp. 725–752.

Freud, Sigmund: *Reflections on War and Death*. Trans. A. A. Brill and Alfred B. Kuttner. Moffat, Yard and Co.: New York 1918. Retrieved 01.08.2014, from http://www.sophia-project.org/uploads/1/3/9/5/13955288/freud_waranddeath.pdf.

Goll, Nicole-Melanie/ Franzens, Karl: "Heroes wanted! Propagandistic war efforts and their failure in Austria-Hungary during World War I". In: Rollo, Maria Fernanda/Pires, Ana Paula/Novais, Noémia Malva (eds.): *War and Propaganda in the 20ᵗʰ Century*. Instituto de historia contemporanea: Lisboa 2013, pp. 90–96.

Grodziski, Stanisław: *Franciszek Józef I*. Zakład Narodowy imienia Ossolińskich – Wydawnictwo: Wrocław, Warszawa, Kraków, Gdańsk, Łódź 1983.

Heine, Thomas Theodor: "Durch!!" *Simplicissimus* (20) 17.08.1914, title page.

"Hofvergnügen in Rußland. Der russische Hofprediger Rasputin erhält den Zaren bei guter Laune". *Der Wahre Jacob* (771) 04.02.1916, last page.

"Illustriertes Schlagwort Serbiens: Wir steh'n nicht allein!" *Kikeriki* (32) 1914.

Jelavich, Peter: "German culture in the Great War". In: Roshwald, Aviel/ Stites, Richard (eds.): European culture in the Great War. The arts, entertainment, and propaganda, 1914–1918. Cambridge University Press: Cambridge 1999, pp. 32–57.

Kelbetcheva, Evelina: "Between apology and denial: Bulgarian culture during World War I. In: Roshwald, Aviel/ Stites, Richard: *European culture in the Great War. The arts, entertainment, and propaganda, 1914–1918*. Cambridge University Press: Cambridge 1999, pp. 215–242.

Kiliç, Sibel: "Contribution of Karagoz humour magazine (1908–1955) to sociocultural transformations of the Turkish society which derives its sources from the Karagoz humour practices and its importance through the perspective of the Turkish cultural history". *The Journal of International Social Research* 4 (16) 2011, pp. 238–247.

Kissinger, Henry: *Dyplomacja*. Philip Wilson: Warszawa 1996.

Mahal, Günther: "Eher Pinsel als Stift. Russland und die Russen in Karikaturen deutscher Zeichner 1870–1917". In: Keller, Mechthild (ed.): *Russen und Russland aus deutscher Sicht. 19./20. Jahrhundert: Von der Bismarckzeit bis zum Ersten Weltkrieg*, vol. 4. Wilhelm Fink Verlag: München 2000.

Moser, Andreas: *Land der unbegrenzten Unmöglichkeiten. Das Schweizer Russland – und Russenbild vor der Oktoberrevolution.* Chronos Verlag: Zürich 2006.

Oroschakoff, Haralampi G.: *Die Battenberg Affäre. Leben und Abenteuer des Gavriil Oroschakoff oder eine russisch-europäische Geschichte.* Berlin Verlag: Berlin 2007.

Tanty, Mieczysław: *Bałkany w XX wieku. Dzieje polityczne.* Książka i Wiedza: Warszawa 2003.

Wolff, Larry: *Inventing Eastern Europe. The Map of Civilization on the Mind of the Enlightenment.* Stanford University Press: Stanford 1994.

Чавдарова, Дечка, "Миф России и стереотип русского в болгарской культуре по сравнению с польским стереотипом". In: Bobryk, Roman/ Faryno, Jerzy (eds.): *Polacy w oczach Rosjan – Rosjanie w oczach Polaków.* Slawistyczny Ośrodek Wydawniczy: Warszawa 2000.

List of illustrations

"Tamerlan". *Der Wahre Jacob* (760) 3.09.1915, p. 8773. Caption un the illustration: "According to the order given to the Russian army, the scorched earth tactics is applied while the army withdraws".

"Der Koloβ auf tönernen Füβen". Kikeriki (34) 1914. Caption under the illustration: "Frenchman and Englishman: Turn back and fire! Russian: My legs are too weak!".

"Die'lieben Juden und Polen' des Zaren". Der Wahre Jacob (734) 4.09.1914, title page. Caption under the illustration: "Dream on, dream on, of bloody deeds and death. Faiting. depair; despairing, yield thy breath" Richard III.

Paspalew, P.: untitled. Baraban 17.09.1916, p. 8. Caption under the illustration: "You son of a bitch, why should I need such an ally?".

"Ein kritischer Moment. *Der Wahre Jacob* (822) 01.1918, title page.

Between paralysis, crisis and renewal: The effects of the war on the polyhedral industrial city of Łódź (1914–1918)

Frank M. Schuster

References

Archival Sources

Archiwum Główne Akt Dawnych w Warszawie (AGAD)

Bericht des Verwaltungschefs Nr. 6, 7, 10.

Kaiserlich Deutsches Generalgouvernement Warschau 1915–1918 (GGW)

Niemeckie władze okupacyjne na terenie byłego Korolestwa Polskiego 1914–1918 (NwotbKP).

Verwaltungschef beim Generalgouvernement Warschau 1915–1918 (GGW VCh) 6, 7, 10.

Archiwum Państwowe w Lublinie (APL)

Kreisamt Lukow 6.

Archiwum Państwowe w Łodzi (APŁ)

Akta miasta Łodzi (AmŁ) 1567, 13583; 13720, 13752.

Archiwum rodziny Biedermannów (ARB) 1, 3.

Główny Komitet Obywatelski miasta Łódzi (GKO), 1.

Łódzka Gmina Wyznaniowa Żydowska (ŁGWŻ) 20; 45, 64, 81, 127, 418.

Związek Przemysłu Włókienniczego w Państwie Polskim (ZPW), 151.

Bundesarchiv/Militärarchiv (BA/MA) Freiburg

N 30/12; 15; 25; 54.

Central Zionist Archives (CZA), Jerusalem

A 15. VIII. 9c.

Z3 149.

Newpapers

Jüdische Rundschau Nr. 2, 8. 1. 1915, Nr. 6, 5.2.1915, Nr. 22, 28. 5. 1915.

Neue Lodzer Zeitung (NLZ) Nr. 192/1915.

Nowy Kurier Łódzki, 1.9. 1914; 22.5. 1915.

Rozwój, Nr. 189/1901.

Bibligraphy

Adler, Jacob: *A Life on the Stage. A Memoir.* Ed. by Lulla Rosenfeld. New York: 1999.

Althaus, Paul: *Ihr und wir.* In: *Deutsche Post* Nr. 18, 24.10. 1915, p. 1.

Althaus, Paul: *Lodzer Kriegsbüchlein.* Göttingen 1916.

Bąkowicz, Stanisław/Nowak, Edward: "Z problemów działalności Głównego Komitetu Obywatelskiego miasta Łodzi". In: *Acta Universitatis Lodziensis.* Seria 1, 41 (1979), pp. 181–187.

Basler, Werner: *Deutschlands Annextionspolitik in Polen und im Baltikum 1914–1918.* (East) Berlin: 1962.

Biskupski, Łukasz: *Miasto Atrakcji. Narodziny kultury masowej na przełomie XIX i XX wieku. Kino w systemie rozrywkowym Łodzi.* Warszawa 2013.

Bogalecki, Tadeusz: *11 listopada 1918 roku w Łodzi. Geneza, przebieg i rezultaty akcji rozbrajania Niemców w Łodzi.* Łódź 1988.

Conze, Werner: *Polnische Nation und deutsche Politik im Ersten Weltkrieg.* Köln, Graz 1958.

Dasyzńska, Jolanta (ed.): *Operacja łódzka. Zapomniany fakt I wojny światowej.* Łódź 2011.

Daszyńska, Jolanta (ed.): *Łódź w czasie wielkiej wojny.* Łódź 2012.

Daszyńska, Jolanta (ed.): *Łódź w drodze do niepodległości.* Łódź: 2013.

Eichler, Adolf: "Der Deutsche Verein im zweiten Jahr seines Bestehens". In: *Jahrbuch des Deutschen Vereins, Hauptsitz in Lodz.* Lodz 1918. pp. 70–86.

Eichler, Adolf: *Das Deutschtum in Lodz.* In: *Deutsches Leben in Rußland* 3 (1925) Nr. 3/4. p. 39–41.

Eichler, Adolf: *Deutschtum im Schatten des Ostens.* Dresden: 1942.

Eichler, Adolf: *Zwischen den Fronten. Kriegsaufzeichnungen eines Lodzer Deutschen.* Lodz 1918.

Fischer, André: *Zwischen Zeugnis und Zeitgeist: Die politische Theologie von Paul Althaus in der Weimarer Republik.* Göttingen 2012.

Flierl, Friedrich: "Der Deutsche Verein für Lodz und Umgegend. Seine Entstehung und Entwicklung". In: *Jahrbuch des Deutschen Vereins für Lodz und Umgegend*. Lodz 1917.

Goerne, Antoni: "Z zakresu statystyki ludności". In: *Informator miasta Łodzi na rok 1919*. Łódź 1919, pp. 25–37.

Goldin, Semion: "Deportation of Jews by the Russian Military Command 1914–1915". In: *Jews in Eastern Europe* (Spring 2000), pp. 40–73.

Goldin, Semion: "Russkoe komandovanie i evrei vo vremja Pervoj mirovoj vojny: Pričiny formirovanija negativnogo stereotipa". In: Budnickij, O.V. et al. (eds.): *Mirovoj krizis 1914–1920 godov i sud'ba vostočnoevropejskogo evrejstva/The World Crisis of 1914–1920 and the Fate of the East European Jewry. History and Culture of Russian and East European Jewry: New Sources, New Approaches. Proceedings of the International Conference. St. Petersburg, November 7–9, 2004*. Moskva/Moscow: 2005, pp. 29–46.

Heid, Ludger: *Maloche – nicht Mildtätigkeit. Ostjüdische Arbeiter in Deutschland 1914–1923*. Hildesheim, Zürich, New York: 1993.

Heike, Otto: "Ernst Leonhardt 1849–1917. Ein Industrieller und Förderer des deutschen Bildungswesens in Lodz". In: Weigelt, Fritz (ed.):*Von unserer Art. Vom Leben und Wirken deutscher Menschen im Raume von Weichsel und Warthe*. Wuppertal: 1963. pp. 85–88.

Hertz, Mieczysław: *Łódzki bataljon robotniczy. Z.A.B. 23*. Łódź: 1918.

Hertz, Mieczysław: *Łódź w czasie wielkiej wojny*. Łódź 1933.

Hetzer, Tanja: *"Deutsche Stunde". Volksgemeinschaft und Antisemitismus in der politischen Theologie bei Paul Althaus*. München 2009.

Hofmann, Andreas R.: "Die vergessene Okkupation. Lodz im Ersten Weltkrieg". In: Löw, Andrea/ Robusch, Kerstin/ Walter, Stefanie (eds.): *Deutsche – Juden – Polen. Geschichte einer wechselvollen Beziehung im 20. Jahrhundert. Festschrift für Hubert Schneider*. Frankfurt a. M. 2004, pp. 59–78.

Hutten-Czapski, Bogdan von: *Sechzig Jahre Politik und Gesellschaft*. 2 Vols. Berlin 1936.

Jankel Adler 1895–1949. Katalog anlässlich der Wanderausstellung 1985: Städtische Kunsthalle Düsseldorf, The Tel Aviv Museum, Muzeum Sztuki w Lodzi. Köln 1985.

Jaskulski, Mirosław: *Władze administracyjne Łodzi do 1939 r.* Łódź 2001.

Karwacki, Wacław Lech: *Walka o władzę w Łodzi 1918–1919*. Łódź 1962.

Karwacki, Władysław Lech: "Włókniarze Łodzi w latach I wojny światowej 1914–1918. Łódzka Rada Delegatów Robotniczych". In: Rosset, Edward (ed.): *Włókniarze łódzcy. Monografia*. Łódź 1966. pp. 90–102.

Kempa, Andrzej/Szukalak, Marek: *Żydzi dawnej Łodzi. Słownik biograficzny Żydów łódzkich oraz z Łodzi związanych.* Vol. 1–3. Łódź 2001–2003.

Krajewska, Hanna: *Życie filmowe Łodzi w latach 1896–1939.* Warszawa, Łódź 1992.

Kulak, Zbigniew: "Memorandum of the Germans form Łódź Concerning the Annexation of Polish Territories to the Reich at the Time of World War I". In: *Polish Western Affairs* 7/2 (1966), pp. 388–403.

Kuligowska-Korzeniewska, Anna: *Scena obiecana. Teatr polski w Łodzi 1844–1918.* Łódź 1995.

Kumaniecki, Kazimierz W. (ed.): *Odbudowa państwowości polskiej. Najważniejsze dokumenty 1912–1924.* Warszawa, Kraków 1924.

Kuźko, Wanda: "Metamorfozy: image trzech pokoleń Biedermannów". In: Kołodziejczyk, Ryszard (ed.): *Image przedsiębiorcy gospodarczego w Polsce w XIX i XX wieku.* Warszawa 1993. pp. 131–150.

Kuźko, Wanda: *Biedermannowie. Dzieje rodziny i fortuny 1730–1945.* Łódź 2000.

Lohr, Eric: *Nationalizing the Russian Empire. The Campaign against Enemy Aliens during World War I.* Cambridge/MA, London: 2003.

Lohr, Eric: Nationalizing; id.: 'The Russian Army and the Jews. Mass Deportation, Hostages, and Violence During World War I'. In: *The Russian Review* 60 (2001), pp. 404–419.

Malinowski, Jerzy: *Grupa "Jung Idysz" i żydowskie środowisko 'nowej sztuki' w Polsce, 1918–1923.* Warszawa: 1987; id.: "The 'Yung Yiddish' (Young Yiddish) Group and Jewish Modern Art in Poland, 1918–1923." In: *Polin* 6 (1991). pp. 223–230.

Matywiecki, Piotr: *Twarz Tuwima.* Warszawa 2007.

Mendelsohn, Ezra: *On Modern Jewish Politics.* New York 1993.

Pelowski, Alfons: *Kultura muzyczna Łodzi.* Łódź 1994.

Podolska, Joanna/Waingertner, Przemysław: *Prezydenci miasta Łodzi.* Łódź 2008.

Protokoll über die Evangelisch-Augsburgische Synode am 18. und 19. Oktober 1917 in Lodz. Lodz 1917.

Prykowska-Michalak, Karolina: "Łódzkie teatry w okresie I wojny światowej". In: Radziszewska, Krystyna/Zawilski, Piotr (eds.): *Łódź i region łódzki w czasie I wojny światowej: Między wielką historią a codziennością.* Łódź: 2012. pp. 119–133.

Prykowska-Michalak, Karolina: *Teatr niemiecki w Łodzi. Sceny, Wykonawcy, Repertuar (1867–1939).* Łódź 2005.

Radziszewska, Krystyna/Zawilski, Piotr (eds.): *Łódź i region łódzki w czasie I wojny światowej. Między wielką historią a codziennością.* Łódź 2012.

Radziszewska, Krystyna: "Korespondencja Związku Przemysłowców Królestwa Polskiego z szefem zarządu Generalnego Gubernatorstwa Warszawskiego 1915-1916. Prezentacja źródła archiwalnego". In: Radziszewska, Krystyna/ Zawilski, Piotr (eds.): *Łódź i region łódzki w czasie I wojny światowej. Między wielką historią a codziennością.* Łódź: 2012. pp. 37-48.

Rosenfeld, Lulla: *Bright star of exile. Jacob Adler and the Yiddish theatre.* New York 1977.

Rozier, Gilles: *Mojżesz Broderson od Jung Idysz do Araratu.* Łódź 1999.

Sandrow, Nahma: *Vagabond Stars: A World History of Yiddish Theater.* Syracuse/ NY 1995.

Schedler, Gustav: *Eben-Ezer, eine Jahrhundertgeschichte der evangelischen St. Trinitatisgemeinde zu Lodz.* Lodz 1929.

Schuster, Frank M.: "Die Stadt der vielen Kulturen – Die Stadt der Lodzermenschen': Komplexe lokale Identitäten bei den Bewohnern der Industriestadt Lodz 1820-1939/1945". In: Lewandowska-Tomaszczyk Barbara/Pulaczewska, Hanna (eds.): *Intercultural Europe. Arenas of Difference, Communication and Mediation.* Ed. by Stuttgart 2010. pp. 33-60.

Schuster, Frank M.: "Zwischen Identitätskrise und Herausforderung: Polen, Juden, Deutsche während des Ersten Weltkrieges in der Textilmetropole Lodz". In: Lasatowicz, Maria Krystyna (ed.): *Der städtische Raum als kulturelle Identitätsstruktur.* Berlin 2007, pp. 95-109.

Schuster, Frank M.: "Zwischen Paralyse, Krise und Aufbruch. Die zentralpolnische Industriestadt Lodz im Übergang 1914-1918". In: Fejtová, Olga/Ledvinka, Václav/Pešek, Jiří (eds.): *Unermessliche Verluste und ihre Bewältigung: die Bevölkerung der Europäischen Großstädte und der Erste Weltkrieg/Nezměrné ztráty a jejich zvládání. Obyvatelstvo evropských velkoměst a I. světová válka*Prag/ Praha 2015, in print.

Schuster, Frank M.: *Zwischen allen Fronten. Osteuropäische Juden während des Ersten Weltkrieges (1914-1919).* Köln, Weimar, Wien 2004.

Silber, Marcos: "Ruling Practiced and Multiple Cultures. Jews, Poles and Germans during World War I". In: *Simon Dubnow Institute Yearbook* V (2006). pp. 189-208.

Skarżyński, Mieczysław: "Akcja pomocy społecznej w Łodzi w okresie działania Głównego Komitetu Obywatelskiego (3 VIII 1914-1 VII 1915 r.)". In: *Rocznik Łódzki* 20 (1975), pp. 265-283.

Skarżyński, Mieczysław: "Polityka niemieckich władz okupacyjnych w Łodzi w okresie działania Głównego Komitetu Obywatelskiego 6 XII 1914-1 VII 1915". In: *Zeszyty Naukowe Politechniki Łódzkiej. Nauki Społeczno-Ekonomiczne* 4 (1977), pp. 91-106.

Skarżyński, Mieczysław: *Główny Komitet Obywatelski w Łodzi i jego działalność w latach 1914–1915*. Łódź 1986.

Skład Komitetów Obywatelskich w dniu 1. Maja 1915 r. s. l.: s. a. [Łódź: 1915].

Skrzydło, Leszek: *Rody nie tylko fabrykanckie*. Łódź 2007.

Stempin, Arkadiusz: *Próba 'moralnego podboju' Polski przez Cesarstwo Niemieckie w latach I wojny światowej*. Warszawa 2014.

Thurstan, Violetta: *Field Hospital and Flying Column. Being the Journal of an English Nursing Sister in Belgium and Russia*. London 1915.

Tuwim, Julian: *Łodzianie*. In: *Estrada* Nr. 2 1918, p. 11–20.

Zilbertsweig, Zalman: *Leksikon fun yidishn Teater*. Vol. 1.New York 1931.

Zilbertsweig, Zalman: *Leksikon fun yidishn Teater*. Vol. 2.Varshe 1934.

Jews, Poles, and Germans in Łódź during the Great War: Hegemony via Acknowledgment and/or Negation of Multiple Cultures

Marcos Silber

References

Bałaban, Majer: "Raport o żydowskich instytucjach oświatowych i religijnych na terenach Królestwa Polskiego okupowanych przez Austro-Węgry". *Kwartalnik historii Żydów* 1, 2001, pp. 35–68.

Bartal, Israel: "Mi-Du-Leshoniut Mesoratit le-Had-Leshoniut Leumit". In Shvut 15, 1992, pp. 183–194.

Bartal, Israel: "Mi-Du-Leshoniut Mesoratit le-Had-Leshoniut Leumit". In: *Shvut* 15, 1992, pp. 183–194.

Ben-Amos, Batsheva: 'A Multilingual Diary from the Ghetto". *Galed* 19, 2004, pp. 51–74.

Bonzon, Thierry and Davis, Belinda: "Feeding the cities". In: Winter, Jay and Robert, Jean Louis (eds.): *Capital Cities at War, Paris, London, Berlin 1914–1918*, Cambridge University Press: Cambridge UK 1997.

Budziarek, Marek: "Konfessionelle Koexistenz in Lodz im 19. und 20. Jahrhundert". In: Jürgen Hensel, Jürgen (ed.): *Polen, Deutsche und Juden in Lodz 1820–1939, eine schwierige Nachbarschaft*. Fibre: Osnabrück, 1999.

Conze, Werner: *Polnische Nation und Deutsche Politik im Ersten Weltkrieg*. Böhlau: Köln/ Graz 1958.

Engel, David: "Ha-She'ela ha-Polanit ve-ha-Tenua ha-Tzionit. Ha-Vikuah al ha-Shilton Ha-Atzmi be-Arei Folin ha-Kongresait". In: *Galed* 12, 1993, pp. 59–66–82 (Hebrew pagination).

Even-Zohar, Itamar: "Aspects of the Hebrew-Yiddish Polysystem. A Case of a Multilingual Polysystem". Poetics Today 11, 1990, pp. 121–130.

Even-Zohar, Itamar: "Aspects of the Hebrew-Yiddish Polysystem. A Case of a Multilingual Polysystem". *Poetics Today* 11, 1990, pp. 121–130.

Fischer, Fritz: *Germany's aims in the First world War*, Chatto & Windus: London 1967.

Frankel, Jonathan: *Prophecy and Politics. Socialism, Nationalism and the Russian Jews, 1862–1917*. Cambridge University Press: Cambridge, 1981.

Geiss, Imanuel: *Der polnische Grenzstreifen 1914–1918. Ein Beitrag zur deutschen Kriegszielpolitik im Ersten Weltkrieg*, Matthiesen Verlag: Lübeck/ Hamburg 1960.

Gilinski-Meller, Chaya: *Mifleget ha-Folkisitim [Folks-partei] be-Folin, 1915–1939* (doctoral thesis) Bar-Ilan University, Ramat Gan 2004.

Golczewski, Frank: *Polnisch-jüdische Beziehungen 1881–1922. Eine Studie zur Geschichtes des Antisemitismus in Ost-Europa.* Steiner: Wiesbaden, 1981.

Grosfeld, Leon: "La Pologne dans les Plans impérialistes allemands pendant la grande guerre 1914–1918 et l'acte du 5 Novembre 1916", *La Pologne au X Congrès international des Sciences Historiques à Rome,* Académie Polonaise des Sciences, Institut d'Histoire: Warszawa 1955.

Grosfeld, Leon: *Polityka państw centralnych wobec sprawy polskiej w latach pierwszej wojny światowej.* Państwowe Wydawnictwo Naukowe: Warszawa 1962.

Guesnet, François: *Lodzer Juden im 19. Jahrhundert. Ihr Ort in einer multikulturellen Stadtgesellschaft,* Simon-Dubnow-Institut für Jüdische Geschichte und Kultur: Leipzig, 1997.

Hertz, Mieczysław: *Łódź w czasie wielkiej wojny.* Skł. gł. Księg. S. Seipelt: Łódź, 1933.

Hertz, Yankl Sholem: *Di Geshichte fun Bund in Łódź.* Unzr Tzayt: New York, 1958.

Herwig, Holger: *The First World War, Germany and Austria-Hungary 1914–1918.* Arnold: London, 1997.

Janczak, Julian: "The National Structure of the Population in Łódź in the Years 1820–1939". In: *Polin* 6,1991, pp. 20–26.

Janczak, Julian: "Struktura Narodowościowa Łodzi w latach 1820–1939". In: Puś, Wiesław/Liszewski, Stanisław (eds.): *Dzieje Żydów w Łodzi 1820–1944, Wybrane problemy.* Wydawnictwo Uniwersytetu Łódzkiego: Łódź 1991.

Janczak, Julian: *Ludność Łodzi przemysłowej 1820–1914.* Uniwersytet Łódzki: Łódź 1982.

Janowsky, Oscar: *The Jews and the Minority Rights (1898–1919).* AMS Press: New York 1966.

Jarausch, Konrad: *The Enigmatic Chancellor, Bethmann Hollweg and the Hubris of Imperial Germany.* Yale University Press: New Haven and London 1973.

Jerzy Holzer/Jan Molenda, *Polska w pierwszej wojnie światowej.* Wiedza Powszechna: Warsaw 1973.

Knebel, Jerzy: *Rząd Pruski wobec sprawy polskiej w latach 1914–1918.* Wydawnictwo. Poznańskie: Poznań 1963.

Komarnicki, Titus: *Rebirth of the Polish Republic, A Study in the Diplomatic History of Europe, 1914–1920.* W. Heinemann: Melbourne-London-Toronto 1957.

Konarski, Kazimierz: *Dzieje szkolnictwa w b. Królestwie Kongresowym 1915–1918* [History of the School system in the ex Congress Kingdom 1915–1918]. Skł. gł. w Ksiaznicy Polskiej w Warszawie: Warsaw 1923.

Kozłowski, Czesław: *Działalność Polityczna Koła Międzypartyjnego w latach 1915–1918*. Książka i Wiedza: Warsaw 1967.

Kulak, Zbigniew: "Memorandum of the Germans from Łódź concerning the annexation of Polish Territories to the Reich at the Time of World War I". *Polish Western Affairs* 7, 1966, PP. 388–403.

Lemke, Heinz: "Die Politik der Mittelmächte in Polen von der Novemberproklamation 1916 bis zum Zusamentritt des Provisorischen Staatsrats". *Jahrbuch für Geschichte der UdSSR und der volksdemokratischen Länder Europas* 6, 1962, pp. 69–136.

Lemke, Heinz: *Allianz und Rivalität. Die Mittelmächte und Polen im Ersten Weltkrieg (bis zur Februarrevolution)*. Akademie-Verlag: Wien,/Köln/Graz, 1977.

Lewin, Sabina: *Prakim be-Toldot ha-Hinuch ha-Yehudi be-Folin ba-Mea ha-Tesha-Esre u-ve-Reshit ha-Mea ha-Esrim*. Tel Aviv University: Tel Aviv, 1997.

Liulevicius, Vejas Gabriel: *War, Land on the Eastern Front, Culture. National Identity and German Occupation in World War I*, Cambridge University Press: Cambridge, 2000.

Mendelsohn, Ezra: *On Modern Jewish Politics*. Oxford University Press: New York/ Oxford, 1993.

Molenda, Jan: "Królestwo Polskie i Galicja, sierpień 1915–Luty 1917". In: Kormanowa, Żanna/ Najdus, Walentyna (eds.): *Historia Polski*, Vol III, part III. Państwowe Wydawnictwo Naukowe: Warsaw 1974, pp. 172–236.

Ogonowski, Jerzy: *Uprawnienia Językowe mniejszości narodowych w Rzeczypospolitej Polskiej 1918–1939* [Language Rights of National Minorities in the Polish Republic 1918–1939]. Wydawn. Sejmowe: Warsaw 2000.

Pajewski, Janusz: *Odbudowa państwa Polskiego, 1914–1918*. Państwowe Wydawnictwo Naukowe: Warsaw, 1985.

Podgórska, Eugenia: *Szkolnictwo elementarne w Łodzi w latach 1808–1914*. Łódzkie Towarzystwo Naukowe: Łódź 1966.

Porter, Brian: *When Nationalism Began to Hate. Imagining Modern Politics in Nineteenth-Century Poland*. Oxford University Press: New York/Oxford 2000.

Puś, Wiesław: "The Development of the City of Łódź (1820–1939)". In: *Polin* 6, 1991, pp. 3–19.

Puś, Wiesław: *Żydzi w Łodzi w latach zaborów 1793–1914*. Wydawnictwo Uniwersytetu Łódzkiego: Łódź 2000.

Radziszewska, Krystyna/Woźniak Krzysztof (eds.): *Pod Jednym dachem. Niemcy oraz ich polscy i żydowscy sąsiedzi w Łodzi w XIX i XX wieku/Unter einem Dach. Die Deutschen und ihre polnischen und jüdischen Nachbarn in Lodz im 19. und 20. Jahrhundert*, Literatura: Łódź, 2000.

Roth, Paul Roth: *Die politische Entwicklung in Kongreßpolen während der deutschen Okkupation*, K. F. Koehler: Leipzig 1919.

Sadan, Dov (ed.): *Zikhron Mordekhai Ze'ev Broda: kovets le-zekher ha-doktor Mordekhai Ze'ev Broda*, Hasifirah hatzionit: Jerusalem 1960 (Remembrance of Mordekhai Ze'ev Broda: collection in memoriam of Mordekhai Ze'ev Broda).

Schuster, Frank M. "Zwischen Paralyse, Kriese und Aufbruch: Die zentralpolnische Industrienstadt Łódź im Übergand 1914–1918", unpublished article.

Schuster, Frank M: *Zwischen allen Fronten. Osteuropäische Juden während des Ersten Weltkrieges (1914–1919)*. Böhlau: Köln/ Weimar/Wien, 2004, pp. 265–269.

Shmeruk, Chone: "Hebrew-Yiddish-Polish. A Trilingual Jewish Culture". In: Gutman, Yisrael et al. (eds.): *The Jews of Poland between Two World Wars*, University Press of New England: Hanover/London, 1989, pp. 285–311.

Sibora, Janusz: *Narodziny Polskiej Dyplomacji u Progu Niepodległości*. Wydawnictwo Sejmowe: Warsaw 1998.

Silber, Marcos: "Hukei Behirot be-Folin ha-Kongresait be-Milhemet ha-Olam ha-Rishona ve-Yitzug ha-Yehudim ba-Mosdot ha-Nivharim". In: *Michael 16*, 2004, pp. 144–164.

Silber, Marcos: "Ruling Practices and Multiple Cultures – Jews, Poles, and Germans in Łódź during WWI". In: *Simon Dubnow Institute Yearbook 5*, 2006, pp. 189–208.

Silber, Marcos: "The German 'Ordinance Regarding the Organization of the Religious Jewish Community' (November 1916–1918)". In: *Studia Judaica* 18(1), 2015, 35–55.

Silber, Marcos: Leumiut shona, ezrkhut shava! ha-mamatz le-asagat otonomia le-yehudey polin be-milkhemet ha-olam ha-rishona. The Zalman Shazar Center for Jewish History and Tel Aviv University Press: Tel Aviv 2014.

Silber, Marcos: *She-Polin Ha-Hadasha Tihie Em Tova le-Hol Yaldeha: Ha-Maamatz be-Merkaz Eropa le-Hasagat Otonomia le-Yehudei Folin ha-Kongresait be-Milkhemet ha-Olam ha-Rishona* (Doctoral Thesis) Tel Aviv University: Tel Aviv 2001.

Stempin, Arkadiusz: *Próba 'moralnego podboju' Polski przez Cesarstwo Niemieckie w latach I wojny światowej*. Neriton: Warsaw 2013.

Stone, Norman: *The Eastern Front, 1914–1917*. Hodder & Stoughton, New York, 1975.

Sukiennicki, Wiktor: *East Central Europe during World War I: From Foreign Domination to National Independence.* East European monographs: Boulder 1984.

Suleja, Włodzimierz: *Tymczasowa Rada Stanu.* Wydawn. Sejmowe: Warsaw 1998.

Ticker, Jay: "Max I. Bodenheimer. Advocate of Pro-German Zionism at the Beginning of World War I". In: *Jewish Social Studies* 43, 1981, pp. 11–30.

Uger, Yeshaya: "Hindenburg Kegn 'Haint'". Haynt Yubilei Bukh, Haynt Farlag: Warsaw, 1928, pp. 11–12.

Vincent, Paul: *The Politics of Hunger: The Allied Blockade of Germany, 1915–1919,* Ohio University Press: Athens OH 1985.

Walicki, Jacek: "Juden und Deutsche in der Lodzer Selbstverwaltung". In: Hensel. Jürgen (ed.): *Polen, Deutsche und Juden in Lodz 1820–1939. Eine schwierige Nachbarschaft.* Fibre: Osnabrück 1999, pp. 215–236.

Weeks, Theodore: "Nationality and Municipality. Reforming City Government in the Kingdom of Poland, 1904–1915". *Russian History* 21, 1994, pp. 23–47.

Weiser, Keith: *The Politics of Yiddish. Noiekh Prilutski and the Folkspartey in Poland, 1900–1926.* (doctoral thesis) Columbia University, New York 2001.

Zechlin, Egmont: *Die deutsche Politik und die Juden im Ersten Weltkrieg.* Vandenhoeck & Ruprecht: Göttingen 1969.

Zieliński, Konrad: "Stosunki polsko-żydowskie w Królestwie Polskin w czasie I wojny światowej (na przykładzie rad miejskich)". In: *Kwartalnik Historii Żydów* 206, 2003, pp. 164–194.

Zieliński, Konrad: *Stosunku polsko-żydowskie na ziemiach Królestwa Polskiego w czasie pierwszej wojny światowej.* Wydawnictwo Uniwersytetu Marii Curie-Skłodowskiej: Lublin 2005.

Zimmerman, Joshua: *Poles, Jews and the Politics of Nationality. The Bund and the Polish Socialist Party in Late Tsarist Russia.* The University of Wisconsin Press: Madison 2004.

Newspaper articles

"Debatn in Lodzer shtotrat vegn di yiddisher natzionale recht". In: *Haynt,* 16.11.1917.

"Der rezultat fun di vahlen in Lodz". In: *Haynt,* 21.1. 1917.

"Di Farzamlung fun yidishn shul farain". In: *Lodzer Folksblat,* 28.8.1916.

"Di Takones fun der zelbst-Fervaltung in Poiln". In: *Lodzer Folksblat,* 24.6.1916.

"Di zelbstfervaltung in okupirtn Poyln". In: *Lodzer Folksblat,* 2.7.1915.

"Di vahl campanie in Lodz". In: *Lodzer Togblat,* 17.1.1917.

"Do wyborców II kuryi". In: *Lodzer Togblat,* 8.1.1917.

"Dos Lodzer Lebn. A farzamlung vegn der yidisher folks-shul". In: *Lodzer Folksblat*, 9.9.1915.

"Dos lodzer lebn. Di unterrichts-shprach in di yidishe folksshuln". In: *Lodzer Folksblat*, 10.8.1916.

"Dos lodzer lebn. Tog notitsen: Ofn shvel fun nayem shul-yor". In: *Lodzer Folksblat*, 28.8.1916.

"Fun Lodzer shtotrat". In: *Lebensfragen*, 14.12.1917.

"Fun lodzer shtotrat". In: *Lebensfragen*, 15.12.1917.

"Jüdische Angelegenheiten – Jüdische Wahlkurien". In: *Deutsche Lodzer Zeitung*, 18.6.1915.

"Mowa d-ra Rozenblata, prezesa frakcji żydowskiej w Łódzkiej Radzie miejskiej". In: *Głos Żydowski*, 1.11.1917.

"Polen". In: *Neue Jüdische Monatshefte* 1, 1916, p. 207.

"Polin". In: *HaTzfira*, 29.12.1917.

"Polin". In: *Hatzfira*, 31.1.1918.

"Russisch – verboten. Die Strassenschilder in Lodz". In: *Die Zeit* (Wien), 3.9.1915.

"Verordnung betreffend Regelung des Schulwesens". In: *Deutsche Lodzer Zeitung*, 7.9.1915.

"Verordnung betreffend Regelung des Schulwesens". In: *Deutsche Lodzer Zeitung*, 10.9. 1915.

"W sprawie stosunków Żydów do Polaków w Łodzi". In: *Wiedeński Kurier*, 22.7.1915.

"Wybory w Łodzi". In: *Głos Żydowski*, 21.1.1917.

Betrayed twice. The German community in the Kingdom of Poland during the Great War

Krzysztof Paweł Woźniak

References

Archival sources

Российский Государственный Исторический Архив , Санкт Петербург.

Fond 821, opis 10, sygn. 534, 1169.

Fond 821, opis 133, sygn. 1068, 1114.

Archiwum miasta stołecznego Warszawy Oddział w Grodzisku Mazowieckim.

Pełnomocnik Gubernatora Warszawskiego w Twierdzy Modlin, sygn. 20.

Archiwum Państwowe w Kielcach.

Kancelaria Gubernatora Kieleckiego, sygn. 98, 1554, 2769, 2987.

Archiwum Państwowe w Łodzi.

Kancelaria Gubernatora Piotrkowskiego, sygn. 2863.

Archiwum Państwowe w Poznaniu.

Spuścizna Alberta Breyera, sygn. 30.

Niemiecki Instytut Historyczny w Warszawie.

Rys historyczny Kościoła Ewangelickiego w Radomiu, v. 1: 1826–1926.

Kronika Zboru Ewangelickiego Lubelskiego, v. 1 (1888–1932).

Printed sources

Caban, Wiesław/Przenioło, Marek/Rokoszny, Józef: *Diariusz Wielkiej Wojny 1914–1918*. Wyższa Szkoła Pedagogiczna im. Jana Kochanowskiego: Kielce 1998, v. 1.

Chrapowicki, Włodzimierz: *Krótki opis topograficzny i statystyczny Królestwa Polskiego*. Zakłady Graficzne Braci Wierzbickich: Warszawa 1912.

Gesetze über die Ländereien der deutschen Kolonisten. Landbesitz feindlicher Ausländer und der Kolonisten. W: Hummel, Theodor: *100 Jahre Erbhofrecht der deutschen Kolonisten in Rußland.* Reichsnährstand Verlags-Gesellschaft, Berlin 1936; Anhang 2. Teil: Enteignungs- und Liquidationsgesetze.

Krzyżanowski, Adam/Kumaniecki, Kazimierz: *Statystyka Polska*. Polskie Towarzystwo Statystyczne: Kraków 1915.

Romer, Eugeniusz/Weinfeld, Ignacy: *Rocznik polski. Tablice statystyczne*. Nakładem Księgarni G. Gebethnera: Kraków 1917.

Strasburger, Edward (ed.): *Rocznik statystyczny Królestwa Polskiego z uwzględnieniem innych ziem polskich. Rok 1915*. Gebethner i Wolff: Warszawa 1916.

Wakar, Włodzimierz: *Rozwój terytorialny narodowości polskiej*. St. Święcicki: Kielce 1917.

Studies

Althaus, Paul: *Lodzer Kriegsbüchlein. Deutsch-evangelische Betrachtungen*. Vandenhoeck & Ruprecht: Göttingen 1916.

Althaus, Paul: *Um Glauben und Vaterland. Neues Lodzer Kriegsbüchlein*. Vandenhoeck & Ruprecht: Göttingen 1917.

Brehmer, Ursula: "Verantwortung als Aufgabe und Lebensgesetz. Josef Alexander Spickermann zum 50. Todestag". In: *Jahrbuch Weichsel-Warthe* 43, 1997.

Eichler, Adolf: "Die Lodzer deutsche Aktivisten und ihre Gegner". In: *Deutsche Wissenschaftliche Zeitschrift im Wartheland* 3–4, 1941.

Eichler, Adolf: *Deutschtum im Schatten des Ostens*. Meinhold Verlag: Dresden 1942.

Eichler, Adolf: *Zwischen den Fronten. Kriegsaufzeichnungen eines Lodzer Deutschen*. Lodz 1918.

Heike, Otto: *Deutsche Minderheit in Polen bis 1939. Ihr Leben ind Wirken kulturell, gesellschaftlich, politisch. Eine dokumentarische Analyse*. Selbstverlag des Verfassers: Leverkusen 1985.

Hensel, Jürgen: *Ewakuacja kolonistów niemieckiego pochodzenia z Królestwa Polskiego "w głąb Rosji" w latach 1914–1915*. In: Borodziej, Włodzimierz/ Wieczorkiewicz, Paweł (ed.): *Polska między Niemcami a Rosją. Studia ofiarowane Marianowi Wojciechowskiemu w 70. rocznicę urodzin*. Wydawnictwo Instytutu Historii Polskiej Akademii Nauk: Warszawa 1997.

Hertz, Mieczysław: *Łódź w czasach wielkiej wojny*. Izba Przemysłowo-Handlowa w Łodzi: Łódź 1933.

Holtz, Edmund: *Der Krieg und die Evangelisch-Lutherische Kirche in Polen. Erweiterter Konferenzbericht verfaßt auf Grund von amtlichem Material im Auftrage des Warschauer Evangelisch-Ausgburgischen Konsistoriums*. Deutsche Staatsdruckerei: Łódź 1916.

Kneifel, Eduard: *Bischof Dr. Julius Bursche. Sein Leben und seine Tätigkeit (1862–1942)*. Selbstverlag des Verfassers, Vierkirchen über München [1980].

Kneifel, Eduard: *Die evangelisch-augsburgischen Gemeinden in Polen 1555–1939*. Selbstverlag des Verfassers: Vierkirchen 1971.

Kneifel, Eduard: *Geschichte der Evangelisch-Augsburgischen Kirche in Polen. Ein biographisches Pfarrerbuch*. Selbstverlag des Verfassers: Niedermarschacht 1964.

Kopczyńska-Jaworska, Bronisława/Woźniak, Krzysztof: *Łódzcy luteranie. Społeczność i jej organizacja*. Polskie Towarzystwo Ludoznwacze: Łódź 2002.

Kossert, Andreas: *"Nieprzejednane sprzeczności?" Napięcia narodowe w protestantyzmie łódzkim w latach 1918 – 1939*. In: Milerski, Bogusław ks./ Woźniak, Krzysztof (ed.), *Przeszłość przyszłości. Z dziejów luteranizmu w Łodzi i regionie. Praca zbiorowa*. Wydawnictwo Ewangelickie św. Mateusza: Łódź 1998.

Kossmann, Oskar: *Es begann in Polen. Erinnerungen eines Diplomaten und Ostforschers*. Verlag J. A. Koch: Marburg 1995.

Krasuski, Jerzy: *Stosunki polsko-niemieckie 1919–1932*. Instytut Zachodni: Poznań 1975.

Krebs, Bernd: *Nationale Identität und kirchliche Selbstbehauptung. Julius Bursche und die Auseinandersetzung um Auftrag und Weg des Protestantismus in Polen 1917–1939*. Neukirchener Verlagsgesellschaft: Neukirchen-Vluyn 1993.

Kucner, Monika: *I wojna światowa w świetle badań literaturoznawczych: kazania pastora Paula Althausa z lat 1915–1917*. In: Rzadziszewska, Krystyna/ Zawilski, Piotr: *Między wielką historią a codziennością. Łódź i region łódzki w okresie I wojny światowej*. Archiwum Państwowe: Łódź 2011.

Kucner, Monika: *Prasa niemiecka w Łodzi 1863–1939*. In: Kuczyński, Krzysztof/ Ratecka, Barbara: *Niemcy w dziejach Łodzi do 1945 r. Zagadnienia wybrane*. Wydawnictwo Uniwersytetu Łódzkiego: Łódź 2001.

Kulak, Zbigniew: "Memoriał Niemców łódzkich w sprawie aneksji ziem polskich do Rzeszy w okresie I wojny światowej". *Przegląd Zachodni* 6, 1966.

Lackner, Franz: *Chronik der Gemeinde und Volksschule Tiefenbach (Nowe Boryszewo, kr. Plock, Polen)*. Ostdeutsche Forschungsstelle im Lande Nordrhein-Westfalen, Dortmund 1959.

Matelski, Dariusz: "Za i przeciw Polsce. Niemcy polscy w Wehrmachcie i Wojsku Polskim w kampanii wrześniowej 1939 r.". In: Nijakowski Lech M. (ed.), *Udział mniejszości narodowych w różnych formacjach wojskowych w czasie kampanii wrześniowej 1939 r*. Wydawnictwo Sejmowe: Warszawa 2009.

Merczyng, Henryk: "Ilu jest ewangelików Polaków?". In: *Zwiastun Ewangeliczny* 5, 1906.

Niemirowicz-Danczenko, Wasilij: "По крестам боев. Под Лодзиою". In: *Русское Слово*, 21.11.1914.

Pruss, Witold: "Społeczeństwo Królestwa Polskiego w XIX i początkach XX wieku. Cz. I: Narodowości, wyznania, sekty, organizacje kościelne". In: *Przegląd Historyczny* 68, 1977, z. 2.

Stegner, Tadeusz: "Protestanci na terenie guberni radomskiej i kieleckiej w XIX i na początku XX wieku". In: *Studia Kieleckie. Seria Historyczna* 1, 1995.

Stegner, Tadeusz: *Ewangelicy warszawscy 1815–1918*. Semper: Warszawa 1993.

Wegener, Tadeusz: *Juliusz Bursche – biskup w dobie przełomów*. Augustana: Bielsko-Biała 2003.

Woźniak, Krzysztof Paweł: "Niemcy w Królestwie Polskim wobec odrodzenia państwa polskiego w 1918 r.". In: *Studia z historii społeczno-gospodarczej XIX i XX w*. 9, 2011.

Woźniak, Krzysztof Paweł: *Niemieckie osadnictwo wiejskie między Prosną a Pilicą i Wisłą od lat 70. XVIII w. do 1866 r. Proces i jego interpretacje*. Wydawnictwo Uniwersytetu Łódzkiego: Łódź 2013.

Press

"Biblioteka Warszawska", 1908, v. 2.

"Deutsche Post", 1918.

"Kurier Warszawski", 1925.

"Русское Слово", 1914.

"Утро России", 1915.

Other sources

http://kronika.sejm.gov.pl/kronika.97.3/text/pl/an-6.htm

War museums at the former frontline between Austria-Hungary and Italy during World War I

Andrea Brait

References

Assmann, Aleida: "Funktions- und Speichergedächtnis. Zwei Modi der Erinnerung". In: Platt, Kristin/ Dabag, Mihran (eds.): *Generation und Gedächtnis. Erinnerungen und kollektive Identitäten, herausgegeben unter Mitwirkung von Susanne Heil.* Opladen 1995, pp. 169–185.

Assmann, Aleida: „Vier Formen des Gedächtnisses. In: *Erwägen Wissen Ethik. Deliberation Knowledge Ethics* 1/13 (2002), pp. 183–190.

Assmann, Jan: Das kulturelle Gedächtnis. Schrift, Erinnerung und politische Kultur in frühen Hochkulturen, München 1997.

Brix, Emil/ Bruckmüller, Ernst/ Stekl, Hannes (eds.): Memoria Austriae I–III. Wien 2004/2005; François, Ettiene/ Schulze, Hagen (eds.): Deutsche Erinnerungsorte, volume 1–3. München 2001.

Casey, Valerie: The museum effect. Gazing from object to performance in contemporary cultural-history museum, www.archimuse.com/publishing/ich im03/095C.pdf.

Große Burlange, Martin: Große historische Ausstellungen in der Bundesrepublik Deutschland 1960 – 2000 (Zeitgeschichte – Zeitverständnis 15). Münster 2005.

Gryse, Piet de: "Introduction". In: Muchitsch, Wolfgang (ed.): Does War Belong in Museums? The Representation if Violence in Exhibitions. Bielefeld 2013, pp. 13–17.

Hirschfeld, Gerhard: "Der Erste Weltkrieg in der deutschen und internationalen Geschichtsschreibung". In: Aus Politik und Zeitgeschichte B 29–30 (2004), pp. 3–12.

Hoffmann, Detlev: „Laßt Objekte sprechen! „Bemerkungen zu einem verhängnisvollen Irrtum. In: Spickernagel, Ellen/ Walbe, Brigitte (eds.): Das Museum. Lernort contra Musentempel (special volume of the journal "Kritische Berichte"). Gießen 1979, pp. 101–120.

Isnenghi, Mario: "La Grande Guerra". In: Isnenghi, Mario (ed.): I luoghi della memoria. Strutture ed eventi dell'Italia unita. Roma/Bari 1997, pp. 273–309.

Keegan, John: A history of warfare, London 1993.

Klein, Hans-Joachim/Wüsthoff-Schäfer, Barbara: Inszenierungen an Museen und ihre Wirkung auf Besucher (Materialien aus dem Institut für Museumskunde 32). Berlin 1990.

Krumeich, Gerd: "Der Erste Weltkrieg im Museum. Das Historial de la Grande Guerre in Pérronne und neuere Entwicklungen in der musealen Präsentation des Ersten Weltkrieges". In: Korte, Barbara/ Paletschek, Sylvia/ Hochbruck, Wolfgang (eds.): Der Erste Weltkrieg in der populären Erinnerungskultur (Schriften der Bibliothek für Zeitgeschichte 22). Essen 2008, pp. 59–71.

Krumeich, Gerd: "Verdun". In: Boer, Pim de/ Duchhardt, Heinz/ Kreis, Georg/ Schmale, Wolfgang (eds.): Europäische Erinnerungsorte 2. Das Haus Europa. München 2012, pp. 437–444.

Lord, Gail Dexter: "Function & Form: Museums in Response to a Changing Social, Cultural and Economic Climate". In: Matt, Gerald/ KUNSTHALLE wien (edd.): Jetzt oder nie. 5 Jahre Kunsthalle Wien. Elfenbein und Disneyland. Kooperationen, Internationalisierung, Globalisierung. Kunstinstitutionen im nächsten Jahrtausend (Schriftenreihe der KUNSTHALLE wien 3). Klagenfurt 1997, pp. 191–200.

Mazohl-Wallnig, Brigitte/ Barth-Scalmani, Gunda/ Kuprian, Hermann J. W./ Bösche, Andreas: "Einleitung". In: Mazohl-Wallnig, Brigitte/ Barth-Scalmani, Gunda/ Kuprian, Hermann J. W. (eds.), Ein Krieg – zwei Schützengräben. Österreich – Italien und der Erste Weltkrieg in den Dolomiten 1915–1918 (Bolzano 2005) 9–21.

Museum von Kobarid. Führer. 1. Weltkrieg – Isonzofront. 1914–1918, [Kobarid 1993].

Nowosadtko, Jutta: "Gewalt – Gesellschaft – Kultur": Ein Ersatz für "Krieg – Staat – Politik?". In: Zeithistorische Forschungen/Studies in Contemporary History, Online-Ausgabe, 1/2 (2005), http://www.zeithistorische-forschungen.de/1-2005/id=4619.

Rauchensteiner, Manfried: Geschichte der Erinnerung. Die Transformation des Ersten Weltkriegs (Vortrag im Rahmen der Tagung Isonzofront 1915–1917: Die Kultur des Erinnerns 29. September 2005 bis 01. Oktober 2005 in Bovec/ Slowenien) [Lecture at the conference Isonzofront 1915–1917: Die Kultur des Erinnerns (29 September, 2005 to 01 October, 2005 in Bovec/Slovenia].

Rothfels, Hans: "Zeitgeschichte als Aufgabe". In: Vierteljahreshefte für Zeitgeschichte 1/1953, p. 1–8.

Schäfer, Hermann: "Zwischen Disneyland und Musentempel: Zeitgeschichte im Museum". In: Museumskunde 60 (1995), pp. 27–32.

Tagungsbericht: "Quo vadis Zeitgeschichte? / L'histoire du temps présent et ses défis au XXIe siècle". 01.10.2014–02.10.2014 Paris. In: H-Soz-Kult. 21.02.2015, http://www.hsozkult.de/conferencereport/id/tagungsberichte – 5841 (28.02.2015).

Thiemeyer, Thomas: "Waffen und Weltkriege im Museum. Wie sich die museale Darstellung der beiden Weltkriege und der Umgang mit Militaria gewandelt haben". In: Militärgeschichtliche Zeitschrift 1/69 (2010), pp. 1–16.

Thiemeyer, Thomas: Fortsetzung des Krieges mit anderen Mitteln. Die beiden Weltkriege im Museum. Paderborn/Vienna 2010.

Wörsdorfer, Rolf: Krisenherd Adria 1915–1955. Konstruktion und Artikulation des Nationalen im italienisch-jugoslawischen Grenzraum. Paderborn 2004.

http://www.kobariski-muzej.si/museum/awards/.

http://www.potmiru.si/deu/.

The Middle East and the Centenary of the Great War

Hassan A. Jamsheer

References

Al-Sadat, Anwar: *Revolt on the Nile*. London 1957.

Calvocoressi, Peter: *World Politics since 1945, VII edition*. London – New York 1996.

Carpetier, Jean & Lebrun, Francois (eds.): *Histoire de la Mediterranee*. Editions du Seuil: Paris 1998.

Cleveland, William I.: *A History of the Modern Middle East*. Boulder – San Francisco – Oxford 1994.

Corme, Georges: *Le Proche-Oriente eclate. 1956–2000*. Paris 2003.

Gelberg Ludwik: *Prawo międzynarodowe i historia dyplomacji. Wybór dokumentów (International Law and History of Diplomacy. Selected Documents)*, Vol. II. Warszawa 1958.

Hart, Liddell: *1953. The Rommel Papers*. London 1963.

Hirszowicz, Łukasz: *The Third Reich and the Arab East*. London 1966; (Polish original edition: Łukasz Hirszowicz: *III Rzesza a Arabski Wschód*. Warszawa 1963).

Histoire de la Mediterranee. Paris 1998 (text of Entente Cordiale, 1904).

Bryg.-Gen. F. J. Moberly (ed.): *History of the Great War, Based on Official Documents. The Campaign in Mesopotamia 1914–1918*, vol. III. London 1919.

Hofstader D. (ed.): *Egypt and Nasser, vol. I–III*. New York 1973.

Kerr Malcolm H.: *The Arab Cold War: Gamal Abd al-Nasir and His Rivals 1958–1970*. London 1971.

L'orient arabe, Arabisme et islamisme de 1798 a 1945. Paris 1993.

Mansfield, Peter: *A Modern History of the Middle East*. London 1992.

Nasser, Gamal A.: *Falsafat al-Thawra (The Philosophy of the Revolution)*. Cairo 1954.

Nasser, Gamal A.: *Egypt's Liberation: The Philosophy of the Revolution*. Cairo 1954.

Nutting, Anthony: *Nasser*. London 1973.

Owen, Roger: *State, Power and Politics in the Making of the Modern Middle East*. London –New York 1994.

The Memoirs of Field-Marshall The Viscount Montegomery of Alamein, K.G.. London 1958.

The Middle East and North Africa 1974–75. London 1974.

The Middle East and North Africa 2000: A Survey and Reference Book. London 2000.

Author Biographies

Dr Andrea Brait studied history, political science and German studies in Vienna. She is a University Assistant at the Department of Contemporary History and the School of Education / University of Innsbruck. She teaches and investigates, with a particular interest in remembrance policy and musealisation, the relations of Austria with its neighbouring countries and the field of history didactics; she has provided numerous lectures and publications on these topics.

Anna Caban has been working as an archivist in the State Archive in Opole since 2003. She graduated from the Faculty of History of the University of Lublin. She is mainly involved in provision, protection of personal data and digitalisation.

Prof. dr hab. Hassan A. Jamsheer, lecturer at the Chair of International Relations of the Warsaw Management Academy. Until 2012, head at the Chair of Middle Eastern Studies, Institute of History, Department of Philosophy and History, University of Łódź. As a historian and specialist in international affairs, he is interested mainly in the Arab and Islamic world. A Member of Oriental Sciences Committee of the Polish Academy of Sciences as well as many other international and Polish expert societies.

Sławomir Jan Maksymowicz – PhD, graduated from the Institute of History at the Pedagogical University (WSP) in Olsztyn in 1995. Since 1995 he has been working as an archivist in the Department of Processing Former German Files in the State Archive in Olsztyn (Oddział Opracowania akt poniemieckich Archiwum Państwowego w Olsztynie). In February 2014 he obtained his PhD degree in history at the University of Warmia and Mazury in Olsztyn. His scientific interests are concentrated on the history of Warmia and Mazury in 1914–1945.

Tomasz Matuszak (1973) – PhD, a historian – archivist. A Director of the State Archive in Piotrków Trybunalski. An author, co-author and editor of 7 book publications. He specialises in methodology of working with archives, in archive studies and in education in archive studies as well as in military history in particular in the history of Polish air forces in 1918–1939.

Kamila Pawełczyk-Dura, PhD. She works in the State Archive in Łódź. Her scientific interests are focused on the history of the Russian orthodox religion, mainly during the soviet period, on the operation of various churches in realities of totalitarian countries as well as on the Russian philosophical, theological and social-political ideas.

Dr Frank M. Schuster, born in 1971 in Bucharest / Romania, studied in Germany and Finland, obtained doctorate at the University of Basle/Switzerland is a historian, literary and cultural studies scholar. Currently he's a visiting professor at University of Łódź and a professor at the Łódź Academy of Humanities and Economics. In addition to his research on World War I and cultural, regional and urban history, his interests primarily focus on the phenomena of multiculturalism, religion and memory in Central and Eastern Europe, as well as on the relationship between history, literature and media, especially photography and film.

Dr Marcos Silber, a senior lecturer at the Department of Jewish History and chair of the Department of Multidisciplinary Studies at the University of Haifa in Israel. He published numerous works on the Jewish experience during WWI in the Polish lands as well as on Jewish autonomism, Yiddish cinema and popular culture and Polish-Israeli relations.

Marek Szczepaniak (1958) – a director of the Gniezno branch of the State Archive in Poznań. In 1981 he graduated from the Faculty of History of Adam Mickiewicz University in Poznań. He is an archivist and a historian, an expert in religious studies and an educator in archive studies.

Grażyna Tyrchan works in the Gniezno branch of the State Archive in Poznań and specialises in the local history and education in archive studies. She graduated from the Faculty of History of Adam Mickiewicz University in Poznań. She completed post-graduate archive studies at the University of Nicolaus Copernicus in Toruń.

Tomasz Walkiewicz (1980) – a historian and an archivist. In 2005 he graduated from the Faculty of History of the Nicolaus Copernicus University in Toruń. Since 2006 he has been working in the State Archive in Łódź as a senior archivist in the Department of Inventory, Information and Access (Oddział Ewidencji, Informacji i Udostępniania).

Dr hab. Krzysztof Paweł Woźniak – a historian and an ethnographer in the Department of the History of Poland in the 19th Century of the University of Łódź. He investigates into the participation of the German population in the social and economic life of the Kingdom of Poland as well as into the modernisation processes, history of the Evangelical Church of the Augsburg Confession in central Poland and the history of multi-cultural Łódź.

Ionela Zaharia, (M.A.) is a Ph.D. candidate at the Faculty of History and Philosophy of the Babes – Bolyai University in Romania. Her interests and her Ph.D.

project are focused on the Romanian military clergy from Austria-Hungary during the Great War.

Piotr Zawilski (1963), a Director of the State Archive in Łódź. He graduated from the University of Łódź (world archaeology) and the University of Nicolaus Copernicus (archival studies). He has been involved in state administration work since 1989. In 1998–2006 he was a Director of the State Archive in Piotrków Trybunalski and since March 2006 he has been the Director of the State Archive in Łódź. Since 2012 Piotr Zawilski has hold the function of the Vice-President of the Association of Polish Archivists (Stowarzyszenie Archiwistów Polskich).

Magdalena Żakowska (PhD) is a historian and a specialist in the field of international relations. She works as an assistant professor at the Faculty of International and Political Studies at the University of Łódź (Poland). She researches into e.g. the image of Russia in the West European cultures, as well as the history and cultural identity of Central, East and South European countries.

Geschichte - Erinnerung - Politik
Posener Studien zur Geschichts-, Kultur- und Politikwissenschaft

Herausgegeben von Anna Wolff-Powęska und Piotr Forecki

Band 1 Machteld Venken: Stradding the Iron Curtain? Immigrants, Immigrant Organisations, War Memories. 2011.

Band 2 Anna Wolff-Powęska / Piotr Forecki: Der Holocaust in der polnischen Erinnerungskultur. 2012.

Band 3 Marta Grzechnik: Regional Histories and Historical Regions. The Concept of the Baltic Sea Region in Polish and Swedish Historiographies. 2012.

Band 4 Lutz Niethammer: Memory and History. Essays in Contemporary History. 2012.

Band 5 Piotr Forecki: Reconstructing Memory. The Holocaust in Polish Public Debates. 2013.

Band 6 Marek Słoń (ed.): Historical Atlas of Poland in the 2nd Half of the 16th Century. Voivode-ships of Cracow, Sandomierz, Lublin, Sieradz, Łęczyca, Rawa, Płock and Mazovia. Volume 1-4. Translated by Agata Staszewska, Editorial Assistance Martha Brożyna. 2014.

Band 7 Maciej Janowski: Birth of the Intelligentsia 1750-1831. A History of the Polish Intelligentsia – Part 1. Edited by Jerzy Jedlicki. Translated by Tristan Korecki. 2014.

Band 8 Jerzy Jedlicki: The Vicious Circle 1832-1864. A History of the Polish Intelligentsia – Part 2. Edited by Jerzy Jedlicki. Translated by Tristan Korecki. 2014.

Band 9 Magdalena Micińska: At the Crossroads 1865-1918. A History of the Polish Intelligentsia – Part 3. Edited by Jerzy Jedlicki. Translated by Tristan Korecki. 2014.

Band 10 Anna Wolff-Powęska: Memory as Burden and Liberation. Germans and their Nazi Past (1945-2010). Translated by Marta Skowrońska. 2015.

Band 11 Thomasz Szarota: On the Threshold of the Holocaust. Anti-Jewish Riots and Pogroms in Occupied Europe. Warsaw – Paris – The Hague – Amsterdam – Antwerp – Kaunas. Translated by Tristan Korecki. 2015.

Band 12 Anna Wolff-Powęska / Piotr Forecki (eds.): World War II and Two Occupations. Dilemmas of Polish Memory. Translated by Marta Skowrońska and Blanka Zahorjanova. 2016.

Band 13 Elżbieta Katarzyna Dzikowska / Agata Handley / Piotr Zawilski (eds.): The Great War. Insights and Perspectives. 2016.

www.peterlang.com